ACADEMIC WOMEN

ACADEMIC WOMEN

Jessie Bernard

A MERIDIAN BOOK

NEW AMERICAN LIBRARY

TIMES MIRROR

NEW YORK AND SCARBOROUGH, ONTARIO
THE NEW ENGLISH LIBRARY LIMITED, LONDON

Library of Congress Catalog Card Number: 64-15066

Permission to quote from the following copyrighted works has been kindly granted by their publishers or authors: American Association of University Professors: "Teacher's Role Book," by Emerson Shuck, *AAUP Bulletin*, copyright 1960. American Council on Education: *Faculty-Administration Relationships*, edited by Frank C. Abbott, copyright 1958; "Anti-nepotism Rules in American Colleges and Universities," by Eleanor F. Dolan and Margaret P. Davis, *Educational Record*, copyright 1960. American Home Economics Association: *The Life of Ellen H. Richards*, by Carolyn Louisa Hunt, copyright 1942. American Institute for Research: *Who Goes to Graduate School?*, by George Leonard Gropper and Robert Fitzpatrick, copyright 1959. *American Scientist*: "Problems of the Scientific Career," by Lawrence S. Kubie, copyright 1953. Basic Books, Inc.: *The Academic Marketplace*, by Theodore Caplow and Reece J. McGee, copyright 1958. Columbia University Press: *The Social Role of the Man of Knowledge* by Florian Znaniecki, copyright 1940. Free Press of Glencoe: *Family, Socialization and Interaction Process*, by Talcott Parsons and Robert F. Bales, copyright 1955. Alice Hamilton: *Exploring the Dangerous Trades*, published by Little, Brown and Company, copyright 1943. Harper and Row, Publishers, Inc.: *America's Resources of Specialized Talent*, by Dael Wolfle, copyright 1954; *Carey Thomas of Bryn Mawr*, by Edith Finch, copyright 1947. Hathaway House Bookshop: *Wellesley College*, by Florence Converse, copyright 1939. Houghton Mifflin Company: *Anthropologist at Work: The Writings of Ruth Benedict*, edited by Margaret Mead, copyright 1959; *The Early History of Smith College, 1871-1910*, by L. Clark Seelye, copyright 1923; *Life of Alice Freeman Palmer*, by George Herbert Palmer, copyright 1924; *A Listener in Babel*, by Vida Scudder, copyright 1903. McGraw-Hill Book Company, Inc.: *Graduate Education in the United States*, by Bernard Berelson, copyright 1960. The Macmillan Company: *Encyclopedia of the Social Sciences*, article by Willystine Goodsell, copyright 1930; *Many a Good Crusade*, by Virginia Gildersleeve, copyright 1954; *Woman as a Force in History*, by Mary Beard, copyright 1946. President and Council of Radcliffe College: *Graduate Education for Women: The Radcliffe Ph.D.*, published by Harvard University Press, copyright 1956. *Sociology and Social Research*: "Personal and Institutional Characteristics of Academic Sociologists," by B. E. Mercer and J. B. Pearson, copyright 1962. University of Chicago Press: *Boys in White*, by Howard S. Becker and others, copyright 1961; *Stipends and Spouses*, by James A. Davis and others, copyright 1962; *Structure of Scientific Revolutions*, by Thomas S. Kuhn, copyright 1962. University of Colorado Press: *Florence Sabin, Colorado Woman of the Century*, by Elinor Bluemel, copyright 1959. University of Minnesota Press: *Maria Sanford*, by Helen Whitney, copyright 1920. John Wiley and Sons, Inc.: *The American College*, by R. N. Sanford, copyright 1962; John Wiley and Sons, Inc.: *The Psychology of Occupations*, by Anne Roe, Copyright 1956.

Reprinted by arrangement with The Pennsylvania State University Press.

CONTENTS

v

PREFACE

This book is not, like others in the "academic" series—*The Academic Man, The Academic Marketplace, The Academic Mind*—a report on a single research project. It began that way, as an evaluation of the contribution of women to the total academic enterprise in the United States, but the amount of background data needed to interpret the original data was so great that presently a dog-into-tail effect was produced. The original research was relegated to appendixes, and the background data were turned into a book.

The book falls into any one of several categories. With respect to the sociology of knowledge it raises, if it does not answer, such questions as: What, if any, is the effect on learning of the sex of the transmitter of human knowledge? What is the effect, if any, of the sex of the innovator on the acceptance of ideas? As related to the sociology of work, or of occupations, it highlights the different career patterns of academic men and women and glances cursorily at the implications. In the area of the problems of modern women, it inquires into the feasibility of combining professional and family life and into the different life or career "calendars" of men and women. In connection with the problems of high-level personnel, it raises questions about the supply of and the demand for highly trained women.

I write, it is obvious, as a sociologist. I have used whatever tool I needed that my discipline has put at my disposal, and I have tried to avoid the use of jargon. I hope the women themselves hide the conceptual framework in which I present them. Where systematic data have been available, they have been used, but in the absence of such data, autobiographical, biographical, and personal-documentary materials have also been exploited, even solicited, and always welcomed, both because of the insights they offer and because they relieve the otherwise relentlessly statistical nature of the data. Most

vii

of the personal documents have been revised in order to protect the anonymity of the subjects, but the essential points have been preserved in all cases. In some instances a document represents my own statement of an interview or conversation which took place some time ago in which case I have, where possible, checked my version with the person involved for accuracy.

Among the new findings which have impressed me most as a sociologist are these: As a whole, the women who receive the doctor's degree are, no doubt because of the greater selectivity involved, superior insofar as test-intelligence is concerned to men who receive the doctor's degree. Yet they tend to be less productive, as measured by published work, than academic men. When the major variables associated with productivity are held constant, however, the differential is reduced, and academic position (college, university, or, in the case of scientists, laboratory) turns out to be a better predictor of productivity than sex. The question must then be raised as to why women tend to gravitate to positions which are less productive. It seems to me that many women have a vocation for college teaching; they prefer teaching to research. The concept of the fringe benefit status has interested me; it is a status whose occupants are on the fringes of their professions but of enormous benefit to the institutions that use them. These women combine marriage, children, and career according to one pattern. Another pattern, even more interesting to me, is that worked out by the women—described at the very end of the book—who are not on the fringe but in the mainstream. The pattern these enormously talented and vigorous women are initiating seems to me to have great significance.

My own biases, I suppose, are clear enough not to require specific articulation. I object to the current approach to high-level personnel in terms of "manpower utilization" or "conservation" or of "using" or "losing" brainpower. I "believe" in women, and I applaud every attempt to institutionalize ways to help them achieve what they want and are able to achieve, but I do not believe that their contribution as academic women is necessarily any better or more socially useful in every case than their contribution as wives, mothers, and community leaders.

I write as an academician. "Man and boy," I have been an academic woman for over forty years. As student, disciple, assistant, associate, and wife of a sociologist, I viewed the academic scene as a semiparticipant observer for many years, and after my husband's death as a full-fledged participant myself. As an undergraduate at the University of Minnesota, Anna Helmholtz Phelan, Alice Felt Tyler, and Marjorie Nicholson were among the academic women who dazzled me, and Maria Sanford was still a living memory. As a graduate student, at the gracious invitation of William Fielding Ogburn—in charge of the then-daring innovation of having a session at the professional meetings devoted to original research, I made my first professional appearance before a sociological audience, presenting a paper based on my master's dissertation. My first taste of independent academic life on the faculty side was at a women's college where Dean Alice Gipson, Alice Parker, Elizabeth Dawson, Mary Talbot, and Florence Schaper, among others, struggled manfully to impose their own meticulous, scholarly, and scientific standards on generations of students already turning away from, if not actually rejecting, the career orientation of earlier college women. At the Pennsylvania State University I participated in the perennial but increasingly salient "polarities" which Bernard Berelson has distinguished in modern academia, the tug and pull between the liberal orientation which academicians bring with them with their doctorates from the great universities and the practical, service orientation which the vocational and professional schools bring from the land-grant ideal.

I write, finally, as a woman—not, however, as a militant feminist, to vindicate the rights of women. I have never, so far as I know, experienced professional discrimination from my colleagues because of my sex (although I was once chased out of the sacred precincts of a faculty club at a great university when I inadvertently stepped over the invisible line). I have, rather, been treated with extraordinary chivalry by administrators, colleagues, and confreres who have made allowances for the demands of maternity—three times—sustained me in bereavement, and rewarded me with many official honors, including the vice-presidency of the American Sociological Society, the presidency of the Eastern Sociological Society and of the Society for the Study of Social Problems, and the secretary-treasurership of the last-named society, as well as membership on important committees, including the research committee of the International Sociological Association.

I write, therefore, without bitterness or rancor, knowing full well that a bland approach is less likely to be appreciated than a rapier thrust. I have enormous pride in my profession; the people who staff our colleges and universities, women as well as men, for all their fairly obvious defects—with which novelists and satirists have had a field day—rank high in my opinion among all professionals, and I concur in the popular polls which have assigned them great prestige.

Much of the thinking in this volume was generated in long discussions with my colleague Margaret Matson and former colleague Judith Kramer, both highly talented academic women. I am indebted to Dr. Otis E. Lancaster, Westinghouse Professor of Engineering Education at The Pennsylvania State University, who was chairman of a university committee on good teaching of which I was a member. Dr. M. E. John, chairman of the Department of Sociology at The Pennsylvania State University, granted me half-time leave to complete work on this book, begun during a sabbatical. I must also express my appreciation for the grant from the National Institute of Mental Health which helped to finance the Matched Scientists Study. Dr. Charles W. Shilling, of the Biological Sciences Communication Project, was of great service in dunning the subjects in that Study, and to the scientists who contributed their time and thought, my deepest appreciation is also due.

Thanks are due to Ben Euwema, my dean for seventeen years, whose own completely unbiased policies with respect to academic women may have biased my own interpretations, rendering me vulnerable to his gentle chiding in the Foreword for not crusading. With a vindicator of the rights of academic women like him, I could afford to eschew any special pleading.

I owe a debt also to David Riesman, whose powerful insights for interpreting the data in this book and whose additional contribution based on his own observations and experience in academia have added greatly to the value of this book.

JESSIE BERNARD

The Pennsylvania State University
March 1964

FOREWORD

So many handicaps bedevil the academic woman that one wonders how she can possibly manage as well as Jessie Bernard reports she does in the following pages. This book is unusually free of the crusading spirit. The author is too much the scientist to become a special pleader. However, as one who has spent over three decades in various types of academic administrative work, I feel that a degree of intelligent crusading is definitely in order.

For, despite the findings here reported, the career woman does still suffer from discrimination: certain departments will hire no women at all; others will not promote women to the higher academic posts; and most departments have a strong prejudice against female administrators. Furthermore, a presumption of spinsterhood implies a sort of tight-lipped prudery and ignorance of "real life" which are themselves prejudicial.

The married career woman has a whole set of additional disadvantages for which many universities make no provision. If she wishes to have children, she will become automatically incapable of pursuing her career during the period of childbearing unless, like the women whose stories are presented as the wave of the future, she gets help. (Although I do recall one woman economics professor who did not interrupt her career in the slightest for two children, both of whom were programmed for the few weeks after the spring semester and before summer school.) When the children are old enough for nursery school, the academic woman is again free to continue her interrupted career, but—again if she gets no help—at what a disadvantage! From now until her children are in their teens, her life will be a mad scramble devoted to baby sitters, the PTA, Cub Scouts, faculty meetings, entertaining, being a chauffeur, being a wife, and being a mother.

I share the appreciation of the services of "fringe benefits" as expressed by the dean quoted by the author. No matter how talented an academic woman is, the family team will most likely have chosen as a place to work an institution selected by the husband as most favorable to his advancement. From then on, the husband's career will come first; the wife, therefore, is denied the professional advantages of mobility. There will be the temptation, when salaries and rank are discussed, to assume that the wife is captive; so long as her husband is advancing satisfactorily, she will have to stay where she is. The situation is an open temptation to exploitation by administrators.

Fortunately, progress is being made. There may now be fewer women in academic careers than we could have expected or hoped for. But this, I trust, is a passing situation. The academic woman is already firmly established on the basis of equality in a number of institutions; and despite handicaps she is doing very well, thank you. To be sure, some institutions still try to enforce antinepotism regulations—some to the extent of hiring no married couples at all, some to the extent of denying the wife tenure—while still others impose varying degrees of discrimination, most of them implicit rather than explicit. But, as this book shows, such rules become increasingly difficult to enforce and must certainly soon be given up as anachronistic. We can no longer afford—if, indeed, we ever could—to shut out one-half of our population from the academic work-force: we need all the intelligence, all the consecrated devotion, all the scholarly creativeness we can get.

The academic task is demanding, and the academic need is immediate. To refuse the assistance we can get from or offer to the academic woman, or to play it down by various forms of discrimination is—in this critical period—entirely unforgivable. Hopefully the great and increasing scarcity of competent and dedicated faculty members should soon attract more women into academic careers. They have much to offer Academe. They are sympathetic, outgoing, and relentlessly verbal; they are interested in ideas but even more so in people. By and large, they may not have risen to as many of the highest academic positions as we might have expected, but they are, every day, adding a distinctive luster to the institutions they serve.

In the long run, the place of the academic woman is secure. For not only can she do almost everything her male colleague can do— and often do it better—but also she can bring to her task certain unique qualities of mind and spirit which Academe can in no way afford to disregard. Hopefully this book will encourage more young women to enter Academe. And hopefully they will receive the welcome they deserve.

BEN EUWEMA

July 14, 1964

INTRODUCTION

It takes art to combine in one work a variety of current sociological styles: demographic or other tabular material; social history gleaned from scattered and inevitably somewhat accidental sources; small-scale empirical studies; biographical data and personal documents; the oblique evidence provided by novels. Some people in the humanities deprecate statistical and microempirical work which they condescend to as "IBM sociology," while some people in all fields distrust the necessarily anecdotal and impressionistic stuff of personal documents as unscientific. Indeed, one of the great works in the latter genre, *The Polish Peasant in Europe and America,* by W. I. Thomas and Florian Znaniecki, is unduly deprecated or disregarded by many young sociologists who know that Herbert Blumer and others have tellingly assailed its probative value. However, if one defines science in an extremely broad way as scrupulous and self-critical use of whatever methods seem appropriate to the tasks of discovery and understanding at hand (including submission of one's data and conclusions and, where possible, of one's own background and potential biases to an audience of fellow scholars), then the use made by the author in *Academic Women* of relevant material from any likely source—from scrutiny of college catalogues over the years to solicited personal statements by both academic women and their spouses and children—is scientific; and the handling of her diverse orders of data is gracefully done.

The study is intended to illuminate both the situation of women in academic life and to contribute to our understanding of academia in its own terms; thus, the book draws on and contributes to the emerging field of the sociology of the higher learning. Take, for example, the findings of a study done by Jessie Bernard, Charles W. Shilling, and Joe W. Tyson of the patterns of communication and of productivity among a group of biological scientists. This research examined the work of some 700 researchers, a tenth of whom were women, in terms of such variables as attendance at professional meetings, informal bull sessions about work, use of the long-distance phone, and so on. It appeared that there was no discrimination as a matter of laboratory policy against the women: they could travel to meetings, use the phone, visit colleagues elsewhere as readily as the men. But they were somewhat less socially aggressive, less given to initiating informal colloquies, although responsive to these when invited. If they were young and unmarried, the author suggests, they may have been inhibited by the fear that initiation of a contact might appear to be a sexual advance. But beyond that, it is clear from a wealth of data that women are trained to be less assertive, to move in narrower orbits, to be (contrary to legend) less exhibitionistic. (Moreover, their voices do not carry as far— one reason given by a dean, even in this electronic age, for confining them to small introductory sections and upper-class seminars in a university and keeping them away from large introductory lecture courses.) While the study of the bioscientists began with the assumption that there might be at least a tacit stag exclusion of women from networks of informal communication, this apparently was not the case. Even so, there are undoubtedly still academic enclaves where women are not felt to belong, and attitudes differ regionally, by status of institution, and by field of work. But in the sciences today, so much depends on what Derek Price terms the invisible colleges and on the spread of information more rapidly than the formal publication systems allow that women suffer if they cannot actively take part on a basis of equality in these processes of give and take.*

---

* In studying the flow of information among doctors and others at the Bureau of Applied Social Research, Herbert Menzel, Elihu Katz, and James Coleman have shown how important position in a network is for any competitive universe that depends on priorities and on concatenations of information that appear chancy in the individual case but systematic in the aggregate. It would appear that women in general make no effort to create a counterculture or "underground" to overcome their disadvantages, being in this respect as in others unlikely to unite as a "minority" for mutual protection and support. For example, when men are thinking of who can fill an academic vacancy, their thought naturally runs to people like themselves, that is, other men, rather than to women who are untypical members of the guild. And while pressure or conscience may sometimes lead them today to search for a suitable Negro to fill an academic post, there is no comparable pressure from today's nonembattled women to help each other out, and the men who are troubled by the professional and academic situation of women are in no way organized.

In fact, there is a fair amount of evidence, though not stressed in this book, that the women are their own worst enemies. The evidence lies in the tacit

The relative noncompetitiveness of women and the shorter tethers of impulse and orbit on which they work show up in other ways as well as in constricting the place and performance of academic women. As the book brilliantly demonstrates, women prefer to be teachers, passing on a received heritage and responsively concerning themselves with their students, while men of equivalent or even lesser ability prefer to be men-of-knowledge, breaking the accustomed mold and remaining responsive not to students but to the structure of the discipline and their colleagues in the invisible university. The topics men study have on the whole more prestige, and men, of course, are likely to teach graduate students in the prestigious major universities, while women, at the more elementary level and in smaller colleges, teach languages, English composition, home economics, etc. Likewise, when a field wants to raise its status, it may do so by avoiding "guilt by association" with teaching-oriented or service-oriented women. For instance, schools of social work, as the author notes, have been gaining in prestige by securing men as their deans; and there is now talk of men in the deanships of colleges of home economics, positions earlier reserved for the "founding mothers" of such institutions. The applied, apparently repetitive, arts of teaching have less academic status than the theoretical and supposedly pure arts and sciences.

The author is perhaps herself sufficiently impressed with this state of affairs to raise as a serious question whether in graduate education the nurturant qualities of women professors are useful or disadvantageous to students—disadvantageous because they might retain in the field some who could not make a contribution. Undoubtedly, many men believe that their toughness and sink-or-swim policy *vis-à-vis* students increase the quality as well as the reputation of their department (although in practice, as in one case presented, the men often talk tough and act sentimentally). There may well be slack institutions the country over where the faculty rightly complain of being baby sitters for self-indulgent young people who want to stay on in school. Yet at major universities, in many fields of the humanities and the social sciences, both graduate students and younger faculty can have their intellectual poise shaken by being caught between factions in a divided department

---

league of educated housewives accusing working mothers of neglecting their families, or the preference of women college students for men teachers, or the dislike of women to be "bossed" by other women.

or by sheer indifference (however unavoidable) from senior men who are models for them. I believe that many potentially gifted researchers are crushed or driven out of the field, and these may sometimes be the very ones, both men and women, who could help reshape the field and reshape the cognitive styles within the field. Sometimes one will find in such a department a woman, possibly a departmental secretary, who helps students in all the little ways that may mitigate anomie. Throughout history, what might be called the "home economics" of women has kept the species going, or rather staying, while the more abstract, idealistic, conceptual or playful and far-reaching outlooks have been more characteristic of men.*

Of course, not all women are nurturant, concrete, and inclined to be teachers rather than men-of-knowledge: one speaks here of overlapping universes and of tendencies; and there are always women who try to beat the game by outperforming in a "male" direction, although perhaps today, as some of the biographical materials in this volume suggest, academic women of this sort are less common and one must look for them, as for other "dated" character orientations, among Negroes and other newly arrived groups.

In general, then, women seem less prone to viewing intellectual life as a game or combat (of course, with the exceptions just noted). Frequently they enter graduate school to please their mentors, without whose encouragement in fact they would be unlikely to overcome the resistance of their families, their boy friends and girl friends, and their own internalized and parochial judgments as to what is properly female behavior. I recall an evening with a group of Radcliffe undergraduates, all of whom were determined to enter professional or academic life, who had invited several faculty members for a discussion of problems they faced in pursuing such careers. A male instructor in history pointed out to them that to get really outstanding grades, they needed to learn to attack in a gamesmanlike way a text or a book or even a teacher; some girls did learn to use this strategy during their four years of college. But the girls of this group declared that they were unwill-

* The interpretation here suggested is not that of the author but is consonant with the writings concerning sex and character of Erich Fromm, Erik H. Erikson, Bruno Bettelheim, David McClelland, Eleanor Maccoby. For a lovely fictional portrait of comparable polarities, see Yukio Mishima, *After the Banquet,* Donald Keene, tr., New York: Alfred A. Knopf, 1963.

ing to make a game of learning or to put on masks to conceal their resiliency. Like many young people today, deeply concerned with identity and integrity, they felt this would compromise them and that such tactics would not be honest where they felt empathy for the work. It goes without saying that all of these young women wanted and expected to marry; several hoped they could stall off the older men who were ready for immediate marriage until they themselves could not only finish college but also define themselves more firmly in career terms so that they might enter marriage from a "position of strength." It occurred to me later, reflecting on this discussion, that some of these young women may have been troubled because marriage gave them an out from the academic and professional competition upon which they were entering. As this book points out, women are given a greater freedom to fail; not everything is staked on a career. But just as some ambitious Negroes fear to fall back on the discrimination against them as a too-convenient, even if justified, alibi, so some young women, now as in earlier times, fear the cushion for modest achievement their femininity provides (achievement, that is, in "male" terms) ; and in addition they may fail to see discrimination where it does exist, in part perhaps because they can find another route, a specifically female one, toward creativity and a sense of accomplishment.

One can but hope that such women, troubled by ambiguity, will have the good fortune, tenacity, and resourcefulness shown by the young academic couples whose poignant and penetrating comments are quoted in the book's final chapter, notably the ability to handle the competitiveness of the outside world as it impinges on judgments as to which of a husband and wife team is "better" in the field they both pursue (cf. the comments of Susan Hoeber Rudolph hereafter). This competitiveness is so very American or more broadly Western in its style that I am led to wonder whether it bears some relation to our progress in scientific work, or rather whether, if women had a larger influence on that work, other sorts of discoveries might not be made, other "laws" emphasized, and altered patterns of scientific and academic organization preferred or discovered. Work such as that of Robert K. Merton on the sources of the scientific ethos is relevant here, and it could be argued that it took a particular set of sex-role attitudes as well as specific religious and cultural values for Western science and technology to develop initially, although to *continue* the work, one might speculate as to whether a different pattern of attitudes might not be productive. In this area, *Academic Women,* which of course could not cover everything, suffers from relative lack of comparative material, although there is continuous comparison with our own historical past, including, for example, reference to the scholarly abbesses of the Medieval and Renaissance periods. However, the author does note that a field such as political science, which emphasizes power, attracts or fosters relatively few women, whereas anthropology, at least where it emphasizes kinship more than kingship, finds much more place for women.*

Since there are so few academic women, however, one must be cautious in generalizing about the relative attractiveness or openness of various disciplines or in interpreting apparent differences of hospitality. As Ruth Benedict's career suggests, well-educated upper- or upper-middle-class women could afford to enter fields which were at the time not paying propositions. As Renée Fox has pointed out in conversation, there is little in the traditional feminine roles to support lonely field work in dangerous places. It seems possible that upper-class position—and I mean here aristocratic values and not simply more money—may give a few academic women a relative freedom from middle-class and lower-middle-class conventionalities concerning sex roles. It is clear from this book that academic women, like college women in general, are of higher social origins than their male counterparts, one reason perhaps why even today, as Chapter 14 suggests, a sizeable proportion remains unmarried. (They are also more divorce-prone once they are married than are academic men.)

While social class comparisons of this sort are suggested in the book, another source of perhaps even more significant comparisons is not touched on, though related to class, namely, the role of ethnicity and religion on the American scene for their bearing on the opportunities women are given and the expectations men harbor for them. The early feminist academicians of the last century, such as Alice Freeman Palmer or Maria Sanford, were

---

* For illustrations of the ability of women to have access in a setting where men might have a harder time, cf. Hanna Papanek, "The Woman Fieldworker in a Purdah Society," *Human Organization,* Vol. 23, Summer 1964, pp. 160–163; Elenore Smith Bowen, *Return to Laughter* (Museum of Natural History—Doubleday Anchor edition, 1964). In Appendix A of *Academic Women* there is a somewhat analogous story concerning the respective sex roles in the development of social work and community welfare administration in which women do the microtasks of case work and men do the macrotasks of administration and theoretically oriented research.

mostly New England Puritans; M. Carey Thomas was a Friend; in a number of cases, they were the daughters of physicians and I suspect that their intellectual fathers sometimes made them into *de facto* "sons." Many of these women were more reform-minded than research-minded, an outlook that took some of them into founding or bolstering women's colleges that would have academic standards at least as high as any Ivy League male institution, while others (and here the author presents material new to me) founded colleges of home economics to spread the new sciences of nutrition and public health and consumer economics.* Since married women can become "men of knowledge" in most cases only with the support or at least nonreluctance of their husbands, much depends on the latter's security, and this in turn depends on the cultural and subcultural definitions as to the proper division of labor among husband and wife. And the case material in the last Chapter suggests that Jewish husbands are less threatened or are more willing to be supportive; they also probably have more money or backing from wealthier relatives. European role definitions may also help settle the sorts of diurnal conflicts that so tragically disrupted Ruth Fulton Benedict's marriage (the author makes good use of Margaret Mead's, *An Anthropologist at Work: Writings of Ruth Benedict*).

Finally, concerning variations among different social strata and ethnic groups in American Catholicism, *Academic Women* has almost nothing to say, despite the fact that the great majority of women's colleges in this country are run by Catholic religious. The Sister Formation Conference is one of the major efforts to improve the academic orientation of the Sisters teaching in these colleges, and inferentially also the lay instructors of both sexes; even so, in most of the women's colleges, except for the most outstanding ones, the faculty's orientation today is toward teaching and not toward research. And in much of diocesan Catholicism, as distinguished from the more intellectual Orders, the women college students are pointed toward family life and parish and perhaps civic responsibility rather than toward boundary-breaking academicism. (Similar pressures operate in a good many of the

---

* Since all women and not only urban women could use the benefits of home economics teaching in the secondary schools, this work could be facilitated through the land-grant colleges as a female form of agricultural extension, whereas social work, more exclusively urban, began its professional career outside the university and only recently has come primarily under academic auspices.

more traditional Southern women's colleges and private women's junior colleges, often against faculty desires.) There is some evidence that even today Irish Catholic men are somewhat more patriarchal and less willing to marry women of higher academic aims than men of Jewish or liberal Protestant backgrounds.* Catholic college girls, like other college girls, want to get married. In talking at several small Catholic women's colleges I have pointed out to the students that the teaching Sisters furnish an example, in the best cases, that it is possible to live a spirited, serene, intellectual, charmingly feminine life without matrimony—a showing that may possibly today be harder to make outside a vocation. In these conversations I did not claim that girls should be sexless or that marriage and a family are not the greatest sources of humanity and growth most of us are capable of; I only intimated that the values of sexuality and marriage as essential for fullness of life may be oversold on the contemporary advertising market, with the result that women frequently make sacrifices, such as marrying dreadfully inadequate men, because no other alternative appears to do justice to life's possibilities. To such a suggestion of mine, the girls have apparently turned a deaf ear; they cannot identify with spinsters—no matter how womanly—possibly because they respect them too much and love them too little.

In a helpful metaphor, the author of *Academic Women* suggests that although the minds of men and women are genetically alike, the "packages" in which these minds come are different and are, of course, responded to differently in a cumulative process of social interaction. Many ambitious women do not like to hear about these differences, although the information might help them—both in college and later—to interpret their own experiences and make better use of the opportunities or circumvent the blockages involved

---

* Evidence here has been elusive and some of it is dated, such as the relative rates of marriage (not controlled for ethnicity) of Catholic and non-Catholic college graduates reported in Ernest Havemann and Patricia Salter West, *They Went to College* (New York: Harcourt Brace, 1947). More recently, a number of Catholic scholars have discussed the question of academic and intellectual orientation of Catholics both in Catholic and secular institutions of higher learning. See Andrew M. Greeley, *Religion and Career: A Study of College Graduates* (New York: Sheed and Ward, 1963); cf. Joseph H. Fichter, S.J., *Religion as an Occupation: A Study in the Sociology of Professions* (South Bend: University of Notre Dame Press, 1961); and, critical of Father Greeley, James W. Trent, "The Etiology of Catholic Intellectualism," unpublished doctoral dissertation, Center for the Study of Higher Education, University of California (Berkeley), 1964.

in their being women; yet they are more allergic to doors being closed than they are interested in searching for alibis and explanations of failure and impasse. The author uses to similar effect a quotation from David B. Tiedman, Robert P. O'Hara, and Esther Matthews: "Women don't mind your asserting that their psyches *are* different; they mind your asserting that their psyches *have* to be different. It is almost as if they don't mind their lot; they merely mind the assertion that there is no escape from their lot." (*Academic Women*, p. 304)

This book should be helpful to career-minded women and to those around such women, especially since it is anything but a rancorous attack on discrimination against women in higher education. It eschews the "manpower" or post-Sputnik approach which regrets the "waste" of talented scientists and technicians either for narrowly Cold War or more broadly generous national aims. The author is not convinced that all intelligent women should be recruited into academic or professional careers; homemaking, less rationalized than our imagery of household gadgets implies, can deploy very great as well as lesser talents. Moreover, she is cautious in interpreting her own data to prove that there is discrimination. If women choose not to compete for graduate fellowships or to drop out before obtaining the Ph.D. or to teach in a secondary school or junior college, such discrimination as there may be occurs earlier in the life-cycle and reflects mammoth cultural attitudes as to proper sex roles rather than specifically academic hostility. Nor does she believe that the nepotism rules militate in any severe way against the careers of academic spouses, since many administrators realize that they can hold a man by giving a perhaps ancillary position to his wife.* In the same direction, the author cites figures from the Woodrow Wilson Fellowship Program and other awards to show that women obtain proportionately as many fellowships in relation to the number and ability of those who apply as men do— this, in spite of the fact that the chance of their actually entering academic life and "producing" at the same rate as men is small.**

* My own limited observations here, not based on any survey, are somewhat less benign. Where husbands and wives are in the same or closely related fields, even large universities may be hesitant to make the double commitment which could actually greatly strengthen a department, precisely because of prejudice against women in the more distinguished universities and the not entirely unjustified fear of a powerhouse combination—a fear less in evidence where the team consists of several men of complementary distinction.

** I myself have sat on fellowship committees where, possibly unduly sensitive to the matter, I have thought that there was discrimination against gifted women

There is also in *Academic Women* a suggestion of the pressures women as cynosures sometimes feel (analogous to those of the first Negro in a previously all-white area) not to let their side down, though these pressures seldom have the intensity of the attacks on President Alice Freeman of Wellesley when she married George Herbert Palmer of Harvard and resigned her post. (Comparison with the Duke of Windsor's romance does not seem out of place here.) There is so little grievance in this book that the author scarcely notes the advantage the male professor has in that in most (over 90 percent) of the cases he has a wife, who even if she does pursue a part-time career, guards her husband's productivity and performance in obvious and in subtle ways, just as her husband's secretary or the woman librarian (which the author does note) speeds him on his way, or is in a group dynamics experiment by Bales, where the task leader is visible and the effective leader remains in shadow. *Academic Women* has an excellent discussion of the woman in "fringe benefit" status who, out of the competition for tenure position or other scarce resources, year after year teaches introductory sections, foreign languages, anatomy classes, and does other "lowly" chores, often part-time.* There is among academic men, as among other American men, a kind of rosy individualism which consciously asserts one's self-made status, neglectful of the infrastructure—governmental, societal, and often female—which makes the visible show possible; narcissism in my own observation is more common among men than among women—and the author does note that in the current roster of academic novels by avant-

applicants on the ground that they would marry and that they should not take the places which would otherwise go to men more likely to stay in the game. This may well be a true judgment and hence technically not discriminatory. The best argument against it seems to me to be a moral rather than a statistical one, namely, a belief that an individual should not be penalized because she belongs to a "race" whose over-all record is in some respects poor. And on the other side, I recall a statement at a conference on honors programs for women by an eminent psychologist that one of his most highly qualified women Ph.D.'s (not a clinician) has never, despite his best efforts, been able to win a university post. Thus she is cut off from access to graduate students and, along with other teachers in the lesser or non-elite liberal arts colleges, is out of the network of publication and communication. The psychologist was not sure he had done his student a favor by encouraging her to enter a subfield still largely stag.
* As Everett C. Hughes has pointed out, academic men in fact work part-time at their supposed jobs, spending the rest in committee meetings, office sociability, and other activities; but by social definition this is full-time work. The woman, however, who teaches regularly and intensively during the hours her children are in school is defined as a part-time worker, even though she actually puts in as many hours as the men.

garde writers, such as Bernard Malamud or Iris Murdoch, the women are pictured as better or less heel-like than the men.

But as I have said, *Academic Women* is noninvidious and quite without malice. This does not mean that it is a bland or a pedantic book. The human documents the author has gathered, either out of her own experience or from the biographies or autobiographies of academic women give it drama. In addition, she draws freely on her own observations as an academic woman. Thus, she writes:

> Sex . . . as a basis for status usually takes precedence over achieved or professional criteria in the social life of a campus. Academic women are thus usually included in the social programs of faculty wives, where their status is uncertain at best. Off-campus, too, the academic women are polarized around faculty wives rather than around fellow professionals. 'I wish hostesses would let me stay with the men, whose talk is interesting,' complained one academic woman, 'rather than insisting on including me among the women, most of whose talk is not interesting to me.'

In my own experience with this pattern, there are differences even among leading universities. At the University of Chicago, for instance, where many faculty wives work in the metropolis and where the University seems to have been little influenced by the stag-precious pattern of Oxbridge, the men and women do not always form two separate circles. At some other universities, academic working wives who want to break out of the small circle of domesticity may have to become quite aggressive about it, hence acquiring what is sometimes called bitchiness, or becoming "castrating females."

The author makes modest claims for her book. She hopes that there will be many other studies of questions and surmises she raises. As I have said, we need comparisons: among countries, among regions, social strata, and ethnic and religious groups in our own country (is the South different?—probably), as well as among the fields and subfields of knowledge where *Academic Women* makes a good beginning. One should not ask more of a book than this.

DAVID RIESMAN

Brattleboro, Vermont
July 20, 1964

AUTHOR'S EXPLANATION

The original date of this book, 1964, shows that it was gestated in the early 1960's, a time of great ferment in the academic world. The student movement which was to charaterize the decade first erupted at Berkeley in 1964 and academia was never to be the same again. *Academic Women* was no such bombshell. It was conceived, researched, and written in the old-fashioned scientific and scholarly tradition, quite well-mannered and subdued. Although appreciatively received—my own University Press granted it the Bell Award and Delta Kappa Gamma an honorary award in 1966—for the most part the response from the academic Establishment was a great big yawn.

Not so, however, the response from the radical young women just entering the academic scene, as women began to emerge from what I had called "the great withdrawal" of 1930 to 1960. (*Academic Women,* p. 37) Like other components of the youth movement they were shaking their fists at the traditional scene. They rebuked me for my lack of militancy vis-à-vis the discrimination against women in academia, my seeming lack of genuine concern for women. As, indeed, David Riesman and my own dean had also. (*Academic Women,* pp. xi, xx, xxiii)

Like all my colleagues everywhere, I stand convicted of not having foreseen this resurgence of feminism in the 1960's. But I can save face by noting that I did sense "augurs of change." (*Academic Women,* pp. 62-63) The changes came thick and fast and the first target for reform was precisely the discrimination against women in academia. It is astonishing to note how much has happened to fight—if not to eliminate—discrimination in less than a decade.*

---

*The Equal Pay Act passed by Congress in 1963 did not include women. The Civil Rights Act of 1964 included women but it did not include educational institutions until March, 1972. An Executive Order (11246) issued by President Johnson in 1965 forbade discrimination on the basis of race by the party to any contract with the government, but it did not mention sex until it was amended by

Discrimination as such was, however, only one of several themes that preoccupied me in *Academic Women*. Another had to do with the sociology of knowledge; (*Academic Women*, p. vii) it sought clues to the question: how does sex influence the development of science? In answer to the question I raised—how does the sex of a scientist influence the problems selected—David Riesman noted that science might have developed along quite different lines if women had had more part in it. (*Academic Women*, p. xix) In a later publication I have pursued this point, noting that the major sociological paradigms are, indeed, defective and deficient because of their male bias.* The same point is also being made by academic women in other social and behavioral sciences as well.

In answer to the question, how does sex influence the productivity of a scientist, Jonathan Cole has arrived at conclusions that expand

---

another Order (11375) which became effective in 1968. Not until guidelines were issued in June, 1970, were women provided with the wherewithall to fight discrimination. Given this tool, which made the courts available, they proceeded to use it. By 1970, charges had been filed against 350 colleges and universities by the Women's Equity League and the National Organization for Women. Women's caucuses were springing up in professional, learned, and scientific societies, and local chapters of the American Association of University Professors were establishing committees on the status of women. "Contract compliance" required that universities take "affirmative action" to overcome discrimination or suffer loss of government contracts. At first the universities paid little attention; not until contract money was actually withheld and forty new contracts delayed did they begin to act. There has been no rush to comply nor has compliance produced striking results. But at least the inertia has been shaken. Part-time appointments with the same tenure and fringe benefits as full-time appointments, maternity leave, paternity leave, are among the changes which are being offered by some of the more liberal institutions. For a résumé of the situation of women in academia in the early 1970's see Alice Rossi, editor, *Academic Women on the Move* (New York: Russell-Sage, 1973).

*Jessie Bernard, "My Four Revolutions, An Autobiographical History of the American Sociological Association," *American Journal of Sociology*, (January, 1973). Women are also showing the sexist bias in the transmission of knowledge by way of textbooks (Carol Ehrlich, "The Male Sociologist's Burden: The Place of Women in Marriage and Family Texts," *Journal Marriage and Family*, 33 (Aug., 1971), pp. 421-430).

though they do not controvert those reported here.* My own research preoccupation in *Academic Women* had been in the part played in the productivity of women scientists by their access to channels of communication. As so often in my own work, what began as the tail (background material on women in academia) began to wag the dog (their place in the communication system as related to their scientific productivity). It was the spate of research projects reported in Appendixes B, C, and D—hand-crafted rather than computerized —that constituted my major concern. That aspect of the book has been less noted than the discrimination aspect. But, as legal and administrative barriers—hopefully—recede, increasing attention is being paid to the subtler "stag effects"** which militate against women. I would like very much to see these barriers breached for the sake of scientific development as well as for the sake of women themselves.

A fourth concern of this book—then quite peripheral—had to do with the impact of motherhood on the academic careers of women. Three cases were presented to show how the problems were dealt with by young women at that time. (*Academic Women,* chapter 15) In a review of *Academic Women* in 1965, Logan Wilson had commented on the anomalous fact that the marital status of academic women was relevant whereas it was not so in a book on academic men.*** Even then we were beginning to study "two-career families." Since then an augmenting, if not as yet an extensive, research literature has appeared on such families**** and much of the effort of activist academic women is directed toward ameliorating the career costs to women of child-rearing by means of maternity leave, paternity leave, part-time appointments with all the prerogatives of full-time appointments, greater flexibility in committee and teaching assignments, and the like.

---

*Jonathan Cole, "American Men and Women of Science," paper given August 31, 1971, at meetings of American Sociological Association.

**See pp. 157, 302. Rita James Simon, S. M. Clark, and K. Galway in "The Woman Ph.D.: A Recent Profile," *Social Problem,* 15 (Fall, 1967)', pp. 221-236, and Martha S. White in "Psychological and Social Barriers to Women in Science," *Science,* 170 (Oct. 23, 1970), pp. 413-416, have corroborated the existence of "the stag effect" and documented in detail the way it works.

***American Sociological Review, 30 (August, 1965), p. 611. Helen Astin found lack of adequate household help to be the greatest single obstacle to career development among women with the doctorate, greater even than professional discrimination, for household tasks took eighteen hours of their time per week. See *The Women Doctorate in America, Origins, Career, and Family* (New York: Russell-

I was especially harsh in 1964 with women as social critics. (*Academic Women,* pp. 124-125) I now believe that the social criticism contributed by women in the last decade has been of enormous importance. I think we understand the nature of the modern world much better because of it.

A final word. David Riesman faulted me for not including the women who were running the Catholic women's colleges. I would like here to make at least partial amends for this oversight by paying my respects to them here. The Catholic college for women I know best— Alverno College—is in the vanguard with respect to the education of women. Its president, Sister Joel Read, is innovative and imaginative and Sister Mary Austin is a dynamic partner. Together they are showing how exciting it can be to pioneer new ways of being academic women.

JESSIE BERNARD

Washington, D.C.
November 10, 1972

Sage, 1969), pp. 147, 148. With respect to discrimination, incidentally, Astin found, as the present book did (p. 50), that the most productive and achieving women reported discrimination more than others did (p. 148).
****Rhona Rapoport and Robert N. Rapoport, *Dual-Career Families* (Baltimore: Penguin Books, 1971; Lynda Lytle Holmstrom, *The Two-Career Family* (Cambridge, Mass.: Schenkman, 1972).

PRELUDE ✿ SYMBOLS, SCHOLASTICS, AND SCHOLARS

It is curious, and worth at least a moment's consideration, that even schools with no women on their faculties are symbolized as cherishing mothers. Even where there are women on the faculties, not they but a mystical female—Alma Mater—nourishes and disciplines and shapes her charges:

> When we stood at boyhood's gate,
> Shapeless in the hands of fate,
> Thou dids't mold us, Dear Old State,
> Into men!
> Into men!

Students of symbolism could undoubtedly explain why it is that colleges and universities are pictured as females. It is not immediately obvious.

Curious also is the association of the intellect with a goddess. There was very little of the cherishing mother, strong but tender, disciplining but caring, commanding affection as well as attention, about Minerva. Though she sprang from Jupiter's brain—not from Metis' womb—she was hardly an intellectual. True, her name was derived from the Sanscrit, Greek, and Latin word for "mind," and she may have invented numbers, but her reputation for brains probably derived from the absence of serious competition on Olympus.

She was goddess of, among other things, war—not, like Mars, however, of violent or aggressive war, but rather of defensive war, of strategy. As a matter of fact, Minerva and Mars were frequently at loggerheads, and they came to blows at least twice. Minerva won both times.

Minerva also presided over the peaceful arts of both men and women—over agriculture, horticulture, and navigation as well as over spinning, weaving, and needlework. She was the goddess of wisdom, of skill, and of contemplation. In addition, she was protectress of cities. All in all, she was quite a character.

There appeared to her devotees to be nothing anomalous in having a goddess rather than a god of wisdom or in having wisdom (Minerva) triumph over violence (Mars), so there must have been at least a few human models for this imaginative conception—women who were strong, even militant, but wise and contemplative at the same time.

Apparently there were, for the learned woman is older even than the academy. Plato's great teacher, Socrates, is said to have gone to school to a woman; he studied rhetoric with Aspasia. Heterae were among the students of both Plato and Aristotle—not necessarily of Minerva's versatility but doubtless women of extraordinary talent.

The convents of the Middle Ages have been likened to women's colleges, and the talented women who staffed them have been favorably compared with their male counterparts: [1]

> No institution of Europe has ever won for the lady the freedom and development that she enjoyed in the convent in the early days. The modern colleges for women only feebly reproduce it, since the college for women has arisen when colleges in general are under a cloud. The lady-abbess, on the other hand, was part of the two great social forces of her time, feudalism and the Church. Great spiritual rewards and great worldly prizes were alike within her grasp. She was treated as an equal by men of her time as is witnessed by letters we still have from popes and emperors to abbesses. She had the stimulus of competition with men in executive capacity, in scholarship, and in artistic production, since her work was freely set before the general public; but she was relieved by the circumstances of her environment from the ceaseless competition in common life of woman with woman for the favor of the individual man. In the cloister of the great days, as on a small scale in the college for women today, women were judged by each other as men are everywhere judged by each other, for sterling qualities of head and heart and character.

There were great women teachers in the Renaissance also. Mary

Beard has traced the fairly considerable contribution they made
to the intellectual life of the time: [2]

> In the fifteenth century and early sixteenth century many Italian
> women displayed the highest technical competence in the study,
> interpretation, and exposition of the revived humanist learning.
> Some of them . . . could hold their own in matters of scholar-
> ship with the best of their male contemporaries and . . . were
> accepted and even acclaimed everywhere. According to Dr. H. J.
> Mozan's *Women in Science,* women took "an active part in the
> great educational movement inaugurated by the revival of learn-
> ing" and won "the highest honors for their sex in every depart-
> ment of science, art, and learning. . . . The universities, which
> had been opened to them at the close of the middle ages,
> gladly conferred upon them the doctorate, and eagerly welcomed
> them to the chairs of some of their most important facul-
> ties. . . ." In nearly every great intellectual center of Italy
> women were lecturing on literature and were studying medicine
> and natural science in the light of pagan learning in these sub-
> jects. Great Italian women teachers of the awakening "sent forth
> such students as Moritz von Spiegelberg and Rudolph Agricola
> to reform the instruction of Deventer and Awoll and prepare
> the way for Erasmus and Reuchlin." . . . Olympia Morata . . .
> was planning to continue her teaching of the classics in Heidel-
> berg, to which she had been invited, when an untimely death
> closed her career. . . . From Italy zeal for classical learning
> fanned out like rays from a sun. Queen Isabella of Spain became
> interested in it through her acquaintance with Vittoria Colonna
> and brought Italian men and women to Spain to instruct her
> courtiers and students in the universities. She studied the classics
> herself. She established a school of the classics in her palace.
> She attended examinations of students. . . . One woman was
> commissioned to lecture on the classics at Salamanca [Beatrix
> Galinda was professor of rhetoric at this university]; another
> on rhetoric at Alcalá. . . . [And Francisca de Lebrixa often
> substituted for her father, professor of history at Alcalá].

The seventeenth century, alas, was not so congenial for intellectual achievements by women. "With the death of Elizabeth we
come practically to the end of the favor accorded learned women." [3]
As a result of "the low estimate of learning, in the first half of the
seventeenth century, as an appropriate pursuit for women . . . [there
was] a great decrease in the number of women who devoted themselves to any form of scholarship." [4]

It was not until the end of the seventeenth century that the pall began to lift and not until the eighteenth century that modern trends began to appear.[5] Our story begins a century later.

CHAPTER 1 ✿ THERE WERE GIANTS IN THOSE DAYS

Introduction: Seven Academic Women

Behind the statistical trends to be presented in later chapters stand human beings. Seven early academic women have so captivated my own imagination that before blurring them in colorless numbers I should like to introduce them briefly, as people and as women. Since they do not constitute a random sample of any statistical universe, I could not justify their selection on any rigorously designed procedure; however, the choice was not entirely capricious.

The first set of vignettes, describing a trio of pioneers—the first woman professor in the United States, the first woman student and faculty member of the Massachusetts Institute of Technology, and the first woman student and faculty member of Johns Hopkins University—, could easily be justified on the grounds that the women were icebreakers. The second set, describing two presidents of women's colleges, could also be justified. Emma Willard and Mary Lyon may have presided over female seminaries, but Alice Freeman Palmer and M. Carey Thomas presided over first-rate colleges.

Why Vida Scudder though rather than, say, Margaret Floy Washburn or Maria Mitchell or Alice Hamilton or Katharine Lee Bates? Here I must confess a personal bias. When, as an undergraduate, I was comparing notes with a friend of mine at Wellesley she spoke with excitement of one of her teachers. "When you touch her, sparks fly," she said. Her conservative banker-father harrumphed at this point that he would never send another daughter of his to Wellesley to be inflamed by those sparks; but there must have been hundreds of other girls so inflamed who, in turn, went back to inflame hundreds of communities with sparks from that torch. It was women of Vida Scudder's ilk who led Calvin

5

Coolidge to comment that the women's colleges were hotbeds of radicalism, and this current of radicalism was a characterizing stream in the story of early academic women in this country.

No one would, it seems to me, gainsay the selection of Ruth Benedict. She was an outstanding example in a field where academic women have been notably and conspicuously successful. For thirty years her books have turned up regularly in students' personal libraries; they all read her. She did more, I think, to shape the minds of thousands of college students than any other academic woman, and for this alone she had to be included. In addition, she is a kind of prototype of contemporary intellectual women. Like them, she wanted nothing more than she wanted love, marriage, and motherhood, and like them, she found these were not enough.

A different selection could easily have been made and the total impact on the reader rendered quite different, but these seven women do not give a distorted picture. Most of them were, if not reformers, at least do-gooders. Many were schoolteachers, for, as Mabel Newcomer has pointed out, the scarcity of men schoolteachers coupled with the increased recognition of the importance of an educated electorate had opened up this profession to ambitious young women; [1] without this recourse some could not have financed their higher education. Two were in the field of science, four were in the humanities, and one—Ruth Benedict—was in a combination of the two; she was a poetic and humane scientist. One had only an honorary degree; four had earned—in the case of Alice Freeman Palmer, semiearned—doctorates. One was justifiably proud of her Zurich Ph.D.; one contemned the Ph.D. Four were married only to their careers. Two were happily married and one unhappily married to academic men.

First Woman Professor: Maria Sanford [2]

Maria Sanford, whom her biographer calls a Connecticut Yankee, was born in Saybrook in 1836. Her father was a cobbler who aspired to be a shopkeeper. He did, in fact, go to Georgia and open a shop; however, it failed in the great panic of the 1830's, and he returned to Connecticut, where Maria was born. He was advised to go through bankruptcy, but declined, and by dint of great deprivation finally paid off his debts. This was a pattern that his daughter was to reproduce in her own life years later.

The home was poor. Maria Sanford said "there was no sordidness in their poverty";[3] however, she was never to rid herself of the scars of that poverty. All the efforts of her sympathetic biographer cannot hide the fact that money was a grand passion with her. She worked like a slave to earn it. She was rebuked both at Swarthmore and at Minnesota for taking so much time from her academic work for outside lecture tours. She was ordered not to accept money for tutoring students. She was accused of making money by renting out books. She engaged in what at this distance look suspiciously like get-rich-quick schemes, failed, and, like her father—refusing the advice of the Governor of Minnesota to file a petition of bankruptcy—had to spend a lifetime in penury in order to pay off her indebtedness. She lived a life of embarrassing frugality. She would pick paper from the campus to start a fire in her classroom, reassuring the students that the University was not paying for it. She dressed so unbecomingly that she antagonized some of her students. Some only made fun of her, but one faction went so far as to petition to have her dismissed. Others, however, rallied to her defense and honored her.

Whatever her peculiarities, on the platform she was a spellbinder, and in the classroom a fascinating teacher. At Swarthmore she taught history and political science, making both subjects come alive for her students. She was especially interested in the bright problem-boys, performing for them what is now called the counseling function. She resigned from Swarthmore for personal reasons in 1879 at the age of forty-three with no other job in prospect. President Folwell of Minnesota heard her at Chatauqua and hired her for his university in 1880. She continued her outside lecturing; she preached; she founded an improvement league to beautify the city; she won a prize in a favorite-teacher contest run by a local newspaper. But she was also in trouble with the Board of Regents. She applied in 1900 for the position of president at the University of Idaho, but was rejected. Her salary at the university was reduced; her colleagues criticized the way she handled her department. Not until two years before her retirement was her salary restored so that she could retire on her Carnegie pension.

Maria Sanford had been self-educated, reading as a young woman under the guidance of John Fiske of Harvard. She was, therefore, overjoyed to receive the degree of Doctor of Humane Letters from Carleton College in 1917. "The greatest day in her life" came when she was asked to give the commencement address at the University of Minnesota in 1909.

The burden of her talk was the duty of the university to teach its students how to solve social problems. Reflecting the characteristic uplift orientation of women of her position, she elaborated the thesis that in great historic class conflicts "the oppressed have always found strong supporters and wise leaders among the upper classes, especially among the educated; . . . so that the rich and gifted may hear the cry that comes up from the poor in their ignorance and squalor, and be proud to come to the rescue."[4]

After her retirement, again reflecting the do-good orientation of early academic women, she spent her life doing what she could "in the interest of any cause for which her help was wanted,"[5] including Negro education, help for the unemployed, child laborers, and the feebleminded. As were the lives of other early academic women, hers "was filled with self sacrificing labor for others, and with earnest endeavor to forward every good cause. She was constantly communicating, through her own vigorous personality, a zealous enthusiasm for education, for character building, and for civic righteousness to all young people with whom she came in contact."[6] Like the other academic women, she was finding great satisfaction in the self-fulfillment which this great new stage for activity—the academic world—was now making possible.

First Woman Member of the Faculty at M.I.T.: Ellen Richards

Ellen Swallow Richards, like Maria Sanford, was also a New Englander, born in Massachusetts in 1842. She also was reared in an ambience that emphasized service: "At that time in that region, . . . earnestness, conscientiousness, and unyielding devotion to duty were breathed in with the air of puritan New England, and self-sacrifice was demanded of women both by tradition and by public opinion."[7] Her father was a farmer who, like Maria Sanford's father, also aspired to be a shopkeeper. Both the father and mother were well educated for the day, graduates of Ipswich Academy, and both had been teachers.

Ellen worked in her father's store while she attended the Westford Academy, from which she graduated in 1862. She taught school, helped in the store and in the household, and at the same time prepared for college. At one time she was so poor that she had to live on bread and milk. At Worcester, where she was teaching, she enjoyed the "opportunity of doing good" both at a mission school and at the local jail.

Still, at age twenty-three, she complained that she had done too little for her Saviour in comparison with what she ought to have done. Between 1866 and 1868 she suffered what—in the light of Nevitt Sanford's researches—we have come to recognize as a common malaise of talented young women, the frustration of unused capacity. In 1868 she entered Vassar as a special student and was "delighted even beyond anticipation."[8] Her chemistry professor believed that "science should help in the solution of practical problems," and under his influence "an unrecognized leaning towards social service . . . led her . . . to abandon astronomy and study chemistry."[9] When her parents wrote telling her about people who asked what she was preparing herself for at college, she replied:

> Tell all such interested individuals that my aim is now, as it has been for the past ten years, to make myself a true woman, one worthy of the name, and one who will unshrinkingly follow the path which God marks out, one whose aim is to do all of the good she can in the world and not to be one of the delicate little dolls or the silly fools who make up the bulk of American women, slaves to society and fashion.[10]

Vassar College seemed a long way from New England, though, and the distance highlighted her appreciation of her New England background: "I never fully realized how much a New England birth was worth. I am so happy that that was my lot. It is a great deal in these days. I feel it so keenly now when I am away from it among strange people almost. Dear old New England is the home of all that is good and noble with all her sternness and uncompromising opinions."[11]

She saved money for a telescope at the expense of clothing, for she had enough "in my head to balance what is wanting on my back."[12] She argued that long graduation dresses and finery hurt the college. "I have lived up to my principles on dress while here and hope that I have done some good."[13]

After graduation, at the age of twenty-seven, she had hoped to go to Argentina to teach, but the plan fell through. Her father was now in a new business—manufacturing building stone—and to help him she wanted to study more chemistry. She was advised to apply for admission to the Massachusetts Institute of Technology. On her twenty-eighth birthday, December 3, 1870, the faculty received her application, and a week later she was accepted. She was, however, not to pay fees so that the president could have an out if he were criticized for admitting a woman; he could say she was not a regularly registered student.

Unlike Maria Sanford or Florence Sabin, Ellen Swallow made friends and influenced people by performing the feminine role in an almost ostentatious manner:

> I am winning a way which others will keep open. Perhaps the fact that I am not a Radical or a believer in the all powerful ballot for women to right her wrongs and that I do not scorn womanly duties, but claim it as a privilege to clean up and sort of supervise the room and sew things, etc., is winning me stronger allies than anything else. Even Professor A. accords me his sanction when I sew his papers or tie up a sore finger or dust the table etc. Last night Professor B. found me useful to mend his suspenders. . . . I try to keep all sorts of such things as needles, thread, pins, scissors, etc., round and they are getting to come to me for everything they want and they almost always find it and as Professor——said the other day, "When we are in doubt about anything we always go to Miss Swallow." They leave messages with me and come to expect me to know where everything is—so you see I am useful in a decidedly general way—so they can't say *study* spoils me for anything else. . . . Professor Ordway trusts me to do his work for him which he never did anybody else. . . . I am only too happy to do anything for him.[14]

No wonder that presently she was an assistant in the chemistry laboratory.

She received her B.S. in 1873 and would have liked to earn a Ph.D., but there was no one around to help or advise her. She went, therefore, into the private practice of sanitary chemistry. In 1876 she became instructor in the so-called Woman's Laboratory, established at M.I.T. that year to train schoolteachers, especially in laboratory techniques. Ellen Swallow, who had married Robert Hallowell Richards, head of the department of mining engineering in 1875, taught at the Woman's Laboratory without salary for seven years and even contributed a thousand dollars a year for its support. When it was torn down in 1883, she felt like a mother whose children have all left home: "Everything seems to fall flat and I have a sense of impending fate which is paralyzing." [15] Fortunately she was made instructor of sanitary chemistry at M.I.T. the next year, 1884, and held this position for twenty-seven years. In addition she established correspondence courses and served, in effect, as dean of women.

If money was a central value in the life of Maria Sanford, power was in the life of Ellen Swallow Richards.[16] She loved to manage things. Her real vocation was that of leader. Upon learning of some social injustice, she wrote in her diary, "We must see to that." [17] "See to it" she did, "from the moment of her own conviction . . . unceasingly wherever and with whosoever she saw an opportunity to improve the material conditions of living." [18]

In the Boston Kitchen, whose avowed purpose it was to change the diet of the working classes in the direction of scientific nutrition, she failed because poor people perversely preferred their unscientific diets to those she prescribed for them. She aroused some antagonism also in her efforts to improve institutional cooking, but she did succeed in establishing a school lunch program. For her, research was always secondary to "sociologic progress." [19]

In 1898 she spoke to the so-called Lake Placid Club on the domestic service problem. There followed ten Lake Placid Conferences; in 1908 the Lake Placid Conference was transformed into a national organization, the American Home Economics Association. She was also one of the founders of what is now the American Association of University Women.

Ellen Richards coined the term "euthenics" for the science of controllable environment, and she became the patron saint of the home economics colleges which sprang up on the land-grant campuses. From her they received the great emphasis on science in the service of human living, an ideal which has guided them ever since.

First Woman Professor at Johns Hopkins University: Florence Sabin

Florence Sabin was not born in New England, but she went to live with her grandparents on the Sabin farm in Vermont when she was twelve, and she became essentially a New Englander in her absorption of the Protestant ethic. She was born in Colorado in 1871, daughter of a mine-owner. Her mother died when she was seven, and from the ages of eight to twelve she lived with her uncle in Chicago before she and her older sister went to stay with their Huguenot grandparents in Vermont, where they attended the Vermont Academy.

> Some Vermont tradition had rubbed off on the two girls at the Sabin farm, and still more was absorbed by them before they finished the Academy. They came to believe that every one was obliged to use all the intelligence he had. Gradually they came to appreciate Vermont virtues—action, not words; good habits; determination; thoroughness. . . . Grandfather wrote . . . that the Sabin heritage was beginning to peek through.[20]

Florence Sabin was interested in music but had to admit she was not good enough to make a career of it. She turned to science and after graduation from the academy in 1889 went on to Smith. Like Maria Sanford and Ellen Richards, she taught—first in high schools and then at Smith—to earn enough to continue into graduate work.

Florence Sabin's biographer suggests a bipolar set of forces operating on this talented young woman. Since she was not pretty and could probably not attract a husband, she therefore had to make a career for herself. Pressure from the other pole came from the outside, from a group of militant fighters for women's rights.

> She began to appraise herself. Her hair, to her way of thinking, was frizzy; her eyes were no good without the glasses that had become almost a part of her. Her hands? They were too small for beauty. There was no question about it—in appearance she was plain. She would never attract any one.
>
> Other Smith College girls went to Amherst and to other men's colleges to parties. They entertained men on campus. She did not even know how to dance with men. She faced the startling fact that she had never had a beau. She probably would never marry and have a home. . . . Florence turned her mirror to the wall. There was no use in her trying to be beautiful,

for she could never accomplish it, no matter how hard she worked at it. What was the future of a woman who wasn't even passably good-looking? Nothing except possibly a career.[21]

She consulted a well-known woman physician, Dr. Preston, who tied her ambitions firmly to the kite of women's rights.

"You see, it's all tied up with the rights-for-women movement. Any woman who wants to be a doctor must work for women as women, and not alone for herself." Florence had never entered into the campaign for women's rights. Somehow fighting wasn't in her makeup. She listened to Dr. Preston's arguments on woman suffrage and, before she went back to her room, had agreed with her that participation in the struggle would not be too high a price to pay for a medical education. . . .
Dr. Preston had said it would be a struggle in which Florence must participate. If there was any fighting instinct in her own pioneer background, it was high time she showed it. If she wanted to become a doctor, she would have to do battle on many fronts. Suddenly she made up her mind to go on with the idea. A doctor she was going to be.[22]

The admission of women students into the medical school at Johns Hopkins University had been, in effect, badgered out of a reluctant board of trustees. It was a group of four women—daughters of trustees—who raised the money which the new university needed so badly and held it temptingly just beyond the grasp of the trustees until they promised to admit women on the same terms as men.
Florence Sabin entered the medical class of 1900, easily passing the entrance examinations, but she was made to feel that she always had to be at the head of her class. The women who had opened Johns Hopkins University to women expected her to justify their faith in her.

The women of the Committee focused their eyes on her, standing ready to assist her in case of need, but expecting high performance in return. She was warned that she must look sharp, being a woman in a man's world. And Florence was reminded . . . that women had to work for women's rights if they expected to become doctors.[23]

The necessity to prove herself intellectually—and hence to justify the rights women were demanding—acted as an enormous spur to her. Her so-called "need for achievement," as it is currently labeled, was not only personal but group-imposed, and she succeeded.

She was awarded the Naples Table Association Prize of $1,000. . . . She was making her contribution to the women's rights movement, and she was having a glorious time. . . . The Baltimore women were more than pleased. She was justifying their faith in women in medicine. She was the reward of all their efforts on behalf of women in the medical school.[24]

The same kind of militancy characterized Florence Sabin's career as a faculty member. It was only when her scientific achievements made the discrimination against her so obvious and blatant that it could no longer bear scrutiny that the university capitulated and appointed her to the faculty of Johns Hopkins as an assistant in the anatomy department in 1902. The battle had to be fought all over again some fifteen years later, however, when the headship of the department became vacant. It was generally felt that the appointment would be hers, but it went instead to a man. The students were outraged and petitioned to have the matter reconsidered and the Baltimore women who had originally raised the money for the medical school complained that the university had let them down. Florence Sabin was offered, as a sop, the position of professor of histology. Her supporters wanted her to fight, but she did not. As a result she felt she had failed both herself and all women. In 1925 she left Johns Hopkins and her career as an academic woman to become the first woman member of the staff of the Rockefeller Institute for Medical Research. She remained there until December, 1938, when she retired at the age of sixty-seven. She then entered upon a third career as protagonist of public health programs in Colorado, where she succeeded in getting passed the so-called "Sabin Health Bills," setting up one of the best state health programs in the country. She was as famous for her reform career as for her academic career.

Driven, brilliant women, these three pioneers—puritans, enormously self-disciplined, filled with abundant energy, do-gooders in an age when this was nothing to be ashamed of, women of strong convictions. Powerful as personalities and able to fight if necessary, but certainly not with chips on their shoulders, they were the very stuff of pioneers.

Two College Presidents, Feminine and Feminist: Alice Freeman Palmer and M. Carey Thomas

Alice Freeman Palmer and Martha Carey Thomas were college presidents. They were contrasting types, one sweetly feminine, one aggressively feminist, and were both, coincidentally, daughters of physicians of modest circumstances. Alice Freeman was born in the rural community of Colesville, New York, in 1855; Martha Carey Thomas, in Baltimore in 1857.

Alice Freeman's home was poor, and she early had to assume family responsibilities to help her mother, who, only seventeen years older than she, was more like a sister than a mother. She taught herself to read at the age of three and was sent to school at four. When she was seven, her father decided to become a physician and her mother, with what resources no one seems to know, supported the family of four children for two years while he—in the modern manner—went to Albany Medical School.

Of course the cares of the household were doubled, yet in so splendid a cause as to fix forever in the mind of one of them the wisdom of sacrificing present comforts to ideal ends. Alice Freeman never forgot those glorious years. They were among the few events of her childhood to which she often referred; for they set a pattern to which she was ever after eager to conform, of noble aims, willing suffering, resourcefulness, persistence, and ultimate arrival at greater ability to serve.[25]

Her father established his practice in the village of Windsor, where there was a good academy which Alice entered in 1865 and from which she graduated in 1872. One of her teachers stimulated her enormously—in addition to falling in love with her and asking her to marry him—and she decided she must go on to college. Her father said he could afford to send only one child, and it must be his son rather than his daughter, but Alice was determined. She promised her parents that if they would help her through college, she would never marry until she had put her brother through college also. She won.

She flunked the entrance examinations at Michigan in 1872 but so impressed President Angell that he recommended she be admitted on a trial basis anyway. She worked extremely hard, making up deficiencies and being tutored while carrying a regular load. Family misfortunes required her to leave the university in her junior year to teach school a term in order to help her parents and to save enough to complete her college work. In fact, "throughout her college course solicitudes over time, health, and money never ceased," [26] but she participated in college activities, was a favorite of President Angell as well as of her professors, and did moderately well in her studies. Despite everything, she was successful.

There were eleven women in her graduating class, and "being pioneers and representatives of many who would come afterwards, they were burdened with a sense of responsibility." [27] Alice took a job teaching in a girls' seminary, and in 1877 began graduate work. "The plan of advanced study was never abandoned. From time to time, as other toils permitted, it was resumed; and though her thesis was never completed, in 1882 the University conferred on her the degree of Ph.D." [28] She taught at Saginaw, Michigan, with great success until 1879 when, after refusing offers from Wellesley in mathematics and in Greek, she finally accepted the headship of the department of history there.

Despite poor health Alice Freeman proved to be extraordinarily successful as a teacher. In 1880 she was asked to become vice-president of the college and acting president for the year. The senior class that year was more than ordinarily "animated" and could hardly wait to have a president not much older than they. She called them into her apartment and told them she had been invited to become acting president. She couldn't do it by herself, she said, but if they would help by taking over the problems of maintaining order, she would then be free to do the general administrative work and could accept. They said they would, and the order was extraordinarily good that year.

From 1881 to 1887 Alice Freeman was at the helm at Wellesley, and by her inventive changes in organization, curriculum, finances, and equipment transformed "a hastily gathered and somewhat distrusted body of teachers and pupils into the firm-built college which, when she left it, commanded universal respect." [29] Among other innovations was that of borrowing faculty from Harvard University. One such loan was George Herbert Palmer, who gave a course of lectures in 1886. In 1887 they were married, and she retired from Wellesley.

Thereafter she devoted herself to the usual causes of the day, especially education. In 1892 President Harper of the University of Chicago insisted she help him with his new university by becoming dean of women. All that was required was that she be there twelve weeks a year, any twelve. She accepted and held the position until 1895. Seven years later she died at the age of forty-seven.

Alice Freeman Palmer appears to have had the buoyant temperament which seems often to go with "consumption," which "ran" in the family. She was the embodiment of femininity, apparently owing her success as much to her personality and charm as to her intellect. The greatest scholars at the greatest universities—Michigan and Harvard—found her completely captivating. She favored women's suffrage but did not fight for it. The few years she served as an academic woman earned her a place in the pantheon far out of proportion to her short career. She was a women first, an academician second.

Not so Martha Carey Thomas who, though only two years younger than Alice Freeman Palmer and also a college president, was her antithesis in almost every way. At the age of fourteen she wrote:

> If I ever live and grow up my *one* aim and concentrated purpose *shall be* and *is* to show that women *can learn, can reason, can compete* with man in the grand fields of literature and science and conjecture that open before the nineteenth century, that a woman can be a woman and a *true* one without having all her time engrossed by dress and society.[30]

Her father, like Alice Freeman's, was a physician, and the family income was small, eked out from time to time by a check from her mother's family. As the eldest child she was early pressed into family service, helping in the care of the younger children. Her father helped to establish a Quaker school, which she attended.

> Outside school hours she and Bessie King felt they must try to learn Greek, since the study of Greek was regarded as harmful to girls and fitting only for boys; and the promise of "going into Caesar" in school, if she did well in her first year's Latin, aroused her to energetic effort. She had the unbounded satisfaction at the end of the school year of winning four prizes.[31]

M. Carey Thomas' biographer looks to her Quaker ancestry to interpret and explain the "rampageous" life of this complex woman, but it is not convincing. Something was driving her, even as a child. She "gloried in combat," had to climb the highest trees, crags, and roofs in sight, explore the wildest streams or woods, pit her mind against intellectual obstacles, test herself in reckless exploits, defy sun or wind—"all to the greater glory of womankind." [32] She was competitive even in love:

> Various . . . of her friends began to fancy themselves in love and, though she experienced no such tender emotion herself for any young man, she felt a little out of the swim in having no affair of her own. But a difficulty arose: "Suppose I should want to fall in love . . . who on earth would there be to fall in love with?" One thing she determined—if she fell in love, she would do so, not tamely like most of her friends, but "with fiery overwhelming passion." Meantime, to uphold her self-respect she must try her hand at flirting and at least outwardly equal her enamored friends.[33]

Whatever the reason for her passionately competitive and feminist orientation, it characterized her behavior from childhood on. She found boys less interesting than girls, and "if she wrote 'boys and girls' in her diary she quickly crossed it out, substituting 'girls and boys.'" [34] She railed constantly against the injustice of encouraging the education of boys but discouraging that of girls. She resented the idea that the best use a woman could make of her talents, no matter how splendid, was by being a wife and mother.

> All her life . . . she had to combat similar complacencies, the more galling because they never ceased to give her an uneasy feeling, as she confessed in her old age, that they might contain a grain of truth. Uncertainty, then as later, doubtless contributed to the overemphatic statement of opposing arguments. . . . "Well! one thing I am determined on is that by the time I die *my brain* shall weigh as much as any man's if study and learning can make it so.[35]

Competing with her cousin Frank, whose college education was taken for granted, she came to feel that she must also go to college. When he died, partly to distract her from grief, her parents consented to send her to Howland Institute, a Quaker junior college near Ithaca. When she graduated, she determined to go to Cornell. Her father demurred but her mother concurred, so at the age of twenty she entered Cornell:

> . . . with *A Purpose* backed by a strong will and an acute sense of everything bearing upon women's position in both education and society. She saw her fellow women students as crusaders,

taking it for granted that they, too, had won their way to Cornell for reasons similar to her own; and, since heretofore she had been a successful leader, she saw herself in the forefront of their militant ranks. To this end, one of her earliest acts on arriving at Cornell was to use her second name, Carey, instead of Minnie, as she persisted in doing . . . for the rest of her life. The added dignity and especially the sexlessness of the name were symbolical.[86]

She was disappointed in her fellow women students; they, on their side, thought her haughty and cold. She was not permitted by her Quaker background to attend dances, but she was good at athletics and understood baseball. Hers was not a socially brilliant college career, but intellectually a stimulating one. When she graduated, she decided she wanted to continue on for a second degree.

Her father was on the board of trustees at Johns Hopkins University, but she was not permitted to register as a regular student. She could, if she chose, study by herself and be examined by the university, but that was all. That was not enough. She tried and struggled along for a while, then gave up; it had to be Germany. As usual, her father demurred but her mother concurred, so in 1879 she went to Leipzig. In 1882 she transferred to Zurich, where she received the doctorate, *summa cum laude*.

Dr. Thomas was excited by the prospects of the new college being established at Bryn Mawr and wanted very much to be its president. The trustees were sympathetic. They considered her intellectually qualified, but she was inexperienced and not quite twenty-seven years old. Her judgment might be rash, and they were not certain of her loyalty to Quaker principles. In 1883 Dr. James E. Rhoads was appointed president and Martha Carey Thomas dean and professor of English.

One of the first things she did was to make a tour of the women's colleges. She used little she learned from them but based the organization of her college on what the men's colleges had done. She emphasized intellectual qualities in judging prospective faculty; the trustees were more interested in character. She agreed with them on curriculum, though her reasons were often different from theirs. She was much more strict than they in her policy for entrance requirements. They were finally won over, and "perhaps nothing that Carey Thomas forced through had such wide and cumulative an influence as these Bryn Mawr entrance examinations. . . . American education, directly or indirectly, benefited for a long time by the rigors of the Bryn Mawr examinations." [37]

As the daughter and niece of two members of the board of trustees, she was in a strategic position to learn what they were doing and to find out what she could or could not do and also, of course, to let them know what she wanted from them. A natural division of labor developed between her and the president, he taking charge of finances, appointments, and general policy and she the internal administrative functions. Actually, in any area that really interested her, she dominated. Her years as dean were, in effect, years of apprenticeship for the presidency, which she finally achieved in 1894.

Her zeal in her job sometimes led to overstepping of legitimate duties. She was accused of despotism and double-dealing, and twice she faced rebellion in her faculty. In 1906 they charged her with, in effect, dishonesty; she learned her lesson and returned to her job. In 1916, however, both the alumnae and the faculty revolted, charging despotism. The bitter fight was carried on in full public view, and in the end the faculty won some measure of self-government and direct access to the board of directors. She could take defeat without collapse of morale. Her faculty respected, even admired, her, but they did not love her.

Two more contrasting models of academic women would be hard to find than Alice Freeman Palmer and M. Carey Thomas— one appealingly feminine, one aggressively feminist. Yet both succeeded in the tough pioneering tasks they undertook. It is possible, of course, that if Alice Freeman Palmer had remained in her position as long as M. Carey Thomas did, she too might have toughened and become more aggressive. The job may have made the woman.

Class Conscious Rebel and Happy—Marxist—Warrior: Vida Scudder

Vida Scudder, daughter of a missionary who died when she was an infant, though born in India was, like so many of the other women who staffed the women's colleges in the early days, also a New Englander. Unlike them, she came from a more comfortable and a more cultured—in the narrow sense—family background. Her father was a graduate of Williams College, and his achievements were considered worthy of a biography. Her mother was a Dutton. There was enough money so that money was completely unimportant.

For the most part, like many New England families of those days, we were not specially concerned as to whether we were poor or rich, but greatly concerned over our vowels, discriminating among our neighbors on grounds not of their possessions but of their enunciation.[38]

Vida—feminine form of her father's name, David—could afford to be radical, a reformer. She could afford to be generous, to feel penned in by her class background, to be a Marxist, to sympathize with—if not to espouse—Russian communism. Her childhood was spent traveling back and forth between Boston and Europe, where she absorbed both cultures. Her mother sent her to the Girls' Latin School in Boston and later to Smith. She did not have to face opposition nor to earn money, and she did not have to work her way through college. She did not even have to take a position after she graduated; there was enough money to free her for whatever she wanted to do. She tried to be an artist and failed; she wanted to be an author and again failed. At the suggestion of Professor George Herbert Palmer, who later married Alice Freeman, she accepted a position at Wellesley, where her radical reformism often put her in an embarrassing position in relation to the college.

I had never considered money; I believe I was over forty years old before I made out a check. My mother once told me that our income, apart from my salary, amounted to $1,200 a year. . . . We moved serenely, shaping our lives by the simple maxim in which I was so well drilled that I practice it to this day: Never let the sun set on an unpaid debt. . . .
I hated my salary. Queer hatred, which would well become a citizen of Utopia, but hardly one in this commercialized world. . . . Yet to live rather on money earned than on money inherited seemed comparatively respectable to me. So my divided life continued. . . . I know that the division of my energies destroyed my chance of amounting to much on any one life; but oh, what fun I have had! . . .
At about the turn of the century, I caught the distaste for "tainted money" infectious among radicals at that time, and joined, if I did not instigate, a vehement protest made by

sundry members of the Wellesley faculty against accepting money from the profits of Standard Oil. The decorous Rockefeller Foundation was far in the future; the scandal of the normal methods of capitalistic competition was shocking many consciences for the first time. Henry Demarest Lloyd's book "Wealth against Commonwealth," had fanned the flame. Now Wellesley was a struggling college, dedicated to the pious education of young women; and that the (much solicited) offer of money could be other than cause of thanksgiving was an inconceivably disloyal notion to our trustees as to our honored President, Miss Hazard. I was not the only one to shrink from that money, but I was the most violent, and I signed, I forget whether by myself or with two or three others, a Memorial more extreme than that sent by the larger group. Many a discussion ensued on the perennial subject of academic freedom. . . .

Our little movement of revolt and inquiry was naturally disconcerting to the Wellesley trustees. From that time on, I perennially bothered them, and myself, by the ever recurrent question of loyalty. I consulted my rector, later Bishop Brent, as to the propriety of resigning from the college. "Stay where you are till they force you out," said he. "The deeper loyalty demands it; loss of the radicals would spell death for the colleges." I stayed, though with increasing discomfort, and I was not tipped out. . . .

Naturally, I disliked making the trustees unhappy. One of them wrote me, anent this "tainted money" business, an indignant letter which I long preserved. It took me sharply to task for stressing the curse which must rest on enterprises built on a foundation of social injustice. . . . Of course the money was accepted; the only concern of the trustees was whether our agitation should reach the ears of the donor and cause him to withdraw his offer. Either he never heard or didn't care; the money was spent on a much needed central heating plant. . . . We radicals were at least glad that the money didn't go into salaries, but I don't think our situation was really improved by the fact. . . . Some of us discussed resigning; but we all stayed on, largely because we perceived that short of fleeing into a hermitage, we could not escape the taint of commercial guilt. . . .

When the time came to retire on a Carnegie pension, the old problem, quiescent but never solved, was acutely renewed for me. I wanted to refuse that money, and I could have done so and not starved. But I took it. I decided that my legal claim on it involved moral responsibility for its use. So I spend it year by year, on radical social causes mostly religious in character and inspired if not endorsed by the Church; thereby seeking to hack off the branch I sit on. . . .

A sensitive radical in the college world is inevitably placed in a false and painful position, if only because the public will insist on holding his institution responsible for his opinions. Freedom is little more than a mirage, as soon as one is committed to group activity of any type. I had my share of the acute distress resultant on knowing that my presence was a practical disadvantage to the College which paid me for my services. The generosity with which I was treated enhanced this distress. I have been shown letters from irate parents threatening to withdraw their daughters on my account; I have been gently asked more than once to explain myself to the trustees; I have been informed of gifts refused because I was a member of the faculty. The most painful to me of these occurrences was when the third President under whom I served, Mrs. Irvine, a woman whom I warmly admired for her intellectual leadership, informed me in so many words that she considered me a detriment to the institution. Then I did feel that self-respect should make me resign. I took my trouble to my uncle, Horace Scudder, who was one of our trustees. He told me sternly to stay where I was. . . .

I went to Lawrence. I attended strike meetings. . . . I visited the workers' homes, bad enough to justify almost any revolt in my indignant eyes. I lunched at the Franco-Belge Co-operative, recognizing in that group, well versed as they were in revolutionary technique, the most competent among the strikers. . . . I spoke at a meeting. . . . I did not go alone. I was not the only radical at Wellesley. . . .

The Wellesley trustees were deluged with letters from both sides. . . . Again, Wellesley stood by her principles. My resignation was not asked. . . . I do not believe the trustees of any educational institution ever acted with more temperate kindness than the trustees and the officers of Wellesley. . . .

I was asked to submit an account of the whole affair to the trustees; and the request was made that I suppress for the coming year my course on "Social Ideals in English Letters." The only thing that grieved me was the attitude of my old friend and colleague, now Head of my department, Katharine Lee Bates. . . . Her first reaction was that I should resign. . . . On her retirement fourteen years later, she failed to recommend me as her successor. . . . I was saddened and grieved, much as I should have disliked the office.[39]

Vida Scudder spent a good part of her life trying to reconcile

Marxism and Roman Catholicism, and she finally entered the Roman Catholic church, although never surrendering her radicalism and never denying that she still had spiritual problems to solve.

She never earned a doctor's degree. She knew that not having one was a professional handicap, but she had too much autonomy—money is a wonderful support for autonomy—to subject herself to the ritual. She did not care to invest the time and energy required. In the years 1893-1895 she took time off but spent the first year doing settlement work and the second at the Sorbonne.

> Truth to tell, I was impatient then, as sometimes now, with Ph.D. research. What I cared for was to keep my students as well as myself in the presence of significant racial experience, embedded in forms of undying beauty; I thought that was what America needed, and I was indifferent to rummaging about in literary byways in pursuit of unimportant information. . . . So I did not then sacrifice much; but I did renounce concern for status. . . . But no Ph.D. for me; and, in that world, a permanently subordinate place.[40]

Different and yet the same is this model of the academic woman. Freed from the nagging necessity of earning a living, sure of herself socially if not ethically, a rebel and a reformer but like other early giants infused with social idealism, though unlike theirs hers was both Marxist and Roman Catholic—that was Vida Scudder of Wellesley, the one who infuriated banker-fathers, trustees, and presidents but who inflamed students who took her idealism home with them and filled countless voluntary and civic organizations with it.

Reluctant Scholar: Ruth Fulton Benedict

Finally, we come to Ruth Benedict—like her forerunners, a do-gooder. For several years after graduation from Vassar, she was a schoolteacher, a social worker, a seeker after fulfillment, but unlike her forerunners, she was trapped in the increasing uncertainties of the twentieth century. No longer supported by the comfortable convictions of the nineteenth century, she longed—or thought she longed—for nothing more than self-fulfillment through motherhood. Denied this, her life became a tortured search for something, for some way of expressing herself. Poetry and prose writing helped, but they were not enough. Not until she discovered anthropology did she discover herself. She threw herself into it with dedication. Her name became a byword, standing for a point of view, a world *Anschauung*, a way of looking at man that took over generations of college students. Her stance made any kind of certainty impossible but implied an almost tender—some thought sentimental—view of man. Perhaps no other person, man or woman, has had so profound an effect on the thinking of so many college students as this beautiful, humane, dedicated woman who out of her own understanding could write so poetically of Apollonian and Dionysian cultures, of chrysanthemums and swords, and of the races of mankind.

Ruth Fulton was born in New York City in 1887. Her father, who died when she was only two, had been a surgeon; her mother a teacher and librarian. From the time she was two until she was seven she lived at the home of her mother's family at Shattuck Farm, Shenango Valley, New York. From 1894 on, the family moved from place to place as her mother's position changed—Norwich, St. Joseph, Owatonna, Buffalo. From 1905 to 1909 Ruth Fulton attended Vassar, and then after some European travel she tried social work in Buffalo and teaching in girls' schools in California.

Like so many other talented young women she suffered from what we might now call the Sanford syndrome. Here she is at age twenty-five:

> It is always very hard for me to feel that year after year is just added preparation—and for what? . . . My aspirations this year have been so many agony points. My longing for understanding had been a bitter cry against blindness; my longing for expression, an impatient contempt of any word I could utter; my longing for service, a dull ache of knowledge of our isolation from each other, and of the futility of our helpfulness; my longing for friendship, a "blanching, vertical eye-glare" of loneliness. . . .[41]

Then, in 1913, at the age of twenty-six, she fell in love with Stanley R. Benedict and everything changed:

> How shall I say it? That I have attained to the zest for life? That I have looked in the face of God and had five days of magnificent comprehension?—It is more than these, and better. It is the greatest thing in the world—and I have it. Is it not incredible? It happened when Stanley came down last week. . . .[42]

It was a marriage that began in ecstasy. At last Ruth Benedict was finding fulfillment. She had never been a feminist; she had been looking for love. Love was one area in which women could equal, or surpass, men:

> . . . this loneliness, . . . futility, . . . emptiness—I dare not face them.
>
> So much of the trouble is because I am a woman. To me it seems a very terrible thing to be a woman. There is one crown which perhaps is worth it all—a great love, a quiet home, and children. We all know that is all that is worth while, and yet we must peg away, showing off our wares on the market if we have money, or manufacturing careers for ourselves if we haven't. We have not the motive to prepare ourselves for a "life-work" of teaching, of social work—we know that we would lay it down with hallelujah in the height of our success, to make a home for the right man.
>
> And all the time in the background of our consciousness rings the warning that perhaps the right man will never come. A great love is given to very few. Perhaps this make-shift time filler of a job *is* our life work after all. It is all so cruelly wasteful. There are so few ways in which we can compete with men—surely not in teaching or in social work. If we are not to have the chance to fulfil our one potentiality—the power of loving—why were we not born men? At least we could have had an occupation then.[43]

She found love but not motherhood. Although neither Ellen Richards nor Alice Freeman Palmer had had children, nothing in their biographies suggests that this grieved them unduly. They had both had the care of younger brothers and sisters in their own youth and knew child-care at first hand, not through a romantic haze. M. Carey Thomas was positively repulsed by the very idea of motherhood, even having the feminist's characteristic antagonism toward her own father for inflicting maternity on her mother. Not so Ruth Benedict. She was the prototype of the mid-century woman who was to seek self-fulfillment in maternity; but there were no children. The entries in her diary trace the slow disintegration of the marriage, entered into with such hope. She needed some avenue of expression, a job, but Stanley Benedict did not see the need. All he wanted was peace and quiet.

> Last night Stanley and I talked. We hurt each other badly, for words are clumsy things, and he is inexorable. But, at any rate, he does not baby me, and honesty helps even when it is cruel. I said that for the sake of our love—our friendship, rather—

I must pay my way in a job of my own. I would not, would not drift into the boredom, the pitiableness of lives like——or——. He said ʃhat, whatever the job, it would not hold me; nothing had, social work or teaching. Children might for a year or two, no more. As for the question of success in such a thing having any value in our relations with each other, it was nonsense; it only meant that I'd discovered now that marriage in its turn did not hold me. If I'd found we lacked friendship now, there was no solution possible—neither of us could change our personalities. He had no faith in the future.[44]

This was 1916; Ruth Benedict was twenty-nine.

In 1922 she took her doctor's degree at Columbia in anthropology and became Franz Boas' assistant at Barnard College. From 1923 to 1931 she held a series of one-year appointments as lecturer in anthropology at Columbia; in 1931 she became assistant professor, associate in 1937, and, finally, in 1948, full professor. She was Boas' first assistant for many years, serving as acting executive officer of the Department of Anthropology in 1936 and as executive officer from 1937 to 1939. During the Second World War she served in Washington as head of the Basic Analysis Section and the Foreign Morale Division of the Office of War Information and as lecturer at the Washington School of Psychiatry. This was Ruth Benedict's brilliant career, the career of a woman who in earlier years had written in her diary that "a great love, a quiet home, and children . . . is all that is worth while," who in speaking of careers had written, "We know that we would lay it down with hallelujah in the height of our success, to make a home for the right man."

It is easy to patronize these pioneering women of an earlier age; to puncture their obsessive reformism and idealism; to translate their cliches into the modern idiom which derides do-goodism and insistence on service; to point out that they were limited in the language available to them, that they had little choice between the language of "women's rights" and the language of do-goodism and service, that, in either event, what they were shouting was, We want out! But it is not easy—at least for me—even in these post-Freudian days, to denigrate them on this account. They really were giants—absurd sometimes, perhaps, amusing sometimes, but admirable and very great people.

The sketches here are, of course, only introductory. We will meet these women again from time to time throughout this book. They are presented here to serve as backdrop to the sometimes relentlessly statistical nature of much of our knowledge about academic women.

CHAPTER 2 ❀ FLOWING AND EBBING TIDES

Who Are Academic Women?

The operation of a modern university or college calls for a great—and increasing—variety of functions. We should, therefore, speak of the academic professions in the plural rather than in the singular. Despite such variety, though, and despite the enormous significance of their contribution, the academic professions constitute an extraordinarily small proportion of the total labor force. Out of a labor force of some 72,706,000 persons (July, 1960), only 382,664 persons —[1]about half of one percent—were in the academic professions (1959–60). Of these, 320,179 were involved in the key or core functions of resident instruction in 283,080 degree-credit courses for an estimated 3,891,000 (1962) graduate and undergraduate students in such courses, and 37,099 were in organized research. Others were engaged in counseling services, in taking care of libraries and museums, and in giving individual lessons, courses by radio or by television, and extension courses or courses by correspondence. In addition, since the distinctively American land-grant university includes among its "students" members of the great agricultural and homemaking publics, a large staff of teachers was busily engaged in such special classrooms as the model farm and the demonstration kitchen.

New functions are constantly called into being as new trends create positions not required even as recently as a decade ago. Specialization, for example, in research-contract negotiation and computer analysis are new developments. New kinds of custodial and retrieving services in libraries demand new kinds of specialists, and admissions problems have brought forth specialists in that area as well. As yet this accelerating proliferation does not show up clearly in the traditional categories into which data are presently tabulated. All the sex differences are not, therefore, revealed.

In this functional "jungle" men and women perform in different ways. Table 2/1 summarizes the variety of types of position held by men and by women in the years 1955–59. The sex differences are not out of line with theoretical expectations based on sex roles. On the theory, for example, that the roles assigned to women in our society are emotional-expressive,[2] the relatively large proportion of women in staff positions for student personnel is understandable. Similarly, the housekeeping or caretaking function assigned to women, as well as the sheltered nature of the work, would also help explain the relatively large proportion of women in professional library positions.

All of these women are "academic" in the sense that they are needed for the successful operation of academic institutions, but our concern in the present study is primarily with the roughly two-thirds who are members of the faculty for resident instruction in degree-credit courses. These women, and those in organized research, make up the smallest proportion of any of the functional categories; they constituted only 19.4 percent of all faculty members for resident instruction in 1959–60 and only 11.4 percent of the professional staff for organized research. These women, performing the most "masculine" functions in universities and colleges, are the academic women who are the subjects of the present study.

Four Periods

The story of academic women in the United States may be conveniently divided into four periods. Since the sociology, as distinguished from the history, of higher education for women in the United States has not yet been researched in depth, the criterion for the classification into periods may be superficial, based as it is on simple comparative rates of increase as shown in Figure 2/1. Periods so delineated, however, do seem to be characterized by concomitant relevant variables and may therefore have some validity, if only as a framework for the data.

Long-time trend data for all women on academic faculties, as well as for those on faculties for resident instruction in degree-credit courses, are given in Figure 2/1; the two curves both differ from one another and resemble one another. Our discussion is limited to the segment of the total delineated below (Table 2/2 B, Figure 2/1B).

The first period, beginning in the middle of the nineteenth century and continuing to about the turn of the century, must be interpolated; it may be assumed to have been one of fairly rapid increase. The second, from about the turn of the century to 1920, was one in which the rate of growth was at its greatest. The third, in the 1930's showed a marked slack in the rate of growth, and the fourth, since the 1930's, has been one of steady decline.

Late Nineteenth Century: "On Trial in the Eyes of the World"

The first period, in the late nineteenth century, was one of great pioneering giants, like those sketched in Chapter 1. It was the period of the founding and proving of the women's colleges. The rise of these colleges created the demand for the services of academic women, and the demand, under the circumstances of the time, created the supply. The great reform ferment which had begun in the 1840's, temporarily decelerated by the Civil War, crested at the turn of the century. Abolition, women's rights, temperance, prison reform, labor organization—these were only a few of the many causes which had been fostered in that great reform movement.[3] The higher education of women had been one of the many.[4]

The women who pioneered this movement were being watched, and they were conscious of themselves as innovators. They enjoyed great distinction. What they lacked in numbers they made up for in enthusiasm. Their situation was analogous to that of the girls in the Hawthorne Plant experiment; they were, in effect, cynosures, and they attracted followers who wanted to share their acclaim.

> The women who came to teach in the women's colleges in the '70's and '80's and '90's knew themselves on trial in the eyes of the world as never women had been before. And they brought to that trial . . . heady enthusiasm and radiant exhileration and fiery persistence.[5]

They were having fun. "Only the women who helped to promote and establish the higher education of women can know how romantic it was to be a professor in a women's college during the past half century." [6]

Many of them were in the New England Puritan tradition, like the women described in Chapter 1. They came from genteel but not affluent family backgrounds and often had to teach school to help finance their own training. They longed to devote themselves to human service, and their dedication attracted young women as models.

1900–1920: Reform in the Elitist Colleges, Service in the Land-Grant Colleges

The second period was one of rapid growth but also of consolidation of gains. It was the period too of the burgeoning land-grant college, with its fostering of the home arts, and of the professional school.

The traditional elitist women's colleges were, in a sense, at war with themselves during this period. The academic women who staffed them were still for the most part women with causes, still reformers at heart, but action was becoming less attractive than contemplation within the ivy-covered walls. The feeling began to grow that the academic role was not an activist one.

Some of the nuances of the conflict between active reform and academic contemplation have been preserved in a novel published in 1903 by Vida Scudder. It is about Hilda Lathrop, a wealthy young woman who refuses a job teaching art at a women's college because she wants to work in a settlement house. Later, disillusioned with that, she becomes a factory girl so that she can infuse work with beauty. Of major interest here, however, is the chapter called "The Academic Mind" in which the author contrasts the nonactivism of the faculty with the heroine's emotional involvement. The academic women cannot accept the heroine's choice of social work rather than academic work. One of them, a professor of biology, has this point of view:

The scholar can no longer live in the seclusion once dear to him. The modern world is one great whispering-gallery, and the wailings that rise from civilization sound insistently in our ears. I—hear—them—but . . . it is weak to listen. To allow one's self to be incapacitated for the honest work that one is best fitted to do by a morbid compassion for suffering that one cannot relieve is a temptation of these latter days.[7]

An instructor in economics comments:

> There are different vocations, and not every one is called to
> serve in the army of reform. The social question has vexed the
> wisest for more than one generation; it will continue to vex
> them long after our day is over. Meanwhile, the great normal
> activities of the world must not be suspended: scholars and poets
> and artists must fulfil the law of their being.[8]

The heroine, who has dreamed that the women's colleges might
become great centers of social movements, as the historic universities
had, is terribly let down. She loves the atmosphere of the college but
protests its lack of reform zeal.

> The whole atmosphere of the college . . . was grateful to
> her; its unworldliness, the strength of its communal interests,
> the simplicity of life, and the spirit of intellectual democracy
> that prevailed. She remembered the great life-communicating
> movements which again and again, proceeding from the historic
> universities—those centres where past and future meet—had stirred
> society to new endeavors. Might not such a movement start from
> the colleges for women, as well as from Oxford, from Paris?
> And of what order ought this living force to be, and whither
> should it flow? It was a democracy under whose fostering care
> these new privileges had been offered to the women of the new
> age, and the ideal of democracy made answer. . . .
> [After discussing her plans with the faculty, however, she be-
> comes disillusioned.] "Oh, this academic fatalism!" she cried.
> "Why is it that thinking seems to congeal the circulation? Where's
> audacity? where's adventure?—You think yourselves free, because
> you enjoy daring theories; but you are bound hand and foot with
> moral hesitancy. It is your type of fatalism which kept our best
> men for years out of politics. . . ."[9]

It seemed to Vida Scudder that success had ruined academic women.
Despite such complaints, though, the academic women in these
colleges remained reformers at heart. As late as 1920, Calvin Coolidge
characterized women's colleges as hotbeds of radicalism.[10] Vida
Scudder herself, as indicated above, was deeply involved in reform
activity, as were her colleagues at Wellesley. One was a convinced
Marxist, " 'sold' . . . to belief in the class struggle as the only means
of salvation."[11] An antiwar attitude was also part of the idealism
of many of these early academic women. Lucy Salmon, of Vassar,
incurred the obloquy of the public for her pacifism during World
War I. Emily Greene Balch was dropped from Wellesley for her

attitudes during the war (she was later awarded a Nobel Peace Prize). Lucy Salmon also espoused socialism and hesitated to accept Carnegie pension money. Other outstanding academic women during this period were made of the same stuff, but the reformist excitement was beginning to cool.

The idealism of another set of women began to take active form in this second period in the so-called home economics movement. These women were uninhibitedly and intensely service—but not necessarily reform—oriented, an orientation which continued to characterize them even when they later became academic women.

The major intellectual interest of the academic women in the elitist women's colleges was the humanities, but among the academic women who brought the home economics movement to the land-grant colleges, it was science. The truly electrifying concept back of the idea of the land-grant college—that the knowledge being created in laboratory and shop should be immediately funneled to the people who could use it—eventuated in this second period in a series of institutions throughout the country which, extending the classroom from campus to farm, home, and community, sent special teachers out to find the "pupils" wherever they were. The departments, schools, or colleges on the land-grant campuses which trained the brand-new profession of science-disseminators were, in effect, teachers colleges. They trained teachers not only for regular schools and colleges but also for the classrooms of the home and of industry.

The women's colleges had used as their model the contemporary men's colleges. Their curricula were almost indistinguishable from those of the best men's schools, and their standards were, if anything, even higher. They were, if not actively antivocational—some of them were—,[12] at least nonvocational. The women who staffed them might be activist in the sense of reformist, as indicated above; but when they contemplated the institutionalization of good works, they preferred schools of social work (Bryn Mawr [13] and Smith, for example) to schools of home economics.

The home economics movement was sparked by idealistic women—college trained but not necessarily themselves on college faculties—who wanted to do good. Ellen Richards, for example, was interested in the problems of the foreign-born, in school lunch programs, in euthenics; Caroline Louisa Hunt was interested in Negro better-ment; Sarah Louise Arnold was interested in child labor and immi-gration problems. All shared an interest in food and nutrition. The so-called New England Kitchen, established by Ellen Richards, be-came a kind of training ground, and it was the source of the first professional home economics magazine, *The New England Kitchen Magazine,* and its editor, Anne Barrow, wrote a cooking textbook.

Colleges of home economics presented different problems; there were no ready-made models for them as there had been in the case of the women's colleges. The women of the home economics move-ment had to innovate, feel their way, improvise; they were pioneer-ing a new effort in human history. It was not necessarily inevitable, although it was certainly not surprising, that the leadership of the home economics movement soon passed into the hands of academic women, or that the land-grant colleges absorbed the movement.

The practical, applied, and service-oriented drive of this cohort of academic women was reflected in the academic programs of the home economics departments, schools, and colleges. Not until the end of this period, around 1920, did the emphasis turn from practical work in cooking and sewing to general educational and to sociolog-ical, psychological, and scientific principles.[14] It was also at this time that home economics colleges began to demand the doctor's degree for their faculties at the top levels. There had been highly trained scientists before—with doctor's degrees from the great universi-ties—[15] but improved standards were making higher degrees of increasing importance for all who aspired to leadership.[16]

The second period in the story of academic women, then, was characterized by a continuing preoccupation with reform in the women's colleges, muted, however, by the pull of academic quietism, and with service in the home economics colleges. They were still women with causes. In the women's colleges there was at least concern for all the reforms then agitating the country; in the home economics colleges there was a strong emphasis on practical activity to serve people by applying science to the everyday activities of the home. The period of the first two decades of the twentieth century was the heyday of academic women.

1920–1930: "Surging flood of disillusion"

The third period heralded a change. By the 1920's the éclat of the earlier years had spent itself, and all of a sudden, as historical and sociological forces operate, the increase in the proportion of academic personnel who were women slowed down. The excitement which had characterized the first generation of academic women ebbed. There was less glamor, apparently, than in the past in the role of learned lady. Once the pioneers had established beyond doubt the ability of women to run and staff top-flight colleges, this fact no longer drew special comment. These academic women were no longer, therefore, in the spotlight, but were taken for granted. Like members of minority groups who strive passionately to be like envied models, once they succeeded they wondered why they should try. They also became less attractive to students as models.[17]

There was, too, the great postwar disillusionment. Most of the reforms of the first years of the century had not panned out, and those that had were disappointing in their results. Vida Scudder sketched this postwar psychological depression of the 1920's:

> On the surface, our Wellesley life flowed serene, clear, and not without sparkle; but there were dark undercurrents. . . . We all found it hard to maintain steady faith in those post-war years. There is a worse type of Depression than the economic; such was shared by most people who in the pre-war period had joyously hailed what seemed the rising forces of social redemption. The Great War had not made the world safe for democracy; intelligent reformers had never expected it to do so, yet it was not easy to watch the surging flood of disillusion which threatened to submerge the idealism and drown the hopes of the world, nor to see the reforms on which hope and effort had centered, hardly with exception halted or destroyed. Those ten exhausted years were the most discouraged I have known, and I say this in 1936.
>
> The loss of old comradeships was one sad natural result of the disintegration in social advance. Some of my friends . . . found refuge in the Roman Catholic Church; others, two in particular, joined the Communist party, where they have since rendered noble service. . . . We who remained doggedly loyal in greater or less degree to the methods and convictions of our pre-war years, felt increasingly lonely.[18]

It was not an atmosphere to attract adventurous young women; the glamor of the early days had passed.

Still the proportion of faculty who were women did increase,[19] however slowly, during the 1920's; it was only the rate of increase which declined. Beginning in the 1930's, however, the proportion as well as the rate of increase declined, almost precipitously.

1930–1960: The Great Withdrawal

Some of the decline in the proportion of academic personnel who were women in the 1930's must certainly be attributed to the great depression, for in such a time preference in hiring is given to men. Other changes were also occurring, however, and the decline continued far beyond the depression. More than economics was involved. The proportion of academic personnel who are women may be thought of as determined by the demand for and the supply of these women. The relative decline, not in absolute numbers but in proportion after 1930, might therefore be interpreted as due primarily either to a slackening of demand or to a shortage of supply.

The bald statement of a supply-demand model leaves unexplained, of course, the size of the supply, itself a complex of many factors, as well as the nature of the demand, and each of these variables depends in turn on many others. The demand for the services of academic women, for example, will depend not only on the number and nature of institutions of higher learning that can use them and on the number of students enrolled in them but also, in part, on such cultural forces as custom, tradition, and convention as well as discriminatory practices which automatically preclude them. The supply, in turn, will depend on such motivational factors as the relative attractiveness of academic positions in competition with other careers, including marriage, and on the costs of preparing for them, including also opportunity costs. Motivational factors will also include reaction to any anticipated impedimenta in the way of participation. In an attempt to explain the decline since 1930, Chapter 3 is devoted to a discussion of some of the factors involved in the demand side of the situation and Chapter 4 to those on the supply side.

Table 2/1 Proportion of Faculty and Other Professional Staff Who Were Women, U.S. and Possessions 1955, 1957, 1959 *

Type of Position	1955	1957	1959	Percent Change 1955–57		1957–59	
				Men	Women	Men	Women
Total Number Different Persons †	(69,475)	(78,496)	(84,690)	16.3 ‡	13.0 ‡	10.4 ‡	7.9 ‡
Total Number Positions †	—	(90,099)	(96,153)	—	—	—	—
Professional Staff for General Administration §	31.3	33.0	21.2	26.8	37.1	22.9	5.9
Professional Staff for Student Personnel Services	—	44.4	44.4	—	—	19.9	17.8
Faculty for Resident Instruction in Degree-credit Courses	20.3	19.9	19.4	14.0	11.3	9.3	6.1
Instructors or above	—	20.3	19.8	—	—	8.6	5.1
Full-time	—	21.6	20.9	—	—	6.8	2.6
Part-time	—	17.5	17.4	—	—	12.4	11.8
Full-time Equivalent of Part-time	—	20.4	19.5	—	—	12.6	6.4
Junior Instructional Staff	—	17.1	17.1	—	—	13.8	13.7
Faculty for Resident Instruction in Other Than Degree-credit Courses	18.4	22.2	22.8	46.4	43.2	16.1	19.6
Extension Staff	28.2	25.9	25.0	‖	‖	1.4	—3.2
Other Faculty, including Staff for Mail, Radio or TV, Short Courses, and Individual Instruction	28.1	25.4	22.6	—6.1	—17.4	28.3	10.1
Professional Library Staff	68.9	69.9	67.2	6.4	7.1	19.1	5.0
Professional Staff for Organized Research	11.2	10.8	11.4	20.8	16.1	13.3	20.5
Elementary or Secondary Instruction	61.5	61.2	59.3	13.5	12.2	10.6	2.0

* Data for 1955 from Office of Education, *Faculty and Other Professional Staff in Institutions of Higher Education* (Washington: GPO, 1959), p. 3. Data for 1957 and 1959 from Office of Education, *Summary Report on Faculty and Other Professional Staff, 1959–60* (Washington: GPO, 1961), table 3.

† The sum of the numbers of persons in each type of position exceeds the number of different persons because some professional staff serve in more than one capacity. Total number of positions represents the sum in all types of positions as classified in the survey questionnaire.

‡ Any percentage less than this indicates a relative decline for that category; any greater, an increase.

§ "Women constituted over one-fourth of the administrators in colleges and universities but were concentrated in women's colleges, according to a study made by the National Council of Administrative Women in Education in 1952. Women held about three-fourths of the administrative positions in women's colleges and one-fifth in coeducational colleges. Positions in which two-thirds or more of the persons were women included dean of women, director of food service, director of residence, and head librarian. Among other college administrative positions, women were from one-third to one-half of the registrars, bursars, auditors or accountants, and directors of student guidance, health, student activities, practice teaching, alumni contact, and student personnel. Over nine-tenths of the women's colleges and about two-thirds of the coeducational colleges had women members on their governing boards. However, women were less than one-tenth of all board members in coeducational colleges having any women on the board, and just over one-third of those in women's colleges" (Jean A. Wells and others, *1962 Handbook on Women Workers*, Women's Bureau Bulletin No. 285 [Washington: GPO, 1963], p. 20).

‖ For extension workers giving courses, 28.8 and 12.7 for men and women respectively; for other extension staff positions, 8.5 and 1.9.

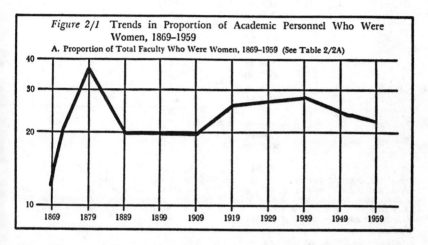

Figure 2/1 Trends in Proportion of Academic Personnel Who Were Women, 1869–1959

A. Proportion of Total Faculty Who Were Women, 1869–1959 (See Table 2/2A)

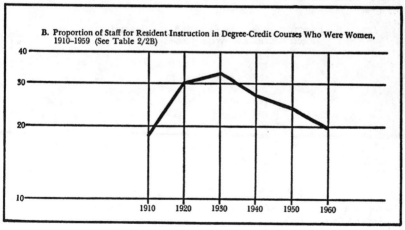

B. Proportion of Staff for Resident Instruction in Degree-Credit Courses Who Were Women, 1910–1959 (See Table 2/2B)

Table 2/2 Trends in Proportion of Academic Personnel Who Were
Women, 1869–1962

A. Proportion of Total Faculty Who Were Women *

Year	Percent
1869–70	12.0 †
1879–80	36.6 †
1889–90	19.6 †
1899–1900	19.8
1909–10	20.1
1919–20	26.3
1929–30	27.1
1939–40	27.7
1949–50	24.5
1951–52	23.5 ‡
1953–54	23.5 ‡
1955–56	23.0 ‡
1957–58	22.5 ‡
1959–60	22.1 ‡
1961–62	22.0 ‡

* Data for 1869–1956 from Office of Education, *Statistics of Higher Education: 1955–56; Faculty, Students, and Degrees* (Washington: GPO, 1958). Data for 1957–58 from Office of Education, *Faculty and Other Staff*. Data for 1959–60 from Office of Education, *Summary Report, 1959–60*. Data for 1961–62 from Office of Education, *Summary Report on Faculty and Other Professional Staff in Institutions of Higher Education, 1961–62*, OE–53014–62 (Washington: GPO, 1963).

† Estimated.

‡ Includes United States and outlying parts.

**B. Proportion of Staff for Resident Instruction in Degree-
credit Courses Who Were Women, 1910–1962** *

Year	Percent
1910	18.9
1920	30.1
1930	32.5
1940	26.5
1950	23.2
1955–56	20.6
1957–58	19.9
1959–60	19.4
1961–62	19.6

* Data for 1910–50 from Dael Wolfle, *America's Resources of Specialized Talent* (New York: Harper, 1954), p. 230. Data for 1955–56 and 1957–58 from Office of Education, *Faculty and Other Staff*. Data for 1959–60 from Office of Education, *Summary Report, 1959–60*. Data for 1961–62 from Office of Education, *Summary Report, 1961–62*.

CHAPTER 3 ❀ DEMAND: THE
THEORY AND PRACTICE OF
DISCRIMINATION

The Great Demand

Once the depression had lifted, the answer to the question of why there were relatively fewer women in academia than there had been earlier could not lie in a scarcity of openings. Both the number of institutions of higher education and the number of college and university students increased, especially after 1950, as shown in Table 3/1. Not a decline in demand but rather a drastic shortage in supply was the major problem in academia in the 1950's and early 1960's. Indeed, the deficit of academic personnel was so great that active recruiting programs were instituted to enlarge the supply, notably the Woodrow Wilson Foundation fellowship program and the Faculty Program of the American Association of University Women.

Institutional and Subject-Matter Areas as Factors in the Relative Decline of Women in Academia

It may be, as has been argued by Budner and Meyer, that the great expansion of institutions and number of students has been more rapid in kinds of institutions which do not have many women faculty members.

> The great expansion in higher education in the past several decades has taken place primarily in secular coeducational schools. . . . These are types of schools hiring few women professors. Thus, the proportion of positions open to women probably has not increased as much as has the field in general.[1]

It is doubtful, however, that this premise could be substantiated.

Among the most rapidly growing institutions have been junior colleges and former teachers colleges, now reorganizing as state colleges, both types being among those which do have relatively large numbers of women on their faculties. The total enrollment in junior colleges increased 12.9 percent between 1957 and 1959, that in four-year institutions, 10.2 percent.[2]

An analogous explanation of the decline in the proportion of academicians who are women as a function of demand could be made not in terms of the rate of growth in different kinds of institutions but rather in terms of the relative rate of increase in the several areas of knowledge. Such areas as the physical sciences and technical disciplines—which are more "masculine" as measured by proportion taught by men—have, it could be argued, been growing at a faster rate than the others, thus creating a greater demand for the services of men than for those of women in academia.[3] This explanation can certainly not be ignored; but some of the "feminine" subjects have also been growing, notably foreign languages, especially since Sputnik. Long-time trends in student enrollments in the "masculine" and "feminine" subjects are not available, but it is doubtful if the differentials have changed enough to explain the trends here under discussion.[4]

If the decline in the relative number of women in academia cannot be attributed to a declining need for the services of academic personnel, nor to the differential rate of growth of institutions accustomed to using women's services, nor, again, to the differential rate of growth of subject-matter areas in which women have traditionally shown interest, is it then due to growing discrimination against them? Economists tell us that supply and demand are specific. If a community prefers white eggs, is "prejudiced" against yellow eggs, and "discriminates" against them, there could still be a shortage despite dozens of yellow eggs in the market. Is the correct image here one in which prejudice discriminates against a large body of well-trained women and excludes them from the many vacant positions?

The only answer offered here is that the decline has occurred in institutions—the women's colleges—known not to be prejudiced against women as well as in institutions whose policies we do not know. The existence of this situation dulls at least some of the force of the discrimination argument.

Decline in the Absence of Prejudice: The Women's Colleges

The case of Wellesley is especially instructive in this connection. Not only did its founder have no prejudice against women, he had a positive prejudice in their favor. He specified explicitly that the faculty must be composed of women (except for the professor of music), and he was willing to accept women who were not themselves college-trained. In fact, he sent some of his appointees to school to learn their trade in order to be able to teach in his college. The policy of positively favoring women persisted until the time of President Ellen Pendleton (1911–1936), who changed it to one of securing "the ripest scholars and best teachers for the College that her budget would permit." [5] In other words, sex per se was no longer to be a criterion in the selection of personnel. Any decline in proportion of faculty who were women would therefore have to be explained on grounds other than sex.

There was such a decline. The trend was similar to that in other colleges. Beginning in 1875 with a faculty entirely of women, with the exception noted above, Wellesley had a rising proportion of men on its faculty, until by 1960 men constituted almost two-fifths of the total. A summary of all officers of instruction and administration between 1875 and 1942, regardless of length of service, showed just under 10 percent to be men. In 1930, the proportion was about 14 percent; in 1940, about 20 percent; in 1950, about 27 percent; and in 1960, about 39 percent. The sciences, at least until the 1950's were able to find and keep women faculty members fairly well, but not so the other areas, as the accompanying data show (Table 3/2). Either women were less qualified than the men or less interested.

Vassar College also began with no prejudice against women, albeit with no such positive bias in their favor as existed at Wellesley. The professorial level of faculty consisted very largely of men, but the teachers were practically all women. As trained women became available, the number of women in the professorial ranks also increased. The proportion of professors who were women rose, reaching a peak in the 1930's, and the proportion of women in the lower ranks declined. Since the 1930's, the proportion of professors who were women has declined, as has, indeed, the proportion of women in other ranks also. From the 1920's to the 1950's, the proportion of all ranks who were women declined from 83 percent to 62 percent, as shown in Table 3/3.

A recent study of eight women's colleges over the period 1940–60 corroborates the above trends (Table 3/4). Six of the eight showed a clear decline in the proportion of faculty who were women, and the other two remained about the same.[6]

Even in professional schools, such as schools of home economics, once almost exclusively the domain of women and, again, with no positive prejudice against women, men have been constituting an increasing proportion of faculties. In the 1960's there was even talk of men becoming deans of colleges of home economics. There might, of course, have been another factor involved here, a desire to upgrade the prestige of a profession by attracting men. That men might be thought to bring prestige to a profession is itself an interesting sociological phenomenon but one that cannot be pursued further here except to note that if it is true that men do upgrade a faculty, then their selection is functional.

Although the conclusion from the above discussion is that a growing discrimination against women in academia cannot be invoked to explain the decline in the relative number of women, the subject of discrimination is such an important one that much more attention is called for. The theme of discrimination bobs up everywhere in analyzing the position of academic women. It is invoked not only to explain the relative decline in the proportion of academic personnel who are women but also to explain the institutional distribution of academic women and their relatively lower professional position. However, as all students of minority groups well know, discrimination, because it implies motivation, is an extraordinary difficult process to delineate, let alone to assess.

The Theory of Discrimination: Autonomous and Judgmental Competition

An analysis in depth of any kind of discrimination involves an analysis of the total allocation system in which it occurs. There are several such systems by which any scarce value—goods, services, rewards of any kind—may be allocated. Competition is one.[7]

Among the others are several systems of arbitrary priorities. One such priority system is segregation of those involved into noncompeting sets on the basis of some ascribed criterion, such as age, sex, race, or lineage. Or the priority may be on the basis of seniority: first come, first served. Distribution on the basis of equality, as in rationing, is another method. Or one can reduce the demand for scarce items by raising the effective "price"—that is, the effort required to achieve them—so high that many decide the candle is not worth the effort; the value is "priced out of the market." Still another way to distribute scarce values is by sheer chance; we toss for them.

If allocation is based on some principle or system of priority, whatever it is, discrimination is built into the process. Discrimination is made by the judge in terms of the criterion involved. You get—or do not get—the scarce value because you are old, colored, a female, youngest-in-service, or whatever. This alternative to competition is, in effect, intrinsically discriminatory in the sense that it involves discriminating among the entities, albeit on a collective rather than an individual basis.

Competition as a method of allocating scarce values is also intrinsically discriminatory. Indeed, it is the function of competition to make accurate discriminations among the competing entities. The existence of individual differences as well as scarcity is one of the conditions of competition. If there were no individual differences among the entities, the scarce value could be allocated on a chance basis.

Competition may be autonomous or judgmental.[8] In the first, the process itself selects the winner; in the second, a human being or committee of human beings does.

In the academic world, the plums—the best positions—are presumably distributed by judgmental competition on the basis of merit as the criterion.[9] Judges decide who the winner is, who is hired. Caplow and McGee have analyzed in some detail the criteria used in selecting winners in this competition.[10] They range from the stiff standards at Harvard, which canvasses the field for the best scholars and scientists, to the personal and sometimes petty criteria used by insecure college presidents looking for flunkies. Sex, they report, is one such criterion, and it is one which, they state, militates against women.

Judgmental Competition: The Functionality of the Criteria

Judgmental competition implies the existence of criteria on which to judge the competitors. Peter Blau and his associates have pointed out that there are both functional and nonfunctional prerequisites for any position.[11] Functional prerequisites take the form of such characteristics as intelligence, education, apprenticeship experience, and the satisfaction of specified legal requirements. There can be little reasonable quarrel with the application of such criteria in discriminating among the competitors in selecting personnel. Discriminations have to be made, and these are reasonable bases to make them on.

The hitch comes when other criteria are demanded, for it is by no means easy to determine whether or not criteria for discriminating among competitors are really functional, or are based on prejudice and custom, or are equivocal.

Is it, for example, functional to take acoustics into consideration when judging the qualifications of a candidate for a position? Here is one dean's position:

> When I plan faculty, I have no prejudice against women. But I do have to keep in mind the requirements for the specific job. I have no qualms about hiring a woman for plant pathology; the classes in that course are always small and even intimate and there are no technical difficulties with respect to acoustics. But for the course in European History I would never hire a woman. The classes are enormous, the acoustics of our lecture halls are not the best, and the general set-up would militate against a woman teacher. In Ancient History, on the other hand, where, again, the classes are small, I would not hesitate to hire a woman.

A determined protagonist might argue that, functional as this dean's criterion sounds, electronic devices could overcome the vocal disabilities of a woman otherwise qualified for the position. Still the dean could probably vindicate his policy with many people.

For both men and women, it would probably be generally conceded, physical appearance suitable for a role—except in extraordinary cases such as that of Albert Einstein—is a functional criterion to apply in selecting academic personnel; but is it functional to make more of it in the case of a woman, to worry that she might have too much appeal for her students or her colleagues, or too little and thus antagonize them? [12]

Is it functional to make congeniality a criterion? This is a much-argued question even in the case of men. If one has to choose between a curmudgeon who publishes extensively but is hard to live with and a pleasant man who publishes moderately but is easy to live with, what is the functional thing to do? [13]

Closely related to this criterion is one which has to do with the drawing power of the candidate. Will he attract good students? Will he attract other good colleagues? This is, essentially, the criterion which most mitigates against women according to Caplow and McGee. Whatever else they may do for a department, a university, and for students, if they do not bring distinction which will make it easier to attract other people, they do not have the qualifications needed.

Is it functional to take into account certain role-related considerations not necessarily related to either the physical or intellectual qualifications of the candidate? Something not in the candidate himself, or herself, such as, for example, "effect on others" or "looking the part" according to role expectations? Here is the dean quoted above on this subject:

> For introductory economics I would be very glad to hire a woman. But for tax economics, no. The tax economist has to go to tax assessors, to tax collectors, to all kinds of record-keepers throughout the state and make contacts with men on a business-like basis. I would hesitate to put a woman in that position in my state. I am sure that she would be as competent as a man in tax theory, in research design; but she would not be as likely as a man to make the practical connections with the laymen in our county offices who are very parochial in their perspective.

Again, a determined protagonist might argue that not the requirments for the tax economics position but prejudice precluded a woman from fulfilling them, prejudice not on the dean's part, perhaps, but on the county tax officers' part.[14] Again the dean could probably vindicate his policy by arguing that educating his student body, not county tax officers, is his job.

However good a case can be made for the functionality of any specific criterion in the selection of staff, Tiedeman and his associates warn against accepting it uncritically. It is often a screen or rationalization for prejudice.

> Rationalizations like these surround the exclusion of the aged, the Negro, the Jew, and others. Equally insidious are rationalizations of preference for the old school tie, one's son or relatives, club affiliations, and the like. . . . [As a result] it is . . . difficult to prove that discrimination exists, and, if it does exist, that it is non-functional. This is particularly true of alleged discrimination because of sex and age.[15]

It is fatally easy to find good reasons for doing what we already want to do.

There is one criterion often applied in the consideration of women for positions which requires special consideration. Ruth Benedict stated it in her diary, quoted in Chapter 1. "We have not the motive to prepare ourselves for a 'life-work' of teaching, of social work—we know that we would lay it down with hallelujah in the height of our success, to make a home for the right man." [16] Is it—considering this attitude—functional to require that commitments be firm and fairly lasting? This is how the situation looks to one department head:

It is sometimes charged that women are unfairly discriminated against in the making of academic appointments. My own concern is that I probably appoint too many of them to graduate assistantships and to the teaching staff—particularly at the instructorship level.

On behalf of the women, it should be said that they are appointed in fair and free competition with male applicants and, so far as can be determined from credentials, they win the appointments because they appear to be superior to their competitors. In competition with some other professional outlets, teaching remains sufficiently undercompensated so that the superior men tend to be attracted to other fields. Women, then, are more available for the comparatively low-paid positions in teaching.

My own practice is to appoint women to about 50 percent of our graduate assistantships and to about 30 percent of our instructorships. My fear that this is too large a proportion of women appointees arises from the considerations: (1) that women are less likely to complete the degree programs upon which they embark; (2) that even if they do, marriage is very likely to intervene and to prevent or considerably delay their entry into the teaching profession; (3) that even when they do become full-time teachers (at whatever level, including the university), their primary sense of responsibility is to their homes, so that they become professional only to a limited degree; (4) that they are far less likely than are men to achieve positions of leadership in their profession, either through research and publication or through activity in academic organizations. . . .

In sum, I think that when the State and our staff invest large sums of money and a great deal of time and effort in the professional development of a woman, we take a far greater risk that this investment will not be professionally productive than when we make a similar investment in a man. For this reason it seems sensible to me that when we are considering male and female candidates of presumably equal calibre, some small preference should be given to the men.

This man and others like him who must judge candidates for a position are, in effect, in a "game against nature": that is, they have to make a decision in the presence of risk or uncertainty. All they can do is play the probabilities. They must weight the qualifications of the candidate by the probability of keeping him in order to arrive at the "payoff." The practical result, however unfair it may be, is often to make the payoff greater for a male candidate than for a female candidate.[17]

The Practice of Discrimination: The Elite

Whatever the theory may be, there is in practice no question that academic competition discriminates against the best women candidates. Dael Wolfle pointed this out some time ago. "The professionally ambitious woman is doubly handicapped in the attainment of her goals, handicapped by the prejudice and competition of men and by the lesser professional ambitions of most women and the employment policies which take account of that lesser ambition." [18]

Furthermore, by an intrinsic sociological mechanism, prejudiced discrimination tends always to make the best competitors its victims. Only the best become competitors in the first place. When there are many disabilities among the competitors, prejudiced discrimination is not needed. Less qualified contestants can be rejected on many functional grounds: They are not well trained, they are not competent, they do not have the skills, etc. It is only when all other grounds for rejection are missing that prejudiced discrimination per se is brought into play. Then it is that sex—or, for that matter, race or age—is relied upon as the criterion for rejection—the discrimination is prejudiced. Thus when a woman with superior qualifications is bypassed in favor of a man with inferior qualifications, prejudiced discrimination may legitimately be charged.

There have been many such cases. The story of Florence Sabin at Johns Hopkins illustrates one, as does that of Ruth Benedict at Columbia, who was kept out of the most exclusive men's club—the

Columbia University Faculty—for many years and was finally admitted only when she had to have status commensurate with her services for her students' sake.[19] Mary Ellen Chase left the University of Minnesota to take a position at Smith in 1926 because "generous as the University of Minnesota had been toward me, I was forced to acknowledge that a full or even an associate professorship in English would probably be denied me on the ground of my sex." [20] Every observer of the academic scene can supply many other cases.

There is a special category among the elite who are particularly vulnerable to prejudiced discrimination, namely the academic women who are in traditionally "masculine" areas. Again, sociological mechanisms are operating against these women. When the informal group structure in any work setting is institutionalized on a one-sex—in this case male sex—basis, the introduction of women upsets established patterns and creates difficulties. To avoid them, women are less likely to be hired. Such, to them irrelevant, considerations are especially bitter for women to take.

Rank and File

However convincing individual cases of prejudiced discrimination are, it is difficult to prove its existence on a large or mass scale. The most talented women may be and, indeed, are victimized by it, but apparently not academic women en masse. At least the evidence from awards and from the number of academic women in proportion to the qualified pool available is far from convincing.

Awards. The National Science Foundation awards in 1959, for example, were given to women in about the same ratio as to men; 12 percent of the applicants were women, and 12 percent of the awards went to women.[21] Ralph Tyler reports that 3 percent of the persons recommended for fellowships at the Behavioral Center at Stanford are women and about the same proportion of successful candidates are women.[22] Despite the fact that the extremely high attrition rate for women Ph.D. candidates is subversive of the aim of the Woodrow Wilson Foundation fellowship program—to stimulate young scholars to enter a career of college teaching—the proportion of Woodrow Wilson Fellows who are women is greater than one-fourth.[23] One study of the younger American scholar reported that "women appear to receive university fellowships somewhat more frequently" than men, but since this particular study excluded teaching and research fellowships and assistantships, the findings are equivocal.[24]

Not at all equivocal, however, are the findings of a monumental study of 33,982 June 1961 graduates at 135 colleges and universities. After detailed analysis, the authors concluded that "women ... have no disadvantage or advantage in offerings" of stipends for graduate study.[25]

Academic Positions. The evidence for discrimination is not very compelling in the overall figures for the proportion of faculty personnel who are women. A test of such discrimination would lie in the answer to the question whether or not women are represented in the academic professions in proportion to some theoretically valid criterion. If they are not, discrimination could legitimately be inferred; if they are, it could not.

Is there any such standard? If we use the situation in other countries as a standard, the results are inconclusive. In Russia today, for example, it is reported that 35 percent of academic personnel are women;[26] in Turkey, Mexico, Thailand, and the Philippines, that "relatively large" proportions are;[27] in Germany, Austria, and Switzerland,[28] that about 10 percent or less are; in France, only some 8 percent; and in Italy only 5.5 percent.[29] Thus, as compared with Russia, the proportion of academic personnel who are women—22.1 or 19.4 percent according to whether one is including all or only core academic personnel—is low in the United States, suggesting the presence of discrimination. As compared with Western Europe, it is large, suggesting the absence of such discrimination. However, we have no way of knowing in any of these countries whether the proportions—large or small—reflect discrimination or not since we do not know what the potential supplies of academic women are.

It is commonly assumed that the proportion of academic personnel in the United States who are women is too small.[30] Whether one believes that women are underrepresented or overrepresented in academia depends on the theoretical basis one uses in judging. If one argues, for example, that since men and women constitute roughly equal proportions of the total population, they should therefore be equally represented on college and university faculties,[31] then even the 32.5 percent of the 1930's would be low. Obviously such a base is invalid; certain qualifications are demanded of academic personnel—the functional criteria referred to above. If one then argues that the proportion of women in academia should be equal to the proportion of women in the total population with more than four years of college education, the results are still unfavorable to women. In 1962 there were 3,171,000 persons 18 years of age or over who had five or more years of college education; 857,000, or 27.0 percent, were women.[32] This percentage was considerably greater than the percentage of women on academic faculties. This theory is, obviously, also fallacious, for it does not take into account the large number of educated women —30.6 percent of those with five years or more of college— who are not in the labor force.[33]

What is really needed is the proportion of those in the labor force with five or more years of college education who are women. This figure as of 1962 was 21.9 percent,[34] suggesting that women were represented in academic teaching positions in roughly the same proportion as they were in the minimumly qualified labor force. If the qualified population is limited to those with the doctor's degree, women are overrepresented in college teaching since they constitute only about ten percent of all doctors and not all of them are in the labor force. No more than in the case of awards do women seem to be discriminated against en masse in the case of academic positions. If the proportion of academic people who are women seems small, it is in part at least because the proportion of women in the qualified labor force is small. One has to ask why this is so, and Chapter 4 attempts to deal with this problem.

Before leaving the topic of discrimination, though, it should be emphasized that discrimination among the top women is in no sense mitigated by evidence that it does not exist among the rank and file. For the women who have the talent and the drive and the will to succeed in academic careers, it is no consolation to know that the top prizes are withheld from them because of policies based on experience with the rank and file. Actually these top women—perhaps more than three "sigmas" above the average —are not in the same statistical universe with the rank and file. They are, statistically speaking, in the same universe with their male counterparts. They do not have the interests of the rank-and-file women, and they are deprived of many of the rewards granted the men. They have a legitimate grievance.

If, then, the decline in proportion of faculties who are women has occurred in colleges known to have no prejudice against women as well as in other institutions and if fellowships and academic positions appear to be allocated to women in at least reasonable relation to the number of qualified applicants and persons in the labor market, prejudiced discrimination, however acute it may be in individual cases—among the most qualified women—can hardly be invoked to explain the downward trend in the proportion of women in academia since 1930.

An alternative definition of the situation emphasizes the supply side of the equation and asks why women are not available for the positions. Why do they seem less willing than in the past to enter the academic world? Chapter 4, as indicated above, attempts to bring relevant data to bear on these questions.

Table 3/1 Trends in Number of Institutions of Higher Education and in Number of Students Enrolled, 1869–1956 *

Year	Number of Institutions	Number Resident College Students
1869–70	563	52,286
1879–80	811	115,817
1889–90	998	156,756
1899–1900	977	237,592
1909–10	951	355,213
1919–20	1,041	597,880
1929–30	1,409	1,100,737
1939–40	1,708	1,494,203
1949–50	1,851	2,659,021
1951–52	1,837	2,319,496
1953–54	1,871	2,534,709
1955–56	1,858	2,661,473
Fall 1959	—	2,947,000
1957–58	1,940	—
Fall 1959	—	3,402,000
Fall 1960	—	3,610,000
Fall 1961	—	3,891,000

* Data for 1869–1956 from Office of Education, *Statistics of Higher Education: 1955–56, Faculty, Students, and Degrees* (Washington: GPO, 1958), p. 6. Institutional data for 1957–58 from Office of Education, *Faculty and Other Professional Staff in Institutions of Higher Education, First Term, 1957–58* (Washington: GPO, 1959), p. 1. Data for 1956, 1959–61 from Office of Education, *Opening (Fall) Enrollment in Higher Education, 1961: Institutional Data* (Washington: GPO, 1961), p. 1.

Table 3/2 Proportion of Wellesley College Faculty Who Were Men, by Academic Areas, 1930–1960

	Mathematics and Sciences	Social Sciences and History	Language and Literature	Art and Music
1930	8.8	29.2	5.9	22.2
1940	7.3	37.5	9.6	55.0
1950	7.3	48.7	15.1	62.5
1960	17.0	59.4	26.0	59.4

Table 3/3 Proportion of Faculty Who Were Women, Vassar College, 1865–1956

Year	Professors	Associate Professors	Assistant Professors	"Teachers" and/or Instructors	Four Ranks
1865	11			95	71
1874–75	22			100	75
1884–85	22	100		100	76
1894–95	29	100		100	66
1904–05	28	86		95	75
1914–15	36	100	100	95	80
1924–25	62	94	94	89	83 •
1934–35	67 •	82	92	81	77
1944–45	63	69	72	84	73
1955–56	58	70	45	66	62

• High point.

Table 3/4 Proportion of Faculties in Selected Women's Colleges Who Were Women, 1940–1960 •

College	1940–41	1956	1960–61
Smith	58.3	37	43.5
Wellesley	90.1	67	62.8
Bryn Mawr	51.8	50	34.4
Mount Holyoke		64	
Vassar	70.0	62	53.0
Barnard		59	
Hunter		59	
Douglass		13	
Newcomb		50	
Goucher	72.1	60	47.8
Agnes Scott		67	
Trinity		82	
Sweet Briar	68.4		66.2
Mills	51.5		51.3
Connecticut College	61.8		57.4

• Data for 1940–41 and 1960–61 from Frances L. Clayton, "A Source for College Faculties," *Pembroke Alumna*, 27 (Oct. 1962), p. 5. Data for 1956 from Woodrow Wilson Foundation, *Report on Activities, 1957–61* (Princeton: Woodrow Wilson Foundation, 1961), p. A–IV–24.

CHAPTER 4 ❀ SUPPLY:
THE MANY USES OF WOMEN

The Perennial Shortage of Women in Academia

There has always been a shortage in the supply of well-trained women academicians, even in the women's colleges. Women Ph.D.'s especially have been scarce. When Bryn Mawr opened in 1875, it appointed only Ph.D.'s to its faculty. There were, according to M. Carey Thomas, only four women Ph.D.'s in the world at that time, two of them in mathematics. "So we could appoint only three including myself as professor of English and the rest of our faculty had to be men." [1]

Even when standards were not as selective, it was difficult to find women to staff the colleges. The presidents' reports for Smith College, for example, were filled with examples of the problems involved in getting a good faculty. L. Clark Seelye noted that although "with the increasing opportunities for higher education, it became less difficult to find women competent to give collegiate instruction, . . . marriage made their tenure of office more uncertain." [2] He complained that "at present there are not enough good teachers to meet the demands." [3] At the turn of the century, President Tyler was made acting dean of the faculty because there was no suitable woman available.

In order to fill the ranks of its faculty, Smith had to "borrow" from Amherst. "I consider the College remarkably fortunate in being able to supply so well its own deficiencies from a neighboring institution," said one president, although he considered it "very important to have a faculty large enough to carry forward the main work of the College without outside help." [4] Wellesley, as noted in Chapter 1, followed the practice of "borrowing" faculty from Harvard.

There have never been very many highly educated women in

any area in the labor force, let alone in academia. The reason lies, first of all, in the high attrition rates of women in school beyond the secondary level. Even if educated, they may not be in the labor force, and if both educated and in the labor force, they tend less often to select academic professions now than in the past.

The Attrition Rate

Up to the age of eighteen, the usual age of high school graduation the proportion of girls who are in school is not markedly less than the proportion of boys who are. Since relatively fewer girls go on to college, however, at age 18 and beyond the proportion of women who are in school falls drastically, increasingly below the proportion of men who are in school (Table 4/1).

Put another way, of the 680,000 males who graduated from high school in 1955–56, 446,000 or 65.6 percent were registered in college in the fall of 1956; the corresponding percentage for women was only 37.7 percent. Of the June 1959 high school graduates, 54 percent of the men but only 39 percent of the women were enrolled in college in the following October.[5]

Some of the differential in college attendance is due to lack of financial backing, for when a family is faced with a choice between investing limited resources in the college education of sons or of daughters, it is usually the son who wins out.[6] (Unless, of course, the daughter is an Alice Freeman or a Carey Thomas.) Some of the differential in college attendance is doubtless due to the preference of young women for marriage, for although marriage no longer necessarily precludes college, as it did in the past, it still does for most young women. As of 1948, the chances are that about 22.7 percent of all eighteen-year-old girls will marry during a given year.[7]

Even if a young woman has financial support and even if she eschews marriage at high school graduation and enters college, the dropout rate for women is so high that the chances for her achieving the bachelor's degree are less than for a man (Table 4/2). The Center for the Study of Higher Education at Berkeley, California, has made a study of women dropouts and reports that although there are varied reason according to ability, one reason is common, namely, a lack of motivation, expressed in an attraction greater toward a vocation, social activities, or marriage than toward learning.[8] Still the differential is not too great. The proportion of those receiving the bachelor's degree who are women is roughly equal to the proportion of women enrolled for resident degree credit (Table 4/5), although there are some fluctuations among types of institutions, being higher, for example, in technological schools than in liberal arts colleges (Table 4/3).

Continued graduate training beyond the bachelor's level has to compete not only with marriage[9] but also with interesting job possibilities, for the last few decades have seen a great increase in the demand for the services of women. There is a broader market for their skills. Many professions seek to recruit them. Because of the general shortage of high-level personnel, there were, in 1962, for example, "more jobs in the market, more competition for graduates and more employers considering women for jobs who wouldn't have done so otherwise," an officer at one university was quoted as saying,[10] and a "a mounting demand for female scientists, technicians and mathematicians as well as for pharmacologists and zoologists" was reported.[11] When the attraction of interesting jobs is added to the pull of marriage, it is understandable that only a small proportion of women who complete college continue on for graduate study. In 1952, only 8 percent of the women who had graduated from college the previous June were full-time students; twice the proportion, or 16 percent, of the men were.[12] Since, apparently, relatively fewer men than women stop for the master's degree, the proportion of all master's degrees that are awarded to women is not markedly different from the proportion at the bachelor's level, roughly a third (Table 4/5).

It is beyond the master's level that sexual selectivity becomes especially drastic. Of those securing the master's degree in June 1951, for example, 12 percent of the men but only 3 percent of the women were full-time students the following year.[13] Even if a doctoral program is entered, the chances of completion are not high. At Columbia University, for example, only about 2 to 3 percent of the women who became doctoral candidates in 1945–51 had earned the doctor's degree by 1956, as compared with 5 to 13 percent of the men who had.[14] At Radcliffe College, the annual attrition rate for women at all stages of graduate study was 17 percent in 1959–60; only one student out of every ten enrolled received the doctorate.[15] Even among Woodrow Wilson fellows, highly selected as they were, the attrition rate for women in

1958–59 was twice that for men.[16] As a result, then, of smaller initial cohorts to begin with embarking on the journey toward the doctorate and of the higher attrition rates, women constitute only a small proportion (about 10 percent) of the total population of Ph.D.'s (Table 4/5).

Compliant Scholars

With the increasing emphasis on graduate training, long-time planning for it will doubtless become commonplace in the future, but until now, "going ahead for the doctorate, which is a prerequisite for long-time professional commitment, seems to be much less the result of a decision and much more the result of drift." [17] If this has been the case for many men, it has been the case for even more women. Their decision to go on to graduate study appears to depend on the kinds of experience they have had as undergraduates. Even the choice of field of study is strongly influenced by faculty contacts.

> In general, fewer women than men *plan* [italics added] on either graduate or professional education. . . . A woman's decision about advanced education is perhaps more difficult than a man's and is generally made much later than a man's. Women who enter graduate school are more apt to have been influenced by experiences at school than the men who enter.[18]

One study of 48 women working for the doctorate revealed that college and high school teachers had been primary influences for 27 percent. Friends, work associates, and even husbands were also influential. In general, teachers were more influential among those in the natural sciences and those from lower socioeconomic status levels; families were more influential among those from higher socioeconomic levels.[19]

The picture that comes through from the various studies is of a bright young woman who has persisted in her studies far beyond other women, happy and at home in the college or university library or laboratories, who finds herself encouraged to continue into graduate work by a professor impressed by her ability, even, perhaps, offered a graduate scholarship or fellowship or assistantship, and who—without relinquishing hopes for marriage—

accepts it, not because she purposively and planfully aspires to an academic career but because, at the moment, nothing more attractive offers itself.[20] Sometimes, graduate study may simply represent postponement of departure from the protection of campus life.

The process by which a compliant young woman may be maneuvered into graduate study even against her own basic wishes has been noted by the interviewers for the Woodrow Wilson fellowship program.

> Instructors, particularly young ones, tend to take a romantic view of female students and to encourage them in academic careers, whether they are so inclined or not. The student, reacting to her professor's interest, sometimes manages to convince herself that she does want a Ph.D., when she really desires a home and family. Often, members of the selection committee ascertain the female candidate's motivation towards scholarship and teaching much more accurately than her own professors, for they view her more objectively. Through questioning, they can lead a young girl to re-examine her own ideas and to save herself from embarking upon a career for which she has small real desire. An experienced interviewer in the program was astonished last year to discover that his own undergraduate assistant was not truly interested in postgraduate study. As his colleagues questioned her during the interview, it became increasingly clear to him that he had himself misjudged her motivation completely. When, rather hesitantly, he informed her that she had been turned down by the selection committee, the girl sighed with relief, remarking that, since the interview, she had realized that graduate school was not what she really wanted. It had taken the objective analysis of the interview to reveal both to the young woman and her instructor what neither had understood before.[21]

The Financing of Graduate Study

However important problems of financing may be in determining the enrollment of women in college, they do not loom up notably greater for them than for men so far as graduate study is concerned. It has already been noted, in Chapter 3, that stipends are as available to them as to men; however, and this is important, women are far less likely than men to apply for them.[22] Among college seniors graduating in June 1961 it was found that:

> Regardless of career field, Academic Performance Index, or marital status, women are much less likely to plan immediate graduate study. Even among girls with no immediate marital plans, the difference is considerable. Examination of the reasons data suggests that the sex difference is primarily due to differences in motivation, not to perceived financial or other external obstacles.[23]

Women constitute a relatively larger proportion of the low-motivation than of the high-motivation group. "Even in . . . fields characterized by high motivation for advanced study, the women show less interest in going on to advanced study immediately." [24]

The high attrition rate of women all along the line, then, from high school to the Ph.D. level, explains the general shortage of women in the pool of educated persons from which all the learned professions must draw. It is a phenomenon of very long standing. We do not have for earlier years as much detailed information as we have for more recent years, but the underlying processes must have been much the same: Financial support at the earlier, but not at the later, stages, lack of motivation, and the competition of marriage and work playing an important part.

Trends in Higher Degrees

The trends in the proportion of academic personnel who are women, which we are trying to explain, appear to be closely related to the trends in the proportion of higher-degree-winners who are women. Figure 4/1 presents data from Table 2/1 and Table 4/4 in graphic form to illustrate this point. For the proportion of master's degrees awarded to women, of Ph.D.'s awarded to women, and of academic faculties who were women, the trends tend to parallel one another. They were up from 1910 to about 1930 and down thereafter, with a possible upward trend in recent years. All were undoubtedly related to one another and to the headlong flight into maternity which characterized women in the 1940's and 1950's.

The Flight into Maternity: "The Feminine Mystique"

In the depths of the great depression, in 1932, in fact, when no one knew that the economic indexes were going to turn up, the marriage rate began to rise, and shortly thereafter the birthrate also. Demographers are still puzzled by the forces which shape the birthrate, pulling it down at one time and up at another. In the 1930's they were studying why people did not have children; in the 1950's, why they did. The reasons are not relevant at this point,[25] but the enormous change in the values of young people, especially women, is.

For women the change in values was to mean a headlong flight into maternity. Whether they wanted babies or not, they felt they should want them. Even motion picture actresses who had once kept their motherhood secret now flaunted their pregnancies. Dress-designers turned their talents to maternity wardrobes. The woman who had four babies could patronize the woman who had only three, and the woman with five or six could condescend to the woman with four.

Mabel Newcomer, tracing the decline in the proportion of women scholars, noted that although prejudices had eased and opportunities increased, "women are now faced with a new handicap of their own choosing—increasingly early marriages and larger families."[26] It was not a situation in which men were slamming the doors of academia in the faces of eager, ambitious women scholars but rather one in which, despite the lures of fellowships, women turned their backs and ran to rock the cradle.

The decline in proportion of faculties who were women, in brief, was due to a decline in the proportion of the educated pool —those with higher degrees—from which faculties are drawn (Figure 4/1). This decline, in turn, coincided with a rapid rise in the birthrate (Figure 4/2).

Augurs of Change?

There are a few straws in the wind to suggest that another change may be in the offing. For both master's and doctor's degrees, for example, there has been a slight recovery since 1950, more marked in some areas than in others (Table 4/6). The recovery has been greatest in education, the arts and professions, and the social sciences; it has been almost imperceptible in the biological and physical sciences. Overall it has been only from 9.3 percent in 1950–54 to 10.9 percent in 1960–61.[27]

Without other indications, these upward trends might be discounted, but it is also reported that whereas only 28 percent of the young women who received their B.A. degrees at Bryn Mawr in 1951 continued their studies into graduate school, in 1960 almost half—46 percent—were doing so. Even married women among them were going on to graduate study in larger numbers. Of the 1951 class only two had done so; of the 1960 class, fifteen.[28]

Relevant also is the decline, or at least the leveling off, in the birthrate in recent years. It may be that younger sisters, seeing large families at close range and in close quarters, may find them less enchanting than their older sisters did at their age. The research of the last decade on the feminine "life calendar" and the widespread efforts to reach college women with programs based on it may be bearing fruit.

The Many Uses of Women

Declining proportions of women in the highly trained pool from which top personnel are recruited is not the whole story. While the proportion of this pool who were women was declining, increasing demands were being made on it by other professions. Graduate study, in and of itself, does not guarantee that recipients of higher degrees will automatically enter academic careers. With the rapid growth of other professions open to those with advanced degrees, it is often less true today than it was when Logan Wilson wrote, that "continuation in graduate school often means a life commitment to academic work."[29] It is still true, of course, that a large proportion of those with advanced degrees do go into academic careers,[30] but there are more and more competing alternatives.

The proportion of faculties who are women depends, therefore, not only on the proportion of the supplying pool who are women but also on competing careers available to trained women.[31] Apparently as the proportion of academic faculties who were women declined, the proportion in other professions who were women increased. Thus an increasing proportion of editors and reporters were women. In 1910, only 12.2 percent were women; by 1950, 32.0 percent were. The proportion of clergymen, lawyers, and physicians who are women has also been rising.[32]

The alternative careers vary in availability according to the field of specialization. For the areas which have traditionally attracted women, such as the humanities, alternatives are relatively few. Chemists, however, find an almost insatiable market for their skills and talents, especially in industry. For psychologists, clinical work is the major alternative to an academic career; indeed, there were more than twice as many clinical psychologists as teaching psychologists among full-time employed scientists in 1956–58. For other scientific fields, research was the most important alternative, being more attractive than teaching for all except mathematicians (Table 4/7). The same conclusion was reached by the Radcliffe study which reported that "research, whether in the natural or the social sciences, whether in government or in private industry or institutions, constitutes a major occupation for married women with Ph.D. training." [33]

Government service appears to be the major competitor of universities and colleges for trained women, especially scientists (Table 4/8). In 1938 women constituted 2.7 percent of all scientists and engineers in government service; in 1954, 4.3 percent; and in 1956–58, 5.1 percent (Table 4/9). Industry, of course, also claims a large part of the pool of trained women. Although long-time trends are not available as in the case of government service, by 1958 private industry was claiming 24.2 percent of all employed women scientists (Table 4/7).

The study of career choices and the factors which determine them is of relatively recent origin, especially in the case of women. Logan Wilson some years ago analyzed the factors influencing persons to enter the academic profession; among them were secure tenure, esteem, working conditions, and leisure.[34] Gustad reports that intrinsic or personal-interest factors outweigh external or situational factors in the decision to enter the academic profession,[35] but Berelson has concluded that young people often merely drift into it.[36] Few young people, at least, start out with the express goal of becoming academic people, women least of all.

A study of 706 college teachers in Minnesota, 27 percent of whom were women, found the women much more tentative, much more modest, and much more influenced by others in their career choices than men.

Few of these women had given any serious thought to college teaching during their undergraduate years; only 1 in 8 reported this as a tentative career choice [even] at graduation from college. . . .College teaching seemed to be a goal far removed from the aspirations of young women, although many planned to become elementary or secondary school teachers (60 percent of the women, 35 percent of the men, reported this goal at the time of college graduation). There was also some indication that parents had encouraged school teaching for their daughters but not for their sons.

Although strikingly similar percentages (78 for women and 74 for men) said that they had looked upon college teaching as a desirable career for other people, fewer women regarded this career favorably as a personal career goal (50 vs. 66 percent, respectively). In other words, there seemed to be a greater disparity for women than men between the generally positive "image" developed of college teachers and their personal career preferences.

To a significantly lesser degree than men, women ascribed their final career choice to factors directly associated with the job itself, such as the possibility of carrying on research (18 vs. 32 percent for men), good working conditions (33 vs. 46 percent), and the academic and social advantages of being a college faculty member (18 vs. 26 percent). External circumstances, such as being counseled in this direction by a respected teacher or counselor (39 percent vs. 19 for men) or by being offered a college-level job (60 vs. 32 percent) had evidently influenced more women than men to join college faculties.[37]

An academic career appeared, from the above findings, to be something almost thrust upon these young women, something which they would not of themselves have aspired to. Some professor, apparently, discerned aptitudes which the young woman herself had not discerned, aptitudes which she might, without his encouragement, consider it pretentious to claim. Presently she was in an academic career. Especially startling is the finding that almost twice as many of the women (60 percent) as of the men (32 percent) had been influenced to become academicians by having a college-level job offered to them. Certainly discrimination against women is not in evidence here.

Nor is discrimination much in evidence in the minds of young women. An interview study of 48 young women graduate students reported that although a majority—56 percent—did actually anticipate prejudiced discrimination, 31 percent felt no grievance on this score; they took it in their stride; it did not deter them. "Several . . . reported they had decided to go into college teaching largely because they expected to find less difficulty there than in other areas of work." [38] In the total set, 20 percent did not anticipate any prejudiced discrimination and 23 percent felt that being a woman would actually be an advantage to them professionally.[39]

Marriage, of course, continues to be a competitor of academic work even after the Ph.D. As many as one-fourth of those who achieve the Ph.D. degree may drop out of their profession, permanently or temporarily, to rear families.[40]

There are doubtless scores of other factors and forces at work determining the supply of women available for academic positions. There may even be changes in the profession itself that make it less attractive than in the past. Budner and Meyer, for example, suggest that the decline in women entering academic professions may "result from the fact that the more 'local' orientation of women professors . . . are precisely those least encouraged by current trends in the academic world. The secularization of academia provides little place for women professors who play more traditional roles."[41]

It has also been noted that student bodies themselves have changed, that the old intimacy of a closed social system, protected from distractions from the outside world, has been eroded away. Students seem different, less satisfying to work with.[42] In addition, the rapidity of change, it is alleged, has increased tension between faculties and administrations. Size and complexity and specialization and government ties vastly increase the demand for administrative activity. Administrative functions which could once be relegated to clerks—and, as historians love to remind us, in the great medieval universities actually were—now run away with the university. New buildings arise for classroom and office use, and before they are completed, large blocks of space are commandeered for administrative uses. The fundamental decisions that have to be made are less and less those which faculties are qualified to make;

increasingly they have to do with maintenance, parking, use of equipment, contractual provisions. In time the office in charge of the dining halls or scheduling classroom space is making policy decisions that affect the academic program, directly or indirectly. The result is a vastly different academic profession from that of the past.[43] The fun, romance, and excitement which Florence Converse referred to and which Vida Scudder corroborated are no more. A great modern "multiversity", as Clark Kerr calls it, "is and must be at war with itself."[44]

Of the two images or myths or definitions of the situation—that the decline in proportion of women in academia is the result of a declining demand for their services, for whatever reason, or that it is the result of a declining supply of women offering their services —the second seems more nearly to conform to the facts. The picture seems to be one not of women seeking positions and being denied but rather one of women finding alternative investments of time and emotion more rewarding, one in which academic professions —because of changing role demands, changing faculty-student relationships, and changing faculty-administration relationships— seem relatively less attractive than in the past.

Trends are not, however, always unidirectional. There are some indications that changes are in the making. Married women are returning to academic positions. Couples are learning how to accommodate marriage to the demands of the wife's career, and new patterns are being worked out. More will be said on these points in Chapter 15.

Table 4/1   Males and Females, 5–34, Enrolled in School, 1962 *

Age	White		Nonwhite	
	Male(%)	Female(%)	Male(%)	Female(%)
14–17	94.2	91.3	89.4	83.7
18–19	52.7	34.6	40.3	27.3
20–24	25.0	9.3	12.2	8.0

* Statistical Abstracts of the United States, 1963, p. 118

Table 4/2   Attrition Rate of College Students, 1949–1960 *
Students Enrolled in the Fall Four Years Earlier Receiving the Bachelor's Degree (%)

Year	Men and Women	Men	Women
1959–60	54.6	57.3	50.3
1958–59	57.1	60.9	50.8
1957–58	58.0	62.9	50.2
1956–57	59.5	64.6	51.9
1955–56	58.0	61.7	52.4
1954–55	60.9	65.5	54.1
1953–54	56.7	58.6	53.5
1952–53	54.6	56.2	51.9
1951–52	58.4	61.4	52.8
1950–51	64.8	69.8	54.4
1949–50	62.3	66.0	52.8

* Office of Education, *Earned Degrees Conferred, 1959–60* (Washington: GPO, 1962), table 1.

Table 4/3 Women Undergraduates and Academic Degrees Awarded to Women by Type of Institution, 1950–60 *

Type of Institution	Undergraduates Who Were Women(%)	Bachelor's Degrees Awarded to Women(%)	Master's Degrees Awarded to Women(%)	Doctor's Degrees Awarded to Women(%)
All Four-Year Institutions	36.0	35.3	31.6	10.5
Universities	29.8	28.0	29.0	10.4
Liberal Arts Colleges	44.2	45.3	42.6	32.4†
Teachers Colleges	49.5	51.9	42.4	12.3
Technological Schools	6.5	4.3	3.1	2.0
Theological and Religious Schools	21.4	12.5	13.3	2.1
Schools of Art	45.2	37.9	33.9	
Others	15.7	8.5	9.4	6.1

* Office of Education, *Earned Degrees, 1959–1960*, p. 9, 11, 13.
† Liberal arts colleges conferred only 2.6 percent of all doctorates in 1959–60.

Table 4/4 Resident College Students and Degree Recipients Who Were Women, 1869–1961 *

Year	Resident College Students	Bachelor's and First Professional Degree	Master's Degree	Doctor's Degree
1869–70	11,126	1,378	0	0
1879–80	37,845	2,485	11	3
1889–90	56,303	2,682	194	2
1899–1900	85,338	5,237	303	23
1909–10	140,565	8,437	558	44
1919–20	282,942	16,642	1,294	93
1929–30	480,802	48,869	6,044	353
1939–40	600,953	76,954	10,223	429
1947–48	—	96,165	13,510	493
1948–49	—	102,476	15,539	522
1949–50	805,953	103,915	16,983	616
1950–51	—	105,009	18,901	674
1951–52	799,982	104,895	19,996	714
1952–53	—	104,037	20,034	792
1953–54	910,489	105,380	18,676	815
1954–55	—	103,799	19,464	826
1955–56	899,954	111,727	19,897	885
1956–57	1,019,000 (Fall '56)	117,609	20,623	939
1957–58	—	122,800	21,362	964
1958–59	—	130,283	22,176	989

Table 4/4 (continued)

Year	Resident College Students	Bachelor's and First Professional Degree	Master's Degree	Doctor's Degree
1959–60	1,228,000 (Fall '59)	139,385	23,560	1,028
1960–61	1,339,000 (Fall '60)			1,180
1961–62	1,467,000 (Fall '61)			

* Data for 1869–1956 from Office of Education, *Statistics of Higher Education, 1955–56; Faculty, Students, and Degrees* (Washington: GPO, 1958), pp. 6–7. Data on enrollment, 1956–61, from Office of Education, *Opening (Fall) Enrollment in Higher Education, 1961: Institutional Data* (Washington: GPO, 1961), p. 1. Data on degrees, 1947–60, from Office of Education, *Earned Degrees, 1959–1960*, p. 3. Where there are inconsistencies in the data from the several sources, the most recent figures are used.

Table 4/5 Resident College Students and Degree Recipients Who Were Women, 1869–1960 *

Year	Resident College Students(%)	Bachelor's and First Professional Degree(%)	Master's Degree(%)	Doctor's Degree(%)
1869–70	21.1	14.7	0.0	0.0
1879–80	32.7	19.3	1.3	5.5
1889–90	35.9	17.3	19.1	1.2
1899–00	35.5	19.1	19.1	6.0
1909–10	39.6	22.7	26.4	10.0
1919–20	47.3	34.2	30.2	15.1
1929–30	43.7	39.9	40.4	15.4
1939–40	42.1	41.2	38.2	13.0
1943–44	49.9	—	—	—
1947–48	—	35.3	31.8	12.4
1948–49	—	27.9	30.6	10.3
1949–50	30.3	23.9	29.7	9.6
1950–51	—	27.3	29.0	9.2
1951–52	34.4	31.6	31.4	9.3
1952–53	—	34.1	32.8	9.5
1953–54	35.9	36.0	33.4	9.6
1954–55	—	36.2	33.5	9.3
1955–56	33.8	36.0	32.5	9.9
1956–57	34.6 (Fall)	34.5	33.2	10.7
1957–58	35.9 (Fall)	33.6	32.5	10.8
1958–59	—	33.8	31.9	10.6
1959–60	36.1 (Fall)	35.3	31.6	10.5
1960–61	37.1 (Fall)	—	—	10.9
1961–62	37.7 (Fall)	—	—	—

* Sources: See Table 4/4.

Table 4/6 Doctor's Degrees Awarded to Women, 1920–1961, by Fields *

Date	Physical Sciences	Biosciences	Social Sciences	Arts-Professions	Education	Total
1920	16	25	22	19	8	90
1921	20	15	28	39	5	107
1922	16	26	33	31	7	113
1923	18	43	40	42	14	157
1924	29	27	48	50	13	167
1925	27	44	51	57	24	203
1926	28	37	56	50	26	197
1927	33	55	45	69	28	230
1928	22	50	66	63	31	232
1929	39	56	84	91	50	320
1930	41	65	68	87	50	311
1931	52	67	82	101	54	356
1932	54	84	81	105	59	383
1933	40	66	85	113	41	345
1934	46	82	72	105	45	350
1935	39	62	84	118	60	363
1936	42	101	84	115	77	419
1937	56	74	100	102	73	405
1938	35	84	108	120	73	420
1939	42	87	98	105	79	411
1940	48	86	84	107	96	421
1941	34	64	88	122	97	405
1942	38	74	80	114	112	418
1943	35	54	87	110	104	390
1944	29	71	61	77	90	328
1945	27	65	55	89	97	333
1946	45	68	80	91	96	380
1947	46	81	90	105	89	411
1948	49	86	81	113	136	465
1949	62	89	121	103	166	541
1950	58	113	122	160	160	613
1951	74	125	160	138	181	678
1952	74	118	160	144	229	725
1953	70	139	166	145	261	781
1954	65	140	171	168	251	795
1955	74	129	212	170	281	866
1956	67	117	182	167	260	793
1957	83	161	236	216	301	997
1958	70	154	268	191	300	983
1959	77	154	264	189	293	977
1960	77	150	268	268	327	1090
1961	103	185	294	256	342	1190

* Lindsey R. Harmon and Herbert Soldz, *Doctorate Production in United States Universities, 1920–1962* (Washington: National Academy of Sciences–National Research Council, 1963), pp. 50–52. The figures from different sources do not always agree in detail. As between Table 4/4 and Table 4/6, the data in the latter are more recent and more nearly correct.

Table 4/7 Full-time Women Scientists, by Work Activity *

Selected Fields	Total	Research	Teaching	Development and Design	Management	Production	Field	Other '
				Work Activity				
Total	8,739**	2,898	2,305	289	190	382	918	1,525
Biological Sciences	2,314	1,034	860	18	51	79	102	142
Psychology	2,047	236	360	197	27	138	760 †	432
Mathematics	1,014	236	455	88	19	47	——	129
Chemistry	1,914	965	280	82	41	52	3	469
Physics	311	144	88	23	12	5	——	33

* National Science Foundation, *American Science Manpower, 1956–58* (Washington: GPO, 1961), table II–I.

** No data for 232 cases.

† Clinical psychology.

Table 4/8 Full-time Women Scientists in Academic and in Nonacademic Types of Employment *

Selected Fields	Total	Educational Institutions	Federal Government	State & Local Government	Nonprofit Organizations	Industry, Business, Self-Employed	Other	No Data
				Type of Position				
Total	8,739	4,098	1,084	637	690	2,098	47	85
Biological Sciences	2,314	1,411	311	139	195	236	11	11
Psychology	2,047	1,058	144	391	189	188	19	58
Mathematics	1,014	538	119	9	40	297	5	6
Chemistry	1,914	573	199	38	174	920	4	6
Physics	311	132	66	1	24	86	1	1

* National Science Foundation, *American Science Manpower, 1956–58*, table II–H.

Table 4/9 Increase in Women Scientists in Government Service, 1938–1954 *

Field	Total 1938	Women 1954	Percent of Total Who Were Women 1938	1954
Total, All Fields	1,274	4,384	2.7	4.3
Agricultural and Biological Sciences	522	613	4.3	4.1
Chemistry and Metallurgy	49	567	3.4	10.9
Mathematics and Statistics	85	881	9.9	17.9
Other Physical and Mathematical Sciences	26	504	2.1	3.3
Economics	230	334	4.6	13.7
Other Social Sciences	200	950	9.9	15.8

* National Science Foundation, *Women in Scientific Careers* (Washington: GPO, 1961), p. 9.

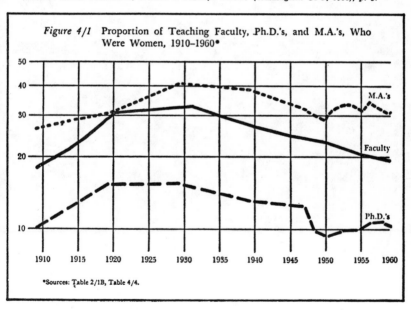

Figure 4/1 Proportion of Teaching Faculty, Ph.D.'s, and M.A.'s, Who Were Women, 1910–1960*

*Sources: Table 2/1B, Table 4/4.

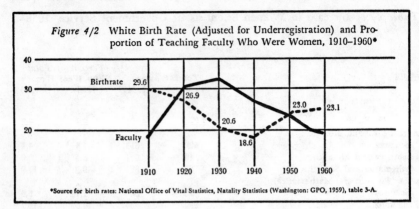

Figure 4/2 White Birth Rate (Adjusted for Underregistration) and Proportion of Teaching Faculty Who Were Women, 1910–1960*

*Source for birth rates: National Office of Vital Statistics, Natality Statistics (Washington: GPO, 1959), table 3-A.

CHAPTER 5 ❋ DIFFERENCES BETWEEN ACADEMIC MEN AND ACADEMIC WOMEN

Shared and Unshared Differences

Viewed as a whole, the academic world is fairly homogenous in the sense that all of its members are associated with books, laboratories, libraries, and the like, and that they are more like one another in background and interests than they are, for example, like long-shoremen. Even a cursory examination of the composition of the population of the academic world, however, reveals marked differences among its components. Careers of a wide variety are pursued in the academic world by a wide variety of people with a wide variety of interests and goals in a wide variety of institutions. Professors differ from administrators, and both differ among themselves. Scientists differ from humanists, and even within the field of science specialists in one area differ from those in another.

Academic women not only share all these differences, they also differ from academic men. The emphasis in this and the following chapter is on the differences between academic men and academic women in class background, in test-intelligence, in age, in functions performed and areas of specialization, and in institutional affiliation. These differences are small in some instances, large in others —so large, indeed, as to indicate the existence, statistically speaking, of separate universes for the two sexes. One kind of difference —in marital status—is so great in its ramifications that its consideration requires a chapter by itself.

Even where academic men and academic women are in statistically different universes, however, the differences—like so many collective differences—are just that, statistical in nature, differences in relative frequency rather than in category. Thus, there are both men and women in the highest and lowest class intervals of social background, both men and women in the highest and lowest test-intelligence brackets, among the oldest and the youngest, and among the married and the unmarried. There are some women in the Top Twelve universities [1] and some men in the poorest colleges. Both men and women occupy all types of functional positions—men on library staffs and women on research staffs—and work in all subject-matter areas—men in home economics and women in engineering.

Sex differences are sometimes less important than other differences. On any land-grant campus, for example, the chances are that the men and women in any one college of a university will differ less from one another in many respects than they will from like-sex members in other colleges. Men and women in agriculture, for example, are more likely to agree with each other on some issues than with members of the same sex in, say, liberal arts. Members of liberal arts faculties—both men and women—are more likely to be stormy petrels, more likely to resist loyalty oaths, restrictions on academic freedom, and interference with their prerogatives than are the men and women on agriculture faculties. The liberal arts faculties are less likely to take to the conditions imposed on the organization man and are more likely to be anarchic, individualistic, last-ditch resisters of bureaucracy. They succumb, when they do, inch by inch, surrendering only under superior "force."

While recognizing that sex differences may be "only" statistical in nature and in some cases less important than other kinds of differences, it is necessary to see the considerable importance of sex differences as revealed by recent research.

Some Caveats

Much of the research on academic women presented here is based on analyses of graduate students and recipients of higher, especially doctoral, degrees. Excellent as this work is, it is nevertheless of limited significance for our purposes, and the defects must be fully recognized. There is, first of all, many a slip between plans for graduate study and graduate study itself, between graduate study and the achievement of the doctor's degree, and between the achievement of the degree and professional status in the academic world. Not all undergraduates who say they plan to pursue graduate study actually do; not all who pursue graduate study win higher degrees; not all who earn the doctorate enter the academic profession. If there were no selective biases operating, it could be assumed that findings for graduate students and for Ph.D.'s were also valid for academic persons. We know that some biases exist; [2] we suspect there may be more.

Even if there were no selective biases introduced in the progress from graduate study to the Ph.D. and on to academia, we would have data for only a small proportion of academic women. Just as all Ph.D.'s do not become academicians,[3] so all academicians do not have the doctorate.[4] Despite these limitations, studies of graduate students and Ph.D.'s appear to be a good, although oblique, source of information about women academicians.

Class Background

Logan Wilson commented a generation ago that the processes selecting the academic man frequently resulted in the choice of a person who came from a fairly low socioeconomic background. Wilson spoke of his "typically plebeian cultural interests outside the field of specialization," of his "generally philistine style of life," of individual instances of "faulty speech, boorish manners, bad dress, and general uncouthness" resulting from a "system of selection that stresses what a man knows rather than how he appears."[5] In the case of academic women the selective processes appear to be somewhat different, for the result is often a person of a higher class-background.

The class background of undergraduate women who plan to continue their education on a graduate level is, in general, higher than that of men who do, as measured by father's education, occupation, or income. Thus, a study of 1,544 undergraduates in 1957-58 reported that 20.3 percent of the men who planned to attend graduate school came from families in which the father had had some graduate training, while 34.0 percent of the women came from such families.[6] Of the men planning graduate training, 45.8 percent had fathers in business, managerial, or professional occupations as compared to 54.1 percent of the women.[7] Almost twice as many women as men (36.4 percent and 19.3 percent respectively) who planned to pursue graduate work came from families with annual incomes of $10,000 or more.[8]

Similar findings were reported for a sample of 33,982 college seniors graduating from 135 schools in June 1961. Among humanities students rating above average in academic performance and hence more likely to complete graduate work, 44.2 percent of the men and 68.6 percent of the women who planned to attend graduate school came from high socioeconomic backgrounds. In the biological sciences, 53.7 percent of the men and 69.0 percent of the women shared high socioeconomic backgrounds. In the physical sciences, there was not this class differential, 48.9 percent of the above-average male students who intended to go on to graduate school coming from high socioeconomic backgrounds compared to 42.4 percent of the women.[9]

These class-background differences between men and women with respect to planning for graduate study also show up in the actual populations of graduate students. Thus about 74 percent of the graduate students at Radcliffe come from professional and business family backgrounds,[10] whereas only about 48 percent of all Ph.D. recipients do.[11]

In one study of college faculties it was reported that even when both men and women came from "middle-and-lower-class homes, in which the fathers had been tradesmen, farmers, skilled or semi-skilled workers, and in which the parents had typically had less than a high school education . . . significantly more women faculty members came from homes where one or both parents had been teachers," [12] suggesting that they came from homes with a genteel, if not middle-class, tradition.

Test-Intelligence

Intellectual ability is admittedly a complex variable. It is a function, among other things, of motivation, opportunity, and stimulation. Whatever its value, the finding is reported that women who receive the doctor's degree are, on the usual types of measure, intellectually superior on the average to men who do.[13] The three measures which produced this finding were high school intelligence-test scores, rank in high school graduating class, and a high school general aptitude test in mathematics and science.

These measures are, of course, far from perfect. Intelligence-test intelligence, for example, is an extremely artificial construct, especially with respect to sex differences.[14] Rank in high school graduating class depends on school grades, and it is generally conceded that girls do better in tests, which determine grades, than boys do. Girls apparently have better test-taking skills; they tend to be more compliant in giving back to the teacher what is wanted. Grade-achieving skills are not necessarily the same as intellectual skills. A similar caveat, though not necessarily to the same extent, is in order with respect to the grade-point average in mathematics and science, the third measure, which also depends on test-taking ability.

Without regard to the question of what qualities other than intellectual ability are involved in academic performance and the question of the relationship of intelligence-test intelligence to creativity, the accompanying figures summarize sex differences in several subject-matter areas, based on the high school records of all those who achieved the doctorate in 1958 and 1959 (Table 5/1).

The test-type superiority of women doctoral recipients can be explained in part by the relatively greater selectivity operating among them. All along the line, the selective factors at work to produce academic women are more stringent than those at work to produce academic men. We have already noted, in Chapter 4, that the attrition rate for women begins at high school graduation and accelerates thereafter. The differential selection diminishes when scrutiny is focused on the higher levels of ability, but it remains even in the top ten percent:

> While various differing estimates have been made as to the total number of higher ability persons who enter college, all are in agreement that fewer high ability girls than boys continue their education beyond high school. For example, a national study conduced in 1957 by the Educational Testing Service shows that three-quarters of the top 10 percent of the boys had enrolled in college the fall after high school graduation, but only three-fifths of the top ten percent of the girls had done so. Of the upper third, 60 percent of the boys but only 46 percent of the girls enrolled in college.
>
> A study of high school graduates for 1955 in Indiana shows that (at the time the study was made, about six months after graduation), of the upper ten percent of the high school graduates, ranked by grades, 85 percent of the boys and 64 percent of the girls had continued education beyond high school . . . .

Other state studies report similar results with respect to differences between boys' and girls' higher education.[16]

As at the high school level, selectivity at the master's level varies for the two sexes, being more drastic among women than among men. The study of 1,544 undergraduate seniors referred to above showed that 59 percent of the male "A" students but only 45 percent of the female "A" students planned to do graduate work; 20 percent of the "A" men and 15 percent of the "A" women planned to go to professional school.[16] In general, the "A" women resembled the "B" men in plans for graduate work (45 and 48 percent respectively having such plans), and the "A" and "B" women resembled the "C" men in the proportions who were undecided or had no plans for advanced education (40 and 50 percent for "A" and "B" women respectively, 45 percent for the "C" men).[17] Low grades appeared to discourage the women more than they did the men.

A relationship between grades and plans almost identical to that for men and women students was reported for the seniors graduating in June 1961. In School Group III, 72 percent of the men with "B" and "B−" grades and 72 percent of the women with "B+" grades planned to attend graduate school. Among School Group I-II, 66 percent of the men with "C+" grades and 64 percent of women with "B" and "B−" grades planned to continue. In School Group III, 53 percent of the "C+" men and 55 percent of the "B" and "B+" women had plans for graduate school. In School Group IV, 47 percent of the "C+" men and 50 percent of the "B" and "B−" women were planning to go to graduate school.[18] In each school group, the proportion of women in any grade-level who were planning graduate study coincided with the proportion of men in the grade-level just below. Fewer of the poorer women students, then, continue into graduate school; apparently only the very best of the good women students do.[19]

Age

Academic women tend to be older than academic men.[20] This is in part a result of a relatively smaller influx of young women into the academic professions in recent years, as indicated in Chapter 4. With respect to the implications of age, it may be pointed out that the forces which were operating in the recruitment of academic personnel ten, fifteen, or twenty years ago were apparently somewhat different from those operating today. Logan Wilson, for example, recognized both competition among institutions for top graduate students and competition among graduate students for top fellowships, but emphasized the competition for fellowships. Today, the situation seems to be reversed. Schools compete for good students more intensely than students for fellowships, as the department bulletin boards, heavy with fellowship announcements, attest. There is more financial support for graduate study today. Older academicians are therefore of a somewhat different breed.[21]

In addition to expected generational differences, the differences between older and younger academic women go deeper than those resulting from age alone. The younger women are more likely to be married than the older women [22] and are more likely to be in coeducational schools.[23]

Academic women in general, young as well as old, are less likely than academic men to be married. Since marital status is so profoundly important in any comparison of the two sexes, discussion of it is deferred to Chapters 14 and 15, where it can be elaborated upon.

"Personality" as Revealed by Subject-Matter Interests

In Chapter 3, reference was made to the subject-matter areas in which women show interest, namely the humanities, and in Chapter 8, the subjects which women teach will be considered. At this point, the subject-matter areas which interest women are used as a kind of projective test to indicate the kind of people they are, for it has been found that different disciplines attract different kinds of people. In the absence of dependable personality studies of academic personnel, studies of differences among persons in the several disciplines are used to give an oblique view of personality differences between academic men and academic women. C. P. Snow's concept of two cultures has accustomed us to the contrast between humanist and scientist.[24] Granted that Snow may have overstated his case,[25] it is true that different disciplines do attract different kinds of devotees, even at the undergraduate level. "Choice of field of study is related to individual differences in . . . characteristics which . . . have to do with the person's inner life—with his thoughts, emotions, and impulses and how he deals with them. . . . This fact . . . indicates what we would of course expect, that a person's intellectual pursuits are integrated in some way with other aspects of his inner life." [26]

The study of 33,982 seniors graduating in June 1961, already referred to, analyzed those in the sample who indicated that they planned to attend graduate school. Those indicating the study of business, law, medicine, nursing, or other than academic professions need not concern us here. Not all who go to graduate school will, of course, become academicians, but it is interesting nevertheless how three sets of values—interest in people, in originality, and in money—and conventionality and political liberalism distribute themselves among different sets of scientists and scholars. [27]

Within the sciences, students in biology, the earth sciences, physiology, and zoology were relatively people-oriented, while at the other extreme those in physics, chemistry, microbiology, and other physical sciences showed very little interest in people. In the social sciences, students of economics and psychology (other than clinical) were less people-oriented than graduate students in general. In the humanities, language students were interested in people, but artists and philosophers were not. "Originality" and "creativity" were highly valued by those in physical science (especially physics and chemistry), in the humanities, and in psychology, but not by those in biology. Money-making was a value for more physical than biological scientists but was not highly esteemed by students in the social sciences and humanities.

On a self-evaluating question on conventionality, the conventional fields were found to be biology, biochemistry, chemistry, earth sciences, mathematics, microbiology, other biological sciences, sociology, and history. Less conventional were physics, physiology, psychology, other social sciences, English, art, and philosophy.

In general, social scientists were politically most liberal, followed by those in the humanities, while students in scientific fields were least liberal.

The significance of these findings is that academic women tend to be in areas characterized by interest in people but not in money and areas which are politically liberal and unconventional. [28]

Most of the detailed research on intellectual interests as related to personality has been done on scientists, for even within the "culture" of science, the different sciences seem to attract different types of personalities, so that physicists, for example, have been found to differ from anthropologists in personality structure as well as in socioeconomic background [29] and social scientists from physical scientists.[30] More surprising is that within any one science those in different subspecialties have been found to show differences among themselves.

In Snow's classification, women—as measured by both undergraduate and graduate specialization—tend to be more than proportionally represented in such humanistic areas as English and journalism, foreign languages and literature, and the fine and applied arts. They tend to be less than proportionally represented in the physical science areas and mathematics. Among the sciences, the behavioral and biological disciplines attract them. Women, in brief, are the kind of people who are attracted to work which involves a concern with people.[31] Although sex differences in interests show up very early in life [32] and may have a genetic component, it is important to remind ourselves here that these differences between academic men and academic women are statistical in nature. Even among those receiving the doctorate in the subject most favored by women, home economics, 15 percent in 1959–60 were men. Interest in people rather than in things characterizes men in the humanities as well as women.

Pieced together from a wide variety of sources, the modal picture of the academic woman that emerges is of a very bright person so far as test-intelligence is concerned,[33] but compliant [34] rather than aggressive,[35] from an above-average social class background,[36] and with a major interest in the humanities.[37]

Table 5/1 Median Scores on Three Specified Measures in Five Specified Areas of Men and Women Receiving the Doctor's Degree in 1958–59 *

Area	Intelligence Test Scores		Rank in High School Graduating Class †		Grade-point Average in Mathematics-Science	
	Men	Women	Men	Women	Men	Women
All Fields	130.0	134.9	127.3	135.1	73.4	78.9
Physical Science	134.6	140.9	127.3	139.7	83.0	87.5
Biological Science	124.6	130.5	114.0	134.8	67.7	82.6
Social Sciences	128.7	137.0	116.4	130.8	62.8	78.5
Arts and Humanities	130.9	136.5	121.4	130.6	70.2	80.3
Education	122.6	124.8	112.0	126.5	61.2	70.5

* Data derived from a study made by Lindsey Harmon. His overall findings are reported in "The High School Backgrounds of Science Doctorates," *Science*, Mar. 10, 1961. The analysis by sex was made by courtesy of Dr. Harmon for this study.

† Rank in class converted to Army Standard Scale.

CHAPTER 6 ❀ INSTITUTIONAL
DISTRIBUTION: CAREER PATTERNS

The Institutional Distribution of Academic Women

There were 1,985 institutions of higher education in the United States and its possessions in 1961.[1] They varied widely among themselves in geographic location [2] (144 in New York State, one in Guam), size, clientele, function, and especially in prestige. Some had tens of thousands of students, others only a few hundred. Some were primarily for Negroes, some for freshmen and sophomores only, some exclusively for women, and some mainly for graduate students. Some were professional, some technological, some devoted only to the liberal arts. Appointment to a chair at one institution might represent the very apex of professional success, while a chair at another might be viewed with contempt.

Some observers of the academic world limit their concern to the elitist institutions,[3] but such a limitation excludes almost two-thirds of all academic women, for the institutional distribution of academic women is quite different from that of academic men. By and large, academic women tend to be associated with the low-status or low-prestige institutions. About one-fourth of them, therefore, were in teachers colleges and junior colleges as compared with less than ten percent of the men in 1955–56.[4] Although almost one-third of the women were in universities (Table 6/1), they were likely to be in the less prestigious ones. Budner and Meyer, studying a sample of social scientists, classified their institutional affiliations in terms of quality and found most to be in the poorer quality schools, in "women's colleges, the Protestant schools and the teachers colleges, colleges which tend to be of low quality."[5] (Table 6/2). Although a wide variety of factors is involved in determining the distribution of academic men and academic women, only four will be discussed here, namely: training, doctoral university, personal preference or vocation as related to institutional function, and geography.

Training

With respect to those lacking the Ph.D. degree, it goes without saying that, with the exception of rare and unusual cases, they will not be considered for positions in the great universities. Since relatively few women receive the Ph.D. degree, it is to be expected that they will be found in the less prestigious institution.

Doctoral University

Even women with the doctorate, however, are likely to be at the less highly ranked institutions. Among the many factors which have been invoked to explain the distribution of academic personnel is doctoral university. In broadest outline, according to Berelson, the process appears to operate as follows: The best universities attract the best graduate students and then place them in the best positions.[6] The doctoral university is, in effect, a great centrifuge which sends its doctors out into lesser institutions according to its own place in the status system among universities.

Enormous, even determinative, importance is thus attached to the doctoral university by most students of academia. It may be more important than ability itself, at least in initial professional placement, for Ph.D.'s of the same ability will be rated higher if they secure their degrees from one university rather than another and will be able to command a better salary and other perquisites. Their doctoral university brings reflected distinction to the departments where they serve.

> Other things being equal, it is to the student's advantage to attend one of the major universities, where . . . "he can rub elbows with the great and serve his apprenticeship under 'big men' in his respective field." Regardless of the candidate's own merit, some of the prestige of the institution accrues to him merely by virtue of his attendance, since he profits by the "halo effect."[7]

Caplow and McGee were even more emphatic in stating the importance of the doctoral university in the distribution of academic personnel.

> The initial choice of a graduate school sets an indelible mark on the student's career. In many disciplines men trained in minor universities have virtually no chance of achieving eminence. . . . The handicap of initial identification with a department of low prestige is hardly ever completely overcome. The system works both in channeling students into graduate school and then in channeling them out into jobs. Thus it affects where students come from and where they go to.[7a]

Berelson views the doctoral institution as practically determinative of later success.

> Just as a person's eventual position in society depends on the class he was born into as well as on his own talent, so his eventual position in higher education depends on the standing of the institution where he took his doctorate as well as on his scientific or scholarly capabilities. . . . The institution where a person gets the doctorate has a determining effect on where he ends up. The higher the institutional level of the doctorate, the higher the subsequent post in academic life.[7b]

Whatever validity these conclusions may have for men—and they appear to be of less than universal applicability— [8] they do not appear to have the same applicability to women, for the Ph.D. university does not have the same significance either in attracting women in the first place or in placing them professionally thereafter. By and large, women receive their doctorates from universities as good as those from which men receive theirs. Berelson reported that about the same proportion of women students (47 percent) as of men (43 percent) received their doctorates from the Top Twelve universities.[9] Many women, however, earned their doctorates after marriage.[10] Their choice of institution for graduate study was not, therefore, as free as it might be for men and was influenced, no doubt, by the location of the husband. It cannot, therefore, be assumed that the best universities were attracting the best students,[11] or, conversely, that because a woman received her doctorate from a less outstanding university she was not one of the best students.

The doctoral university does not have the same determinative professional consequences for women as for men. If it did, the institutional distribution of men and women Ph.D.'s would be the same. This is not, however, the case.

Tables 6/3 and 6/4 show the differing career patterns for two sets of men and women scientists: for those from all universities (Table 6/3) and for those from the Top Twelve (Table 6/4). Expecially striking, of course, is the vastly greater proportion of women dropouts among both zoologists and chemists.[12] Also striking is the greater proportion of men in university positions. The far greater industrial market for chemists accounts for their difference from zoologists in the proportion in the "other" category.

If the distortion introduced by the disproportionate number of dropouts is eliminated by concentrating only on those who were active scientists and for whom data were available, as in Table 6/5 and Table 6/6, an arresting situation shows up. The absence of male chemists in college teaching positions continues, of course. Among the zoologists, almost twice as many women as men from the Top Twelve are in college positions, 22 percent as contrasted with 12 percent.[13] In general, the institutional placement of the women Ph.D.'s is lower than that of the men Ph.D.'s from the same doctoral university level. This differential is due in part to the institutional placement of the married women being determined to a large extent by their husbands' positions. Thus several of the women from the Top Twelve were teaching in junior or teachers colleges; none of the men were.

In the case of the unmarried women, institutional placement was still not commensurate with doctoral university status. The colleges were able to attract more women than men from the Top Twelve universities; the men they were able to attract were not so likely to be from the Top Twelve, a fact which confirms the Wilson-Caplow-Berelson theory.

An interesting relationship between doctoral university and career was noted in the comparison of the number of women zoologists and chemists who were still active scientists ten to fifteen years after receiving the doctorate. More of the women from the Top Twelve were active scientists than women from other doctoral universities (Table 6/7). Conversely, more active scientists than dropouts came from the Top Twelve (Table 6/8).

Personal Preference and Institutional Function

Some of the differential in the institutional position of academic men and academic women, especially among those from the Top Twelve, is doubtless due to discrimination.[14] Since a substantial proportion of women Ph.D.'s do go into university positions, however, it cannot be argued that all were being seriously discriminated against in explanation of why so many accepted college posts. They may actually have preferred college positions, as some people apparently do.

A bias is introduced into any study of academia which limits itself to elitist populations. Among such populations it can be assumed that everyone is indeed competing for positions at the best universities, that everyone would like to be associated with them, that all are in the same race for the same prizes. Actually, however, this is not the case in the total academic population. The almost obsessive preoccupation with status which characterizes the elitist academic population does not characterize all segments of the academic world.[15]

Evidence will be presented in Chapter 14 to suggest that many of the Top Twelve university doctors prefer college positions; many may even have a vocation for college teaching. Vida Scudder felt guilty because she found her life as a college professor so delightful.[16] Mary Ellen Chase has described the great pleasure she felt in her career as a college professor.[17] It is perhaps on women of this bent that the survival of some—especially women's—colleges may ultimately depend.[18]

The processes by which those who wish to be college professors go into and remain in college positions and those who do not wish to be move out of the colleges are illustrated by the following documents. The first is by a young woman still uncertain of her destiny; the second by a man who, knowing exactly what he wanted, bet everything he had on the opportunity to escape from a college position.

> If you hear of any jobs that might suit me both personally and professionally, please keep me in mind. The college here has treated me well; they have given me a decent salary and released time in the spring. So I'm under no pressure to leave. But the 15-hour teaching load, the slow promotions, and the general atmosphere of a subway college remain as disagreeable as ever. I know there are no academic paradises but I'm sure

there are places better suited to my temperamental affinities for involvement and performance—and not too isolated from sources of unmarried men. . . .

I suspect that my specifications, such as they are, are most likely to be found on either coast—New England or California. I continue to have reservations about women's colleges. The women I know teaching at even the best of them complain of a combination of mental and social isolation. . . .

I will write to Professor Blank as soon as I have recovered sufficiently from the last push through the semester to think clearly. It sounds like a possibility to consider. What do you think? I wish I knew enough about these places to be capable of almost rational consideration, but that's asking too much of the academic marketplace. No doubt, whatever develops in the next year or so will be a result of both my professional interests and fortuitous circumstances—be it jobs or men. I'm incapable of sustained systematic strategies and inclined to follow my personal bent—and whatever chance brings. . . .

Tentative, uncertain, ambivalent, in conflict between professional and marital aspirations, her future institutional affiliation will, as she frankly recognizes, depend on forces outside her control as much as those within it. She is clearly not one with a vocation for college teaching.

Nor is the man who wrote the following document. In contrast to the young woman, he was determined to be, academically speaking, master of his fate. He knew he did not want to remain in a college, and he did something about it.[19] He practically climbed the walls, in fact, to get out.

With the view firmly held that I did not want to teach in a small college—I was brought up in Siwash College where my father taught—I found jobs in my specialty very scarce in 19— whereas they had been easy to get in the period a decade earlier. It was at this time I was doing graduate work because I had spent five years in the air force immediately after my B.A. Consequently I tried a technological school job, which it turned out I did not like. In 1951, with the chance to go to——, which is not so small as colleges go, and which has fantastically good students, I accepted the statement of both dean and chairman at face value that they would encourage research. The only difficulty proved to be that their idea of research and my idea of research bore little relation to each other. As I became discouraged at the prospects of a lifetime there . . . I began to bend every effort to get out. . . . [He accepted fellowships which took him away from his campus, took leave without pay, and finally resigned outright.]

I am now in a potentially permanent position in a university, but must satisfy everyone around me before I attain it. Needless to say, I have even stronger feelings about small colleges for people like myself than I had acquired from watching my father's career. . . . It is a shame that the facts have not been, and possibly cannot be, made widely available in print as to just what can be expected in colleges as opposed to univer-sities. . . .

Small colleges . . . are fine places for some people. Part of the staff at —— are happy as clams with their situation. Some of the teaching, particularly by members as they get older, is not worthy of the sort of student they are dealing with almost exclusively. They really are terrific, about like the top 5 to 10 percent at Columbia, for example. I fear for the future of the good small colleges as a couple of decades of not keeping up catch up with them. . . .

Henry Noble McCracken has also commented on the process which weeds out of the colleges those who do not have a vocation for college teaching.[20] Caplow and McGee found that 22 percent of voluntary terminations were due to personal causes,[21] many no doubt like those described in the above documents, part of the process by which people and institutions accommodate themselves to one another.

There may also be functional reasons for the institutional dis-tribution of academic women. The university is more likely than the college to demand the man-of-knowledge function, and as suggested in Chapter 8, women are not as likely as men to perform it. The college, on the other hand, is usually dedicated to the teaching function, and in it women are more likely to be called upon.

Geography

In addition to training, doctoral university, personal preference or vocation, and institutional function, geography also acts as a var-iable influencing the institutional distribution of academic person-nel. There appears to be a tendency for both men and women to prefer positions in the same general region of the country as that in which they were born. In one study, ten to fifteen years after receiving the Ph.D. degree, 46 percent of the men and about 60 percent of the women were holding positions in the general area of their birthplace. In the Eckert-Stecklein study of Minnesota teachers, 44 percent of the women had been born in Minnesota and only 25 percent of the men had. The authors concluded that "women tend to be residentially more immobile than men." [22] Caplow and McGee refer to the "El Dorado" theme as a reason for changing positions.[23] It may be that people feel more comfortable in institutions near their birthplaces. In the case of women, proximity to family of orientation may also be a factor. For whatever reasons, the influence of birthplace appears to be one of the many factors in the institutional distribution of academic personnel.

The differences between academic men and academic women documented in this and in the preceding chapters—in social background, test-intelligence, age and marital status, "personality" as revealed by intellectual interests, institutional affiliation, and functional position—mean that academic women constitute a different population, statistically speaking, from academic men. In the world of academic women, career patterns develop along different lines. Women tend to serve in institutions which emphasize different functions, and they themselves are attracted to different kinds of functions. Further, they tend to be in areas which are not in strategic positions in the academic marketplace and which are not as productive as the areas which attract men.

In Chapter 7 some of the characteristics of the women in this academic domain are explored. The focus of attention is not on the differences between the worlds of academic men and academic women but rather on differences within the world of academic women itself.

Table 6/1 Full-time Equivalent Faculty Members with Rank of Instructor or Above, United States and Possessions, November 1955 *

Type of Institution	Full-time Equivalent Men		Full-time Equivalent Women	
	Number	Percent	Number	Percent
Universities	86,792	54.9	13,154	32.0
Liberal Arts Colleges	33,613	21.3	15,586	37.9
Teachers Colleges	8,154	5.1	5,031	12.2
Technological Schools	6,685 ⎫		234 ⎫	
Theological Schools	2,021 ⎬	11.0	298 ⎬	4.4
Other Professional Schools	8,633 ⎭		1,279 ⎭	
Junior Colleges	12,315	7.7	5,551	13.5
All Institutions	158,199	100.0	41,133	100.0

* Office of Education, *Statistics of Higher Education: 1955–56* (Washington: GPO, 1958), p. 39.

Table 6/2 Distribution of Men and Women Social Scientists According to Quality of School *

	Women		Men	
Percent in Schools of:				
High Quality		22		38
Medium-high Quality		23		32
Medium-low Quality		39		22
Low Quality		16		8
Total cases	(264)	100	(2158)	100

* Stanley Budner and John Meyer, "Women Professors," p. 7.

Table 6/3 Institutional Position of Men and Women Ph.D.'s 10–15 Years after Receiving Degree *

	College		University		Other		Dropouts and No Data	
Biologists								
Men (77)	13	17%	36	47%	20	26%	8	10%
Women (77)	16	21%	21	27%	15	20%	25	32%
Chemists								
Men (49)	0	0%	11	24%	30	61%	8	16%
Women (40)	9	22%	5	13%	14	35%	12	30%

* The women include all those receiving Ph.D. degrees in their field in a given period of time; the men are a random sample of men receiving the degree at the same time.

Table 6/4 Institutional Position of Men and Women Ph.D.'s Who Received Doctorates at Top Twelve Universities, 10–15 Years after Receiving Degree *

	College		University		Other		Dropouts and No Data	
Biologists								
Men (36)	4	11%	18	50%	11	30%	3	9%
Women (38)	5	13%	10	26%	8	21%	15	40%
Chemists								
Men (16)	0	0%	4	25%	9	56%	3	19%
Women (19)	4	21%	3	16%	8	42%	4	21%

* Subjects from same sources as in Table 6/3.

Table 6/5 Institutional Position of Professionally Active Men and Women Scientists 10–15 Years after Receiving Degree

	College		University		Other	
Biologists						
Men (69)	13	19%	36	52%	20	29%
Women (52)	16	31%	21	40%	15	29%
Chemists						
Men (41)	0	0%	11	27%	30	73%
Women (28)	9	32%	5	18%	14	50%

Table 6/6 Institutional Position of Professionally Active Men and Women Scientists Who Received Doctorate at Top Twelve Universities, 10–15 Years after Receiving Degree

	College		*University*		*Other*	
Biologists						
Men (33)	4	12%	18	55%	11	33%
Women (23)	5	22%	10	43%	8	35%
Chemists						
Men (13)	0	0%	4	31%	9	69%
Women (15)	4	27%	3	20%	8	53%

Table 6/7 Doctoral University of Women Scientists 10–15 Years after Receiving Ph.D.

	Doctoral University			
	Top Twelve		*Other*	
Biologists	38		44	
Dropouts *	7	18%	13	30%
Active †	31	82%	31	70%
Chemists	19		21	
Dropouts *	4	21%	7	33%
Active †	15	79%	14	67%

Table 6/8 Doctoral University of Women Scientists 10–15 Years after Receiving Ph.D.

	Doctoral University			
Field	*Top Twelve*		*Other*	
Biologists (82)	38		44	
Dropouts (20)*	7	35%	13	65%
Active (62) †	31	50%	31	50%
Chemists (40)	19		21	
Dropouts (11) *	4	36%	7	64%
Active (29) †	15	52%	14	48%

* Dropouts are defined as women who are not listed in the 1960 edition of *American Men of Science* and for whom there are no data available from the alumni office of their doctoral university and those for whom data from alumni office gave no evidence that the women were engaged in professional work.

† If a woman was in *American Men of Science*, she was considered to be an active scientist. In some cases women not in *American Men of Science* had returned to an active career after varying periods of inactivity. They were considered active despite several years of previous "dropout" status.

CHAPTER 7 ❀ "HER INFINITE
VARIETY": SOME DIFFERENCES
AMONG ACADEMIC WOMEN

Heterogeneity

The population of academic women is itself no more homogeneous than is the total population of academia. It is as diverse with respect to all the variables discussed in Chapters 5 and 6 as the population of academic men. Academic women differ among themselves in class background, ability, age and marital status, "personality" as indicated by subject-matter interest, training, and institutional position. This chapter is devoted to the added differences between women in different kinds of colleges (specifically, elitist women's colleges and home economics colleges), between women who have professional status and those who do not, between women in colleges and in universities, and between women who are in academic positions and women with equal training who are not.

Academic Women in Elitist Women's Colleges and in Home Economics Colleges

In 1955, there were 15,586 "full-time equivalent" women in liberal arts colleges, a large proportion of whom were in women's colleges.[1] In 1959, there were 2,859 persons in college and university teaching and research in home economics,[2] all but a small proportion of whom were women. These two sets of academic women have quite different traditions, different preoccupations, and different problems.

In the great academic status system, the status of the home economics colleges in relation to the traditional women's colleges parallels that of the land-grant, especially agricultural, colleges to the traditional colleges and universities. The students at traditional women's colleges tend to come from higher socioeconomic backgrounds than do those at home economics colleges.[2a] Even on the same land-grant campus, in fact, women students in liberal arts tend to have higher socioeconomic backgrounds than do women in home economics.

It is quite likely that a home economics faculty might call on a graduate of a traditional women's college to fill a position. Some of the pioneers in the home economics movement were, for example, products of Vassar (Ellen Richards, Katharine Blunt) and Smith (Alice Norton). It is less likely that an elitist traditional women's college would call on a graduate of a home economics college.

If the academic women who staff the home economics colleges have ever been aware of any invidious distinctions, however, they have made no note of them. Indeed, they have all but ignored them. Busy, engrossed, challenged by their fascinating assignment, they have shown little interest in such status matters. They have their own world, their own reference groups, their own status system, their own role conceptions, their own self-images. The elitist women's colleges and the home economics colleges have had different kinds of academic women at their helms. The great academic women in the elitist women's colleges have tended to be in the humanities—classical scholars, historians, literary scholars; those in the home economics colleges, in the sciences—biochemists, economists, psychologists, and sociologists.

In the home economics movement, academic women are themselves an elite of scientists and entrepreneurs in the classic sense. They have been innovators who, if they have not always known precisely what they wanted, have known at least how to get it. Against competing demands on university budgets they have managed to get funds for building up a remarkable series of colleges which for decades have turned out the teachers who have brought the results of research to homemakers.

The academic women in home economics colleges continue to be service-oriented. The women's colleges have long since ceased to be "hotbeds of radicalism." The conflict between reform and academic aloofness which Vida Scudder delineated at the turn of the century (referred to in Chapter 2) was resolved in favor of quietism. There may still be political liberalism among academic women in the elitist colleges, but it is likely to be more impersonal and abstract than the concrete, immediate desire to be of service to specific people in specific communities which is characteristic of those in home economics colleges. No study is available of the political orientation of academic women in different positions, but it is likely that those in home economics colleges are more conservative than those in liberal arts colleges.[3]

There is something open, extrovert, and outgoing in the ethos of the academic women in colleges of home economics, something more withdrawn and introspective in the ethos of the academic women in the women's colleges. The educational issues involved in preparing women for life in today's world are likely to find the two kinds of faculties lined up on different sides. The traditional elitist women's colleges show intense preoccupation with the development of individual identity in their students. They continue to resist vocational courses [4] and any idea that women require a different kind of education from that of men. Not so the colleges of home economics.[5] Studies of home economics alumnae stress their far-flung services throughout the world; studies of elitist traditional college alumnae, their adjustment problems.

The top-ranking women who staff colleges of home economics are not—or have not been so far—themselves doctors in home economics. The situation in colleges of home economics is analogous to that in medical colleges where much of the scientific training is done by those with Ph.D.'s rather than with medical degrees.[6] It is only the clinical or applied aspects of the training that are taught by medical doctors. So in the case of home economists, albeit on a less advanced student body, the members of the teaching faculties are likely themselves to be doctors in biochemistry or psychology or economics or sociology.[7]

This situation is, however, changing. In the 1950's an apparently successful movement to accelerate and improve facilities for training doctors in home economics was begun.[8] In 1950–51, only 20 doctorates in home economics were granted, but by 1954–55 this number had more than tripled, to 61. The number fluctuated between 34 and 58 in the succeeding years, and was 50 in 1959–60. The change between 1950–51 and 1959–60 represented an increase of 150 percent, compared with an increase of only 33.9 percent in all fields.[9]

If this trend in the direction of degrees in home economics continues, the academic women in colleges of home economics in the future will not be doctors of biochemistry, economics, sociology, or psychology but doctors of foods and nutrition, clothing and textiles, child development and family relations, home economics education, and "general home economics." [10] It is too early to tell whether this new trend will lead to parochialism and narrow specialization or to improved training, but it may be that the increasing amount of knowledge which research is constantly creating demands a high degree of specialization.

Most of the doctor's degrees in home economics are granted to women, but not all of them. In some areas men outnumber women. Thus, for example, in 1959–60, five out of nine dissertations in the area of guidance of school age children were by men as were five of the nine in the field of family life. In the same year, four of the eleven in nutrition and foods were by men.[11]

The trend from 1949 to 1959 in doctoral degrees showed a decline in the proportion awarded in the field of foods and nutrition (from 60 percent to 18 percent) and a marked increase in the proportion awarded in the field of child development and family relationships (from 8 percent to 28 percent). Despite the relative decline, however, foods and nutrition remained by far the most popular area for all degrees combined, accounting for 131 theses. Next in order were: home economics education, 103; clothing and textiles, 76; child development, 55; housing and equipment, 40; family economics and management, 23; family life, 21; and art, 6.

There has been some speculation about the future of the traditional women's colleges. The president of Vassar has predicted that they will either become coeducational—since their programs are as suitable for men as for women—or cease to exist. Financial support is especially difficult, since families with money prefer to endow men's rather than women's colleges. The college of home economics faces no such threat; it is already coeducational, and it is assured of support. There is, however, no guarantee that it will not be taken over by men.

Professional and "Fringe Benefit" Status

Budner and Meyer interpreted many of their findings with respect to women social scientists in terms of lack of professional involvement. They explained this withdrawal from genuine professional commitment as, in part at least, a result of unequal rewards. It may, however, at least in some cases reflect a preferred status.

Academic women may meaningfully be classified into two status categories in terms of commitment, namely professional and "fringe benefit." The ultimate distinction between the two categories may be based on tenure; those in the "fringe benefit" status do not have it. They might appreciate having it, but they are not interested enough in getting it to meet the requirements.[12] But there are many other distinctions more immediately relevant to the position of academic women.

The term "fringe benefit" implies a status which is on the fringe of the profession; it implies also, however, that the person occupying this status is of great benefit to the institution where the work is done. There may be occasional men in this status, but by far the majority are women.[13] For the most part, they are the wives of deans, professors, instructors, graduate students or, often, even of townsmen. They constitute an elastic labor pool, hired and furloughed as needed. They carry a large share of the backbreaking load of introductory work in English composition, modern languages, history, mathematics, natural sciences, and the like.

Academic women in professional and in fringe benefit status differ basically in career motivation, reference groups, role conception, and levels of aspiration. They may or may not differ in training.

The career motivations of women in fringe benefit status tend to differ from those of women in professional status and especially from those of their male colleagues. Women in the fringe benefit status often do not "have" to work. They work because they very much want to. In some cases they may be escaping the tedium of an uncongenial marriage, as in Ruth Benedict's case, or escaping from community chores,[14] or from intolerable ennui. They may be trying to keep up with a successful husband, or their work may be a sheer labor of love. In some cases, these academic women are the prototypes of the new woman who returns to the labor force when her maternal functions have been performed.

The reference group of many of the women in fringe benefit status is not composed of her teaching colleagues or professional confreres in the invisible university but rather of the wives of other professors or businessmen, often bored with their bridge clubs, who are impressed with the professional achievements of the women in fringe benefit status, however minor they may appear on the campus. The fringe benefit woman feels satisfied with her position because it is superior to that of other women in the community. Prestige inheres in her connection with the college or university.

Academic women in fringe benefit status pose fewer role problems for their male colleagues than do the professionals. They usually conceive of their role as simply that of teacher. Their problems are similar to those of any working wife, especially of teaching wives. Their work is a job which they do with as much dispatch and efficiency as any other teacher. They probably enjoy it greatly, but it is not necessarily an absorbing career. They can take it or leave it, since they have other than academic sources of satisfaction.

The professional status of the woman in fringe benefit status is distinctly lower than that of the regular professional staff. She comes and goes as she is needed. If her husband is an academic man, she is often content to be Professor Smith's wife rather than Professor Smith herself. But the suitable reaction is not necessarily one of "pity-the-poor-woman-professor," for she may be quite satisfied with her niche; her level of aspiration and her level of achievement may coincide fairly well.

The distinction between academic women in the professional and fringe benefit statuses is very real. Ignoring it and combining all academic women together tends to distort the picture and thus invalidates certain comparisons between the sexes, making both the position and the contribution of professional academic women appear somewhat inferior to what they are. It is, however, by no means clear how to assign women to one or the other of these status categories. The same women may pass from one to the other, in either direction, that is, from professional to fringe benefit status or, conversely, from fringe benefit to professional status.[15]

In general, a single woman with the rank of professor, a Ph.D. degree, and tenure would almost certainly be in the status of a professional. But if she married and moved to another community she might well have the status of a fringe benefit in some other institution. Conversely, a woman instructor with no doctorate,[16] without tenure, might be as committed to her work as any of her colleagues and take it just as seriously.

Since the term "fringe benefit" refers to a status rather than to the personal characteristics or traits of those in the status, what proportion of academic women are in fringe benefit status at any given time is not determinable from a study of the traits of academic women themselves.[17]

Antinepotism Rules and Fringe Benefit Status

A large proportion of academic women in the status of fringe benefits are wives of academic men.[18] The tenure status, if not the characteristics, of this category of academic women has been the subject of systematic study in connection with so-called antinepotism laws and practices.

One study of 68 schools with less than 3,000 students, found that 54 percent would employ faculty wives and pay them on the same basis as other faculty members, but not all of them would promote them on the same basis or grant tenure and retirement privileges to both husbands and wives.[19] Another study of 124 institutions—most of them publicly controlled and of small size (2,000 to 5,000 enrollment)—reported that only 43.5 percent had no restrictions on the hiring of faculty wives.[20] The American Association of University Women found that 55.4 percent of 285 institutions had no antinepotism rules; 26.3 percent had such rules of varying degrees of flexibility; and 18.2 percent had very flexible rules.[21] It also found public institutions more likely to have restrictions than private ones.

Whatever the official rules may be, however, in practice the stringency of the demand for academic personnel has eroded away the structure of antinepotism even where it existed in theory. Exceptions must be made, evasions resorted to. The American Association of University Women study, for example, reported comments like this:

> "Employment of persons from the same economic unit shall be discouraged except when it becomes necessary because of the shortage of qualified personnel. . . ." "We have made exceptions . . . for temporary periods of time. . . ." "It is understood . . . that husband and wife are not employed. We employ [wives] on a temporary basis. . . ." "We have from time to time employed both husbands and wives but, also, with one of them on a visiting faculty status. . . ."

One president admitted the impracticability of antinepotism restrictions; despite a strong antinepotism rule at his college, "during the last three years . . . with the increasing shortage of qualified college teachers, exceptions have been made to this rule. My strong impression is that this will shortly become the rule rather than the exception."[22]

Even in institutions which retain antinepotism rules, if academic men and women marry, both are usually permitted to retain their professional status. A special problem, it is thought, results when both husband and wife are in the same department. Apparently, this kind of situation, in which husbands and wives are in the same department, is the rule rather than the exception, and it is expected to continue.[23]

Still, in institutions which do not have antinepotism rules, there appears to be general satisfaction with the arrangement of permitting wives on their staffs. In general, the satisfaction results from the competitive advantage which such a policy offers in attracting good men.

[This state college] operates under a policy which permits us to employ staff members related by blood or marriage. . . . It has been most advantageous in securing people with excellent qualifications who otherwise might not have been available to us.

[This state] university employs wives of our faculty members. . . . We consider ourselves fortunate when we are able to find a married couple qualified for positions in our institution. We have found that it is one of the best ways to hold our personnel if we can provide satisfactory employment for the man and the wife.

This policy has worked out quite well, and the university has been able to secure the services of many well-trained and experienced women for faculty positions. It is our feeling here that, with the present shortage of competent teaching personnel, well-trained faculty wives will provide a source of very competent teaching personnel. The only objection to this policy is that if the husband resigns to take another position, it means the loss of two staff members instead of one.

We are happy when we can find a wife who may be able to participate in the activities of our collegiate program.

We are delighted to have both members of a family on our faculty.

I can certainly state that [this] university has benefited from such arrangements; and we certainly plan to keep this policy.

This college has rather deliberately avoided antinepotism regulations on the assumption that our ability to offer employment to a couple would be in our favor in the coming struggle for good teachers.[24]

The Contribution of the Women in Fringe Benefit Status [25]

It is not only the contribution of the couple that is appreciated. The contribution of the woman in fringe benefit status herself is, at least in some cases, judged to be indispensable. Although there is no reported systematic research on this subject, the following comments, made by a dean of liberal arts in a land-grant university, are illuminating.

> We would find ourselves in something near catastrophe if we were suddenly forced to operate without the services of the women, mostly faculty wives, who are our part- and some-time teachers. They teach many of our introductory sections in composition, in the foreign languages, and in our laboratory sciences. They would like tenure, of course, with all the security that goes with it. I frankly admit that I do not like the idea of filling the permanent ranks of my faculty with these women—competent as they are in the work they are doing—because for the most part they do not have doctorates. I recognize that the doctorate may be a ritualistic requirement, but so long as accrediting agencies use it as a measure of a faculty's quality, I intend to comply with it. One notable case comes to my mind. Mrs. X is an excellent introductory mathematics teacher. She wants what most normal young women want: a home and family. She also wants to teach. She came to me to ask if she could be given enough work to gain tenure so that by the time her last child was in school she could resume full time as a tenure member of the staff. I demurred and explained to her exactly why. If she were willing to undergo the rigors of achieving the doctorate I would be willing to cooperate with her. But as it turned out, she was not willing to endure the additional hardships—and, indeed, why should she—involved in getting a degree. So she continues to teach with the outlook excellent for work as long as she cares to teach, but without tenure. I think this policy protects me also with respect to the nepotism rule on our campus. So long as wives do not have official tenure we can sidestep that rule.

Valuable as they are, however, the presence of women in fringe benefit status does introduce some problems. Because of their status they may be relieved of student advising and of committee work, thus adding to the load of the regular staff. If they are given advanced courses to teach, members of the regular staff may feel discriminated against.[26]

However simple the status of the woman in the status of fringe benefit may be to her, she does introduce inconsistencies into the status structure of a department.[27] The wife of a professor—herself without a degree—may nevertheless have higher status socially than the professional woman with a Ph.D. The wife may associate socially with the president and the dean. Not so the academic woman who has a certain position in the hierarchy that she may not transcend. The status of the wife is ascribed to her on the basis of her husband's position; that of the professional woman must be achieved by the woman herself. In her role as teacher, the woman in fringe benefit status has a lower position than that of a professional colleague; in her role as wife of a professor, it may be higher.

Two Cases

Two cases are introduced here to illustrate some of the facets of the fringe benefit status. The case of Ruth Benedict illustrates the difficulty in assigning women to either the professional or fringe benefit status. She belonged to a transitional generation of academic women, one foot in the nineteenth century and one in the twentieth. Like her prototypes, the first generation of academic women, she had been filled with idealism as a young woman, a longing to be useful, to serve. She tried many kinds of service, but it was not until she fell in love with Stanley Benedict that she found fulfillment, thus constituting in a way, a prototype herself of the current model of academic woman. As traced in entries in her diary, the story of the disintegration of her marriage, which began in ecstasy, is filled with pathos. Little by little estrangement grew into destructive silence; she and her husband could not communicate with one another.

Her entry into the academic world was an escape from this emotional trap. Through the good offices of Franz Boas, she became the assistant to Elsie Clews Parsons. An academic position was out of the question: She didn't need the money, she was in the status of a fringe benefit, and the faculty of Columbia University could not admit women.

In the very tight economy of those days jobs were for those who needed money. The wife of a professor at Cornell Medical College did not need money. The position at Barnard College, which would have been the appropriate one for her, Boas was planning to give to Gladys Reichard, who was not married and did need a job. Ruth Benedict was just too old for the fellowships which were opening up—thirty-five years was their upper limit. As Stanley Benedict was fundamentally repelled by the idea of her taking up a profession, communication between them—always difficult, always dependent upon intensity as a medium—became still more difficult. She felt that she must earn a sufficient living to support herself on the days when she stayed in the city to work for anthropology, and not ask Stanley to underwrite this. By 1926, they were even discussing the possibility that she might have to teach in some other city and that they might have to meet for weekends by plane instead of by train as they were then doing. But in Boas' eyes, she was a wife, amply supported and with the obligation of a wife, someone for whose talents he must find work and a little money, someone on whom he could not make extreme demands and for whom he need not be responsible.[28]

It was not until Ruth and Stanley Benedict separated that Boas granted her full academic recognition.

> Boas entrusted more and more teaching to her, but until 1930, she held only the position of lecturer, which sometimes paid a little and sometimes nothing at all. Hard as she worked, devoted as she was, she still seemed to him . . . essentially a visitor from afar who might go away.
> Then, in 1930, the slow, painful process of estrangement between Ruth and Stanley Benedict came to the point of separation. . . . At this time Ruth Benedict presented Boas with a need for professional standing that was accompanied by some reward in money, a need that he recognized. Now when it was necessary, he went to work and got her an assistant professorship which became an associate professorship in 1936. It was now clear that she had come to stay.[29]

The second case illustrates another facet of the status of fringe benefit, its function in the total life pattern of a modern woman, as well as its function in the university.

> For many years my chief contribution to the university was as the wife of a division head. I had entertained—that is, "rushed" —prospective faculty members in an ingratiating way so they would want to work with my husband. I protected my husband against all the daily annoyances of running a home and rearing four children. When he had to go off during the summers for research and professional reasons I had struggled by myself with

household maintenance, camp preparation for the children, community and church obligations. During the years when he left us promptly after dinner to return to the laboratory to watch a delicate experiment or down to his study to work at home, I again took over all the family problems. In this way he was free to devote himself to his work and he was extremely successful, both as an administrator and as a creative person in his laboratory.

When our last child was finally away at [boarding] school I felt I had earned some consideration for my own interests. I had had some graduate work years ago and was anxious to get back into academic life on my own. I went to a neighboring university to get a Ph.D. It took longer than I had expected to get caught up with my field, which had more than tripled since my graduate work. I had to start almost from scratch. Everything had changed in the 25 years I had been away, both in knowledge and in laboratory equipment. I kept at it for three years and then decided that I had had enough for my purpose which was only preparation to teach. At my stage of life there was no particular value in the doctor's degree. So I returned to my husband's university. I was given a section of the introductory course to teach and a lab section. Soon it was two sections. After while I was being shunted in whatever direction current registration or absent personnel indicated need. One term it might be one course, the next, another. I had to be willing to prepare for almost any course, within limits, that had to be taught with no one available to teach it. I do not object. I love teaching, especially the lower-level students who need motivation but whom my [male] professional colleagues shun like the plague. I work extremely hard. I never enter the classroom without knowing exactly what I want to accomplish that hour. My reward is the appreciation of my students. The time I devote to preparation of my lectures, reading lists, and demonstrations, and to the reading of laboratory note-books, research reports, and examinations is not taken from my husband but from the time I used to have to devote to the rearing of my children. I still act as hostess for my husband. I am very happy with the present arrangements. I don't spend a great deal of time around the laboratory. I tend to my business with students and that's about it. I am not interested in departmental cliques and politics. All I want is to do a good job in my teaching, help my students, and then leave.

At the end of Chapter 15, three other cases are presented which illustrate the newly emerging pattern in which academic women retain professional status throughout their marriages. It will, however, doubtless be a long time before the current fringe benefit status for academic women becomes wholly obsolete.

Nonacademic Women

In Chapter 4 the decline in proportion of faculties who were women was explained in part by the rise of alternative careers for women in the pool of qualified personnel. Even if women had contributed relatively more to the qualified population—those with higher degrees—the demands of the nonacademic market would probably have drained them away from the academic market.

The question arises: How, if at all, do nonacademic women differ from academic women? Are there differences between them or do they all belong to the same population? In Chapter 5, the basic control in studying academic women was sex, and it will continue to be throughout our discussion; we are comparing academic *women* with academic *men*. But it is also of interest to compare *academic* women with *nonacademic* women.

A study of academic women as compared with nonacademic women must recognize the enormous heterogeneity of the universe "nonacademic women." Which particular segment should be included depends, obviously, on the nature of the questions to be asked. A comparison of academic women with charwomen would answer certain questions; a comparison with actresses, other questions. Unless carefully defined, almost any control contaminates the "nonacademic" variable. In the present discussion an attempt is made to keep the variables—academic and nonacademic—as clean and uncontaminated by such other factors as degree of training and alternative careers as possible by limiting the comparison to Ph.D.'s in a given speciality, zoology. The findings would certainly be different if the comparison were between academic and nonacademic classicists or historians or Shakespearean scholars, or even in academic institutions are themselves probably different from chemists. The differences between women chemists in industry and those between women zoologists in government and in academic institutions. This caveat is offered to place the following discussion in perspective.

A comparison of academic and nonacademic women zoologists, ten to fifteen years after they received their doctorates (Table 7/1), shows the former to be somewhat older than the latter. This suggests that the competitive attraction of nonacademic positions was somewhat greater for the younger than for the older women.[30] The academic women were somewhat older when they received the doctorate. The academic women were somewhat less likely than the nonacademic to have taken their degrees at the Top Twelve universities.[31] They were, however, members in more scientific and professional organizations than the nonacademic scientists.[32] The academic scientists were less likely than the nonacademic scientists to be married.[33]

The small size of the differences—and their absence in the case of chemists—suggests that with the exception of the greater incidence of marriage (and perhaps quality of doctoral university) the academic and nonacademic women seem to differ hardly at all. They seem to be drawn from essentially the same population so far as the above items are concerned.

Indeed, some women move from one career to another without great difficulty. They are academic women at some stages of their careers and nonacademic at others. There were sixteen such women among the zoologists. Of these, ten, at the time of the study were in nonteaching positions, three were in colleges, and three were in universities. With respect to practically all of the comparable items, they tended to resemble other women in the same positions as those they were then occupying. The implication is that a certain amount of experimentation had taken place in the years after earning their doctorates during which they had tried out several possibilities and then hit upon the one that best suited them. Or, in some cases, they had accommodated their careers to their husbands'.

The commonest pattern was from a university position to a laboratory position (four). Three women reversed this pattern, leaving a laboratory position to go to a university. The other eight women traced varying patterns: college, laboratory, university; university, laboratory, university; college, university; university, laboratory, university; college, university, laboratory; college, university, college; laboratory, university, laboratory; college, university, college, laboratory. In the case of three other women, the influence of the husband's career was clearly visible. One of them went from a laboratory into high school teaching; one went from a university to a laboratory to a university and then to a college; and, finally, one went from a laboratory to a junior college to a university to a high school to a junior college. They were, in effect, interchangeable academic parts.

As a whole, these mixed-career academic-nonacademic women differed from the straight-career women in the comparatively large proportion married—60 percent—and in the relatively younger age at which they received their doctorates (28.5).

College and University Academic Women

The overall comparisons between academic and nonacademic women made above and the picture of the mixed-career academic-nonacademic women obscure some interesting differences between academic women in colleges and those in universities, at least among the scientists just described.

The academic women in colleges were about four to five years older than those in universities, and they were older when they received the doctorate, the median age being 32.8 for them and 29.5 for those in the universities. The college women averaged membership in more professional and scientific organizations, 3.5 versus 2.6. Finally, the college women included only one who was married; whereas almost half of the university women were.[34]

Of great significance was one specific kind of college scientist, the woman who went straight from her doctoral university to a college position and remained in a college position for the next ten to fifteen years. She was a rather clear-cut example of the type first mentioned in Chapter 6 in the discussion of the processes which distribute academic personnel institutionally—a woman with a vocation for college teaching. In the 1950's, with scientific personnel in short supply, at a great premium, such a woman scientist could undoubtedly have found another position if she had so desired. Still she entered and remained in a college position. Her type deserves detailed consideration.

This academic woman was older than the others; she was 47 in 1960. She was older than the others when she received the doctorate; she was 33. She had memberships in more scientific and professional organizations than the others; the average number was 4.1. And she was not married.

As a scientist she was interested in students more than in research. She enjoyed teaching. Research was of secondary interest to her. She measured her scientific productivity in terms of students stimulated rather than in terms of articles written. In a questionnaire study, the following kinds of comments appeared:

Teaching . . . is my dedication. . . .

I am very interested in stimulating greater emphasis on science in the preparation of teachers. These, in turn, will because of their interest and know-how inspire youngsters to enter the field of science. . . .

Teaching means more to me than publication. . . .

These scientists, in brief, viewed their contribution to the scientific world primarily as teachers. They "measured" their productivity in terms of students inspired, of teachers trained, or of knowledge disseminated. They were not unaware of the status implications of their choice. Some may have felt defensive about their professional preference, but others prided themselves on their achievements as teachers.

The conclusion seems inescapable that as an end-result of the processes which distribute personnel among academic institutions, those who enter and remain in college positions are there because they prefer making their contribution to scholarship and science by way of teaching rather than by way of research. These are the women who have time for students, who do not think of them as natural enemies robbing them of time they need for their own research; these are the women who sponsor clubs, entertain students in their homes, accompany them on trips. These are women who are married to their careers.

In general the women who went directly from their doctoral university to a university position (seven were in professional schools), tended to fall between those in college positions and those in nonacademic positions with respect to the items here under discussion, that is, in age, age at receiving the doctorate, and percent married (one-third were). They resembled the nonacademic women in average number of professional and scientific memberships, and the college women in proportion taking the doctor's degree at the Top Twelve.

It would doubtless be profitable and interesting to pursue the subject of differences among academic women and between them and nonacademic women. It would be interesting to know more about the differences among those in different subject-matter areas, among those in different parts of the country, among those in different kinds of institutions. But as yet sufficient detailed data are not available for such comparisons.

Table 7/1 Summary of Differences between Academic and Nonacademic Women *

	Academic Women † (31)	Non-Academic Women ‡ (16)
Median Birth Date	1917	1920
Median Age at Doctorate	32.5	28.7
Percent with Doctorate from Top Twelve	35	56
Average Number Memberships in Professional and Scientific Societies	3.3	2.7
Percent Married	32	50
Median Age at Marriage	25.5	29
Proportion Married before Ph.D.	23	25
Percent of Married Who Have Children	60	50
Average Number of Children among Those who Have Children	2.1	1.25

* All subjects were biological scientists receiving their degrees during the same time period. One Negro scientist is not included. Source: *American Men of Science* (Tempe: Cattell, 1960).

† Includes 12 in colleges, 12 in universities, and 7 in professional schools in universities.

‡ Includes 4 women in nonteaching laboratories connected with universities, such as university hospitals.

Table 7/2 Summary of Differences Between Academic Women in Colleges and Academic Women in Universities *

	In Colleges (12)	In Universities (19)
Median Birth Date	1915	1919
Median Age at Doctorate	32.8	29.5
Percent with Doctorate from Top Twelve	33	43
Average Number Memberships in Professional and Scientific Societies	3.5	2.6
Percent Married	8	48
Median Age at Marriage	31 (1 case)	25.8
Percent of Married Who Have Children	——	31
Average Number of Children among Those Who Have Children	——	1.9

* All subjects were biological scientists receiving their degrees during the same time period. Source: *American Men of Science*.

CHAPTER 8 ❀ TEACHERS
AND PROFESSORS: SUBJECT-MATTER
AREAS

Academic Institutions as the Natural Habitat of Learning

Institutions of higher education perform many varied services in our society. They conserve accumulated knowledge and transmit it to succeeding generations, they create new knowledge, and they interpret, criticize, and honor knowledge. They serve as the natural habitat of learning. They create a certain kind of ambience which is important just by the fact of its existence. They serve, that is, merely by being places where people can sit and think,[1] where ideas are valued for themselves.[2]

It takes a great many people in many roles to insure that all these services are performed. Of all the functional positions required, as described in Chapter 2, two are of special relevance for our discussion here: the key or core professions subsumed under the rubrics "faculty for resident instruction in degree-credit courses" and "professional staff for organized research." Women, it will be recalled, constituted 19.4 percent of the first and 11.4 percent of the second category in 1959–60.[3] What, exactly, were they doing, and how well were they doing it?

Teaching and Professing

A college or university, then, is much more than a place where generations of students are processed for later life. It is a place where, even if there were no students, ideas would flourish. Face-to-face teaching may be important, although it has long been pointed out that since the invention of printing the strictly information-conveying function of teaching has become anachronistic. Motivated people can learn by reading materials themselves. The so-called teaching boxes, in fact, can do the job of this kind of teaching faster and better than the human teacher.

Much more than teaching, however, is involved in the atmosphere of a good college or university. There must be people around who are enthralled by their subjects. Students must learn that there are people vitally interested in ideas, people to whom ideas are important. There have to be people who "profess," debate, argue, stand for something, live their subject. It is worthwhile for the student to know that there are such people in the world, not that he will necessarily take them as models—students in most universities won't. In later years, however, the student as board member, executive or voter will know that there are people desperately attached to certain values and that these values are good and must be protected. The man who has never been exposed to men-of-knowledge will be cavalier about voting support for a community "culture"—in the narrow sense—center. The man who has been exposed to a great Shakespeare scholar—who may have been a poor teacher or lecturer—may live a no more "cultured" life for the exposure, but he will be aware of "culture" and the public that loves it.

Teacher Role and Man-of-Knowledge Role

In order to understand the contribution which women have made to the academic enterprise in the United States a distinction between the roles of "teacher" and "professor" or "man-of-knowledge" is useful. This distinction is not identical with one commonly made between "discipline loyalty" and "institutional loyalty," though it may be related, nor is it identical with the ancient "teaching" and "research" polarity, though, again, it may be related. The professor or man-of-knowledge may or may not also be a researcher.

It is a distinction more like Franz Adler's between means and ends. If we view both professors and teachers as performers (as well as models), the following statement shows how their roles differ:

The performer may be defined as a middle man between the author and the publics. Performance may be divided into two classes; those that are more or less ends in themselves and those that are means for facilitating the presentation of a work. The first kind is produced by a "charismatic mediator," the latter by a performer who may be called a "tool." The charismatic mediator deserves to be considered as an author in his own right. His authorship comes into play after rather than before that of the official author. In this it differs from most kinds of true authorship. The performance of the charismatic mediator tends to carry high prestige and is rightly regarded as a sign of creative ability. The performance of the tool is less likely to carry a high prestige, and whatever prestige it does carry derives from technical perfection rather than from creativity.[4]

The role of the teacher, in brief, is to serve as an instrument of communication; the role of the man-of-knowledge is to serve as a collaborator with the original author.

We are here speaking of roles; the same people may perform both roles at different times. Generally, however, as the following discussion indicates, the tendency has been for women to perform primarily in the teaching role. The professor or man-of-knowledge role has been performed primarily by men.

A second distinction between the teacher and the professor or man-of-knowledge roles has to do with the nature of the materials dealt with. The teacher often deals with the established, hence usually elementary, aspects of his discipline. He is conserving, not innovating. Again Adler:

> Where orthodoxy or exact performance is emphasized, the teacher will be under specifically heavy scrutiny by members of the general public, his colleagues and, if such exists, the hierarchy of performers. And woe indeed to him who becomes a heretic while instructing. . . . This is easily understandable if the tremendous potential influence of the teacher is considered. The teacher is believed because he is a teacher. It is assumed by his audience that what he is going to tell them is true, that is, orthodox. If he is found out, then, to teach opinions of his own and not those shared by his colleagues or his superiors he will find himself rapidly discredited except where he is able to assume the role of a new author and is recognized in it. It will take a special public for such a recognition. . . . The performer in general and the teacher in particular are factors for the maintenance of existing forms and contents and serious obstacles to innovation. As they transmit orthodoxy to future authors and performers they are instrumental in shaping future works and

their presentations. As they transmit orthodoxy to members of publics they shape their expectations and their readiness to accept or reject new works and new performances.[5]

The professor or man-of-knowledge deals with controversial, hence usually with advanced, aspects of his discipline. He stands for a point of view in the field, a fact which leads students to say "I would like to study with Professor Blank at Kanwisota University." [6] He does not take orthodoxy for granted. He modifies, performs exegesis, tells his listeners that this author is clearly wrong, that one mistaken. Although he may never do much writing of his own, the performance of his role as a man-of-knowledge requires a kind of effort quite as rigorous as that of research. As systematizer he has to make sense out of the vast torrent of findings that pour from the laboratories and libraries. He puts findings in their place, in perspective. He has to see implications, relationships, total structures, and gestalts as well as small details. He must know less about more rather than more about less. He is, in brief, a generalist. The professor or man-of-knowledge role calls for a heavy load of intellectual baggage. It requires that the performer keep his eyes open for trends in a wide variety of areas. The performer of this role is the one who makes use of the researcher's findings, often conferring more value on them in this way than the researcher does. It is in this sense that, as Adler pointed out, the man-of-knowledge becomes a collaborator with the original author.

Naive people do not understand the difference between the function of the man-of-knowledge role and the teacher role. Thus, for example, members of the American Legion or the Veterans of Foreign Wars or other conservative organizations feel called upon to scrutinize what is being taught. If what they find is contrary to the accepted patterns of thought in the community, they raise a hue and cry. This is not what they pay teachers to do. It is the academic person performing the man-of-knowledge function who is most likely to have problems with academic freedom. Indeed, it is the institutionalization of academic freedom which alone makes possible the performance of the man-of-knowledge role at all. Without it, the man-of-knowledge role would be assimilated by the teacher role.

The fact that women are more likely to be in the teacher role than in the man-of-knowledge role and hence less likely—even in the social sciences—to be dealing with controversial materials may help to explain why they were found to be less apprehensive than men in the McCarthy era, as reported by Budner and Meyer.

A third difference between the roles of teacher and professor or man-of-knowledge has to do with the complementary role of student. The teacher is often performing his role in a required course, one in which the interest of the student cannot be taken for granted. The relationship between teacher and student is influenced by this fact; it is peculiar in that the teacher is, so to speak, at the mercy of his students to the extent that their achievement is a test of his competence. The importance of student achievement often gives a kind of stark urgency to the relationship from the teacher's point of view. Because the student can use refusal to learn as a strategic weapon against the teacher, the teacher is usually surrounded with powerful weapons of deterrence or defense—an apparatus of grades and attendance requirements which serve as potential threats. The teacher pushes; the student often resists. The score is evened up by the weight of the institutional support back of the teacher.

There is less likely to be this kind of conflict between the student and the professor or man-of-knowledge. He invites the student to share his enthusiasm for the subject matter. There exists, theoretically, a joint enterprise in which motivation is assumed on the part of the student. To the extent that he performs as a professor rather than as a teacher, the academic person does not need the institutional apparatus of grades and compulsory attendance for support. Znaniecki has described the professor-student relationship as follows:

> What binds this group of professors and students together is knowledge as such—the scholarly type of theoretic, systematically ordered, absolutely true knowledge. Its cultivation and perpetuation is the primary task of the group and the chief reason of its existence; if it ceased to perform this task, it would also cease to be a center of higher intellectual education. No matter what psychological motives induce particular individuals to seek admission to the group, so long as they are its members they are bound to accept its appreciation of knowledge as the highest common value.[7]

A final difference between the two roles is a corollary of the third one. Both the teacher and the man-of-knowledge must be as well as do, that is, they must serve as models for the young. But they do so in quiet different ways. One author has distinguished at least five model-related demands which students may legitimately make of teachers: (1) that they be cultural and aesthetic examples; (2) that they exhibit serious scholarship; (3) that they have social sophistication, that is, poise and self-assurance; (4) that they show professional responsibility, that is, a serious attitude toward their jobs, their colleagues, and their environment; and, finally, (5) that they serve as ethical and moral arbiters, willing to make known their commitments rather than hide behind a facade of objectivity or neutrality.[8] The great teacher, according to these specifications, has to be a certain kind of person as well as do certain things:

> Every genuine teacher is concerned with assisting his students to develop and to educate themselves. And beneath all the trappings of pedagogy and erudition one of the most significant means of doing this is by his own example, whether he wishes it or not. The old saw, "What you do speaks so loudly I cannot hear what you say," applies with painful accuracy to the student-teacher relationship. To be a teacher means the acceptance of that responsibility, no matter how embarrassing, enervating, or humbling the prospect may be. While we lament, as we so often must, that students just don't listen to us, we must also remember that they do note with frightening accuracy what we stand for. When we become discouraged about their seeming resistance to much we try to tell them, we must remember that very fleeting impressions may have far more effect in the long run than hours of very laborious exposition in some good cause.[9]

As the transmitting function imposes hazards on student-teacher relationships, so also does the model-serving or socializing function. At more elementary levels the community often demands that its schoolteachers behave much better than other citizens. Until fairly recently they were not permitted to smoke, and their recreational life was strictly policed. They are required to be conservers of the mores as well as of knowledge. At the college and university level the model is less circumscribed— [10] except, perhaps, at conservative church-affiliated schools—but there still remains a barrier. Indeed, the resulting *persona* often becomes so fixed that some college teachers can be spotted as such in a crowd.

The kind of socialization for which the man-of-knowledge is responsible is of a quite different kind: He must socialize the student into his intellectual, not his citizenship, role:

> A secular university is an association of mature persons in

which professors have positions of authority. Although, like every other social group, it exercises some control over the conduct of its members, yet it does not try to educate them physically or morally, to guide their personal evolution so as to make them fit for social participation, since it presumes that this has already been done during their childhood and early youth. . . .

The school of higher learning performs the specifically social function of an educational institution only because its main activities are not social but scientific,[11] do not aim to contribute to the maintenance of the social order but to the maintenance of knowledge as a supersocial domain of culture supremely valuable in itself. Therefore, the chief personal duty of every member is to share in the activities by which knowledge is maintained, even if only by faithfully assimilating that relatively small portion of knowledge which is transmitted to him during the period when he is a mere student.

Academic Women as Teachers

These functional distinctions between the roles of teacher and man-of-knowledge help to explain why women, by and large, have made their most important contributions to the academic enterprise as teachers, both at the bottom of the academic hierarchy and at the professional school level, and to a greater extent in some subjects than in others.

The earliest catalogs of both Vassar and Smith College showed only two ranks, professors and teachers. The professors were, for the most part, men and the teachers, women.[12] The distinction by sex at Smith did not, however, last very long:

Among the men and women on the Faculty no discrimination in rank or tenure of office was made on account of sex. The title "professor" was not at first given to the women, because most of them preferred not to receive what seemed an absurd and pretentious appellation, which had been retained, apparently, for men only by force of an ancient tradition. In the earliest official circulars, the women were designated simply as teachers, but it proved a needless and vain attempt to emphasize feminine distinctions and was not long continued.[13]

On the basis of a survey of college catalogs over a century and of more recent studies in several different kinds of institutions, it may be said that women have carried a disproportionate share of the heavy, "back-breaking"—anyone who has ever sat grading examination papers will recognize the literalness of this adjective—load of introductory instruction. At Vassar—and the situation was essentially the same in other colleges—women constituted almost the entire "teaching" or "instructor" faculty until well into the twentieth century (Table 8/1). No doubt much of this introductory work has been, and is, done by women in the status of fringe benefits, but some of it is doubtless done by professionals, at least by women with Ph.D. degrees, as suggested by the rank of Chicago Ph.D. women (Table 12/3). It is suggested here that there may be a functional reason for the distribution of academic women by rank, that they are likely to be found at the lower ranks in part, at least, because they teach the less controversial, more standard, aspects of their subjects.

The Elementary Level of Instruction

A glance at Table 8/2 shows that the proportion of, for example, mathematics teachers who were women (1954–55) was much greater than the proportion of women receiving the doctorate in mathematics (1955–56). (The difference in date must, of course, be taken into account in interpreting these figures, for the teachers with Ph.D.'s in 1954–55 reflect doctorates of previous years, but the difference is not great enough to nullify the point being made here.) In brief, a great many college and university mathematics teachers were women without doctorates and hence, presumably, were not teaching advanced courses. A similar comment might be made with respect to the physical sciences, to the health professions, to business and commerce, to education, to English, journalism, and foreign languages, to fine and applied arts, to home economics, and to library science. That women without doctorates were probably teaching elementary courses does not mean that those with doctorates were necessarily teaching the advanced courses. The relatively low rank even of those with doctorates (Table 12/3) suggests that they were not.

Women as Teachers in the Professional Schools [14]

Further evidence that academic women tend to be teachers of the more stable subjects and the more elementary levels may be adduced from the situation in professional schools. The teacher-professor distinction helps to explain the anomalous fact that women entered the faculties of the great universities at the level of the professional schools. At Harvard in the 1920's and 1930's women came as instructors in child hygiene, in nutrition, and in vital statistics.[15] At the University of Michigan there was a woman professor of public health nursing in the 1920's, the only woman among 209 professors, but with the obvious role of teacher.[16]

The acceptance of women in professional, especially medical, schools, which are of graduate level standing, more readily than in Ph.D.-granting faculties reflects a difference in the nature of the training for the several doctoral degrees and in the faculties which confer them. The M.D., for example, is not a research degree and does not call for the same kind of relationship between faculty and student. The M.D. calls for the absorption of a certain amount of scientific knowledge, the acquisition of technical skills, and socialization into a certain occupational culture. The faculties of such schools reflect a division of labor with respect to these functions. Those who convey the theoretical knowledge are primarily teachers of science; those who serve as clinical teachers are practice-oriented.[17] The teachers of the sciences are likely to be Ph.D.'s,[18] the clinicians, M.D.'s.

Among the Ph.D.'s on the faculties of professional schools, some perform the teacher role primarily, others the professorial or man-of-knowledge role. In relation to medical school faculties, the following account is illuminating:

> There is undoubtedly a relationship, although not a necessary one, between style of teaching in these courses and advances in science. Gross anatomy is a morphological study, and the morphology of the body has been known for many years. Teachers of the subject are somewhat in the position of Latin teachers in high school. There is an old discipline with many teaching traditions. . . . Physiology and microanatomy are rapidly advancing fields; outmoded knowledge must be constantly replaced by the results of research and new knowledge integrated with old. . . .[19]

Both teachers and professors are required, the first for the settled areas of science, like anatomy, and the second for the evolving areas, like physiology. Women have been successful in performing the teacher role, even at this advanced level, especially in the field of anatomy.

In a study of the proportion of women on the faculties of twenty leading universities in 1960, for example, anatomy stood out as especially hospitable to women. Disregarding for the moment such subjects as home economics, library science, and education, we find that it leads all other subjects, with 15.6 percent of those teaching anatomy being women, almost twice as many, proportionately, as those teaching physiology (8.4 percent). They achieved top rank in this subject more often than in any other, 9.4 percent of the professors of anatomy being women. The next subject below anatomy in proportion of women professors was music (5.9 percent). There were no women professors of physiology.[20]

Without pressing the suggestion too far, it does seem that the character of the subject matter taught is a relevant variable in explaining the contribution which academic women have made. They seem to have done most in the stable areas of learning. For all subjects, this would be at the introductory level; for some subjects, it would also be at the professional level.

There are, to be sure, anomalies. Alice Hamilton became a member of the Harvard University medical faculty in 1918; she came as an assistant professor and retained this rank until she became emerita in 1939. Hers was certainly a growing field—indeed one to which she was herself a major contributor—and should, therefore, according to the suggestion offered above, have been preempted by a man. It so happened, however, that she knew more than anyone else in the world about industrial medicine. It was a choice between filling the post with her or leaving it unfilled. But her rank conformed to her sex; it remained low to the end.[21]

The Social Sciences [22]

The distinction between the roles of teacher and professor helps to explain also the areas in which women have made their most important contributions, as well as the levels at which they have done so. It is, to be sure, only one factor. The subjects women teach are related to market demand and to their interests. The under-representation of women in the physical sciences, for example, can be plausibly explained by the lack of interest of women in this field. No matter how great the market demand and no matter how stable the introductory aspects, women are not attracted to it.

Women are also under-represented in the social sciences. Next after the physical sciences, the social sciences are the most "masculine" subjects. As shown in Table 8/2 (and in Tables 12/2 and 12/3), the proportion of women teaching in these subjects is low.

A possible interpretation of the relative under-representation of women in the social sciences, especially in the great universities, may be sought not in lack of interest on the part of women[23] but in the nature of the subjects themselves. Except for statistics, the social sciences are less standardized than, for example, grammar, rhetoric, mathematics, or the physical and biological sciences. In these areas the teacher is conveying relatively fixed and standardized knowledge. The teacher can usually rely on the authority of fixed principles, little subject to controversy. Grammar is grammar, atoms are atoms, cells are cells, at the elementary level, however controversial they may be at advanced levels. The same is less true in the social sciences, where there are more likely to be many schools of thought[24] and more room for interpretation and controversy. Even elementary textbooks reveal many different points of view as reflected in the selection of materials and the relative emphasis given to them. The teacher is therefore often on controversial ground,[25] dealing, furthermore, with issues on which the opinions of women often do not carry much weight. In many matters in the social sciences the experience of women is not always judged to be relevant.[26] The teacher is also often on the opposite side of the fence from his students politically.[27]

Another aspect of this situation has to do with the function of the social sciences in the university as sources of social criticism. At the elementary levels of the social science disciplines a bland picture of the functioning of our society is presented according to theory, but at the higher levels the defects as it actually operates are, of necessity, also presented. The great social critics, from Veblen, Beard, Ross, Commons, and Hart, to Galbraith, Riesman, and Mills have been academic men. This is an integral part of the role of the academic man as man-of-knowledge. The one area in which women have traditionally served as social critics has been that of the place of women in our society, and even here their contribution has often been one of waspish special pleading rather than serious, responsible social criticism. The great reformers among academic women, noted in Chapter 1, were just that, reformers primarily rather than social critics.[28] Conscience, not science, was their forte.

It has been in languages and literature—English composition, French grammar, German grammar, Spanish grammar, and the like (sometimes euphemistically classified with the humanities)— and the elementary levels of the several physical and biological sciences, and mathematics that women have traditionally made their major contribution.[29]

In the areas and at the levels where women have made their major contributions as teachers, then, they have had behind them the weight of definitive bodies of knowledge about which relatively little controversy or few differences in interpretation exist. They did not have to defend themselves, being primarily agents or "tools" of transmission. Sex as such is apparently no handicap in this kind of role, but in less defined and stabilized and established areas the problem of competence becomes more difficult even to concept-ualize; the professor or man-of-knowledge role seems to be de-manded. In addition, the function of social criticism, which is part of the man-of-knowledge function of the social scientist, has not been one customarily assigned to women, except in limited areas.

Among the consequences of the differences between academic men and academic women in areas of interest is one of special relevance. Academicians in different fields have different positions in the market. Some, because of great demand, are in better bar-gaining positions than others and hence can demand better rewards. Others do not have good bargaining positions. In general, these differences in bargaining power tend to operate against women, since they are more likely than men to be in the areas with poorer bargaining power, namely the humanities.

That the major contribution of women to the academic enter-prise should have been as teachers is related also, presumably, to the fact that the role of teacher is consonant with that of other roles assigned to women in our society. As mothers, women have been traditionally conservators and transmitters of non-controver-sial knowledge.

Academic women, then, have performed some of the hardest work that has to be done by academic institutions, the grinding drudgery of unchallenging introductory courses, and have thus re-leased academic men for the more rewarding assignments, graduate courses in new and more exciting areas, of the professor or man-of-knowledge role.

Table 8/1 Proportion of Professorial and Instructor Ranks Who were Women in Four Subject Areas, Vassar College, 1865–1956

Year	Science and Mathematics Profes-sorial	Instruc-tor	Language and Literature Profes-sorial	Instruc-tor	Social Science and History Profes-sorial	Instruc-tor	Art and Music Profes-sorial	Instruc-tor
1865	25	100		90				100
1874–75	50	100		100				100
1884–85	50	100		100				100
1894–95	43	100	25	100	50	100		100
1904–1905	29	100	40	100	50	100		50
1914–15	17	100	57	100	40	100		60
1924–25	63	92	91*	90	57	100	20	71
1934–35	87*	85	77	100	56	57	22	60
1944–45	58	86	78	82	71*	100	29	63
1955–56	67	67	71	68	55	60	17	77

* High point.

Table 8/2 Doctors in Specified Fields, 1955–56, Who Were Women and Teachers in 673 Institutions Who Were Women, 1954–55 *

Field	Percent Doctors Who Were Women	Percent Teachers Who Were Women
All Fields	9.9	22.0
Agricultural and Biological Sciences	9.0	10.3
Mathematics	4.3	14.2
Physical Sciences	4.1	6.0
Psychology	13.6	13.4
Geography and Anthropology	6.4	15.5
Health Professions	4.9	46.9
Business and Commerce	0.0	20.2
Education	17.8	36.9
English, Journalism, Foreign Languages	17.0	27.5
Fine Arts	13.2	27.3
Social Sciences	10.0	10.6
Library Science	6.6	71.5
Home Economics	84.8	96.4

* Data on doctorates adapted from Office of Education, *Statistics of Higher Education: 1955–56* (Washington: GPO, 1958), pp. 96 ff. Data on teachers, National Science Foundation, *Women in Scientific Careers* (Washington: GPO, 1961), p. 9.

CHAPTER 9 ✱ TEACHERS
AND PROFESSORS: THE QUALITY
OF ROLE PERFORMANCE

The Evaluation of Teaching

It is of interest to know not only the extent and area of participation of women in the academic enterprise but also the quality of their contribution. How well have they performed in their academic roles? Both autonomous and judgmental competitive processes may be used to evaluate teaching. In autonomous competition, it will be recalled, success is measured by the process itself: the teacher whose students learn most, for example, is, ipso facto, the best teacher. In judgmental competition, someone decides who is best.

M. Carey Thomas, after observing men and women at Bryn Mawr for thirty-seven years, was convinced that "women make exceptionally successful teachers." [1] When Henry Noble Mac-Cracken came to Vassar he was surprised at the excellent quality of the teaching there, "definitely better than I had known at either Harvard or Yale." [2]

These statements illustrate judgmental competition. They are to be respected, coming from careful observers with many years of experience in judging academic performance. Yet such judgments are fallible: Different judges often arrive at different conclusions on the basis of the same evidence. Students differ from peers, peers from administrators. [3]

It is usually felt that it is possible to judge the really superb teachers and the obviously incompetent ones; it is in the great middle range and along the borderline where it is difficult to differentiate among or to grade teachers. Even the best judgments are subjective and difficult to prove. Students, for example, can be found at the memorial services for almost any college or university professor who will paint glowing pictures of the deceased as teacher. [4] It has, in fact, been found to be practically impossible to remove academic personnel on the grounds of incompetence because there is always someone—student or colleague—who will swear that so-and-so is a wonderful teacher.

Nor is there even consensus on the criteria to apply in making judgments. Different judges may use different criteria, and the subjects may not know on what basis judgments are made. Thus, they are at a loss to know what they must do to win good "marks." [5] The absence of clear-cut criteria for judging teachers for promotions or raises has, in fact, been offered as one of the reasons for faculty-administration conflict.[6]

The "Vote" of Students

There is one form of autonomous competition in which success is measured by popularity among students. This is, literally, an "election." The criterion here is the "vote" of students. Almost every campus sooner or later develops great traditional teachers. Everyone just "has" to have a course with "Daddy" So-and-So or with "The Great One" or he really hasn't been to Kanwisota. William Graham Sumner was such a tradition at Yale for many years. Usually, though, such teachers are only local giants. They contribute flair or charisma or glamor or a rallying point at which diverse elements can come together. Their function, though often contemned, is important and valuable, both students and institutions becoming more interesting because of their contribution.

Sometimes the top-ranking teachers are known, not for their glamor, but for the quality of their courses. Word-of-mouth accounts among students dwell on the organization, depth, and thoroughness of their courses rather than on their personalities or on their success as performers.

Women as well as men can reach the top level in both kinds of teaching in women's colleges; in coeducational institutions, women are probably more likely to succeed in the second than in the first. They are, probably better known as substantial, conscientious teachers than as personalities that everyone should be exposed to.[7] But that there are great personalities among academic women in coeducational institutions is illustrated by the story of three great teachers presented below.

Success in teaching as measured by popularity is sometimes

taken as prima facie evidence that it is being bought by lowered standards or easy grading. Since it is so difficult to hold constant the many variables involved, this alleged relationship is hard to prove. The student grapevine seems to convey the message that women are easier graders than men, or at least more susceptible to persuasion, bullying, blackmail, or pity, if not to sex appeal.[8]

In view of the difficulties involved in any kind of evaluation, it is not surprising that none of the many published studies evaluating teaching performance have attempted to evaluate men and women separately. Several unpublished experimental studies (see Appendix B), however, while not definitive, are relevant and interesting. On the basis of these experiments, it is safe to conclude that women are entirely competent in teaching a standard body of knowledge; they may be somewhat handicapped in teaching controversial material.

Experimental Studies

The first experiment was in the field of mathematics. The evaluation process was autonomous: The criterion of success was student achievement. The controls were as tight as it was possible to make them. The results showed that, as measured by student achievement, the women mathematics teachers were not as good as the best men teachers, but on the other hand neither were they as bad as the worst; they tended to approach the average. Of special interest was the fact that the women tended to be relatively better with the poorer students than they were with the superior ones, suggesting that patience rather than stimulation was their forte. The suggested picture is certainly not one of two discrete universes, one for each sex, nor even one of overlapping universes, but rather, apparently, of a less variable universe within the limits of a more variable one.

The second experiment was in the field of English. Here it turned out that even in the status of fringe benefits, the contribution of women teachers was at least average in success. It was, incidentally, judged better by colleagues than by students.

The third experiment, in the "masculine" field of sociology, appears to have the most interesting theoretical implications and to offer the most illuminating insights into the role-related hand-

icaps of women in teaching students, especially in areas of knowledge which do not have the weight of established tradition behind
them.

Role theory states that roles are always reciprocal, that their
performance always involves a mutual response: Roles cannot be
performed alone, in isolation. No matter how well one person
performs his role, if the other person or persons do not respond,
the role is not, in effect, being performed at all. The success of
any role performance depends, therefore, as much on Alter's performance of the complementary role as it does on Ego's performance of his role. Thus the question may well be raised, quite apart
from their intellectual qualifications, whether women, no matter
how well trained they are or how skillful, actually do for students
as teachers what men can do.

The experiment reported in Appendix B suggests that the
same material presented by a man and by a woman may not
have the same impact on students. In the particular situation of
this experiment, the man aroused more emotional response—hostile
in this case—and was accused of bias and prejudice. And yet,
despite this fact, what he said was accepted as more authoritative
than what the woman said. She did not, despite her communication skills, carry the weight that the young man did.[9] She did not
"look the part." Her performance of the teacher role was, therefore, in a way less successful than his, for no reason that she could
do anything about.[10]

The fourth study had to do with speech (see Appendix B).
Some 911 students in 56 sections of an introductory course were
asked to "assist us to determine what students think about" the
course in question. The overall differences between the replies
from students in sections taught by women and those from students
taught by men were negligible. In general, the students of the
women teachers were more likely than those of the men teachers
to consider the instruction very good and less likely to consider the
course poorly taught. Of special interest was the fact that the
women-taught students were more likely than the men-taught
students to give extremely favorable replies to questions dealing
with the teacher's performance. In some cases the proportion who
found the teacher's performance either highly valuable or extremely
valuable was about the same for those taught by women and by
men, but the tendency was for the differences in the "extremely
valuable" category to favor the women.

The relative favorableness to women of the replies was especially interesting for the item dealing with "conferences with instructor." One-fourth of the women-taught students found such conferences "extremely valuable," whereas only 16 percent of the men-taught students did; that is, about 56 percent more of the women-taught than of the men-taught students found such conferences "extremely valuable." Written comments did not show such a great disparity. The implication can only be that it was the personal confrontation between teacher and individual student which so many of the women-taught students found so valuable. It was in this situation where the academic women seemed to be especially effective.

Academic Momism?

The greater patience of academic women implied in the mathematics teaching experiment reported above and the reputedly greater leniency among them raise the question of too great a dependence of students of academic women, or "academic momism." We shall have more to say on this subject below in connection with graduate students; at this point a document is introduced which shows how skillfully one academic woman used her relationship with a young male undergraduate for learning purposes and how she terminated the "transference" so consummately that the whole episode left a glow in his memory of it. She knew how to use dependency creatively.

Tutor Meets Advisee [11]

As a junior at ——— College in 1957 I had become interested in a research problem concerning voting patterns of Catholics in the United States. I began a rather active search for a faculty member who could direct my research, hopefully toward a thesis project required of all senior honors candidates in the college.

Everyone acknowledged that there was only one person well acquainted with the area of voting, Dr. Helen Patrick. I asked her to read a paper I had written on the subject, and when I returned for her comments, she said little. She gave me a reprint of a recent article she had written to illustrate methodological flaws in voting analysis. She asked me to return in a week with comments on how her article bore upon my problem.

There was, frankly, little bearing of this article upon my problem, I discovered, other than one point: analysis of voting requires methodological sophistication uncommon among analysts up to that time. It was clear that if I were to embark on such analysis, I would have to develop this sophistication. Another point was implicit: Dr. Patrick was the person competent to develop this talent.

At our following meeting the next week I agreed to the necessity of methodological precision, and asked her with a bit of foreboding whether she would undertake to advise my thesis on this topic. She responded with enthusiasm, and we began laying plans for the next few months. It was clear that I was dependent upon her technical competence and would have to adhere to her directions closely.

She also expressed a slight suspicion at my motives for this research. I was a rather vital Catholic, and the possibility of either dual intellectual allegiance or rigidity of interpretation concerned her. She suggested that I begin "reading between the lines" when I interpreted actions or pronouncements of Catholics. I found it necessary to emphasize that I was politically uncommitted at the time. My only outlook was one I interpreted as "liberal." The issue of my motivation finally exhausted itself, but in the process I had become more firmly attached to Dr. Patrick as a tutor. For the only means for achieving a successful thesis was by perceiving action of Catholics with a cool, methodologically analytic eye. I had, intellectually, loosened myself of all supports save her orientation. Once having adopted it, the intellectual task ahead seemed viable to both of us.

Although our personal relationship retained the customary university formality—addressing each other by highest title—our work together assumed rather energetic proportions. She arranged for me to visit the Survey Research Center at the University of Michigan, where she had received her own graduate training, for obtaining data during the summer. In preparation she introduced me to many folkways of research she had acquired there. Her attitude was both instructional and supportive.

After a very profitable research period in the summer, we resumed our weekly tutorial sessions in the fall of 1957. She required more frequent meetings than did most tutors, though in substance they were similar. I would present a problem and then be expected to work it out while she acted as a sounding board. Our sessions retained the original formality until time became so pressing about four months later that our meetings were held at lunch hour. This atmosphere elicited conversation of a socio-emotional nature, though never about personal affairs. She began calling me "Mike," and I called her "Mrs. Pat."

Throughout these sessions she remained extremely supportive.

At one point I had incurred a $40.00 bill for card duplication which she examined, put into her folder, indicating that funds were available for payment of it. When I began writing the thesis, she commented on the drafts assiduously, almost line-by-line. At one point she asked me not to continue writing until she had commented upon my work to date.

My dependence on Mrs. Pat was also demonstrated in my plans for graduate work in social psychology. Since I had not decided upon a graduate school, I turned to her for expert advice. When I indicated I would like to remain at the university if for no other reason than because I was satisfied with their program, she emphatically discounted my rationale. Since I had few other criteria upon which to choose among the few schools which offered such a program, I chose Michigan mainly because of her example of a successful career as a graduate. Again she played a supportive role in writing several personal letters to friends at Michigan in an attempt to secure some financial assistance for me.

If the notion of dependence seems overdrawn, for in many cases the action seems merely that appropriate to that of any adviser, one negative instance may provide further support. After finishing my presentation of data in the thesis, I turned to inquiring about the generality of my findings. I drew upon rather wide sources, both in political science and the religious spheres. I employed a less terse, more elegant style in the presentation. She made few comments on these chapters, save that they were discursive and added little to the thesis except weight. I felt her comments were imperceptive at best and asked a political scientist to read the same material. He agreed that the chapters were central to a rounded interpretation of the problem, and that they were unobjectionable stylistically. I have interpreted her objections to be due partly to my assertion of certain independence in my presentation. Concurrently our meetings became very infrequent, mostly replaced by an occasional telephone call. Our relationship had entered its terminal stage, with the two parties becoming both physically and psychologically distant.

The last two months before graduation pulled each of us into his own direction. Mrs. Pat was leaving for the west in a month so that her time was nearly totally committed. I similarly had to terminate my affairs before returning to my home for the summer and to Michigan in the fall. I found it strange, though, that upon my having received the grade Magna cum Laude on the thesis I received no invitation for celebration when I telephoned the news to her.

We have exchanged only one letter since then, and that was upon my entering graduate school at Michigan. This has been a typical termination of a relationship in the academic life, I feel. It concluded a most satisfactory tutorial relationship, extremely rewarding academically—a relationship distinguished by a more supportive role of the tutor in a case in which the advisee was extremely dependent. When there was no longer occasion for dependence, however, the relationship quickly became attenuated.

Three Great Teachers

That there are very great teachers among academic women, and in the great universities, is illustrated by the following description of three teachers at Stanford University by a former student. These women won the "votes" of students. The criteria on which success was based differed widely among the three; there is, apparently, no single standard type of successful teacher.

An Unusual Triumvirate of Academic Women [12]

When I was an undergraduate at Stanford University, from 1942 through 1946, there was on the campus a very unusual trio of women professors. To the best of my knowledge, they all received their education at Stanford and were all employed as faculty members during the presidency of Dr. Ray Lyman Wilbur, 1916–1943, who must have had a very enlightened view of academic women. By the time I arrived on the campus, all three of these women had been renowned members of the campus community for many years. Two of the three taught courses that were considered to be "must" courses for the student who wanted to include in his curriculum the best that Stanford had to offer. All three were campus "characters," each in her own way. None of the three ever married.

Dr. Margery Bailey stands out as the most colorful of the three. She was a genuine campus "character" of heroic proportions. She struck fear into the hearts of many a lowly undergraduate. She was famous for one special course. She was an English professor, and her course on Shakespeare may well have been the most famous course offered at Stanford in my day. At least it so stands out in my memory.

Marge Bailey was an austere and dramatic person of fierce

likes and dislikes. The only picture of her that I ever saw printed anywhere was very true to her type. It was taken full profile, John Barrymore style. She had a strong profile with a rather prominent acquiline nose. Her eyes were dark and stern. She wore her hair in a severe style, pulled up and back from her face and fixed in a bun at the back of her head. Her jaw was stubborn and her mouth set. She was a large-boned woman, not heavy, but solid. She was rather handsome in a stark and massive way. Her voice was quite deep and full. She wore tweedy, tailored, severe clothes.

Taking Marge Bailey's Shakespeare course was a rather masochistic pleasure. She was very demanding and regularly practiced ridicule in the classroom. Woe be to the poor student who didn't perform up to standard or who made any attempt to be bold with Marge Bailey. Women students were especially vulnerable. Marge Bailey hated women, reserved special hatred for sorority women, and made no secret of it. She took special pains to break down the composure of any poor girl who happened to make herself conspicuous in class. It was to the advantage of a girl in Marge Bailey's class to stay as anonymous as possible, especially if she had a faint heart or tender emotions. Marge Bailey sent many a girl student weeping from her classroom. Boys fared better.

And yet the students lined up to get into that class. Marge Bailey's name was synonymous with Shakespeare to Stanford students, and she perpetuated among them a great and often lasting interest in the Bard of Avon. Her style was dramatic and an aura of Shakespearean tragedy enveloped her like a living spirit. On occasion she could be persuaded to sing old English ballads, which she did in true folk style. Her singing voice was not mellow or beautiful. The songs were not gay. But her deep, unembellished tones, accompanied by no musical instrument, lent authenticity to the tragic old ballads of early England.

Marge Bailey had charisma. She attracted students to her as moths are attracted to a flame. Some students considered taking her course like playing a game. It was an exhilerating challenge to their courage as well as to their intellects. You wanted to get close enough to her to watch her and hear what she had to say. But you didn't want to get too close. There was a wall between Dr. Bailey and her students. But beyond that wall stood large numbers of Stanford students spanning several generations who braved the tempest to get close enough to sit at a calculatedly safe distance from the feet of the master.

Dr. Edith Mirrielees was, like Dr. Bailey, a professor of English. I believe that she had been at Stanford since around the turn of the century, first as an undergraduate, then as a graduate student, and, finally, as a faculty member. If my memory serves me correctly, she was a founding member of the Cap and Gown Society (Stanford's equivalent to the Mortar Board Society). She was one of the old alumnae who resisted affiliation with the national Mortar Board Society, much to the annoyance of some of my contemporaries who were undergraduate members of Cap and Gown at that time. Miss Mirrielees became emerita during my years at Stanford but remained an active and beloved member of the academic community until her death two or three years ago. Stanford University Press had published her latest book just prior to her death. The book was about some phase of Stanford history. Stanford and Miss Mirrielees were inextricably bound together by a bond of mutual affection during all the years of her adult life. Hers was a true vocation.

Miss Mirrielees appeared to be a person of uncomplicated personality and simple tastes. She was slight of build and had a friendly and gentle nature. She was extremely quick and intelligent but never overpowering or awe-inspiring. She was not famous for any one course that I knew of. She was sympathetic and lovable and drew students to her by her understanding and affection as much as by the scholarly content of her courses. I don't know what her prestige rating was in her discipline. I do know that among many generations of Stanford students Miss Mirrielees was loved and her courses were popular.

Dr. Hazel Hansen was a professor of classics. She was primarily an archaeologist, and she loved to spend her summers digging in Greece. She had a special interest in Cretan art and folk history. The glory of classical Greek civilization was her passion. I did not know Dr. Hansen personally, so my knowledge about her is mostly heresay. Hers was a very familiar face around the campus. Everyone knew who she was even though her courses were not as popular as those taught by the other two women. Possibly this was because the classics were not considered very important by my generation of Stanford students—we were the Second World War generation and were much influenced by what was going on in the world at the moment. Dr. Hansen was reputed to be just as good a teacher as the other two women. These students of my acquaintance who did take her courses were devoted to her and some became classics scholars because of her influence on them. She had a rather small but dedicated following. My husband took a course from her and thought very highly of her. It is my judgment that her knowledge of and devotion to her field attracted students to her rather than pull of a charismatic personality, which I do not believe she possessed. She was a thoroughgoing professional in her field and commanded respect by the quality of her scholarship.

These women were all of an older generation. Dr. Mirrielees, the oldest, was probably close to twenty years the senior of Dr. Hansen, the youngest of the three. But even Dr. Hansen received her doctorate no later than the twenties. Marge Bailey and Hazel Hansen both had mannish, blunt personalities. They practiced no feminine charms. Even Edith Mirrielees' gentle nature could not be associated with femininity as we know it today. Each of these three women possessed a special kind of individuality and personal integrity which marked them as unusual people and attracted anew each succeeding generation of students. Once they had served out their years and become emeritae, no one replaced them. It may be significant, in considering the academic woman, that no new women professors of their caliber have appeared at Stanford in recent years. Is it because their generation allowed them as women a measure of personal growth that has not been possible to attain in recent years? Was there a militancy about women's rights during their formative years that had a lasting influence on their adult personalities? Or were these women merely unusual mutants who occur rarely but consistently over the years? If the latter is true, how did three of them happen to be in one place at the same time? And why haven't new women of this type appeared to succeed them?

Teachers as Models

The research and the cases presented above use criteria which minimize the model-serving function of the teacher's role as sketched in Chapter 8. The question might legitimately be raised, however, whether women can serve as models for young men at all. Is it that no matter how good they are, they are incapable of performing successfully in the model-aspect of their role? Could it even be argued that they are dysfunctional to men students as models? That the better they are, for example, as cultural and esthetic models, as serious scholars, as sophisticated professionals, as responsible academicians, and as ethical and moral arbiters, the more dysfunctional their contribution would be? That their very success would tend to associate cultural values (in the narrower use of that term) with women and hence something effeminate, to be rejected by men? [13] At least this line of reasoning has, in fact, been urged against the preponderant influence of women at lower levels of instruction and also even against coeducation.[14]

It is difficult to evaluate in any systematic way the success of academic women as models, but there is case or anecdotal evidence. The biographies and memorial addresses devoted to great teachers are usually filled with tributes to them by students documenting the very real impact they have had as models on both young men and women.

Usually, to be sure, women are thus memorialized by women students, but the following incident involving a male student refers to an academic woman who, apparently, was successful as a model.

> One day the students on our campus were rioting because they had been refused a holiday before a football game. They were going from classroom to classroom chanting loudly and inviting all the students to walk out on their teachers. The men teachers in the college capitulated; they dismissed their classes. But not Miss Blank. She told us this was a matter of principle with her. She didn't like to be pushed around. She feared mobs; she thought they were wrong. "Come on!" the mob cried. "She can't do anything to you if you leave," it shouted to us, and "You're not teaching them anything!" it shouted to her. I guess she thought she was. For fifty minutes she stood there, facing them down. For a while it was almost nip and tuck who was going to win out. There was a kind of restlessness and shuffling for a while. It would have been easy just to leave. The mob was right. There wasn't anything she could do to us if we left. But somehow or other the sight of that little old gray-haired, dowdy woman, unintimidated, standing up to a howling mob, got through to us. We settled down to complete silence. We couldn't let her down. And we couldn't be less brave than she was. Only one student out of about 50 in the class left and you could see that the rest disapproved of him. She won. The mob finally gave up. I sometimes wonder how I would have acted in her place. I wonder if I would have had the guts to do what she did. I hope I would.

The Man-of-Knowledge Role

Although the major contribution of academic women has been as teachers, there have been many who have also contributed in the man-of-knowledge role, more successfully in some aspects than in others. Since in our day the criterion of success in the man-of-knowledge role is usually in terms of publications—"it is neither an overgeneralization nor an oversimplification to state that in the faculties of major universities in the United States today, the evaluation of performance is based almost exclusively on publication of scholarly books or articles in professional journals"— [15] evaluation of the performance of academic women in this aspect of the man-of-knowledge role is postponed to Chapter 10, where productivity is discussed in detail.

Caplow and McGee report that the evaluation of professors as men-of-knowledge is more difficult in some areas than in others, most difficult in the "feminine" subjects like English and least so in the "masculine" subjects like physics. They found the difficulty of evaluation in the social sciences to lie between the complexity of the humanities and the relative simplicity of the physical sciences. Whether any specific categorization or classification of academic men in terms of content of their contribution, method, or political stance was considered good or bad, they found, depended, of course, on the evaluator. In any event, they concluded, it was based on "performance and is as equitable as conflicts of viewpoint permit." [16]

With respect to the criteria used, whatever their nature, according to Caplow and McGee, "women scholars are not taken seriously and cannot look forward to a normal professional career." [17] When they are hired, they are hired as teachers. It is not that they have low prestige, but that "they are outside the prestige system entirely and for this reason are of no use to a department in future recruitment." [18] The presence of a woman in a department will not serve as a lure to attract either good students or outstanding personnel.

Before flunking women so unequivocally in the professorial role, however, an examination of their credentials as scholars and scientists is in order, a task to which Chapter 10 is devoted. At this point, though, a brief statement with respect to academic women as graduate student mentors is in order.

Graduate Student Mentor

In addition to organizing and interpreting a field of knowledge, the professor or man-of-knowledge is called upon to induct graduate students into the profession. Much of the socialization of the graduate student is a result of his association with professors. He learns how to be a man-of-knowledge himself by living and working with men performing this role, taking over their definition of professional roles, and modeling his perspective on theirs.

Of special significance is the relationship between the graduate student and his mentor. It may take any one of several forms: great man-disciple, master-apprentice, teacher-pupil, employer-employee, or coach-trainee, among others. The relationship, whatever form it may take, is especially sensitive because so much of the graduate student's future career depends on it. Because he has not yet been tested, the graduate student is not sure of himself; he is in a peculiarly difficult stage of his professional career, a fact which magnifies the ordinary human relations problems that arise in any situation where people interact.

The position of the graduate student is one of great tension. Unless a member of the graduate faculty is willing to take him on, his chances for survival in the grueling ordeal are poor. Unless he is promising, the chances that he will be taken on are not good either, for on the side of the professor there is a desire to invest his time and energy only in the best students; the others take time he would rather use on his own work. If the student is promising, several faculty members may want him, and he may, as a result, be caught in a cross fire. Sniping aimed at his mentor may be deflected toward him. He may become the Albania of one professor or the Yugoslavia of another.

The association of the graduate student with his mentor may make all the difference between success or the lack of it in his subsequent career. If a top man takes him under his wing, doors will open for him and he will be in the club. If no one takes him on, or if a lesser faculty member takes him on, he may never arrive professionally. He will not be recommended for the best jobs; he will not be in.

The graduate professor, on his side, also has a stake in the graduate student. Good students carry on his work. At least they will cite him in their own. The time may come, to be sure, when the cubs turn on the old bear. They become his competitors rather than his disciples, and in time they may even attack him. But for a while, a graduate professor and his brood may constitute the in-group of a specialty and dominate it professionally.

Between the good students and their mentors there often arises a warm relationship that may last for years; neither is altogether unaware of the assets of such a relationship. But the subtleties are such that sensitive people may find them difficult, however pleasant.[19]

A careful search of the literature has uncovered no systematic study of the performance of women in the training of graduate students. Scrutiny of the catalogs of academic institutions shows that women have been most active, as noted earlier, in certain fields at both the lower undergraduate level and at the professional school level, where the transmission of knowledge and the imparting of technical skills constitute a straightforward instructional job. The Ph.D. degree is different, since it is still a research-based degree. The program which leads to it is less structured, course by course, than a professional degree. The candidate is not part of a cohort, progressing simultaneously along a given course with given hurdles. He is more on his own, more dependent on his own initiative, and more dependent on his relationships with his mentor.

Cora Dubois has asked if there is not some distinctively feminine contribution which women can make to academia.[20] The answer is that it is precisely the feminine contribution which many of the great universities reject.[21] One function of the professor or man-of-knowledge—and presumably some of the candidates for the doctorate are being groomed for this role—is to serve as a fighter-for-truth, and much of his training is, directly or indirectly, designed for this end. Even the terminology—"defense of the thesis"—bears the stamp of this design. The doctoral candidate has to learn how to be a fighter, has to be toughened for the grueling battles ahead of him. The oral examination becomes a kind of hazing in which the candidate is judged on how well he can defend, not his thesis, but himself.

There is not only an absence of a nurturing aspect in the format of the great graduate universities, but a positive rejection of such an attitude, a tough-minded approach to learning which they prize. A latent function of discrimination against women is, in fact, to keep learning tough.

In the absence of systematic studies of women in the role of graduate student mentor, dependence on individual cases becomes necessary. The following almost random cases, from biographies in two instances and pieced together from several interviews in the others, are offered only for what they may be worth. In one of them, an academic woman raises the interesting question of whether her great concern for students—"academic momism"—was actually subversive of the academic enterprise.

Florence Sabin had a professorial conception of her role. When a student once asked her to speak more slowly so that he could take better notes, she appeared astonished and replied, "You are not supposed to take notes on my lectures. The facts are all in the textbooks." [22] She had the reputation of being a hard taskmaster, brutally frank, but she was almost compulsively eager to help her students. One of them noted: "One of my vivid memories is of her sitting beside me as I looked through a microscope at a histological preparation. She cared so much about my seeing the important points on the slide that she all but lent me eyes for the occasion." [23] Many of her students came back to work with her later in their careers.

Ruth Benedict illustrated a kind of exalted momism. For years she had been a second self to Franz Boas "in his sense of responsibility to ethnology, its students, its problems, its methods. He could ask her to give the opening lectures or to go over a field problem with a student. . . . He could talk over with her the problems which students' behavior presented." [24] Soon almost the entire work of running the department fell on her shoulders, including finding jobs for students and money for their research, as well as putting their manuscripts into shape. Some serious male students felt uncomfortable working under a woman with so much power over them.[25] Still "without her help, her students would have been completely lost." [26] Her concern for her students became legendary:

> By the spring of 1948 . . . more graduate students had to be provided for. . . . Money . . . released a great burst of creative group effort, but it had not essentially changed the style of work which had developed under Boas, in which each person gave as much as he could and was paid as much money as there happened to be—or nothing if there was none—and each participant was treated fully as a human being, his special skills and defects, his culturally and occupationally defined strengths and weaknesses, his blind spots, his babies, his love affairs, and his psychoanalysis, all taken into account. When people were

out of temper, they would say, "Ruth can't tell the difference between research and therapy." In an age when sympathy and willingness to listen and, if necessary, to agonize with the one who speaks have become highly professionalized, and when most people consider that the proper answers to most problems involve visits to a psychiatrist, Ruth Benedict held fast to the position she had taken long ago—that self-realization through congenial work is vitally necessary and that the teacher has an obligation to help the student find himself.[27]

Despite this momism, or perhaps even because of it, Ruth Benedict turned out a top-grade product, and with her as with Florence Sabin, a professional could garner prestige by saying "I did graduate work with Ruth Benedict."

The remaining cases are presented in, so to speak, collage form. Since they are in no sense a random sample and since there are no controls in the form of male mentors to compare the performance of these women with, they may only illustrate the hazards of doctoral study, not the hazards encountered by students of academic women. Whatever their value, here they are:

I sometimes toy with the idea that perhaps women are not only not valuable but actually subversive elements in modern academia. I sometimes ask myself: do the values they represent as women [read: their expressive-emotional roles] interfere with the achievement of the [instrumental] goals set for university students?

John Brown was an attractive young man, the kind who is instantly on the inside, ingratiating, who makes the right contacts. He is now dean at a small college. He did his master's degree with us and I supervised his thesis. It was a very creditable little study. He was duly grateful for my help. He brought me candy, told me I was more than only a teacher. Alarmed, the head of the department assigned him to another adviser for his future work. He left our university and the last time I saw him was when he came back for help with his doctoral dissertation, which he was writing for a degree at another university.... [She then asks: "Was this a case of your academic momism? Had my supervision weakened instead of strengthening him?"]

[At the other extreme was the case of Tom Smith, told by another academic woman:] Smith worked out a design for his dissertation and then went off to teach at a college in the South. He returned at the end of the year with a suitcase full of data.

He laid it at my feet with a flourish. I looked at his material and said, fine, now write your dissertation. He looked hurt. He thought this load of data *was* a dissertation. There began then one of the strangest academic tussles I have ever heard of. It got to the point where communication had to be through an intermediary, first his wife and then the chairman of the department. He could not humiliate himself to the extent of taking supervision from a woman. I could not sign his dissertation. [This woman asks: "Was this a case of academic bitchiness, as subversive in its way as your momism?"]

During a transition period in our department, Paul Green had been kicked around from one adviser to another. He had problems that this kind of treatment didn't help. When three people had finally had their fill of him he was turned over to me to salvage. But by this time the damage had been done. I worked with him intensively and we had a next-to-the-last draft of a thesis ready when he broke down. I withdrew all pressure from him, of course. With everything done except the final polishing-up of details, he dropped out of school. No one knows where he is or what has become of him. [Question: "Would a bit more momism earlier in his career have salvaged him? Or, conversely, is the question, should he have been salvaged?"]

Henry White, intimidated by the confusion in our department, was, in spite of great natural ability, having a rough time of it. A long-conquered tic was returning. He flunked his languages twice. He asked if he could have me for his adviser and his request was granted. He was the ulcer-type and I think that without emotional support, brilliant as he was, he might not have made it. ["If this is what you call momism, I think it was worthwhile; he is now doing a fine job at a state university."]

No one wanted to be Mary Jones' adviser. A woman, after all. No disciple-harvest here. Of course she was turned over to me. She was conscientious, hard-working, a durable woman. She wrote an excellent dissertation and is among our more successful doctors. ["No momism here; none needed."]

One informant, not herself a graduate student adviser, upon being told of the above cases asked: "Shouldn't those who need the momistic approach have been weeded out of the profession? Should people with such dependency needs be allowed to enter the academic profession? Is it good for them? Is it good for the profession?" Good questions.

One case illustrates the fact that momism is not necessarily identical with low standards:

> A colleague of a woman in our physics department told me that it was generally felt by the men in the department that Dr. X. was a little too motherly, too sympathetic with the students. They sometimes expressed concern for departmental standards. A week later he stated, somewhat sheepishly, that she was the only member of the department who had refused to pass a student for the master's degree that all the others felt too sorry for to fail. Concern [momism] in her case did not mean low standards; it did not mean susceptibility to pressure; it just meant more genuine concern.

The last case illustrates not momism in the protective form described above but in the form of protecting a student from cross fire among other faculty members:

> The dissertation of one graduate student in our department had been rejected by his committee in part because the student's adviser—brilliant, erratic, undisciplined—was not in the good graces of his colleagues. (He was without a doctorate, still by far the most popular member of the staff with graduate students.) They were plodding technicians, excellent on form, unimaginative on content. The student was turned over to me. I knew my job was primarily to salvage what was original, if possible, and at the same time placate the more pedestrian ones. (I am one myself.) The result was a fiasco in my opinion —neither fish nor fowl nor good red herring—but it passed muster.

Until more systematic research becomes available, including data with male controls, the success of the professorial role performance of the academic woman cannot be adequately evaluated.

CHAPTER 10 ❀ SCHOLARS
AND SCIENTISTS: PRODUCTIVITY

Intellectual Ability, Productivity, Creativity

Three phenomena must be distinguished in the discussion of the performance of academic women in the role of scholar and scientist. One is intellectual ability as measured by tests; another is productivity, measured by volume of published work; and the third is something which for the present will be subsumed under the currently fashionable rubric "creativity," measured by originality or, in the case of science, priority. There is no necessary or intrinsic relationship among the three.

With respect to intellectual ability as measured by tests, data presented in Chapter 5 showed that women both as undergraduates and as Ph.D.'s were superior to men on the average. Whether or not intellectual ability, so measured, is related to productivity, or creativity, it cannot be invoked to explain differences between academic men and women. Whether or not intellectual ability, so measured, is necessary for productivity, academic women have it at least to the same degree as do academic men. This fact does not make the problem of explaining relative productivity any easier; indeed, it makes the problem more difficult. Sheer intellectual ability as measured by tests has to be rejected. Factors not reached by these tests are involved.

As research digs deeper into the nature of those who make the basic contributions to our culture, there is less talk of "genius" and even of "talent" and more of "top-level personnel." For, as Lindsey Harmon—whose whole career is devoted to studying them—points out, most of the work of scientists today is devoted to the pedestrian task of filling in.

Creative . . . activities or achievements are relatively rare, and persons who characteristically operate in these ways are also

146

rare. A few creative people can spark the work of many lesser men. Most of the work of most scientists is likely to be somewhat more mundane. The careful teasing out of the fine structure of fact along lines which some earlier creative act has suggested; the testing of hypotheses derived from an accepted theoretical framework; the accumulation of data which, most of the time, will reveal no important divergencies from the customary way of thinking about our world—this is the workaday world of most of the research people.[1]

These are the productive people; they may or may not be "creative" also.

Measures of Productivity

Most of the research on academic personnel deals with productivity rather than with the more difficult phenomenon called "creativity." In the absence of adequate measures of even this relatively uncomplicated variable, simple counts of publications are usually relied upon. Thus Berelson, for example, used a count but distinguished single from joint authorship. The Budner-Meyer study, recognizing the difficulties of fine gradations, distinguished only those above and those below average, the average itself being based on a simple count. The Radcliffe study used a combination of books and articles.

The defects in this simple count as a measure of productivity are obvious. Quite aside from quality of contribution, should the same weight within any given subject-matter area be given to a factual as to a theoretical article, assuming the level to be high in both cases? Does an article on technique have the same value as a measure of productivity as an article reporting substantive findings? Should length be considered?

Comparisons across disciplines add new complications. Different disciplines have different rates of productivity, as measured even by simple counts; the so-called "data" subjects have a higher productivity rate than the so-called "word" subjects, according to Berelson's findings.[2] It is not, therefore, legitimate to compare the productivity of historians, say, with that of chemists since historians have a low rate and chemists a high one. Biologists, further, have an extremely complex pattern of publication. Their bibliographies distinguish contributions to the "open literature," notes, abstracts, technical reports, progress reports, reports to such special publics as governmental commissions and legislative committees, in addition, of course, to books, chapters in books, and the like.[3]

These are among the more salient problems that are simply swept under the rug in measures of scholarly and scientific productivity. It is assumed, however, that every published item must meet at least the minimum standards imposed by editors who, in turn, must have the confidence of their colleagues. Beyond that there are few clear-cut standards to serve as guides in evaluation. It is with full recognition of these defects of the measures used that the following studies are here reported.

Reported Productivity of Academic Women

Budner and Meyer studied the productivity record of 264 women respondents who taught the social sciences; they constituted 11 percent of the total sample of 2,351 social scientists studied by Lazarsfeld and Thielens for their report on the academic mind. The index used was a "summary count of the teacher's publications." [4] They reported that, holding age and type of school constant, the women were less productive than the men (Table 10/1 and Table 10/2). In this sample, however, only 52 percent of the women, as compared with 72 percent of the men, had doctorates, suggesting that a number of them may have been in fringe benefit status.

A later study of women sociologists corroborated the lower productivity of women. In this study the measure was number of articles in the two major professional journals, the *American Journal of Sociology* and the *American Sociological Review*. Between 1949 and 1958, women constituted between 8 and 19 percent of all persons receiving doctoral degrees in sociology, but they contributed only between 5 and 13 percent of the articles in the *American Journal of Sociology* and between 2 and 10 percent of those in the *American Sociological Review*.[5]

The Radcliffe study—42.4 percent of whose subjects were academic women—had the advantage of being limited to those with doctorates; it was therefore unlikely to contain a large number of those in the status of fringe benefit. It did not, however, like the Budner-Meyer study, hold subject matter constant. Since women, as noted in earlier chapters tend to be in the "word" rather than in the "data" fields, overall comparisons between the sexes become blurred. As in the Berelson study, the Radcliffe report found that scientists were more productive than nonscientists (Table 10/3).[6]

The Radcliffe study compared Radcliffe Ph.D.'s in several institutions with the women on the faculty of one women's college which places great emphasis on publication. Then, within the faculty of this one college, it compared the productivity of men and women. The first comparison thus "measured" the influence of institutional environment and encouragement on productivity; the second comparison held this factor constant and "measured" the influence of sex.

In order to have some basis of comparison of this general publication record of Radcliffe degree-holders, the reports of all those who hold the position of professor or associate professor in any college or university were separated out. Persons of such academic status are sufficiently mature in their professions to afford an indication of published accomplishments. These accomplishments can then be compared with those of a control group. The group chosen consisted of the professors and associate professors of a large women's college in the East. Even on this basis, unfortunately, the comparison is not exact. The control group included both men and women; not all the professors compared held a Ph.D. degree and some of them taught subjects that were not purely academic; the periods during which publication took place were not identical; and the college maintains two series of publications which provide convenient media for the publication of monographic material of its own faculty. But the comparison, though limited, is still of interest.

It is of interest in two respects. First, the women faculty members at this eastern college, both professors and associate professors, publish more than the Radcliffe Ph.D.'s of like rank in various institutions. Although the absolute numbers are too small to compute percentages, in each rank the college professors who have engaged in extensive publication outdistance the Radcliffe graduates by about two to one. [This point indicates the influence of institutional environment.] And second, the men of coordinate rank run far ahead of the women in the same institution: 69 percent of the men professors had published extensively, and 56 percent of the women. Among the associate professors, the percentage of men was 73, of women, 27. [This point indicates the influence of sex.] [7]

In the absence of a subject-matter breakdown, and in the presence of such "contaminated" variables, the above findings are certainly not unequivocal. They are, nevertheless, summarized in Table 10/3.

Corroborating the results of these studies is a more recent one based on a sample of 262 sociologists who received the doctorate during the years 1945–49 inclusive, 37 of whom were women. The women were over-represented in the low-productivity brackets and under-represented in the high. Only two had published more than five articles at the time the study was made, as compared with 55 of the 225 men. As in other studies, it was found that the women were not proportionately represented in the major universities. Institutional affiliation was not, however, controlled in the analysis of productivity.[8]

Reasons Given for Low Productivity

Budner and Meyer interpret the inferior productivity of their sample as related to a "psychological withdrawal" or "lack of involvement." There is evidence for this conclusion, not only among those in fringe benefit status but also among professionals. Thus, "being less firmly identified with the occupational role of the college teacher, the women included in the Minnesota study may have felt less of the ego involvement on which a long-range commitment to this field may depend." [9]

Budner and Meyer explain the withdrawal or lack of involvement itself as a product of discrimination, which they document, in the form of inferior rewards to serve as incentives to produce:

> For every age and productivity group, the women professors are much less likely than the men to have received large salary increases. . . . This is true for all types of schools. . . . On each age and productivity level women are much less likely than men to have reached one of the higher ranks. Again . . . this is true for each type of school, including women's colleges.[10]

As a result of such discrimination, they conclude, academic women have less incentive to be productive and less stimulation to become professionally involved.

A wide variety of explanatory variables is offered by the Radcliffe report to account for the relatively inferior record of the subjects, all related in a circular manner. Inadequate training is not, of course, among them, for these women were trained at Harvard. But both "environmental," that is cultural and social, and "psychological" or motivational factors are invoked. Among the environmental factors are tradition, colleague and administrative attitudes, and inducements:

> The relatively low productivity of Radcliffe Ph.D.'s can hardly be ascribed to their training as such. It is more likely to result from the environment in which they find themselves, the tradition of scholarship, the amount of time and facilities available for research and writing, the attitude of their colleagues and the college administration, and the material inducements to publish. . . . In many smaller colleges atmosphere and opportunity are much less conducive to research and publication. Relatively few Radcliffe women hold professorial status in large institutions where scholarly pursuits are inspired by faculty and demanded by competition.[11]

Among the explanations given by the Radcliffe subjects themselves were these: more domestic responsibilities; more attention required for appearance; less motivation, as pointed out by Budner and Meyer, because of lesser rewards for women than for men, and also less need to earn money to support a family to act as incentive; greater difficulty now than formerly in getting material published because channels have not increased as rapidly as potential authors; less stamina; and more committee work, advising, club sponsorship, and teaching.[12]

It is quite possible, however, that what Budner and Meyer call withdrawal or lack of involvement is merely the reflection of the fact that women are just not as interested in research as an activity as men are. In a study of 33,982 seniors graduating from 135 colleges in June 1961, it was found that students going into the "feminine" areas, notably languages, English, fine arts, other humanities, sociology, and biology were not interested in research.[13] Among 440 men and 440 women psychologists who received their Ph.D. degrees between 1921 and 1940, almost twice as many men as women (19.0 percent and 10.6 percent respectively) reported professional work—research or teaching—as a major source of satisfaction. Work contributed more than any other interest to the life satisfactions of more men (42.1 percent) than women (26.9 percent). Work contributed less than other satisfactions in the case of 28.9 percent of the women but only 1.6 percent of the men.[14] Women, in brief, were less likely than men to put all their emotional eggs in one basket. The women, therefore, spent less time on the average in professional reading and less in research and writing, than did the men; these relations held for both full-time psychologists and less than full-time psychologists.[15] These women had other more satisfying uses for their time.[16]

The Budner-Meyer study controlled for discipline and type of school, but not for training. The Radcliffe study controlled for training, type of school, but not for discipline, nor, with any rigor, for sex. The Fava study did not control for institutional position. The Babchuck-Bates study did not control for institution either. The Matched Scientists study was designed to control as many as possible of the variables known to be related to productivity, namely, subject matter, training, academic position, and length of postdoctoral career.

The Matched Scientists Study

The subjects for this study were 222 women scientists and 224 men scientists, approximately matched [17] with respect to the four relevant variables listed above, who were in academic positions ten to fifteen years after securing the doctorate, and 6 women and 4 men in laboratory positions.

Because of the complexity of publication forms in this science—zoology—the items in the lists of publications of these subjects were classified into several categories: (1) books and articles; (2) "notes" and short articles (less than 5 pages); (3) abstracts (not published elsewhere as articles or papers); (4) short, usually laboratory, reports; (5) longer reports (including agriculture experimental station bulletins and longer laboratory reports); (6) reports to special publics (wildlife commissions, legislators at hearings, the profession as a public, etc.); and (7) teaching aids (films, laboratory manuals, charts, demonstration materials, translations, and bibliographies). As Table 10/4 makes clear, although there were no sex differences in the number contributing to the first three categories—46 men-items versus 42 women-items—there were sizeable differences between the men and the women with respect to the remaining categories—32 men-items versus only 12 women-items.

For these latter categories, in fact, there appeared to be a kind of sexual "division of labor" with respect to the several categories of publications. Apparently anything that had to do with the "foreign relations" of the discipline, that is, with relations with the public and with students (categories 6 and 7), fell to the men, although in this connection it should be noted that by far the most successful scientist addressing the public recently (category 7) has been a woman, Rachel Carson.

Accounting for "domestic relations," that is, the work of the laboratory in the form of progress reports (category 4), came in this set of scientists mainly from two women in laboratory positions. The production of long technical reports (category 5), however, was almost exclusively the domain of the men scientists. It should be noted again that the one woman scientist who did produce in this category was far more productive (23 items) than the eight men who did (24 items) but that she was the only woman producing in this category.

With respect to category 3, women tended to produce more than men; the reverse, in general, was true with respect to category 2. Women were more likely than the men to publish their work in the form of abstracts. "Notes," which tend to characterize the work of naturalists—often descriptions of rare or unusual specimens or of new and interesting examples of wildlife behavior—were, by and large, commoner in this set of scientists among men than among women (Table 10/5).

These differences in forms of publication reflect the fact that even among scientists in one specialty widely different careers are pursued, men and women tending to gravitate toward careers with different characteristic patterns of publication. Not ability but interest would seem to be involved since the women who are in "masculine" writing areas are apparently as successful as men.

The first category—articles, chapters in books, papers—was, for our purposes, the most important, for this is the form in which contributions to science—in contrast to contributions which happen also to be scientific—are most likely to be cast. Comparisons based on these items are therefore of relatively greater importance than those based on the other categories. They are shown in Table 10/5.

Although ordinary tests did not justify a clear-cut conclusion that the differences in productivity between men and women scientists were statistically significant,[18] several considerations—the existence of any differences at all under the rigorously controlled conditions of the study, the consistency of the differences for most forms of publication in favor of the men, and the greater variety of publication forms characteristic of the men as noted above, taken together with the results of former studies—forbid the unequivocal conclusion that they were not actually, as contrasted with statistically, significant. All that can be said is that if enough variables are controlled, sex differences in productivity are reduced almost to insignificance.

What can, however, be said without equivocation, is that academic position, if not sex, is inextricably related to productivity. Scientists in universities, whatever their sex, are more productive than those in colleges, whatever their sex. Women in universities, for example, are more productive than men in colleges. In brief, academic position is a far better "predictor" of productivity than sex.

Even if position should prove to be a better predictor of productivity than sex, however, this is not the end of the story. The question then arises as to why some people—men and women alike—tend to gravitate to the positions which are less productive. Is it because, as Budner and Meyer so contemptuously ask with respect to women, they *like* these positions? The answer may well be a positive Yes. There is some evidence that both men and women who teach in the less productive institutions do, in fact, like their positions. This came out in comment after comment among the Matched Scientists. Many of those in colleges were, for all intents and purposes, in a different profession; scientific productivity for them took the form of teaching. That was what they preferred to do.[19]

In evaluating the effect of sex on the relative productivity of academic men and women, it is suggested here—soberly, without facetious intent—that some adjustment factor should be applied to take account of time—not to mention thought, emotion, and drive—invested in the bearing and rearing of children. How many more articles would a woman have produced if she had not produced a child instead? The idea is not that children and articles can or should be equated but only that if our aim is to determine as far as possible the influence on productivity of sex per se, aside from all the other factors inherently and even inevitably associated with it, then the deflection of time and interest resulting from maternity is a relevant variable. The 28 women in the Matched Scientists study had produced 14 children at the time of the study, and one had had to stop work in order to satisfy the requirements of an adoption agency. If, instead, these women had devoted the time to producing articles, would their total output have equaled or surpassed that of the men? Can each child be rated as the equivalent—in time, at least—to one, two, or three articles? The problem is easier with respect to teaching. If an academic woman takes a term off to have a baby and teaches part time until the child is of school age, it is simple to calculate the number of student-hours she has missed. Is anything analogous in order with respect to scientific productivity?

The effect of marriage and children on career is discussed at greater length in Chapter 15. It may be noted here that children do, indeed, affect the careers of women [20] and that any assessment of the effect of sex on productivity must certainly take this fact into account.

Incentive and Drive: Productivity Types

Some of the Matched Scientists data suggest that there are at least two types of scientists with respect to productivity of articles and chapters. Figure 10/1 shows the distribution for the entire number of subjects. Examination of the actual arrays suggests that the gap in the 9–13 interval was not a chance fluctuation but rather a reflection of a genuine characteristic of the distribution. The overall distribution appeared to consist of two quite separate subdistributions. Figure 10/2 illustrates the nature of the two separate distributions if the cases in the 4–8 interval are divided into two parts and assigned to the two separate distributions. The result is that one of the distributions is perfectly symmetrical and, without the necessity of testing, obviously statistically different from the other.[21] The overall data appear to include two types of scientists with respect to productivity.[22] One type makes teaching rather than research its major emphasis; the other, in varying degrees, gives more emphasis to research.

A study of the productivity of physiologists also suggests the possibility of two types with respect to productivity. The distribution of papers written in the last three years was found in this study to be: none, 8 percent; 1–2, 18 percent; 3–4, 23 percent; 5–6, 17 percent; 7–8, 8 percent; 9–10, 9 percent; 11 or more, 15 percent.[23]

Even so, these fragmentary data by themselves would certainly be inadequate to demonstrate productivity types. Lawrence Kubie has also explored this possibility, however, basing his thinking on psychoanalytic insights. He explains differences in productivity among scientists in terms of unresolved neurotic anxieties. Studying the problems of the scientific career, he found that unconscious factors often impelled some scientists to select problems that would take years to solve; they did not want to expose themselves. Some scientists, on the other hand, were impelled to publish frequently and selected their problems to facilitate quick publication.

[Unresolved neurotic anxieties] may impel one over-anxious young investigator to choose a problem that will take a lifetime or, alternatively, may drive another into easy, get-rich-quick tasks, which yield a yearly paper, a yearly acclaim, the yearly promotion. The former tendency to postpone the day of reckoning indefinitely occurs in the young scientist who deals with his anxieties by pretending that they do not exist. The latter is found in the man who finds it impossible to endure suspense and uncertainty for more than a few months. Neurotic anxiety can take either form; and young scientists frequently walk a tightrope between these two alternatives, that is, between the annual piecework type of productivity and the long-drawn-out tasks which postpone indefinitely any ultimate testing of theories against experimental data and observations of nature.[24]

High-producers, it appears, organize their lives about their work; productivity is, in fact, a way of life for them. They are "driven" by "curiosity," "ambition," "need for achievement," "neurotic anxiety," or whatever we wish to call it.

Because women have so many more outs for failure, because they are less sex-driven,[25] because they are less involved,[26] because they have less at stake,[27] and because of a dozen other sex-linked factors, it is quite possible that they are less likely to be in the driven, high-producing category.[28]

Two documents are presented here which illustrate motivation in two cases. The first illustrates the delaying-tactic productivity type, both illustrate the integration-through-work type.

I really dread completing a project. While I am working on

one, it organizes my life. I know just what I have to do. When I am not engaged on a project I feel at loose ends. So I write because I have to, to keep myself integrated. But I don't like to finish. I have been working on my current book for eight years.

All I ever knew was that the library was my natural habitat. I love libraries and feel completely myself only when I am in one. I turned down a job in the midwest so I could continue to come to the Library of Congress weekends and holidays. When I have a desk in the stacks it is like a religious retreat for me. Return to the womb, one critical friend of mine calls it. Be that as it may, I am only a visitor in the outside world, not really part of it. I do my work, as required, conscientiously. But I mind time away from my work in the library. I also have the historian's dread of finally stopping the accumulation of notes and putting them together. . . . I should have entered a contemplative religious order.

The Communication System

The original hypothesis of the Matched Scientists study had two parts: (1) scientific productivity is a function of position in the communication system, those with easy access to channels of scientific communication having greater productivity; and (2) women are less likely to be in favored positions in this system because of the so-called "stag effect," which prevents them from participating freely in the system.[29] As it turned out, the first part of the hypothesis could be accepted, but not in any causal sense. Those in universities, men and women, were more productive and had better positions in the communication system, both no doubt as a result of a common career-determining factor.

The second part of the hypothesis revealed only limited clews. Of special interest was the difference in use made by men and women of professional meetings. More men (60 percent) than women (23 percent) reported that the intellectually most productive conversations at meetings of professional societies were those with persons whose work was only recently becoming known. This suggests something about the processes which actually go on at such meetings. Either the men are more alert than the women to the emerging trends in their field and seek out the scientists identified with them, or there are barriers—of the "stag" kind, perhaps as noted by the Radcliffe Ph.D.'s—which restrain the women from seeking them out.

Two sets of scientists showed widely divergent positions in the communication system, the university men and the college women. The university men more than other scientists were likely to have coworkers. They were more likely than other scientists to find the professional activities which took them off campus to be educational; that is, they sometimes or often learned something relevant to their own scientific work. Finally, they were also more likely than other scientists to find professional society meetings useful in providing new contacts which they could follow up through correspondence or in other ways.

At the other extreme were the college women, by far the least favored of the scientists so far as position in the communication system was concerned. Fewer of them than of other scientists had students who ever called to their attention something they might otherwise have missed. They were less likely than other scientists to find meetings of professional societies useful in providing general knowledge of what work was being carried on, where, or by whom. They were less likely than other scientists to be on the regular mailing list for the reprints of researchers. They were less likely than other scientists to be consulted by mail for advice or for information. None of them used correspondence with authors or researchers as a way of having current developments in their field called to their attention; about one-fourth of the other scientists did. None of them had regular mailing lists for their own reprints; about two-thirds of the other scientists did.

Although it was not possible to pinpoint the relationship between productivity and position in the communication system and express it in a single statistical measure, it was true that the scientists who were most productive were also those in the most favored positions to know what was going on in their field, in closest contact with people and laboratories doing the most important work, in closest and most frequent contact with leaders in their field, and most likely therefore to get the unexpected, unanticipated, even accidental information which, as Menzel rightly points out, is so essential in this day and age.[30] The women teaching in colleges were the least favored. These are factors which must undoubtedly be taken into consideration, along with many others, when attempting to explain the relative productivity of different sets of academic persons.

The rather unexpected results of the Matched Scientists study tended to corroborate the original hypothesis that place in the scientific communication system was related to productivity, but they suggested it was academic position (university or college) rather than any "stag effect" which was the decisive factor in determining position in a communication system.

Another study, however, of 673 laboratory bioscientists, 68 of whom were women, indicated that sex could not be ignored. As in so many such studies, not the magnitude but the general consistency of difference was what was interesting. These women were slightly less productive than the men. There was nothing in laboratory policy which appeared to discriminate against them so far as opportunities for informal communication were concerned, but opportunities for informal communication which depended on taking the initiative in making contacts, or which depended on invitation from others, tended to be less available to the women. The women were less aggressive than the men in actively seeking opportunity for such communication except by mail, and they were less often sought for such communication, even by mail. So far as informal communication was concerned, the women were more passive, although when the opportunities were offered to them they took advantage of them about as much as did the men. Not necessarily a "stag effect" but perhaps a certain diffidence resulting from role training may help to explain this finding.[31]

Table 10/1 Productivity of Men and Women Professors by Age Group *

Age Group	Percent who Are Highly Productive	
	Women	Men
Under 40	19% (85)	30% (1,031)
41–50	39% (70)	60% (544)
Over 50	44% (107)	68% (548)

* Stanley Budner and John Meyer, "Women Professors."

Table 10/2 The Age Specific Productivity of Men and Women Teachers in Various Types of Schools *

	Percent at or above Median for Age Group in Productivity †	
	Women	Men
Secular Coeducational Schools of High Quality	53% (30)	79% (954)
Secular Women's Colleges	47% (93)	61% (124)
Teachers Colleges	34% (47)	38% (148)
Secular Coeducational Schools of Low Quality	28% (25)	48% (258)
Catholic Women's Colleges	26% (31)	60% (20)

* Budner & Meyer, "Women Professors."
† The use of the particular index of productivity employed here somewhat inflates the difference between women and men in all but the first type of school. This is true because the correlation between productivity and type of school is greater among older professors than among younger ones. Since in each type of school the women are older than the men, the sex differences in the schools with lower productivity are slightly exaggerated.

Table 10/3 Productivity of Radcliffe Ph.D.'s *

	Two or More Books or 20 or More Articles		One Book or 10-19 Articles		3-9 Articles		1-2 Articles		No Publications		Total	
	No.	%	No.	%	No.	%	No.	%	No.	%	No.	%
A.B. before 1920	20	28	18	25	16	22	7	10	11	15	72	100
A.B. 1920–1934	22	15	27	19	28	19	24	17	43	30	144	100
A.B. 1935–	0	0	5	5	25	25	35	34	36	37	102	100
Total	42	13	50	16	69	22	66	21	91	29	318	100

* Radcliffe College, *Graduate Education for Women, The Radcliffe Ph.D.* (Cambridge: Harvard Univ. Press, 1956), p. 26.

Table 10/4 Men and Women Scientists Who Contributed Items in Specified Bibliographical Categories

Category	Men (28)	Women (28)
Articles, Chapters, Papers	22	20
"Notes" and Short Articles	18	13
Abstracts	6	9
Short Reports	1	2
Long Reports	8	1
Reports to Special Publics	8	2
Teaching Aids	8	2
Miscellaneous	1	0
No Publications	6	6

Table 10/5 Average Number of Items Reported in Specified Publication Categories for Different Sets of Subjects *

Set	Articles, Chapters, Papers	Publication Category "Notes" and Short Articles	Abstracts
Men	14.5 (22)	7.0 (18)	2.5 (6)
Women	9.5 (20)	5.3 (13)	4.5 (9)
University	14.0 (24)	6.0 (17)	3.5 (8)
College	4.5 (10)	3.5 (8)	2.5 (2)
Other	16.5 (8)	13.5 (6)	7.0 (5)
University Men	15.5 (13)	9.0 (9)	3.0 (3)
University Women	11.0 (12)	4.5 (8)	4.0 (5)
College Men	4.0 (5)	3.5 (5)	2.0 (1)
College Women	4.0 (5)	1.5 (3)	3.0 (1)
Other Men	12.0 (4)	13.5 (4)	4.0 (2)
Other Women	17.0 (4)	13.0 (2)	17.0 (3)

* The median was used to describe the data because the nature of the arrays seemed more conformable to nonparametric than to parametric assumptions. See the discussion on technical problems of testing in Appendix C. The general trend of the differences is not altered by the use of the arithmetic mean.

Table 10/6 **Proportion of Productive Laboratory Bioscientists, by Sex** *

Proportion Who Reported They Had:	Men (605)	Women (68)
Given Papers in Last Year	50.7	27
Published Articles	87.3	88
Written Chapters in Books	28.7	23
Written Books	14.5	4
Written Technical Reports	33.8	15

* Biological Sciences Communication Project Study. See Appendix D.

Table 10/7 Median Productivity of Laboratory Bioscientists, by Sex*

	Men †	Women †
Papers Given in Last Year	.56	.64
Articles	16.3	14.7
Chapters in Books	2.3	2.8
Books	.8	3.5
Technical Reports	4.2	5.0

* Source: See Table 10/6.
† Number varies by category; see Table 10/6.

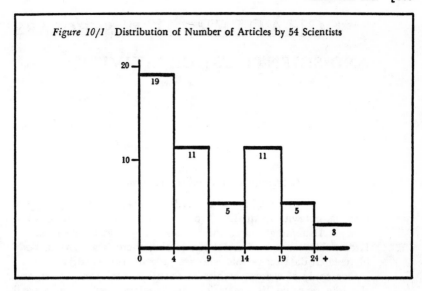

Figure 10/1 Distribution of Number of Articles by 54 Scientists

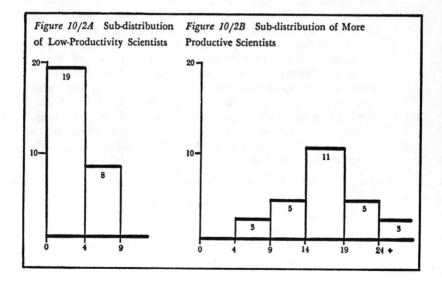

Figure 10/2A Sub-distribution of Low-Productivity Scientists

Figure 10/2B Sub-distribution of More Productive Scientists

CHAPTER 11 ✤ SCHOLARS
AND SCIENTISTS: CREATIVITY

Academic Creativity and Intellectual Ability

The discussion in Chapter 10 dealt only with quantity of production, not with its quality. Productivity, important as it is, is not enough. Increasingly attention is now being paid to the presently fashionable concept of creativity, so that there is a growing body of research data on people who are judged to be creative.

One study of writers, architects, scientists, engineers, artists, and the like reported little relationship between intelligence—beyond 120 IQ—and creativity.[1] There are, however, several areas of creativity, and it may well be that the kind which is characteristic of academic achievement, as contrasted with the kind involved in composing music or writing epics, for example, is more related to intellectual ability per se than nonacademic kinds.[2]

It is true that academic people do sometimes write novels, plays, and poems and that they do paint, make sculptures, and compose music. Increasingly, colleges and universities have artists-in-residence. For the most part, however, the kind of creativity which characterizes academic work is not the same as the kind which characterizes musical composition or mural painting. Turner's interpretation of American history in terms of the frontier is more characteristic of creativity in academia than Katharine Lee Bates' composition of the poem "America the Beautiful." For this kind of creativity, intellectual ability above 120 IQ would seem necessary.[3]

The focus of attention in the present discussion, then, is on academic creativity. The problem here is to determine the qualitative nature of the contribution which academic women have made and, if possible, to interpret it. The problem is not to assess the contribution of women in musical composition or in archi-

164

tecture or in painting, that is, but in the areas of scholarship and science.[4] Since most of the research has been done in the area of science, the concern here is even more restricted, limited to the contribution of academic women in that field.

The criterion of creativity in science is originality or priority, for the development of a science is not a matter of simple accretion. Granted, as Lindsey Harmon has said, that most scientific work is not creative, that is, innovative, still there must be some creative contributors. There must be great leaps or mutations, as well as growth, according to the usual growth curves. This distinction —between the great jumps and the organic growth thereafter—is an important one to make in evaluating the contribution of academic women scientists, for it seems to take different qualities to succeed in the two aspects of scientific development. No one can successfully challenge the ability of women to contribute at the level of filling in, as the discussion of productivity above makes clear. It is as bold innovators, not as patient followers, that their record is inferior to that of men.

Creativity and Productivity

There is no intrinsic relationship between productivity and creativity. In a study of significant contributors to the field of psychology, for example, as determined by an elaborate judging by peers, it was found that some psychologists were very productive, but their contribution was not judged to be significant.[5] In contrast is the case of Lord Rutherford who, it is reported, published an article a month for years, each one a major contribution.

Reported Creativity of Academic Women

The research data available to assess the creativity of academic women are very limited, indeed almost nonexistent. The authors of the Radcliffe study noted, almost casually, that Radcliffe Ph.D.'s tended to select subjects for study that were of restricted rather than of general interest.[6] A study of significant contributors in the field of psychology reported that women were far less than proportionately represented among the significant contributors (Table

11/1), constituting about one-fourth of all psychologists but only about 5 percent of the "significant" contributors.[7] Mabel Newcomer found that whereas women constituted 7 percent of all scientists, they constituted only 3 percent of outstanding scientists.[8] One department chairman, on the basis of many years experience, concluded that "on the whole the quality of term projects and theses written by women is less robust, less imaginative and daring, and makes less of a contribution than that, on the average, produced by their male competitors—although the scholarly production by the women is likely to be more orderly, more precisely directed toward indicated goals, perhaps more thorough, and more dependably produced on schedule." The array of data is not extensive, but it does not take systematic research to note that women are conspicuously underrepresented on the rosters of innovating scientists.

Before proceeding with the analysis, a brief caveat is in order. Attempts to explain the inferior creativity of academic, or, for that matter, any other, women run squarely into the difficulty that too often they deteriorate into an apologia or into an ad hominem attack or into an attempt to assess guilt or to blame someone or other. As in the case of race, it is extraordinarily difficult to seine out, even analytically, the sexual factor per se in explaining creativity. For practical people it may not even seem very important. They are confronted, as President Cleveland is quoted as saying, by facts, not theories. The statistical, not the biological, psychological, or sociological, facts are what concern them. If most women are thus-and-so, it matters little to them why they are. For the scientist, however, the relative absence of scientific creativity in a set of human beings whose intellectual capacity is unquestioned presents a tantalizing challenge. Even if nothing can or should be done about it, as a sheer intellectual puzzle the problem is fascinating. The discussion here is not designed as an apologia or as an assessment of blame. It does not even assume that apologies are needed or blame called for.

Reasons Given for Lower Creativity of Academic Women: Psychological, Cultural, and Social

That there are differences between men and women in verbal facility, hand skills, spatial conceptualization, number ability, mechanical assembly, and in the application of general principles, as well as in interests, is documented by numerous studies, some of which have been reported in earlier chapters. It is even alleged that women differ in "psyche" or "mentality" from men, that "they think differently." [9] With respect to differences backed by research, there may be agreement, although the research is less unequivocal than it appears. In one study of young men and women of college age and boys and girls of high school age, sex differences in "thought-ways" were very difficult to prove. Groups of four, with varying sex composition, were asked to discuss two topics—one dealing with a hypothetical accident and one with the moon-shot—and the discussion was tape-recorded and transcribed. The transcriptions were presented to twenty-six judges who were asked to decide on the basis of the transcriptions alone what the sex of each speaker was. If the judges had been able to see the discussants, they would have been correct 100 percent of the time; if they had judged on a purely chance basis, they would have been correct 50 percent of the time. Actually they were correct 60 percent of the time. This degree of success was slightly above chance and could be accounted for on the basis of such role-related phenomena as frequency of talking, frequency of questions, use of sex-typed words, and the like without having to import the concept of different thought-ways between the sexes. The experimenter notes that the results are not conclusive until the study is repeated for older men and women; while in school, boys and girls are dealt with alike, but after twenty years of differing experience, differences might be expected to occur.[10]

Whether such differences in thought-ways between the sexes are accepted or not, controversy arises when explanations are offered, for some explanations are more acceptable than others. Usually cultural explanations are more acceptable than genetic ones. The wholly unwarranted implication is that if differences are cultural or social in origin they are somehow or other less basic than if they are biological, that if they are cultural or social, they can be more easily modified, if not wholly eliminated.[11] The "ineffable if" is invoked. "If" women had equal opportunities, or treatment, or status, or whatever, "then" there would be no differences in creativity. The logic is impeccable, but the situation is more complicated than the logic suggests. The interrelations between the biological and the social and the cultural are not mechanical, but organic.

The Package Metaphor

A "package" metaphor is here proposed to suggest these inter-relations between natural ability, whatever that may be, and sex. Suppose an identical chemical is packaged under two brand names. The package for Brand A is of a material that keeps out light but not moisture; the material for the Brand B package keeps out moisture but not light. Thus, even standing on the same shelf they tend to be transformed into somewhat different chemicals. Suppose, further, that it so happens that as a result of the changes brought out by packaging industries on the maritime shores find one brand better for their purposes while those in the drier high-lands prefer the other. The brands are therefore used in different ways. In packages that admit and reject different outside influences, in environments that exaggerate these differences, the originally similar chemicals become increasingly different.

Analogously, the brains of men and women are packaged in different containers. The brain packaged in a woman's body has different muscular and glandular equipment at its disposal; it is sensitized to different kinds of stimuli; it is protected from exposure to certain other kinds of stimuli. Even though there were originally no intrinsic differences between it and a brain packaged in a man's body, it inevitably becomes different because of its different packaging, and this quite independent of cultural or social factors. But, of course, in addition, the brains packaged in a woman's body, to pursue the analogy, are also used for different purposes, thus the original divergence is accelerated.

The effect of the "package" is vividly portrayed in the following document based on a chance interview with a male patient during the first stages of his rebellious convalescence in the solarium of a hospital:

> For the first time in my life I think I can begin to understand what it must feel like to be a woman, to be physically weak and slow in a world where men are strong and fast. To have to figure out your capacity before doing anything—can I make it to the sun parlor. To be aware of your feet. To have to wangle favors from more powerful people, like nurses. To be dependent on brisk, competent, though inferior, attendants. To be hemmed in, robbed of autonomy because if you displease people they can just physically overpower you and put you back in your place. This experience has changed my whole

personality. Temporarily, of course, I hope. I was never con-descended to, patronized, before. I have to resist the attitude of the nurses or I become like a child. I become devious. I have to outwit them by strategy, since I don't have either physical strength or hospital rules on my side. The whole situation has even affected my relations with the other two men in the room. We feel and act like conspirators. Even our logic was affected. The nurses behaved according to the logic of hospital rules, which seemed to us to be all in their favor. If a few weeks of being without superior strength and the support of rules can do this to a man, what can years of it do to women? It makes you think.

Implications of the Package Metaphor

In answer to the question regarding the paucity of innovating scientists among women, a twofold reply is suggested here for ex-ploration. First, it is suggested that most women do not, or cannot, want to be innovators.[12] Elaboration of this point involves, in addition to the discussion of the package metaphor, a discussion of the structure of science as an institution, of the role of the innovator in the processes of science-building, and of the kind of person it takes to perform this role. Second, it is suggested that innovation implies a certain kind of relationship with a public of peers and that this relationship is less likely to obtain in the case of women than in the case of men.

The Structure of Science and the Processes of Science-Building

The logical and the historical aspects of science have long been studied, but the sociological aspects have only relatively recently come under scrutiny. When they are noted, it appears that a process is at work in the development of science which is analogous, though, of course, not identical, to what takes place in religion as an institution. In the study of religion, it takes the form of sectarian-ism, so called, a process by which established denominations spin off innovators who, in turn, themselves finally stabilize and insti-tutionalize their position and become denominations, with vested interest of their own in the status quo against which new sectaries or innovators rebel.

In the development of science, we do not speak of sectarians, and rightly so, for the implications of the term do not fit. But the processes in which innovators take part are similar to those in which sectarians do. Znaniecki distinguishes between "discoverers of truth" on one side and "creators of knowledge" on the other; the second are a new phenomenon.

> All new developments in the history of knowledge have been due to those scientists [13] who did more in their social roles than their circles wanted and expected them to do. . . . Now we come to an extremely interesting phenomenon for which there is no precedent and no parallel, except perhaps in modern poetry and art. We find individual scientists who specialize, so to speak, in doing the unexpected. They may be metaphorically termed *explorers*, for they are seeking in the domain of knowledge new ways leading into the unknown. Originally they were for the most part aberrants from socially recognized ways. Some of them, however, have attempted to have this type of activity recognized as a regular social function and to construct a new pattern of the scientist's social role, implying a new conception of knowledge itself. So long as they remained isolated from one another, they were unsuccessful; but with the growing facilities of communication, their number slowly increased. The first initiators found followers in various intellectual centers and eventually there developed a world-wide solidarity of explorers in every scientific field.[14]

But "explorers," though like sectaries they begin as rebels, tend to become conservative, like members of denominations. As knowledge becomes systematized, its professors acquire a vested interest in its stability. They do not welcome new ideas which interfere with their intellectual security.

> It is thus obvious that a discoverer of facts, freely roaming in search of the unexpected, has no place in a milieu of scientists with well-regulated traditional roles. He may be a solitary, independent individual with no interest in professional traditions or else a rebel against established intellectual authority. Neither of these types is actuated merely by curiosity or by the desire for adventure. Curiosity alone does not make men search for facts objectively unknown, not yet observed by other investigators; on the contrary, it is rather stimulated by social communication. . . .

[The discoverer of facts] is mainly desirous to throw off the intellectual yoke of professional science. Often he is an unsuccessful technologist, sage, or scholar who could not or would not conform with traditional requirements. . . . His rebellion, however, is not a mere personal problem of subjective misadaptation. It becomes depersonalized and objectified as a problem of the validity of the very knowledge cultivated in those scientific circles against which he revolts. He tries to undermine this validity by discovering facts hitherto unknown which will conflict with recognized generalizations.[15]

Those who have a stake in keeping things as they are do not take kindly to those who defiantly overturn the apple cart. The literature on the sociology of knowledge documents in great detail the conflict between the innovator and those who have a vested interest in the scientific status quo.[16]

An even more recent analysis of the processes of science-building, based largely on the physical sciences, views these processes not in terms of the sect-denomination model but in terms of the Darwinian natural selection model. There is competition between an established "paradigm" or accepted pattern of thought and a new one which arises when the anomalies resulting from the established paradigm become intolerable to the scientific community.

The process described . . . as the resolution of revolutions is the selection by conflict within the scientific community of the fittest way to practice future science. The net result of a sequence of such revolutionary selections, separated by periods of normal research, is the wonderfully adapted set of instruments we call modern scientific knowledge. Successive stages in that developmental process are marked by an increase in articulation and specialization. And the entire process may have occurred, as we now suppose biological evolution did, without benefit of a set goal, a permanent fixed scientific truth, of which each stage in the development of scientific knowledge is a better exemplar.[17]

The competition among paradigms may be extremely intense; success often results for exponents of the new one merely from outliving exponents of the old one. Resistance to the new may, according to this analysis, serve an important function:

By ensuring that the paradigm will not be too easily surrendered, resistance guarantees that scientists will not be lightly distracted and that the anomalies that lead to paradigm change will penetrate existing knowledge to the core.[18]

As the creating of new knowledge by way of science has become institutionalized, resistance to innovation has become less aggressive, even perhaps less patent, though no less real. It takes the form, for example, of sheer inertia rather than aggressive attack. How much of all this vast amount of new knowledge do I have to assimilate? Is this paradigm going to win so many adherents that I can't afford to be left out? How much of what is new can I ignore? A professional scientist who has to relearn and rethink his discipline several times during his professional life finally gets tired. He waits to see which of the numerous lines of development are going to catch on and prevail before he decides which to invest his time in. Even so, he resists as long as he can.

Competition among Innovators

The creator of knowledge, or the new paradigm, then, is up against a status quo, against a structure of vested interests, against inertia. What incentive is there to buck it? The personality motives will be discussed presently; here interest attaches to the institutional reward system, for if an innovator is successful in gaining acceptance of his contribution there are enormous rewards, especially if he is first with the innovation. If there were not such rewards, many potential innovators might wonder if it were worth the price; they might seek other channels of rebellion. But enough do find the rewards worth the price so that the innovators are not only in conflict with the status quo but also in intense competition with one another to be first.[19] Again the sociology of science has shown the mechanisms at work in this competitive race.

Robert Merton, for example, has traced the system of "eponymy" which rewards those who make the great leap.[20] In addition, there are honorific awards, medals, and prizes; memberships and fellowships in honorary societies; admission to lists of distinguished persons. In all these rewards, priority is most highly weighted. The great leapers, the innovators, the first-ones-there are the winners; they receive the homage, and theirs is the prestige.

Innovator as Rebel

Priority is a social and a sociological phenomenon. If there is a first, then there must be a second and succeeding cases. We are at once in a social situation that raises a number of questions. What, in terms of intellectual ability, is the difference between the first and the second person? The intellectual equipment necessary to understand the new contribution is present in the second person; what else, in addition, did the first person have? It used to be said there were only twelve persons in the world capable of understanding Einstein's contribution; scores now understand it, and perhaps hundreds, if not more, can use or apply it without necessarily understanding it. The difference between the first and the second is sometimes an accident of timing, as the story of virtually simultaneous discoveries illustrates. Sometimes it is a matter of position, or of chance.

In many cases, however, the difference is one, not of sheer intellectual ability but of rebellion, however well mannered. Znaniecki, in the quotation given above, referred to innovators as "aberrants" and rebels. Psychological studies of outstanding scientists tend to corroborate this point of view. Anne Roe, for example, has found in them "a general need for independence, for autonomy, for personal mastery of the environment." [21] Donald W. MacKinnon has reported for his subjects independence, curiosity, skepticism, emotional commitment to one's work, energy, nonconformity, egotisticalness, and a "sense of destiny." [22] Kubie has pointed out that "a drive for 'originality' may cloak a difficulty in mastering existing facts and techniques, or it may serve to disguise an unconscious hostility to all existing authority." [23] Getzels and Jackson report more "aggression and violence" in both the verbal and pictorial responses of their highly creative adolescents as compared with their high IQ subjects.[24]

The successful innovator, then, in addition to being intellectually superior, must also be responsive to the reward system established by science as an institution. He must be aggressive and competitive and have what it takes to reject the status quo. He has to have some of the qualities of an exhibitionist, or at least be willing to shout, Look at me! He has to have a personality that can bear the weight of publicity, and he has to be able to stand the spotlight. All of these characteristics—this "sense of destiny"—are independent of sheer intellectual ability. No one knows how many times brilliant creative ideas have occurred to humble people unable or unwilling to proclaim them. No one knows how many were lost because no one picked them up and carried them through.[25] Creativity in this sense is far more than the act of individual innovation. It is a social act, indeed, almost a societal act.

Application to Women

These processes of innovation and resistance and the kind of personality required for performance of the innovative function help to explain the otherwise very strange paucity of great women scientists.[26] The innovative role is an instrumental one and not consonant with the emotional-expressive role assigned to women in most societies.[27] Women are socialized into a role whose function is conserving, stabilizing, appeasing.

The women who achieve the doctorate apparently have little difficulty in the passive art of mastering existing facts and techniques, at least as this aptitude reveals itself in the ability to do well on tests. This mastery is consonant with the emotional-expressive role. To the extent that they are successful in this mastery, on the basis of Kubie's insights, they would find it less necessary to hide their deficiency by a plunge into originality. In general, also, they have been processed to accept authority and whatever resentments they might feel toward authority; resigning themselves to it is less wounding to their self-image than it is for men. If true, this circumstance would also detract from the need for a plunge into originality.

Merton lists a second norm of science as an institution, namely modesty and humility, noting that "the social organization of science allocates honor in a way that tends to vitiate the institutional emphasis upon modesty," [28] so that most male scientists would rather be known for being first than for being modest. This is less likely to be the case with women. If women tend to have less motivation toward the priority norm, they seem to have more motivation toward the modesty or humility norm. It is more consonant with the emotional-expressive role. Here, for example, we have Vida Scudder boasting of her lowly status,[29] and Lucy Salmon hesitant about accepting an honorary degree because of her modesty,[30] always soft-pedaling rather than proclaiming her originality.[31]

The Part Played by the Public in Innovation

The importance attached to priority has other implications than those discussed above. It highlights the importance of followers or, in the case of science, of the public qualified to judge innovations. If an innovation is not recognized—even if recognition takes the form of rejection and a fight—it is dead.

> The author's work must be "consumed" to have social relevance. . . . The scientific work has to be read and put to work in practice. . . . If the author's creations are not used in this manner, then they remain dead for all practical purposes.[32]

The creative act has not only to occur but must also be "sold" to a frequently resisting public.

If, as noted above, acceptance of new ideas is difficult when they are presented by aggressive, ambitious, competitive men,[33] it is even more difficult when they are presented by women, whom we are not accustomed to seeing in the idea-man or instrumental role. We are simply not used to looking for innovation and originality from women. Margaret Mead is of the opinion that lack of recognition of women's contribution is due to the unfamiliarity of the feminine style: "New ideas cast in the new style will be twice suspect, once because they are new and once because the style is unfamiliar." [34] But sometimes they are not even recognized when they occur.

Typical is the case of Agnes Pockels, whose ideas were rejected out of hand by the great German scientists of her day.[35] When two scientists, a man and a woman, make the same contribution at the same time, it is likely to be credited to the man rather than to the woman.[36]

The willingness of the public to listen to women, as we have had several occasions to note, differs in different areas. As noted earlier, observations and interpretations of preliterate societies made by women are more likely to be accepted as valid than those made of industrialized societies by women. It is felt that women may even have better access than men to the basically important relationships in preliterate societies, which are based on kinship. But it is often felt that they do not have even as good an access as men to the fundamentally important relationships in an industrialized society, that their experience does not qualify them to understand the structure of interpersonal or power relations among men. In sociology women are listened to more attentively in the field of marriage and the family than in, say, the field of industrial sociology. They are more listened to in pediatrics, say, than in agronomy.

It was noted in Chapter 9 that identical material presented by a woman appeared to have less authority than it had when presented by a man. Similarly, identical ideas presented by women seem to have less power to trigger acceptance than when presented by men. Only a shred of evidence if offered here, and it may be biased. It is the statement of a young academic woman in a social science.

> For several years before and after I took my degree I was associated with the great man of my discipline. Many were the times when my ideas appeared under our joint authorship. They were accepted, sometimes acclaimed, included in all the bibliographies, and always cited in footnotes. After my marriage I had to break the relationship and move to another position. My work was, so far as I can judge, just as good as ever. But when it appeared under my name alone, it was hardly even noticed, let alone acclaimed.

The following informal experiment is reported at this point not because it is immediately relevant to the relationship between the innovator and the public but because, though somewhat tangentially, it does offer some insights. A social psychologist, on the basis of an informal experiment, noted that a man may give the same amount of homage to a distinguished woman as to a man, yet when the question is asked, "Who are the top ten in your field?" the woman is not likely to be among those named. When this was pointed out to the subjects, they tended to look sheepish and say they never thought of her. She was not in the same image of their profession as were the men. The social psychologist tried this "experiment" several times, once in his own field, once in the field of scholarship in English literature, and once in the field of college presidents. In the field of anthropology, he found, women were included among the top ten. It is not that the work of distinguished academic women scholars was not taken seriously; it was only that in most disciplines the image of the profession did not include them.[37]

Table 11/1 Level of American Psychological Association Membership and Sex of Significant Contributors and Control Groups *

Sex	Year in Which Doctoral Degree Was Received					
	1930–34		1935–39		1940–44	
	Significant Contributors	Psychologists in General	Significant Contributors	Psychologists in General	Significant Contributors	Psychologists in General
Male	49	144	45	148	48	151
Female	1	56	5	47	2	55
Number	50	200	50	195	50	206

	Total, 1930–44 Significant Contributors	Psychologists in General
Male	142	443
Female	8	158
Number	150	601

* Clark, *America's Psychologists:* (Washington: American Psychological Association, 1957), p. 72

CHAPTER 12 ❀ COLLEAGUES:
ACADEMIC COMPETITION

Channels of Ascent in Academia

There are several channels of ascent on any campus. We have already discussed the teaching channel and the relative success of women in it in Chapter 9. Some academic persons, however, look for their rewards in the recognition they receive from their peers in their discipline in the invisible university. They want to see their work cited, commented on favorably, used as a basis for further research, incorporated into the corpus of their discipline; they want to be elected to membership in honorary societies, to office in professional societies, to committees of various kinds; they want to become "names." There are women who rank high in this channel but, as noted in Chapters 10 and 11, they are handicapped with respect to both productivity and creativity in this channel. Since much competition in this channel is judgmental in nature, the fact that they are often not taken seriously is against them. Men, as noted in Chapter 11, may not even think of women as being in their status system. Even if they recognize their work as excellent—and put them on an academic pedestal for it—they do not feel they have to assess it on the same scale as that used to evaluate the work of other men.

When the competition is autonomous, women may be very successful. This fact is illustrated by the case of a one-of-a-kind economist who took no pains to conceal her satisfaction in being able to command the top fee for her consultations with industry. She was even at some pains to make this very clear to those who sought her services or advice. She enjoyed the discomfiture of those who, because she was a woman, expected her fees to be lower, when she told them what her price was. They had no bargaining power with her. Since she had a monopoly on her know-how and skill, it was her service or no one's. They paid, both in embarrassment and in money.[1]

Currently, status in some universities is measured in terms of the number and size of research grants or funds brought to the campus. The man who knows the sources of funds, who gets money just on his name, is the new kind of Big Man on Campus. The rise of the grant system has had the effect of transforming many academic persons into independent entrepreneurs, freeing them from control by the institutional hierarchy. They have their own little fiefs, their own vassals. Or, to change the metaphor, the university is like a modern Hollywood studio in which independent producers in effect rent space to do their own work. The part played by the great foundations in transforming academic life was already beginning to be significant when Logan Wilson made his sociological analysis of academia a generation ago. But since that time the impact of grants from government and industry has overshadowed that of the foundations. It is no longer a matter of getting a personal grant, that is, a grant to carry on an individual project. It is now a matter of large-scale enterprise. The person who receives the grant is no longer a researcher but an administrator, charged with assembling personnel, working out budgets, procuring equipment, keeping records, and a host of related administrative functions. If he leaves, he may take his enterprises with him. All this is new as a status system, and the implications for men as well as for women have not yet become clear.[2] Presumably women can be as successful as men in this system when they care to be.

There are, finally, the channels of ascent by way of rank, the administrative ladder, or positions of power and influence with colleagues through election to important policy bodies; these are variants of ascent in any hierarchic bureaucratic system.[3]

Administration

Despite the existence of such vivid exceptions as M. Carey Thomas, the administrative channel for upward mobility is not one in which academic women have been preeminent. Although, as indicated in Chapter 2, a substantial proportion of academic women are in administrative positions, they are likely to be in such staff positions as personnel and counseling rather than in line positions. There were, to be sure, in the 1950's some 120 women college presidents, 20 in coeducational institutions. Their success will be discussed in Chapter 13. At this point we merely note that administration does not appear to be a common channel of upward mobility for many academic women.

Academic Rank

The academic rank of women is inferior to that of men in all kinds of institutions, as shown in Table 12/1. This is true even of women with the same qualifications as men, whether measured by the doctorate (Table 12/1A) or by productivity (Table 12/1B). The differential varies according to type of institution (Table 12/2). It also varies according to subject matter, women constituting a larger proportion of the upper ranks in some areas, such as home economics and library science, than in others, such as the sciences (Tables 12/2 and 12/3). The only study which measured rate of professional ascent for the two sexes, although quite limited, found no significant difference at least among sociologists.[4]

Salary

In the United States the median salary of women professors ($7,899) in 1959–60 was about a thousand dollars less than the median salary of men professors ($9,179); for instructors, the medians were $5,161 for men and $4,855 for women. The overall figures were $6,906 and $5,865.[5] Since the differential was smaller for instructors than for professors, the implication is that it was declining. In the very tight academic market of the 1960's, women were apparently in a better bargaining position than women had been in when the professors entered upon their academic careers. Still there was a differential even among the instructors. Some of the salary difference was probably due to differences in institutional affiliation, women tending to be in schools which pay less; some of the difference was probably due to differences in subject matter taught, women tending to be in fields—the humanities, for example —at a competitive disadvantage in the market.

Why, it might well be asked, do academic women tolerate such status inequalities? Why don't they do something about it? Why don't they respond more enthusiastically to leaders who, in effect, tell them they have nothing to lose but their chains?

Part of the answer no doubt lies in the fact that many of the women are in the status of fringe benefits teaching elementary courses, as suggested in Chapter 8, with reference groups among nonacademic women rather than among their male colleagues, as indicated in Chapter 7. Part of the answer lies also in the fact that women are by and large less status-driven occupationally than men and are less competitive.[6]

The Noncompetitiveness of Women

It is a common diagnosis of the characteristic problems in the relationships between the sexes today to say that they result, in part at least, from the fact that men and women are in competition with one another. In industry, in the professions, in the home, in fact everywhere, it is alleged, a competitive atmosphere exists which embitters the relationships between men and women. Although there is a surface appearance of validity in this allegation, a deeper probing of the situation suggests that the precise opposite is—and has been—true for most women.

Indeed, a major grievance of men with respect to women in the labor force is that they refuse to compete for the values men set up. Women make the same charge.[7] In addition to the psychiatric evidence cited in Chapter 10, there is a convincing body of research data to corroborate these statements,[8] for most women, with what must be frustrating consistency, refuse to compete for the top jobs.

Dael Wolfle has summarized some of the earlier studies of competitiveness, or rather, noncompetitiveness, in working women, and concludes: "Taken at their face value these studies point clearly to the conclusion that the typical goal of an employed woman is not promotion and advancement in her chosen field. The strongest wish is for marriage and a home. When that wish cannot be realized, continuation in the same or a similar job is a more frequent goal than is promotion. The typical employed woman, in short,

is not wholeheartedly in competition with the employed man." [9]
He warns against taking the results at face value and suggests that
perhaps the noncompetitiveness of women may be a defensive
reaction against sex discrimination.

The same secondary evaluation of the job as compared with
marriage and family shows up, in varying degrees, in all the studies.
A study of 48 women Ph.D. candidates at Pennsylvania State University in the early 1960's reported that all of them, married and
unmarried alike, placed marriage above career in their value
systems.[10] Bernard Berelson cited an NORC survey that reported
as many as 15 percent of women graduate students did not want
professional work in the first five years after receiving their degrees.[11] James A. Davis reported that up to the age of 35 a substantial proportion of women graduate students in liberal arts—about
two-fifths—still expected to marry.[12]

One study of 440 women and 440 men receiving the doctorate
in psychology between the years 1921—40 reported clear-cut differences between them in attitude toward professional advancement.
Almost twice as many women (14.3 percent) as men (8.9 percent)
were "content to hold present job without promotion or salary
increase until retirement." [13] Only half as many women (4.1 percent) as men (8.1 percent) were "ready for promotion and will
not be content until it is received." [14] Less than half as many
women (2.0 percent) as men (4.5 percent) were "somewhat discon-
tented" because promotion had been delayed.[15] But, interestingly,
when conditions got quite bad—"promotion long overdue"—more
women (2.0 percent) than men (1.2 percent) were "quite dissatisfied." [16]

Despite the fact that far fewer women (43.7 percent) than men
(65.6 percent) had "reasonable expectation of promotion and
increased salary in present work," more of the women (41.6 percent) than men (37.7 percent) were "satisfied with [their] job." [17]

Attention has already been called to the fact that fewer of the
women psychologists than of the men found their professional work
a major source of satisfaction; far more women than men reported
work satisfaction as secondary to other kinds.[18] Women tend to
invest less of themselves in their work than men.

In the Matched Scientists study, women tended more than men
to explain their productivity in noncompetitive terms. Such reasons,
for example, as "a publish or perish" policy at their institutions,
a strongly competitive atmosphere at their institution, or stimula-

tion from colleagues and confreres constituted almost two-fifths (37 percent) of those given by men but only about one-fourth (25 percent) of those given by women. Conversely, reasons such as "fascination with a problem or problems" that they could not throw off and preference for research over other professional activities constituted about half (48 percent) of those given by men but three-fourths (75 percent) of those given by women.

Documentary evidence is available also to corroborate the statistical findings. The enormous preoccupation with status and prestige among academic men, illustrated by the emphasis accorded it in Logan Wilson's study of the academic man and by succeeding studies, seems almost obsessive to many academic women. For instance:

> Although I was often nominated for a position on the Academic Council of our university, it wasn't until I had been on the faculty for about a dozen years that I was finally elected. I couldn't have cared less for the "honor," which, so far as I was concerned, merely meant more time-consuming meetings. But each time I was defeated, my male colleagues offered me their condolences, showing clearly how bad they would have felt to be in my position.

Another case illustrates the motivation of one academic woman and how it looked to a male confrere:

> I have been deeply involved in research with——for many years. I published a series of papers on it that won me a little reputation of sorts and flattering recognition. I kept on with it even after that because I loved what I was doing. When I met a former fellow graduate student a few years ago he asked me what made me run so hard, I'd made it, hadn't I? He had done his major work primarily to win a promotion. Once he had made the grade he stopped producing. He couldn't understand why I worked so hard just for the fun of it.

And, finally:

> It seems to me women want recognition all right, but not necessarily as the best in the field or even necessarily as better than someone else. It's like wanting your husband to notice your dress, not to remark that it's prettier than some one else's or prettiest in the world.

Willingness to compete is a sign that one accepts the values competed for; refusal to compete implies rejection of, even contempt for, the values competed for.[19] Refusal to keep up with the Joneses, for example, is a way of saying that one does not share the Joneses' values.[20]

It is true that some men also reject competition. Despite the strong emphasis on upward mobility, it is a common complaint that many workers are not competitive. They do not want to be foreman or chief or head. They are willing to take their upward mobility in the form of better wages won for them by the union rather than in the form of better pay for a higher job. There are many academic men who do not want administrative positions, who in fact give up such positions in order to have more time to devote to their research work. But competitiveness is still characteristic of enough men to keep the academic race sharp—and predominantly masculine.

Competition among Status Channels

Not only is there competition within the several channels of ascent, there is also competition in prestige among the channels themselves.[21] Those in which women are likely to be successful—especially teaching and service to students—have less prestige than the others.[22] With the relatively rare exceptions, therefore, of those who achieve success in the administrative channel and in the invisible university, the success of academic women tends to be denigrated, disparaged. Their contribution to the total academic enterprise tends to be less highly prized than that of those who take part in the competition of more prestigious channels.[23]

A Successful Academic Woman

That it is possible for academic women to achieve top positions in even the more prestigious channels and also in the less prestigious ones—in all channels, in fact—is illustrated by the following case of an academic woman who was high in the administrative hierarchy, in rank, in the invisible university, in the teaching channel, and high also in the service-to-students channel.

Dr. H. received her bachelor of science degree from a small local college in 1943 and her doctor of philosophy degree from the University of Chicago in 1951. In the interim she taught in the public schools and at her alma mater.

She came to the University as an assistant professor in 1951, became an associate professor in 1955, and chairman of the department—the first woman to head a major science department at the University—in 1961.

Her work as a scientist won widespread recognition; she received a number of grants for basic research and also for the development of research projects and seminars at the University. She had few equals in either the laboratory or the classroom.

Her classes were jammed each semester. In 1954 she was given a $500 University award for excellence in student counseling and teaching of freshmen and sophomores. She was noted for her aid to students, in whose achievements she took great pride. One pre-med major recalled being "roused out of bed at 3 a.m. by a phone call from Dr. H. who had just hit upon a solution to a problem which had been plaguing his research project. She was so excited and she knew he would want to know immediately. He did."

She served as a sponsor for a junior women's honorary organization. When, after her death, students, faculty, staff members and friends launched a drive to raise money for a memorial fund in her honor, at the request of her students "who knew she was interested in all facets of learning, the financial assistance would not be restricted to students in her specialty."

She was extremely popular with fellow faculty members as well as with students. She was a skilled raconteur, had great interest in music, and was often called on to entertain her friends by playing the guitar and singing folk songs. She had been treasurer of the local chapter of Sigma Xi, had served on the University's budget committee, on the committee for self-evaluation, the public lectures committee, and on the committee on degrees with highest distinction.[24]

It would be difficult to find a more successful academician—man or woman—distinguished in so many status channels.

Status Inconsistency

The existence of several channels for status mobility often leads to the phenomenon which sociologists have come to label status inconsistency. If a person is high in status as measured in terms of one set of criteria—achieved or ascribed—and also in terms of other criteria, he knows where he stands, and others know how to behave with respect to him.

If, however, a person is high in status as measured in terms of one set of criteria but low in terms of other criteria, uncertainties and difficulties may easily arise with dysfunctional consequences. It is this phenomenon of differing status positions for an individual in differing status systems which has been called status inconsistency. The concept has been found useful in explaining a number of kinds of phenomena, such as disturbed interpersonal social relationships, unstable self-images, anomalous rewards, social ambiguity, and even stress symptoms.[25]

Academic personnel, men and women alike, are peculiarly subject to status inconsistencies. In relation to the institutional framework in which they must operate, professors are in an anomalous position. As faculty members they are part of a bureaucracy whose absurd structure and anarchic functioning have been noted by both social scientists like Logan Wilson and novelists like Mary McCarthy. As men-of-knowledge they belong to quite a different status system also. The man-of-knowledge has an exalted, though narrowly restricted, position. He may spend his life dealing with the most important, fundamental, inspiring problems of mankind, in a position to condescend to Plato or poke amused fun at Einstein. He knows more than his audience, has power over them, and is high in status. But the very attributes necessary to remain up in his field are precisely the attributes that may make him inept in the day-by-day chores of managing a college or university. Accustomed to large thoughts, he finds the details of bureaucratic operation not only distasteful but positively repulsive. Used to the company of Shakespeare, Kant, and Gibbs, he finds himself having to take orders from the buildings and grounds staff with respect to parking. He comes from the lecture hall where he has traced the development of a great major trend in human development to a faculty meeting where he must vote on whether or not to permit the journalism department to add a course on public opinion against the opposition of the sociology department.

The incongruity between the status of the almost god-like classroom lecturer, at home in the most abstruse areas of thought, and the shabby man, sometimes indifferent to his appearance, often inept in his ordinary contacts, perhaps abstracted and absorbed in his own thoughts, and not very high in the bureaucratic status system, is striking. It may even be confusing to the student.

Reference was made in Chapter 5 to the fact that the academic person is often of a lower "social" status than the students he lectures to or teaches. At the same time he is part of a system that has something to offer—a degree—that many people of high "social" status want. The resulting discrepancy between the status of his role as academician and his status in the "social" system often shows up in the embarrassment both student and teacher or professor sometimes feel when they meet off-campus, especially if the student arrives in a Cadillac and the academician in a Volkswagen. To the extent that academic women have a higher class background than academic men, they are less susceptible to this form of status inconsistency.

The relative prestige of the several channels of mobility also gives rise to some inconsistencies. The person who is in the system which awards high status on the basis of popularity with students may find himself denigrated by his colleagues who are in a system which awards high status on the basis of, say, position in the administrative hierarchy. Practically all studies, as indicated above, show academic women to be more involved with students than academic men are. Success in this area is not highly prized by those in other channels of ascent.

One interesting form which status inconsistency takes is that between the intellectual's assessment of his occupational status and that assigned to him by the public. Academic social scientists were reported in one study as imagining their status, as judged by businessmen, congressmen, and college trustees, to be lower than that of a branch bank manager, an account executive in an advertising agency, and a lawyer. Actually, public opinion polls rank professors higher than every nonpolitical occupation except that of physician, about as high in prestige, in fact, as important businessmen, bankers, and corporation directors.[26] Since academic women are not likely to be running in this race, they are spared this sense of invidious failure.

All the kinds of status referred to above are achieved, but sex is accorded a status by ascription. This ascribed status leads to inconsistencies. Sex, for example, as a basis for status usually takes precedence over achieved or professional criteria in the social life of the campus. Academic women are thus usually included in the social programs of faculty wives, where their status is uncertain at best. Off-campus, too, the academic women are polarized around faculty wives rather than around fellow professionals. "I wish hostesses would let me stay with the men, whose talk is interesting," complained one academic woman, "rather than insist on including me among the women, most of whose talk is not interesting to me."

There is the further inconsistency which occurs when the academic woman who is in the fringe benefit status has, as wife of a professor, or a graduate student, a different social status from that of her departmental colleagues and professional peers. If her husband has a high position in the status hierarchy, she may be on warm personal terms with the president of the university; her professional colleagues, men and women, have no such access to the higher administrative echelons.[27]

Table 12/1   Professional Status of Academic Women

A. Rank of Chicago and Radcliffe Ph.D.'s Teaching in Universities and Colleges *

	Before 1911 Men	Before 1911 Women	1911–1925 Men	1911–1925 Women	1926–1938 Men	1926–1938 Women	(Radcliffe Ph.D.'s)
Date of Receiving Degrees							
Number	236	20	679	91	1009	231	(136)
Percent with Rank							
of Professor	94.0	85.0	78.4	56.0	43.2	32.4	(32)
Associate and Assistant							
Professor	5.5	5.0	21.2	40.7	42.0	43.7	(54)
Instructor	0.5	10.0	0.4	3.3	14.8	23.8	(15)
Total	100.0	100.0	100.0	100.0	100.0	100.0	101.0

* Mabel Newcomer, *A Century of Higher Education for American Women* (New York: Harper, 1959), p. 203. Radcliffe data from *Graduate Education for Women: The Radcliffe Ph.D.* (Cambridge: Harvard, 1956), p. 24.

B. Proportion of Men and Women Professors (of Social Sciences) Who Are Associate or Full Professors, According to Age and Productivity *

Productivity	Under 40 Women	Under 40 Men	41 and Over Women	41 and Over Men
Age				
High	25% (16)	52% (307)	81% (74)	92% (697)
Medium or Low	13% (89)	18% (724)	56% (103)	75% (395)

* Stanley Budner and John Meyer, "Woman Professors."

C. Proportion of Academic Ranks Who Were Women in 98 Institutions, 1958–59 *

Sex	Full Professors	Associate Professors	Assistant Professors	Instructors	All Ranks
Men	90.5	92.0	79.2	69.3	80.9
Women	9.5	8.0	20.8	30.7	19.1

* Helene Ward, American Association of University Women report.

D. Proportion of Academic Ranks Who Were Women in 20 Leading Universities, 1960*

Sex	Full Professors	Associate Professors	Assistant Professors	Instructors	All Ranks
Men	90.6	95.3	89.9	83.9	90.6
Women	4.7	10.1	10.4	16.1	9.4

* John B. Parrish, "Women in Top Level Teaching and Research," *Jour. Amer. Assn. Univ. Women*, 55 (Jan. 1962), p. 102.

Table 12/2 Percent of Total Faculty Who Were Women in Two Types of Universities, by Teaching Area, 1960 *

Discipline	Ten High Endowment Universities	Ten High Enrollment Universities
All Disciplines	6.7	11.1
Physical Sciences	1.7	2.3
Biological Sciences	7.4	6.4
Social Sciences	3.7	5.2
Humanities	6.7	12.0
Selected Other Fields		
Education	24.4	23.6
Home Economics	66.1	93.1
Library Science	42.9	21.8
Psychology	7.3	7.3
Mathematics	3.3	9.8

* Abridged from Parish, *Jour. Amer. Assn. Univ. Women*, 55 (Jan. 1962), p. 107.

Table 12/3 Percent of Total Faculty Who Are Women in Twenty Leading Universities by Selected Disciplines and Rank, 1960 * .

Discipline	All Ranks	Professor	Associate Professor	Assistant Professor	Instructor
All Disciplines	9.4	4.7	10.1	10.4	16.1
Physical Sciences	2.0	1.2	2.1	1.6	5.7
Biological Sciences	6.8	1.3	6.7	7.1	16.3
Social Sciences	4.5	1.9	5.7	5.4	7.6
Humanities	9.9	4.2	9.2	11.1	14.9
Selected Other Disciplines					
Education	23.8	12.3	21.8	28.5	39.1
Home Economics	86.4	86.7	94.5	75.0	91.0
Library Science	25.9	53.8	13.2	40.0	25.0
Psychology	7.3	2.7	11.1	10.4	8.3
Mathematics	7.3	0.4	7.3	10.1	16.7

* Abridged from Parish, *Jour. Amer. Assn. Univ. Women*, 55 (Jan. 1962), p. 102.

CHAPTER 13 ❈ COLLEAGUES:
CONFLICT

Intrinsic Issues in Academic Conflict Today

Most of the differences discussed in Chapter 5 between and among academic personnel are integrative in nature. As an aspect of the division of labor, they are necessary for the functioning of the individual college or university and of the total system of higher education. Sometimes, however, there arise differences which are not integrative in nature but divisive. They give rise to issues, and cleavages form to support or to oppose them.

Berelson finds certain issues—he calls them "polarities"—to be intrinsic in modern academia:

> In the nature of the case, there is an inherent clash of interests between service and standards, teaching and research, the college and the university, academic and professional objectives, different classes of institutions, different fields.[1]

It is suggested here that there is a tendency for women to be identified with the first of each of Berelson's pairs of poles and that these are precisely the ones that are tending to decline in the influence exerted in academic decision-making. Women, that is, may be more interested in service than in standards, in teaching than in research, in the college than in the university, in academic than in professional objectives,[2] in the less prestigious, the less technical, the smaller institutions than in the opposites, and in the humanities than in the more technical fields.

Conflicts in Academic Roles

The teacher is, in effect, in a running battle with his students. There need be no hard feelings between them; there may be warm affection and admiration.[3] But let the demands of the teacher exceed the limits considered proper by the student culture of the campus and the resistance becomes palpable. Or let the teacher fail to hold the interest of his students and belligerence appears. Almost every teacher knows that the day he returns examination papers he will be able to do little effective teaching; the hostility is often solid enough to touch. The final bargain between teacher and students is usually a compromise between the standards of the teacher and the effort the students are willing to put forth.

There is also a strong conflict component in the man-of-knowledge role. Of the six historical types of scholars which Znaniecki has distinguished, one of them—the fighter for truth—performs in the role of protagonist in a battle of minds.[4] The man-of-knowledge is obliged to participate in these conflicts. He has to represent the "truth." The "battle" may take the form of an extensive research program to test the correctness of a hypothesis or the form of learned treatises evaluating the pros and cons of different theories.

Conflict in the form of debate is also part of the academician's role as member of a faculty governing the university, a role performed with notorious incompetence.[5]

In addition to issues intrinsic in academia today and conflicts built into the roles of academicians, there are also personal conflicts, based not on fundamental issues or institutionalized demands but rather on personal incompatibilities.

Interpersonal Conflict

Academic personnel are notoriously sensitive to slights. Because there are so few objective criteria for judging the worth of a person and because so much academic competition is judgmental in nature, academic people depend on recognition from one another to a greater extent than do those in professions where autonomous competition is the rule. The slightest evidence that they are not valued as highly as a colleague—whom they know to be inferior to them but whose inferiority is difficult to demonstrate—as expressed in office space, salary, privileges of one kind or another, or prerogatives, course allocation, or whatever arouses great anxiety.[6] This sensitivity has been noted in women as well as in men.

Here, again, as in the case of Berelson's major issues and the conflict component of the academic role, inevitability must be assumed as part of the conditions of academic life. Henry Noble MacCracken who, as president of Vassar for many years, had occasion to observe faculties in operation, had this to say about such interpersonal conflicts.

I never succeeded in eliminating faculty tensions. Some folks just do not like others. I came to two conclusions in the final consideration. The first is, that tension is inherent in intellectual life; when workers live too much to themselves, the mutinous emotions, left to themselves in the preoccupation with the intellect, take their revenge in breaking down the restraints which life in a wider community enforces! Lifelong association, at very close quarters, is not easy at best, as all apartment house tenants well know. Unlikenesses and inequality of abilities tend toward friction, which a common love of scholarship does not succeed in overcoming.[7]

Some of this interpersonal conflict is independent of sex; it occurs among both academic men and academic women, as well as between them. Sex only complicates, and often exacerbates, the situation. Sometimes the conflict is intrasexual:

Conflicts within departments were often the result of some sex antagonism. A woman who sought the favor of the masculine [sex] was pretty sure to incur the hostility of the other women, and was likely to lose her post when the man retired. One department was so split over this that no meeting of its members could take place, and I was forced to assume a temporary chairmanship to enable them to organize.[8]

Sometimes, however, the conflict is between the sexes, as in the following situation recalled by MacCracken:

In three departments the man-woman tension led to splitting of the departments into two independent ones where the subjects of instruction permitted it. Thus geography was separated from geology and became a social science, and botany left the shelter of zoology. Unhealed splits occurred in other departments which remained in name only.[9]

More subtle cleavages masquerade as sex conflicts. There was at Vassar, for example, the cleavage between those whom Mac-Cracken labelled the "analytics" and those he called the "creatives." By and large, although not exclusively, the women tended to fall into the first category and the men into the second.

The chief cleavages did not run along the sex line. The academic animal, it seemed to me, was rather sharply divided into two groups. The first group, and the more numerous, might be called the analytical. Its nature was reflective, studious, industrious, but not dynamic. It sought a leader and was content to follow guidance. It was disinclined to physical exercise. Poor health often dogged such teachers, and timidity and inferiority controlled their feelings. They tended towards group life, since low spirits love company. They worked well in chosen grooves, preserving the great tradition of learning, but they would never add much to it, or alter its course.

The other group might be called creative. They were active, independent, aggressive, and had a surplus of energy with which to combat disease. They led faculty action, and loved the scent of battle. The college was too small a field for them. They left the protection of college rooms, and lived in town, where they participated strenuously in civic life. They worked for suffrage, against child labor, against economic inequality and other forms of injustice. It was whispered of one of them that she had defended the right of an unmarried woman to bear a child and rear it. One or two, it was darkly hinted, were socialists. One even dared to be a Unitarian. Dangerous women, all of them. They rejoiced in every conflict of ideas. . . .

The creative group was as a whole superior to its station, the analytic group in danger of submitting to its handicaps. For the first my task seemed to be to further their projects, and support them. . . . But it was the large group of analytics that became my particular charge. They were not all women, by any means. Indeed, in a college for women, the men who accepted posts were likely to leave soon for other fields if creatively disposed, leaving the analytics to carry on.[10]

MacCracken's account of his "creatives" is reminiscent of the rebels at Wellesley as presented in Chapter 1.

Status Conflict and Sex

In some instances of academic conflict an apparent cleavage along sex lines is really a cleavage along status or power lines. The conflict would exist even if the parties were not of different sex, but sex may exacerbate it. The form the conflict takes is somewhat different according to whether the superordinate party is a man or a woman.

The following excerpt from MacCracken's book illustrates conflict when the status relationships are along conventional lines, that is, the male in the superordinate p~ ~:

> The men of the faculty   a quarter of the whole
> body, and nearly all   of departments. Natu-
> rally, therefore   there ensued a strife
> of the insubordinate bloc against the imposed domination of
> the male. Sometimes the unexpected self-assertion of women
> professors came from the same dynamic that makes professors
> absent-minded—devotion to truth in one's special field. . . .
> Sometimes women's aggression came from the sudden recognition
> of newly acquired powers. . . .
>   In general, the men in self-defense became conservative, op-
> posing every change, while a triumphant women's majority
> drove them from pillar to post in faculty reform.[11]

Problems of status inconsistency slant academic conflict in a peculiar direction when it is the academic women rather than, as at Vassar, the men who are in the superordinate positions. As hierarchical superiors, the record of the academic women who administrate colleges of home economics illustrate how successful academic women can be, despite the fact, noted in Chapter 12, that administration is not a common channel of ascent for them. But there is some evidence that they are not always successful, especially when men are involved in the subordinate positions. MacCracken said that he "could not honestly recommend a man to apply for a place in any department headed by a woman." [12] Virginia Gildersleeve described the devious conflict strategies indulged in by a woman in an administrative post at Barnard, feuding with the bursar, quarreling with the president and, when she differed from him, playing the trustees off against him, enlisting their sympathies for herself.[13]

Even the academic women in home economics colleges have had their problems. The self-driven women who created these remarkable colleges had, like all such vigorous entrepreneurs, aroused resistance and disaffection among their less dedicated staff members. Married to their professions, agog with the excitement of fields to conquer, of jobs to be done, of services to be performed, willing themselves to put sixteen to eighteen hours a day into their work, exemplifiers of MacCracken's "creatives", they could not always see why less strenuous colleagues—the "analytics"—did not care to follow their example. There were the usual faculty frictions, the resentments at being "pushed around," assaults on professional dignity, and the like.

The introduction of men in the 1950's complicated the situation. Men were being recruited at first primarily in the field of marriage and the family, but as housing expanded to include wider community and sociological aspects, men came into this area also. By the 1960's there was talk of male deans of home economics colleges.

How, in this novel situation in which women were superordinate, could the conventional sex roles and statuses be preserved? How could men work "under" women employers? Industrial sociologists have shown that even among the humblest workers in a restaurant, men cooks resist taking orders from women waitresses; sex is far more salient than role as determiner of status.

As it happened, the influx of men into the home economics colleges coincided with a stringent shortage of personnel, especially in the areas where men were specializing. In the area of marriage and family there was a seller's market. Deans were in serious competition with one another for the short supply of teachers. This situation tended to give the men strategic advantage. If they did not like what was done or how it was done, they had only to refer to other offers to win their point.

Professional Status and Conflict

One of the arguments sometimes advanced in favor of antinepotism rules is that a husband-wife team, expecially if they are in the same department, can form a powerful coalition and dominate policy. Actually, though, in most cases the woman in fringe benefit status is not likely to be an active participant in interpersonal conflicts, nor is she likely to take active part in campus or even in departmental politics. She is often not that involved, having other uses for her time.

Women in professional status, however, may be as deeply involved as their male colleagues, as capable at infighting, and as ruthless. There are probably few campuses that could not duplicate cases like that of Dr. X., who pursued an enemy relentlessly and implacably until she finally "got" him on a morals charge—in Mexico.

Role Anomalies and Conflict

The concept "role conflict" has become almost a cliché in analyses of the position of modern women, and the implication is that it is the women who experience the conflict.[14] But role conflict is often the lot of those, especially men, who have to deal with women who are performing in anomalous roles.

Since academic women are performing multiple roles, it is sometimes confusing to others, who don't always know what roles to assume themselves. The dean at one university once reassured a new member of the faculty that he did not have to perform all the chivalrous rituals for her; he was more nonplussed than relieved. It was easier for him to treat all women as women rather than have to discriminate between women in different roles.

Any role can be performed in many ways or modes. In the case of women, the mode may be neuter, sexy, feminine, or womanly. The attempt to perform in the neuter mode often results in an imitation of male role performance, with anomalous results.[15] Men respond to women in the role of sex object. In the game of pursuit and capture, of dueling, of the bargain, they understand and feel comfortable. They also understand women performing roles in the feminine manner, defined as weak, capricious, dainty, frivolous, coquettish, appealing; they feel comfortable in the complementary masculine role. They understand also the womanly mode, though they may feel less comfortable in the complementary role since the womanly mode implies a good deal of strength.

Whatever the mode of performance, men must always decide how they must respond. In an academic setting this may become confusing. Here is how the anomaly looked to one academic man in relation to a certain woman:

> There she stands. A beautiful woman. Above her neck she is talking about the most abstruse subject. From the neck down her body is saying something altogether different. She wears good clothes. They show her body off to good advantage. And yet she acts as though she were completely unconscious of it. She acts as though she were a man, like the dog who thinks he is a human being. Sometimes it strikes me almost as freakish, this split between the way she talks and the way she looks. The two don't go together. Which message am I suppose to be getting?

Some men find their relationships with talented women easy and pleasant if the woman has a husband; they know how to deal with women in such a relationship. Her status as a wife sets clear-cut boundaries in her performance of other roles. These same men may be stumped, however, when they have to deal with talented women who are not married. The existence of a husband establishes a role pattern that is familiar and comfortable. But what is the role definition of a man in relation to a professional woman who is not also a wife?

One young woman describes role confusion after her divorce:

> When Jack and I were graduate students together I was as much a part of the groups we ran with as he was. What I had to say was listened to; I was in. I was brighter than Jack; more original, quicker. He admitted it; it was generally accepted. But after our divorce my position changed. The men who had viewed me primarily as an interesting person who was Jack's wife now viewed me as a possible sex conquest. They were wolves as well as fellow students. A definite change came over my position in the group.

This experience is, of course, common among divorcées; it differs only in its academic setting from that of other women.

The status of disciple or protegée—literally, a protected one—may also serve to mitigate role conflict among men in relating to a woman. The withdrawal of such protection may lead to uneasiness:

> When Professor Smith was alive we used to go to professional meetings together and I was admitted to all the discussion groups without comment; no one paid any particular attention to me. Afterwards we would discuss what had taken place and apply what we had learned to what we were doing at our own laboratory. He always was generous in crediting me with ideas and always expressed his indebtedness to me; we published jointly. It was a satisfying relationship. After he died it took quite a while before it dawned on me that I was no longer able to enter the discussion groups at meetings on the same basis as before; the men were, or seemed to me, self-conscious about me. I felt isolated, as though I were talking to myself. It became pretty discouraging.

It would be much easier for men if they did not have to think of professional colleagues as women; having to take the sex of a colleague into account complicates any relationship. It is complicated for the women as well:

> There is great pressure on women, on me, at least, to define

roles in masculine terms. I have found myself resisting this pressure, reassuring myself of the validity of the values that I represent as a woman, reassuring myself that I was justified in being a woman, in protecting my own definition of my role. I am an inner-directed person, a spontaneous person, a non-authoritarian person. Both by temperament and by conviction I am an opponent to enforced conformity. I have never, therefore, capitulated to the pressure to think of myself as a man. In my written work I have not aggressed against others. I have not felt my confreres and colleagues to be my competitors. I often receive letters addressed to me as Mr., implying that there is no sex differentiation here. In face-to-face relationships, where there was a possibility of conflict, I have tended to assume the professional role when the situation was an intellectual one, but the feminine role when it was a social one. The switch has sometimes been confusing to my colleagues.[16]

Two Examples

Mode of role performance is especially important when women are performing roles not customarily assigned to them. There is, as noted in Chapter 11, nothing in the biology of men and of women which allots the instrumental function to one and the emotional-expressive function to the other. There is, however, much social logic in it, and hence most cultures do assign these functions to different sexes.[17] We therefore become accustomed to the idea that the feminine role is primarily emotional-expressive and the masculine role, instrumental. When either sex performs a function usually assigned to the other, the mode of performing it has to be adjusted to take care of the anomaly. Two examples are offered here, the first unsuccessful, the second, successful.

The administrator of a certain laboratory was accomplished and highly successful in his role until a woman assistant was added to his staff. She was a brilliant scientist, innovative, and creative. She performed an instrumental function, throwing out ideas, suggestions, inventive plans by the dozen. The administrator performed the emotional-expressive role, and had managed to keep a set of extraordinarily talented scientists highly productive for years. He had relied on them for ideas. It would have been possible for his assistant to perform the instrumental role in a feminine manner; many women do, as James Barrie showed us in his play *What Every Woman Knows*. But she did not. She performed it in a masculine manner. Presently the entire staff, men and women alike, were demoralized. She herself was frustrated. The laboratory appeared to be falling apart. She could not get done what she thought should be done; she attacked the administrator; she almost destroyed him. He lost confidence in himself. The psychoanalyst might have called her the "castrating female" in archetypical form. The damage she did was almost irreparable. Fortunately she was replaced by a woman scientist who was able to perform the instrumental role in a way that was not destructive.

Virginia Gildersleeve was an example of a woman who learned to deal successfully with the anomaly of a woman performing an instrumental role. Despite the greater verbal facility of women, the feminine role in relation to men is defined as that of listener, as that of the absorber rather than as that of the dispenser of words. Part of the emotional-expressive role is to listen, to soothe the emotional hurts and shocks of others, to just be there.[18] One of the most resented traits in women is violation of this function. The woman who talks too much—and sometimes almost any amount seems too much—is a stock character for ridicule, hatred, or contempt as the case may be. If her talk is mere chatter, it can be ignored or shut out, but if it is meant to be taken seriously, it seems role-anomalous.[19] A good deal of the talk of the academic woman is meant to be taken seriously; the academic role includes much talking. If she is to be successful she has to learn how to listen more than men and how to talk without making men feel either like children or inferiors. This is how Virginia Gildersleeve learned to handle the anomaly of her role:

> Men dread the prospect of having a woman around. Their worst fear is that she will talk too much and often irrelevantly, that she may get emotional in seeking to have her own way. My natural instinct was to begin very gently. I spent hours and hours just sitting quietly, listening to discussions of the University budget or whatever was before us, speaking rarely and briefly, to comment on the business, to ask intelligent questions, occasionally to make a suggestion. If a woman just sits quietly and says nothing at all, then the men will think she is timid or stupid and uninterested. If she is to gain any influence, she must establish herself as a pleasant, amiable, but intelligent human being, no trouble but rather a help. The men can then turn to her in any puzzling questions involving women,

perhaps enjoy her protection in warding off attacks by militant feminists from outside, and in time will lend an attentive ear to her own projects.

This technique of mine, which I drifted into naturally because of my own temperament, was a slow-moving one, not at all spectacular in its results. . . . It [would] not, perhaps, have been effective for the pioneers in seeking opportunities for women. Probably they had to batter at the doors rather violently and spectacularly [20] before I could get in and sit there peacefully in a friendly atmosphere, "boring from within." Actually, after I got going on any one of these committees or commissions, I was not really "boring from within." I was just one of a group of human beings, all trying together for the best possible solutions of the important questions before them.[21]

Attraction

Disturbing as conflict between the sexes may be on a campus, undue attraction between them may present even greater problems.[22] Novels of campus life are spiced with scandals and sexual intrigue. In *The Severed Head*, the heroine has an incestuous love affair; in *The Party at Cranton* the heroine is practically promiscuous. (Both are anthropologists.) But Henry Noble Mac-Cracken is of the opinion that such behavior is not in the common American tradition, and in all his experience he knew only two such cases, one at Harvard and one at Smith.[23]

But neither novelists nor administrators are reliable as sources, the first because they must find illicit relationships and the second because they'd rather not. Illicit attachments between members of faculties are doubtless present at some time or other on most campuses, but by the nature of the case, except if there is a public scandal, they are difficult to learn about. In the first place, the partners are not immature undergraduates, and therefore they are likely to be appeasingly discreet. Unless someone wants to make something of it, there is every incentive not to notice such a relationship. If it is at all possible, administrations are likely to remain ignorant; they prefer not to have their attention called to such situations; they even resent those who force them to notice the personal lives of their faculties.[24]

Minor sex playfulness, however, is omnipresent and acceptable. One academic woman makes the following comment:

> I am always impressed and surprised, no matter how often it happens, by how near to the surface thoughts about sex always are in men's minds. A committee is sitting around a table busily absorbed in some piece of academic business. The concentration is intense. After a few minutes of this a man nearly always releases the tension and nearly always by a sort of sex-tinged joke. Nothing obscene or objectionable, just titillating and unexpected. It would never occur to the women. They'd be more likely to bring in the coffee.

Women are no longer offended by evidence of this preoccupation of men with sex, although there was a time when they would have been required to be.[25]

It is difficult for a Negro, a Jew, or a Catholic who sees himself as an individual to realize that the world sees him as part of a larger whole. So it is with women. They think of themselves as individuals, "just like anyone else," and it often comes as a surprise to them to find that their sex is very much in the minds of those who are observing or interacting with them. They might, under certain circumstances, forget they are women, but men do not.

Balance Sheet

If there are disadvantages in the position of the academic woman because of her sex, there are also advantages. One of the most important of these is less vulnerability and less apprehension with respect to her social and political opinions. The radicalism of the women's colleges in the first two decades of the century has already been discussed in Chapter 1 and in connection with MacCracken's comments on "creatives" above. Women could "get away with" a considerable amount of radicalism. Budner and Meyer analyzed the data on women from the Lazarsfeld-Thielens study of the academic mind and found that they were less likely than men to be attacked in "the difficult years" of McCarthyism. If they were taken less seriously by administrators in allocating rewards, the reverse was also true: They were taken less seriously by those attacking academic freedom. Budner and Meyer conclude that "women are considerably less apprehensive than men apart from the major factor producing apprehension." [26] This is quite an advantage.

Protected by her sex, it is also often easier for a woman to stand up to hierarchical superiors. "I miss Charlotte," says one department head, "she used to stand up to me; I knew where she stood and where I stood. The men seem afraid to speak up." Another illustration:

> On one occasion a committee of my colleagues invited me to a meeting at which we were to draw up a list of grievances against our chairman. We worked hard to make them clear-cut and provable. When the list was all typed up we were to sign it. Only one of my colleagues and I did. The others reneged, to a man. I finally sent the list to the dean over my own name. Another woman colleague and I went to the dean. We won what we asked for.

It was probably easier for the woman than it would have been for a man to stand up to the student mob also, as described by her student in Chapter 9.

Less important, perhaps, but comforting nevertheless is the supporting bond, often reported among minority group members, which may be helpful:

> If my professional experiences are indicative, you might have a word to say about the "feminine fraternity" in the academic world—the comfort and support offered by a community of peers—everything from ladies' room grapevine to behind-the-scene-help about jobs and publishing. Or is it just selective perception on my part?

A young attractive woman may be the indulged "mascot" in a large graduate department where she is thus protected from the infighting among the men. The women who "man" home economics colleges have an advantage also; it is hard for legislatures to turn down symbols of home and mother.

Women are more protected than men from the hazards of student entanglements. Someone has said that the relationship between a male teacher and a female student is an ideal setup for seduction. It used to be required in some colleges that whenever a male faculty member had a woman student in his office the door had to remain open. The protection was for him as well as for her.[27] Because the age and status differentials between academic women and male students are not in the conventional direction, the risk of incidents is less great. Only two cases of advances by male students to academic women—as distinguished from teaching graduate students—were uncovered, although, it must be confessed, no systematic search was made for them.

A final advantage is that if academic women fail to live up to their own aspirations, there are always available outs. They can marry and say, in effect, "I never wanted the prize in the first place." Or, if they cannot marry, they at least have the face-saving device, which they share with minority group members, of "It wasn't my fault."

Images

However good or bad the academic woman may look to her colleagues, however anomalous her role or inconsistent her status within the academic system itself may be, her image as projected in popular fiction is rather favorable than otherwise. Indeed, as contrasted with the image of the academic man, she shows up rather well. A cursory scanning of several novels dealing with academic life suggests that the women (with the exception of anthropologists) are more likely than the men to be moved by idealism and to have ethical rather than merely personal conflicts; they are less likely to be involved in intrigue. It is interesting to note in passing that a surprisingly large number are anthropologists and that the anthropologists behave somewhat less well than the others.[28]

CHAPTER 14 ❀ SPINSTERS

The Marital Status of Academic Women

As a result of the change in values referred to in Chapter 4, it is not surprising that academic women today are more likely to be married than were those of the past.[1] There were, to be sure, great academic women in the past who were married; the romance of Alice Freeman, president of Wellesley, and George Herbert Palmer, professor at Harvard, was one of the great idylls of the time.[2] For the most part, however, the women who staffed the women's colleges and pioneered the home economics colleges were not married.[3]

Even today, with the rise in proportion of academic women who are married, they still are less likely to be married than academic men,[4] and, more to the point, they are also less likely to be married than are women in comparable professions.[5] Nor is the discrepancy eliminated if the comparison is made between women with identical training and professional or scientific interests.[6] Thus, among the women biologists who, ten to fifteen years after receiving the doctorate were in non-academic positions, 56 percent were married; among those in academic positions, only about half that many, 29 percent, were. Clearly there is no artifact here. There is something about the academic profession which makes it, or at least, has to date made it, inimical to marriage among women.

There are doubtless many forces at work to produce the low marriage incidence among academic women. Only three of them will be discussed here, namely: a monastic tradition in the academic world, a vocation for celibacy among some academic women, and a shortage of suitable men in the world at large.

Monastic Tradition

The monastic tradition in academia was referred to in Chapter 4 where Margaret Mead was quoted to the effect that "the academic world is fundamentally hostile, by tradition . . . to those aspects of femininity which involve child bearing." [7] Academic women, she has noted, as students and as faculty members, must forego their interest in their appearance and attractiveness and assume interests which were first set by monks.

The monastic tradition meant, of course, in addition to asceticism, no marriage. Learning and domesticity were not compatible; they made conflicting demands on people. The implication, in the case of women, was not only that married women were not likely to be employed but also that they left the academic profession when they married.

As a crescive norm, this rule was not usually formulated; it was just understood, taken for granted. It was, however, openly articulated during the public debate which attended the resignation of Alice Freeman from the presidency of Wellesley to marry George Herbert Palmer:

> Private fulfilment against public service was brought widely into debate. There were heated partisans on each side. On the one hand it was strongly argued that in proportion as one develops capacity for public things he should treat his personal desires as matters of little moment. Others should treat them so too. Priests cannot marry, and kings only those who are likely to promote the interests of their land. . . . It is not tyranny to regulate the marriage of soldiers and sailors. Possibly artists should remain single. Responsibility carries with it trusts which cannot be cast away at will. Civilization rests upon dedicated lives, lives which acknowledge obligation not to themselves or to other single persons, but to the community, to science, to art, to a cause. Especially base was it for one who had proved her power to win an unwilling public to look with favor on the education of women now to snatch at the selfish seclusion of home, and so confirm the popular fancy that a woman will drop the weightiest charge if enticed with a bit of sentiment.[8]

The same arguments were not, of course, used for academic men; the monastic tradition was not so demanding for them.[9]

Whatever influence the monastic tradition may have exerted in earlier times, however, it can no longer be invoked to interpret the low incidence of marriage among academic women, even today.

Vocation for Celibacy

The counterpart of the monastic tradition or set of expectations, and a second possible explanation for the low marriage incidence among academic women, is a vocation for celibacy, not only among Catholic [10] but also among many non-Catholic women.

This preference for a celibate life may characterize as many as one-fifth of the unmarried academic women at the graduate school level (who, themselves, constitute about 71 percent of all the women graduate students in liberal arts) and, because of the dropping out of those who marry, an even larger proportion of those who finally become professional academic women.[11] Thus whatever force the monastic tradition or set of expectations may have exerted on the marital status of academic women, it was probably strengthened by the selective forces which channeled women into and out of the academic world. Early academic women like Alice Freeman who preferred marriage to their careers left the fold, much to the consternation, incidentally, of the presidents who had to replace them.[12] Those who remained, therefore, and made a success of their work were celibate by preference.

Maria Sanford gave up the man she loved at Swarthmore, and when marriage became possible at the age of 60, she declined.[13] Florence Sabin, it was rumored, was engaged before she entered medical school, but the young man died and thereafter "medicine was to be her one romantic interest." [14] The staunchest antiwoman of them all, M. Carey Thomas, who dropped Martha from her name as soon as she entered college in order to render it sexless, wondered in later years if her life might have been fuller, more varied and useful if she had married, but finally decided in the negative.[15]

It was Vida Scudder, however, who gave the frankest and most candid presentation of the case for celibacy for women, as a positive value in itself and not as a second-best choice. After Maria Sanford's Dionysian account of her great love affair, the bland, Apollonian style of Vida Scudder's account, about a generation later, presents a startling contrast. But she makes a strong statement:

> My imagination is immune from shock; but I do not see why one should pay so much attention to one type of experience [sex] in this marvelous, this varied, this exciting world. I was walking once in the Alps with two women of recognized charm and distinction, each of them happy in a large following of disciples and devotees. Having fully enjoyed the glaciers, settled the world's economic future, and talked about the latest plays, we were moved to personal confidences; and were presently telling one another that no one of us had ever had a love affair. I at least was not mortified by the fact; we were all aware that many women with satisfying and fruitful lives are in the same case. I know that something perhaps, humanly speaking, supremely precious has passed me by; but had it come to me, how much it would have excluded!
>
> I want to register my conviction, and I wish I might have a great many masculine readers at this point, that a woman's life which sex interests have never visited, is a life neither dull nor empty nor devoid of romance. I did not always think so. What young thing could, if she read the novels, saw the dramas, in which sex relations are the staple? Until I was thirty, I wanted terribly to fall in love. I didn't care so much about being loved; almost any woman can manage that if she cares to try. But I was eager for the experience without which, all literature assured me, life missed its consummation. Once or twice I tried to compass it, but I couldn't. . . .
>
> I suppose I do soberly think that for most people, possibly for myself, life devoid of sex experience lacks fulfillment. But my feeling to this effect is due to my respect for authority, not to any personal sense of lack. And I confess that married life looks to me often as I watch it terribly impoverished, for women.[16]

That there still are women with a preference for a celibate life, despite the current disparagement of it, is evidenced by the data presented above. It is from among their numbers that college professors in women's colleges are, apparently, or were, to a large extent recruited. This is the life they, like Vida Scudder, want to live. They do not aspire to marriage.

The complete reversal in attitude toward celibacy which took place in the second and third decades of the twentieth century greatly reduced the number of women who were willing to espouse it. As a result of the work of the "less responsible psychologists and psychiatrists," as Virginia Gildersleeve pointed out,[17] unmarried women came to be pictured as inhibited, frustrated, and somehow or other not complete human beings. To escape this obloquy, most of the young women wanted to marry;[18] indeed, they seemed determined to.

Virginia Gildersleeve watched the impact of this revolution in attitudes from a position as dean of a women's college. From a tradition which, in effect, forbade academic women to be married, let alone to become mothers, to one which, in effect, required them to, was a remarkable jump to take. One moment she was having to protect married women; the next, unmarried women.

> It was right to do what we could at Barnard to aid married women teachers; but of recent years another aspect of the question has troubled me. I have occasionally thought that in schools and colleges there has arisen a particularly cruel and unwholesome discrimination against *unmarried* women for some teaching and administrative posts. This is due in part to the attitude towards the unmarried of certain of the less responsible psychologists and psychiatrists of the day, which tends to voice disrespect for spinsters in the teaching profession as "inhibited" and "frustrated." [19]

Attitudes had come full circle. Little wonder that even academic women wanted very much to be married, now that celibacy, once honored if not imitated, was so disparaged.[20]

Still, despite this strong pressure toward marriage, the number of unmarried academic women remains high. Neither the monastic tradition nor a bent toward celibacy can explain it today, however relevant they may have been in the past.

Lack of Peers

Are academic women rejected by men? Helene Deutsch implies as much. She believes that "only exceptionally talented girls can carry a surplus of intellect without injuring their affective lives" and that "woman's intellectuality is, to a large extent, paid for by the loss of valuable feminine qualities." [21] Intellectual ability makes them less than women.

An alternative explanation has been suggested: "The damage

to the feminine core development may result from the injury to the woman's self-concept that results from *society's views* of intellectual activity in women, rather than from the process of intellectualization itself." [22]

Still another possibility suggests itself with respect to academic women. They do not begin with damaged femininity. Many have entered graduate school as compliant scholars, in part to please their professors, as reported in Chapter 4. Like most young women they hope to marry men they can "look up to." They want husbands who are at least their equals, and preferably their superiors, intellectually, men with whom they can happily accept a subordinate position, to whose careers they can contribute.[23]

They are, however, not ordinary young women. They are superior, at least so far as measurable intelligence is concerned. Height offers an interesting analogy. Suppose that instead of being superior in measurable intelligence, they were superior in height, that they were, on the average, taller than their male fellow students. Most young women want to marry men who are taller than they are, just as most young men prefer wives somewhat shorter than they. The young woman is not "to blame" if she is tall. She would have been just as tall if she had not continued to graduate school.

Those in charge of graduate programs often note that many of the young women are—unknown even to themselves—abler than the young fellow students they marry. In many cases the young women are willing, even eager, to subordinate their own degree programs and careers to those of their husbands. It is sometimes a rude and unwelcome surprise to them when they realize that the husbands are less likely than they themselves are to make the grade.

Whatever the deforming effect, if any, on femininity, it is not due to the intellectual gifts of the young woman but to the relative deficit of young men superior to her to perform the masculine role to her feminine one. The so-called marriage gradient complicates the situation even more; it reflects the tendency of men to marry somewhat—though not greatly—below them in both ability and social position.[24] Thus when one notes the characteristics of the unmarried population, among women it is often the cream of the crop who are not married; among men, the rejects.[25]

Some of the talented young women, unwilling to keep on intellectually stooping all their lives in order not to appear intellectually "taller" than their husbands, forego marriage and find feminine fulfillment as assistants or associates to men they can happily subordinate themselves to. The relationship of a researcher or scholar and his female associate may often take on the role nature of a husband-wife relationship, just as that of a businessman and his secretary may result in the so-called "office wife" role. One well-known scholar pointed out that when he first came to his university none of his plans went right until Miss Jones arrived on the scene as his assistant; thereafter everything clicked and went just fine. For decades he was acclaimed for his scholarship; his assistant felt amply repaid for her contribution by basking in his reflected glory. She was, in effect, a second wife.

Unmarried and Married Academic Women

The academic women who are married—whether in the status of fringe benefits or of professionals—are likely to have had a somewhat different career pattern than either the unmarried academic woman or the academic man. If they were married as graduate students, the financing of their study was different; they "have high rates of support from husband's jobs. To put it simply, it appears that married women can afford to go to graduate school only if their husbands can support the entire family, whether or not there is a child." [26] The author just quoted infers from this that "while a man's graduate training can be considered an important investment, graduate training for married women is an economic luxury, and the high-income levels of the married women probably stem from the fact that married women typically go to graduate school only when their husbands are making enough money to pay for such a luxury." [27] The unmarried woman, however, probably has to finance her own doctoral program, and this fact no doubt helps to explain why—in the Matched Scientists study—she tended to be somewhat older when she received her degree and why she was less likely to receive it from one of the Top Twelve schools (Table 14/1).

Not only the financing of graduate study but other aspects of the careers of married and unmarried academic women as well seem to be different. The unmarried reported considerably more memberships in professional and scientific societies. But the most striking difference between the married and the unmarried academic women in this set of subjects was in institutional distribution. With so few cases that one or two can make a great difference, disparities have to be large in order to be convincing. It is large between the proportion of the married and the unmarried in college positions. A very large proportion of the unmarried—almost all, in fact—were teaching in colleges (Table 14/1) .[28]

For the fourth time now we meet the dedicated academic woman. First, in Chapter 6 we noted the processes by which academicians distribute themselves among institutions. We documented the importance which availability of marriageable men assumed in the decision-process of a young woman trying to plan her career. Again, in Chapter 7 we met her when comparing academic women in colleges and in universities; in Chapter 10 she appeared again as the teacher rather than as the researcher. Now we meet her as the unmarried woman who devotes herself almost exclusively to her work. She is the woman who has time for her students, time to sponsor organizations, time to talk to them. She is the woman without competing demands from husband or children. She is, almost without any doubt, in professional status—as evidenced by her large average membership in professional societies— and her major interest, as noted in Chapter 10, is almost certainly teaching, not research.[29]

Table 14/1 Married and Unmarried Academic Women *

	Married (18)	Unmarried (29)
Birth Date (Median)	1919	1916
Age at Doctorate (Median)	29.5	32.3
Percent Married at Time of Receiving Doctorate	61	
Average Number Years Married before Doctorate	5.5	
Percent Married after Receiving Doctorate	33.3 †	
Average Number Years after Doctorate	5.3	
Percent Receiving Doctorate at Top Twelve	61	31
Average Number Memberships in Professional and Scientific Societies	2.4	3.3
Teaching in Colleges (Percent)	8	92
Teaching in Universities (Percent)	42	58
In Other Occupations	56	44

* Women biologists receiving doctorate at same period of time. Data from *American Men of Science* (Tempe: Cattell, 1960).

† One woman married same year as doctorate received, not included in tabulation.

CHAPTER 15 ❀ WIVES AND MOTHERS

"The Feminine Mystique"

The great waves of change that sweep over populations from time to time have not been as carefully researched as smaller, more immediate forms of collective behavior.[1] We do not have at our disposal as carefully fashioned conceptual tools for analyzing them. We do not, therefore, completely understand one such change that swept over many parts of the world in the last few decades, to which reference was made in Chapter 4 in discussing the reasons for the decline in proportion of faculties who were women. The change took the form of a kind of reproductive mania.

There was a reevaluation of the family. After rejecting maternity, as measured by the birthrate, for several decades, women seemed suddenly not able to get enough of it. They wanted to get married young and have babies.[2] Between 1940 and 1960, the birthrate for third children more than doubled, for fourth children almost tripled, for fifth children more than doubled, for sixth and seventh children, increased by half. The change even among college women was so great that it was called revolutionary.[3] The result, as noted in Chapter 14, was an increase in the relative number of married academic women.

Academic women in the status of fringe benefits are, almost by definition, married, and the married academic woman is likely also to be in the status of fringe benefit. If she is young, she is not likely to be also a mother; if she is older, the chances are that she is, but that her children are fairly well grown. In either case, her role as academic woman is, as indicated in Chapter 7, secondary to her role as wife and mother. Since she is not likely to undertake academic responsibilities unless her family approves, or at least consents, there are not likely to be many severe difficulties involved in her activity. If she fails as a mother, the failure can scarcely be associated with her role as academic woman. The children of such women are often pleased that their mothers can perform successfully in the academic role.

The academic women in professional status are not so likely as the academic women in fringe benefit status to be married, but a significant number of them are. A considerable—as yet indeterminate—number of academic women are married to men in the same general area of specialization. In some instances this makes for especially close ties,[4] but the possibility of a competitive relationship is also present.[5] Sometimes, despite a determined effort not to outshine her husband, she shows up better professionally than he does.

The Stability of the Marriages of Academic Women

The stability of the marriages of academic women is hard to evaluate. In some cases marriages are stable despite, or perhaps because of, the fact that the partners teach at different institutions. Budner and Meyer found in their sample of social scientists that 7 percent of the women and 1 percent of the men were in the divorced marital status.[6] Among 440 men and 440 women doctors of philosophy in psychology—not all academicians, however—5.3 percent of the women and 1.6 percent of the men were in the divorced status.[7] It is not clear what these figures mean.

For the total population 15 years of age and over, the (adjusted) figures for those in the status of divorce were 2.2 percent for males and 3.1 percent for females in 1950.[8] Actually, however, divorce is less common among the more highly educated. The 7 percent of women in the social sciences and the 5.3 percent of women in psychology in the divorce status are thus rather high; conversely, the 1 percent of men social scientists and 1.6 percent of men psychologists are unexpectedly low.

On the basis of the above two samples, either the marriages of academic men are far more stable than those of academic women and of the general public, and those of academic women much less stable; or else academic men remarry sooner after divorce than academic women and the general population;[9] or divorce brings back into the professional ranks women who had left their positions at marriage.[10]

In addition to the above data, the study of the psychologists reported that 2.3 percent of the women, but only 0.7 percent of the men were so dissatisfied with their marriage as to wish a divorce.[11] More of the women (6.8 percent) than of the men (2.6 percent) were dissatisfied, but not enough to want a divorce.[12] More men (91.7 percent) than women (79.4 percent) were fairly well satisfied or well satisfied and enthusiastic about there marriages.[13]

Effect of Marriage on Career

The only data to throw light on this question refer to psychologists, not all of whom were academic persons. Although the effects were somewhat different for those with full-time employment and for those with less than full-time employment, the general picture is one in which 28 percent of the married women report marriage to be a professional asset and 34 percent report it a hindrance.[14] Among the part-time psychologists, about one-fourth (23.9 percent) gave marriage as the chief factor in abandoning their careers.[15] By way of contrast, 72 percent of the men found marriage a professional asset and only 5 percent found it a hindrance.[16]

Effect of Career on Marriage:[17] A Husband's-Eye View of an Academic Wife

How does the academic woman look to her husband? There are probably as many kinds of images of her as there are kinds of academic marriages. Here is only one:

It takes a lot of getting used to—a great many adjustments by both husband and wife. My wife was tentatively and temporarily academic when we were married; just enough to help earn my way through graduate school; enough also to demonstrate her capacity and to whet her appetite. Then she did what marriage meant to both of us—settled back into the roles of wife, mother, hostess, and housekeeper.

For ten years these demanding jobs kept her occupied, though not contented. I became excessively self-centered, with her help and connivance. The whole family's welfare depended on me: for income, status, and hope for improvement of our social and economic circumstances. Family life was organized to encourage and assist my intellectual life, my community activities, my writing, my teaching, the broadening and deepening of my interests.

Then, as our girls were old enough to go to school, I began to notice significant changes in her feelings and behavior. She no longer responded enthusiastically to my successes and recognitions. In fact, she began to resent them so positively that I felt absolutely rejected and concluded our marriage was at an end. My earnings were now more than adequate for our needs; but simply because the monthly pay check was not so much needed it came to be little appreciated. Socially, professionally, and economically we had "arrived" to the degree that no longer was there a need of concentrated family effort to help me bear the banner forward.

For a period of several years she manifested a genuinely (medically) neurotic rebelliousness against her own subordinate and unsatisfying situation, most commonly manifesting itself in open resentment against me because I had so much that she lacked and wanted. Her feelings were further aggravated by uncertainty as to what she could do about it.

When, finally, she made the heroic effort of returning to graduate school for two years of gruelling study, breaking through the shell of ten years of non-intellectual housewifery, both she and I reacted badly. She became as awkwardly self-assertive as are adolescents, and for almost precisely the same reasons: the strongly urgent need to assert her own independence, and lack of any practiced or approved mode for doing it. I, meanwhile, felt myself rudely shoved out of the spotlight to become a spectator of her central role as an emergent scientist, then teacher. Since I was so much superior to her both as scientist and teacher, it was doubly difficult to see my own achievements ignored and her bumbling efforts become the center of attention. I tried very hard to be nothing but admiring and encouraging, but it was a very difficult period.

As she finally emerged into professional competence, the strain eased for both of us. A new partnership feeling developed. My pride in her achievements matched hers in mine. Slowly and hesitantly we became able to discuss serious questions with serious regard for one another's opinions. The growth of comradeship proved worth the cost. But no one should be deluded into thinking it was easy. Any woman who is both wife and mother has to earn her way back into academia, and the cost to both her and her family is certain to be very great. And so may be the rewards.

Academic Women as Mothers [18]

Many academic women are also mothers. Like regulations with respect to nepotism, colleges and universities differ with respect to their policies on teaching during pregnancy. In some, women are expected to take maternity leave, with or without pay.[19] In others they are permitted—even, in some women's colleges, encouraged—to teach as long as they can.[20] Pregnant women in the classroom appear today to be no more anomalous than at the supermarket.

By and large, academic women have fewer children than do women with comparable training who are not academic women, and the number of children is related to the extent of professional involvement, as shown in the accompanying figures for Radcliffe Ph.D.'s (Table 15/1). Since these Radcliffe figures are prevalence rather than incidence figures, they do not show the different patterns over time. Sometimes the same woman can appear in a different category, or several different categories, all within a rather short period of time:

> After receiving the Ph.D. from the University of Chicago I taught at Kanwisota University for two years . . . and did part time research for the University of Winnemac for one year. But, unable to arrange for satisfactory care of my children, I quit paid professional work until last February when my youngest child was in kindergarten. At that time I became a part-time instructor and intend to broaden my professional work with research within the next few years.

Some women in fringe benefit status become involved only after their children are older:

> I have been employed as lecturer at the local college. This has been on a part-time basis since I am also raising four children. Except for publishing my thesis . . . I have engaged in no research since receiving my degree. . . . Since 1952 I have

been teaching approximately two-thirds time . . . except for a leave while having my fourth child and a year abroad. . . . In addition, I have occasionally given relief to the regular staff when excessively large enrollments or sabbaticals required such assistance.

Effect of Children on Career

The above comments require no amplification to document the effect of having children on a woman's career. One woman in the Matched Scientists study jotted down on her questionnaire "[having] baby took two years from professional work." Another indicated that it was not the biology but the sociology of the situation that influenced her career:

Combination of a research career with marriage to a fellow researcher, in the absence of children, presented no problems to me in either area. The introduction of children, however, to the situation has made for difficulties in the "career" in that my time for it has been reduced. We are adopting children, and I had no choice but to quit working in order to get the children (agencies won't place with working mothers). I didn't really "quit" but just stopped doing experimental work and earning money; I have, however, kept up with literature and have been writing up work done prior to getting children. As soon as they are in school I'm going back in the laboratory. Combining career and marriage-children requires some compromise in both areas and pulls a woman's energy and thoughts and time in many directions at once. I can speak only from the standpoint of a scientific research career, but wouldn't advise any woman to combine that with marriage unless she had a husband who thoroughly understood the special demands of that career, was in sympathy with them and wanted his wife to pursue them. To be successful at both marriage and career a woman must "choose" her mate carefully! [21]

Statistical findings corroborate the evidence from documents. Among psychologists—almost half of whom, it will be recalled, were probably not academic women—"25 per cent of the mothers report their children as professional assets, and . . . 60 per cent of the mothers report their children as professional liabilities." [22] The attitudes of the women with full-time employment differed from those with less than full-time employment, twice as many of the first category (28.2 percent) as of the second category (14.6 per cent) reporting children as "definitely an asset." Conversely, more than one-third (34.6 percent) of the mothers with less than full-time employment reported that children were the "chief factor in the abandonment of career" as contrasted with only 3.1 percent of those with full-time employment.[23]

The authors of the above report summarize their findings with respect to the effect of marriage and children on men and on women as follows:

> If we compare marriage and children as professional assets and liabilities, we find that marriage and children are about equal as assets for women and as liabilities for men. Marriage (72 percent) is a greater asset for men than are children (29 percent). Children (60 percent) are a greater liability for women than is marriage (34 percent). That all makes sense. The men are helped professionally by the social status of marriage and in that respect a wife is more important than children. . . . It is clear that the careers of women are balked to a considerable degree by the responsibilities of childless marriage and even more by motherhood.[24]

A closer look at the allocation of time among these psychologists helps to explain the effect of children on career. Women averaged 14.1 hours per week on "familial or domestic activities," as compared with 10.6 hours for men.[25] Three or more hours per week were spent on child-training and guidance by 29.4 percent of the women, on physical care of children by 24.5 percent, and on special problems of children by 10.2 percent.[26]

Interpretation of the above findings will vary according to one's point of view. If the observer is interested in the profession, if he is observing the subjects as actual or as potential professionals, then he will tend to take a pity-the-poor-woman-professor point of view and measure her performance as a scientist or professional by certain standards. He will emphasize her disabilities as a woman. If, on the other hand, the observer is interested in marriage, family, and the role of women in our society, he may view her as a working mother and judge her by the effect her work has on her family role performance.[27] Most studies, especially of scientific personnel, tend to be made from the first point of view and hence imply that if women drop out of their professional role, or suspend it temporarily, they are somehow or other deviants; something must be done about it. They are not measuring up to certain standards. The women may see themselves in a quite different light. They are happy to pay the asking price career-wise for the satisfactions derived from children. There is no assumption here that the time and energies of women would always be better spent in the lecture hall or laboratory on campus than in the rearing of children.

Effect of Career on Children

The effect of the work of academic women on their performance as mothers has not been researched in any systematic way, but we do know in general that occupation (as an index of class) is a standard variable in sociological studies of the family and is usually found to be significant. Child-rearing practices, as well as marital stability, have been found to be related to occupation. Even within given class levels, type of occupation—entrepreneurial or bureaucratic—has been reported as significant with respect to child-rearing practices.[28]

The children of professionally involved academic women are subject to the same hazards as are the children of any working mothers, with the addition of a few others peculiar to the academic occupation. Success in an academic career, as noted in Chapter 10, makes inordinate demands on time and energy. The absorption in subject matter which is required of a successful academician is, if not all consuming, at least consuming of enough time, energy, and emotional substance to affect all other relationships. Until the last ten to fifteen years, furthermore, the kind of work which brought recognition had to be done in addition to regular teaching assignments. Being an academic person therefore required enormous preoccupation with professional work for many hours a day, usually at the expense of family contacts.[29] In rapidly growing areas of knowledge, reading alone takes great chunks of time. The professor has to read dozens or scores of periodicals in his own area even if the contents yield no golden nuggets. He has to know what Newman is writing about even if Olds says it is bosh. He has to know what is coming out of the great laboratories at the great universities even though there is little he can use in his own lectures. If, in addition to being a passable teacher, he wishes also to make a contribution to his specialty, an even greater investment of time is required.

It is, understandably, more difficult for the academic woman thus to brush aside her obligations to her family than it is for the academic man. The enormous preoccupation which academic work requires is hard enough for the family to bear when it is the husband and father who is so absorbed. It can be catastrophic when it is the wife and mother. If a man resigns from the world to carry on in the field of his profession, his wife can keep him anchored. It takes two to make a career.

But the academic woman cannot expect the same support. However much understanding her husband may show of the demands on her time and energy, her children, at least when they are small, can hardly be expected to do the same. All the problems of the working mother, therefore, may be present and, in addition, the extra preoccupation even when she is at home.[30] Like many other working mothers, the academic woman is likely to make a special effort to counteract any of the anticipated hazards of her work in relation to her children, sometimes, as in this case, with doubtful success:

> I used to think I was being ingenious when I did much of my professional work at home. At least the children knew I was there. I wasn't off somewhere. But it soon turned out that it was better for me to be physically out of their sight than for me to be there in the flesh at my desk but absorbed in my own thoughts. If I was out of sight, at least I wasn't rejecting them. But if I sat there thinking my own thoughts, shushing them, rather than responding to them, it bothered them. They could take my absence better than they could take that.

There is possibly an additional hazard for the children of academic women related to academic work, namely that of being held to exceptionally high standards of both behavior and intellectual achievement.[31] The behavior of the children of parents in some professions is expected to be better than that of other children. The children of ministers, for example, are often more carefully watched than those of other parents.[32] The children of psychiatrists or of clinical psychologists or professors of child development or of family sociology are similarly exposed to special hazards; they are expected to exemplify their parents' knowledge[33] and intellect. If one's father is a professor, that is hard enough; but if one's mother is, the standards are even higher.

There have been some spectacularly successful mothers among academic women. Millicent MacIntosh and Mary Bunting come immediately to mind. There have, of course, been some equally spectacular failures—delinquency, crime, suicide, emotional disturbance. The question of how these outcomes—successful or unsuccessful—were related to the professions of the mothers has as yet not been studied. Until it is, the effect of academic occupations per se, as contrasted with other kinds, cannot be accurately assessed.

In the absence of systematic research on the children of academic women, the following cases are presented without analysis or probing, and with no estimate of their representativeness.

Child's-Eye View of Academic Women

It's very hard for me to think of my mother as an academic woman. She seems like just a mother to me. Once when I was a little girl I was shagging tennis balls for students on our campus. The students finally asked me what my name was. When I told them, they asked was I Professor Blank's little girl? I smiled disparagingly and shrugged my shoulders, "Oh, you mean mother." As I grew older and people commented on how much my mother had achieved, raising four children, teaching, doing research, and all that, it seemed strange to me that they would think this unusual. That was my idea of what a mother did. She raised children and held down a job. I think it has set a hard pattern for me. I do not have any strong career drives. I want to marry and have children. But I fear that won't be enough for me. I'll feel that I have to have some kind of career, too. You can't just shake off a pattern like that even if you want to.

I learned when I was very young that my mother [a widow] was an absent-minded professor. I always had to check up to see that the electric burner on the kitchen stove was turned off, that she had a key when she left the house so she wouldn't be locked out, that the record player was turned off. I had to know where her glasses were, her brief case, her pile of notes, her textbook. Especially her purse. She was always putting it somewhere and forgetting where. I had to remind her to be sure to cash a check; we were always running out of cash at the most inopportune times. There were some weekends when we actually didn't have enough money to buy food; she had just forgotten to cash a check. I don't know how many bottles of vermouth we accumulated buying just anything in order to have the liquor store cash a check on Saturday. She was greatly distressed by all this and kept complaining that she was surely becoming senile. Since she had always been that way as long back as I could remember, I couldn't see that age had anything to do with it.

My mother was always leaning over backwards to see that we weren't deprived of anything other children had. She kept explaining until we were bored to death with the subject just why she had to work. We couldn't have cared less. It just meant that we had more freedom than other children whose mothers were always butting into our affairs. We were neither especially proud or ashamed to have her teaching at the college. Everyone in that town was connected with the college. If she taught instead of typed or cleaned it didn't seem very important to us. I can't see that her particular position at the college made any difference to us one way or another.

Both my parents taught at the college. I didn't mind the fact that they taught. I just minded being so poor. That I did mind. And if we would have been even poorer without my mother's working, that would have been terrible. She was around about as much as we needed her anyway.

My mother and I are friends in a cold sort of way. I admire her and feel inferior and embarrassed when she visits me and my husband. He comes from a very humble family and he had only two years of college. She tries not to condescend to us but I know she's just being polite. She always manages not to be with us when my husband's mother is here.

My mother [a divorcée] taught at State. I was a campus pet. Everyone made over me. But my mother never had time for me alone. I think she enjoyed the picture she made walking cross campus with me. But it was for the audience's benefit, not mine. Even when we were alone she seemed preoccupied, as though even then she was with her students, not me. When I was tiny there was a periodic crisis when the arrangements for taking care of me hit a snag. She always seemed more concerned about missing her classes than about me. I felt that my relationship to her was more to project an image at the college of a womanly woman than a genuinely mother-child relationship. She was a great success as a faculty member; the students worshipped her. As soon as I was old enough she shipped me off to boarding school. You can supply the rest. I was a problem child. I never finished high school. I married the first chance I got. My mother was shocked. My husband was far beneath her socially. But he's genuine, not a phony in his relationships with other people.

Unmarried Mother

The academic woman is by no means exempt from the crises, or immune to the hazards, which beset Everywoman. Like Maria Sanford of Swarthmore or Mamie Gwinn of Bryn Mawr, she may fall in love with a married man. Her marriage may end in scandalous divorce. Or, like the author of the following document, she may become an unmarried mother.[34]

Dear Dr. Blank:

This is certainly a long overdue letter, but one that I did very much want to write.

I have a little girl who was born on————and is a prize package if there ever was one. She was, of course, my reason for leaving my job and I was extremely sorry to have to leave, because I enjoyed my work very much, and also I much regretted not being able to tell you about my pregnancy at the time. However, as I had tremendous decisions to make during that period and about as much pressure as I could handle emotionally, I felt that it was definitely better not to do so at that time. I went to great lengths to keep the situation from possible discovery by students and townspeople and I certainly hope for the sake of the department that I succeeded. I do feel that my work suffered very little and I have personally felt satisfied and happy about my teaching in general during the fall semester. I hope that I can eventually continue in college teaching because I like it very much.

At this point I am hoping to be able to keep my little girl—if it can possibly be arranged in a manner that will not seriously harm her future development. She is certainly a much loved child. If it does not appear possible, she will be adopted. I will decide by fall and will tell my family at that time. I have felt that in order to make as responsible and realistic a decision as possible I must wait before telling my parents.

In the fall I shall begin teaching in a school for exceptional children. I am looking forward very much to the beginning. I will live in this cooperative community, which I have enjoyed tremendously during the past year, again during the coming year and my child will be cared for during the day by close friends of mine here.

The young man, who came to breakfast with me at your house, is her father and has given as much support—moral and financial—as he could. He wanted you and my parents to know who he was because we felt that you would want to know him. We would have married if our circumstances and feelings had permitted, but unfortunately, it didn't seem at all wise to do so.

At this point I feel that while there has been a tremendous amount of sadness for me, there are no serious psychological scars and there have even been a few very worthwhile outcomes. I look forward as much as ever to the possibility of marriage and a family, but with perhaps more insight in many directions. . . .

I wish you and the department a very pleasant and fruitful year and I hope that if you are ever here you will stop and have dinner and a chat with us.

Sincerely,

The Returnee

Since a considerable amount of hope for increasing the number of college teachers is now invested in the return of trained or trainable women into the profession, it is a matter of interest to know not only how they perform academically in the status of fringe benefits—as evaluated in Chapter 7—but also how their return affects their families. The trials and tribulations of one such woman are described below. The situation she portrays contrasts with that in which, from the outset, the plans for the family include careers for both husband and wife, as illustrated by the documents that follow this one.

I have been a housewife and mother for almost sixteen years. Except for two minor ventures, I have never held a job away from home. When I was a senior in college, I worked as a teaching assistant for a professor of economics. This involved grading papers and doing odd administrative jobs such as keeping records. The year following my graduation from college I was an unpaid intern in the state government. . . . My internship lasted from September, 1946, until the end of the following April when I got married and settled down to being a housewife.

Now, sixteen years later, I am back in college hoping **to get** a graduate degree and go on to a professional career. My decision to do this was a long time in the making and its effects on my personal outlook and on my family are mixed—some good, some not so good, and (probably the most important ones) not yet established. I hope that my present course of action will lead to a productive personal experience that will improve my attitude toward myself, my home, and my family and allow me to have a satisfying life after my children are grown. By acquiring some professional competence and entering a career I hope to avoid some of the pitfalls of the years beyond middle age when the career of parenthood has been exhausted by the passing years.

I have a career-oriented husband. Thus far we have had mutual interest in our children and their upbringing to keep us in contact with each other. But he is very involved in his career and always has been. I assume he always will be. I fear that if I don't have a personal commitment to a career of my own I will become overly dependent on my husband for emotional support after the children leave home. I think we'll be happier together if I am involved in affairs beyond the confining walls of our home.

I was definitely career-oriented when I was young. I had negative reactions to the thought of being tied down to housework. It seemed menial and extremely unrewarding to me. I planned to prepare for a career and, if I got married and had a family, to earn the money to hire a housekeeper. But that isn't the way it worked out. I had not gotten launched on a career by the time I was married, and we started having our family immediately. Our first child was born just thirteen months after we were married. Within six years we had four children. When our first child started to kindergarten I had a twenty-two month old child and infant twins still at home, and there was no time to give thought to a career for many years.

From the time we were married until we came to Kanwisota a year ago, we lived in large metropolitan areas—Washington, D. C., Pasadena, California, and then New York City for ten years. We lived in the suburbs and my husband spent two hours a day commuting to and from work. He was away from home on professional trips much of the time—occasionally for several months at a time. His work took him all over the world. While he was becoming ever more of a cosmopolite, I was becoming more and more parochial. I hated it, but alternatives were non-existent during those years. We didn't have the money to make it possible for me to accompany my husband on his trips.

We had no relatives close by to help care for the children. I was so exhausted at the end of each day that I couldn't read to keep myself abreast of the changing world scene, much less to try to build up professional competence that would give me a lead back into the outside world when my family was older.

During the years when I was confined to home, I tried in many ways to find activities that would give me a sense of creative satisfaction. One year I took a sewing course and spent every spare minute sewing until I hated the sight of the sewing machine. Another year I took a course in folk guitar and spent my spare time singing folk songs to the children. We all enjoyed this, but it wasn't the outlet I needed. One year I baked all of the bread we used. This was time-consuming and made me popular with my family, but it was just another empty diversion. The old-fashioned housewifely tasks aren't practical any longer. They have lost their significance, because they are not important contributions to the welfare of the family.[35]

My family learned to take for granted the extra things that I did around the house for so many years. Ironically, this is a handicap to me now as I try to change my family's image of me so that I will have time to study and prepare for a career.

Several years ago, after my children were all in school and I had peace and quiet for a few hours each day, I started reading again. I quickly deserted fiction and started reading books on education, religion, philosophy, and sociology. Concern with the quality of the education my children were getting caused me to develop an interest in educational philosophy. I took exception to much that my children were getting in school, and I objected to the parochial and outdated religion they were learning in Sunday School. All of this led to more reading as I tried to discover what I did believe in. Each book that I read led to others, and my re-education was underway.

I found great pleasure in my reading, but the time came when I had to face the fact that I didn't want to spend the rest of my life just reading. I wanted to be involved in something, too. My reading had made me aware of the cause of my dissatisfactions, but it didn't solve the problems.

In high school and college I had participated in extra-curricular activities. When my children got into school I was soon doing PTA work, serving on school committees, and having to face the prospect of being a Cub Scout den mother or Brownie Scout leader. I found these civic activities very unrewarding and felt that I would find greater satisfaction in using my time in other ways. This is when I began to think about a career.

Thinking about a career meant doing some soul-searching. Since my marriage I had been pushing aside some of the values that had been important to me when I was younger. When I married I accepted the idea that a woman's place is in the home. I was sufficiently socialized by my upbringing to feel that I should accept the time-honored "womanly virtues" and work at building a home and marriage within that frame of reference. Unfortunately, I didn't feel the way a satisfied housewife should feel, and I didn't have the knowledge to understand the reasons for my dissatisfaction. I resented my lack of freedom, and I thought there was something wrong with me because I did. I didn't enjoy housework. I felt trapped and resentful and blamed my husband for much of it. I was jealous of his freedom. I envied him his trips abroad, and sometimes I wasn't a very good sport about it. I felt that he should be as tied down as I was. Yet my attitude made me feel guilty and selfish.

My initial reaction, when I finally faced my problems, was one of alarm. It was hard to admit that I had doubts about the validity of the values I had been upholding for so many years. However, when I could admit it and was able to recognize that my doubts might have some merit, two things happened to me. First, I felt betrayed—the way a child must feel when he discovers that the lovely myths of childhood aren't really true after all. Then I felt relieved, as though I had just taken off a *very* tight shoe. This has been my re-birth, and it has left me free to plan quite a different future for myself than that which I had originally anticipated.

I feel good about my new image of myself, but it isn't easy to convince my family that the new image is either real or good. They expect many little services that I am no longer willing to perform. I expect greater cooperation in running our household than my family has given in the past. I think that the conflicts will resolve, slowly but surely, without causing anyone undue anguish.

My husband isn't yet convinced that I am wise to want a career—at least yet. He thinks I should wait until the time is more propitious. But the time is never propitious. It's like waiting until you can really afford children. If you do, you find you can never really afford them. He is willing to agree to my career in view of my strong feeling of need for it. But he fears that two careers in the family will have a divisive influence on our home life. He thinks that I should be backing him up rather than seeking a career of my own. I believe that my involvement in the professional world will make us more compatible in years to come. I agree with Kahlil Gibran that a married couple should "drink from each other's cups but not from the same cup."

One further problem confronts me as I look toward a career at my time of life. My knowledge in my original field of interests is very outdated, and pursuit of a career in that field is now impractical. I had once wanted to go into the State Department and have a career in the Foreign Service. But my interests have changed, and, in any case, my family commitments would make this type of career impossible. I can't choose the location of my job. Since I am interested in interpersonal and intergroup relations, I think that I can combine a job in this field with my family responsibilities. Job opportunities in this field, either teaching or research, should be available wherever my husband's job might take us.

It is clear that—as all the research and all the documents demonstrate in vivid detail—the future career of any married academic woman depends very largely on her husband. Whatever plans are made for the recruitment of women—and this would hold for any learned profession—must of necessity include men. The preparation of men is as intrinsic a part of preparation for women's careers as that of the women themselves.

The Wave of the Future: Three Cases

Chapter 1 of this study began with the stories of some academic women in the nineteenth and early twentieth centuries. Chapter 15 now ends with stories of academic women of the present time which illustrate the wave of the future. They show what is possible. They show also how important the preparation of men is for career plans of women. As noted earlier, it takes two to make a career.

To talented young women contemplating the paths open to them, these stories should be revealing. They show how scientists and scholars, working together as a team, can realize the wife's potentialities without sacrifice of the more personal values of the family. History in biographical form is as revealing as it is in statistical form, and far too eloquent to require exegesis.

Scientists

Like many other husband-wife teams in the sciences, Keith and I met in graduate school, took our degrees in the same department and had parallel research interests. Unlike some others we even worked as a team before we were married, so continuing to work together seems the best possible arrangement for us.

Both of us worked in research after college before going on for our advanced degrees and I had done some teaching including a couple of years at Sarah Lawrence. It was almost by accident that I discovered pharmacology since I'd never even heard of it in my undergraduate days. Once introduced to the systematic study of drug effects on the brain, however, I settled down to this investigative field and then went back for my Ph.D. in pharmacology at the University of Illinois Medical School and Graduate Colleges.

Keith and I started working together just before the much publicized "Miltown" hit the market and we started out our research program with a view to uncovering how tranquilizing agents act on the brain. Almost ten years later we are still trying to find out how these drugs alter the mental state—but now of course the field is burgeoning and there are almost too many such drugs even to know all their names. In the course of this investigation we had had to realize we don't really know how the brain works or how it directs behavior so we are also deeply engaged in fundamental neuro-physiological and behavioral studies. . . .

When Keith and I were first married our schedule didn't change much although there was a momentary panic in the department of anatomy at UCLA Medical School because of strict nepotism rules. The final result was that Keith was appointed in pharmacology instead (a not illogical place for a pharmacologist after all) and we went right on working together in the same lab as before. We found ourselves doing the same fifteen hour experiments the same six or seven days a week but without any of the problems our other married friends had seeing their long-suffering spouses. And whenever we could we would be off for a two day breather in the mountains without worrying about out of phase schedules. We didn't really divide up the lab work formally—we just did what came to hand.

Our schedules, or rather my schedule, changed abruptly just about 18 hours before our daughter was born four years ago. Anne Louise was (and is) a charmer. I didn't work officially during her first six months although I often tucked her in her infantseat and took her to lunch at the lab with some visitor I wanted to see. Or after dinner I took her down to the lab and put her to sleep in her carriage while I helped finish up a long experiment. The rest of her first year I worked mornings cleaning up projects for the move to Stanford.

When in 1959 we came to the Stanford Medical School we again had to shift our arrangements. Keith's teaching responsibilities to the medical students, the need to build labs from the bare walls out, and our responsibility for pre- and post-doctoral students meant we couldn't afford the luxury of always working together on experiments. Again I worked half or three quarter time, saving part of each day for Anne Louise.

After Paul was born 18 months ago I managed four months at home and then went back to part-time research. At first it was part of every day but at the moment I spend three full days in the lab and do my reading and paper work at home evenings. This seems a happy arrangement for now—especially since Keith and I usually manage a couple of experiments a week together. We divide up more these days: while he runs the conditional behavior program in the morning I do the surgery for a neurophysiological experiment. In gathering data on drug effects on brain spontaneous and evoked electrical activity we either work together or, more often, relieve one another on and off depending on our other responsibilities for the afternoon. Almost inevitably Keith finishes up while I go home to start the children's baths, supper, etc.

At the moment I'm fortunate in having my mother living in the next town so she supervises the children when I'm at the laboratory and both they and she enjoy it hugely.

What my schedule will be by the time this feature comes out I haven't the least idea. Anne Louise goes to nursery school two mornings now but may 'graduate' to three or four a week in the fall. Paul, in contrast to his sister who spoiled us, is an uppity little character already into everything, so for a few years at least, how this husband-wife team divides up the work will be a continuous variable depending on two delightful little generators of random activity.[36]

Scholars

Both of us are members of the Department of Government at Harvard, although our specialities are somewhat different. Lloyd concentrates on comparative politics, more particularly on the American, British and Indian scenes. I have always been interested in Indian government and history. When Lloyd settled on Western politics as a graduate student, he thought he ought to understand at least one non-Western area, to widen his comparative approach. At this point he met me and his choice of a non-Western area was more or less solved by marriage. I became interested in India partly in consequence of some work with Helen Lynd at Sarah Lawrence on China. That work led to the economics and politics of developing areas, and since China seemed an inconvenient developing area to be interested in—one couldn't visit it—I thought I might study India instead. I have been at it ever since. Lloyd teaches a course on "Bureaucracy in Modern and Developing Societies," and a seminar in "Comparative Administration and Economic Development." I teach a course called "History of Modern India, 1858 to the Present," and another, "American Character and Social Structure," with David Riesman. In addition to that, we teach one course in common, "The Government and Politics of Contemporary India."

Our work is both separate and joint. We teach and write together, and do some things separately. Collaboration took some learning. It is my recollection that our first joint articles produced a good many tears on my part and a lot of set teeth on Lloyd's part. At that time, collaboration in fact took the form of extended mutual criticism sessions, hard on both of us. We were young, had scores of intellectual and stylistic weaknesses, and both felt that our intellectual identity hung on every finely shaped but overdone sentence. Over the years, we have gained confidence, and collaboration now takes the form of long talk-athons in which we discuss the subject, develop new points, downgrade old ones, and sharpen our wits on each other's thought. They are no longer mutual criticism sessions but rather occasions in which one of us is stimulated by what the other has to say.

Over the years—we were married in 1952, in the middle of our graduate school careers—we have developed considerable similarity in intellectual styles, a similarity that has grown gradually. It certainly did not come that way. Lloyd thinks we are rather like doubles partners in tennis, each of whom learns to perfect his own style even as he is becoming familiar with the style of the other, and developing a joint game. As with doubles partners, we go in for a certain amount of specialization within our joint fields. Lloyd is particularly interested in the theory and practice of administration, in political institutions, especially parties, and in a sociological viewpoint. I find that much of my own work has been in history and intellectual history as well as in psychology and literature. While even in these fields we overlap considerably, we can cover more than one person otherwise might, and still preserve a unity of approach. In practice, this means that we have collaborated on a series of articles and are in the process of collaborating on a full book.

As far as teaching is concerned, our joint course like our collaboration in writing grew over time. We thought it very painful the first year. We lacked confidence, as most teachers on their first teaching round are apt to, and were very critical of one another. Each of us claimed he wanted the criticism of the other, and yet it hurt when it came. We learned not to ask for it or give it very frequently, and over time it became less necessary anyway. Another thing we had to learn was how to disagree on a point without bringing out the bullfight instincts in our students. We wanted to be able to disagree, because among other things we needed to, but also it was good for teaching. On the other hand, we did not like the prospect of students gleefully rubbing their hands, saying that the Rudolphs taught a class together and boy, did they fight! About the time that we were teaching our first joint course, both of us were also working with David Riesman in his course on "American Character and Social Structure." He taught us something about "debate" versus "discussion." We found that when the younger staff in his course had a public discourse for the benefit of the students, it really turned out to be a discussion rather than a debate, an occasion for cooperating in some sort of quest for the truth, or at least for the ranges in which truth might be found, rather than an occasion for making debating points. Having a discussion of this sort involves something more than merely the outer tactics of communications. It involves something further, which touches on a more cooperative inner condition of the psyche as well. And this inner condition is something we have tried to develop in our own course and has been strengthened as our confidence in ourselves and in each other has grown. After four years of teaching our course, we feel pretty good about it, feel that we give reasonably good lectures, which are broken up by discussions between us which pretty soon involve the entire class. In consequence, we seem to have high morale and a participative setting, which both of us prefer greatly to impersonal lectures.

I suppose one of the more difficult issues for any husband and wife team, especially where both work in the same field, is the problem of being measured against each other. It is a problem from which both of us have suffered. It was one thing to have Lloyd judged better than myself in some compartment—that both of us could somehow live with. After all, the culture says husbands ought to be "smarter" than their wives. But if the reverse happened, then both of us suffered. I in my confidence that I was a "real woman"—isn't it mannish (and who wants to be mannish) to be better than one's husband in some department?

And what about Lloyd's dignity as a male? Managing this problem was certainly related to our relative self-confidence as independent scholars, and our confidence in each other. Probably it depended more on Lloyd's confidence than on mine. If he had suffered greatly on those occasions when I managed "better," I would have had to make one of two decisions: to let him suffer, which would surely have damaged our marriage, or to quit being good at what I was good at, which would have meant being less myself. As each of us has grown surer of his various competences, (and learned to live with his shortcomings, with which we must after all all learn to live) comparative measuring has bothered us less, although it can still give us pinpricks.

One of the most surprising and satisfying circumstances surrounding our collaboration is that over time, as we have begun to establish a small reputation as a team in our own academic community and to some extent outside it, people have come to accept us as a team. This is true institutionally as well as otherwise. The Ford Foundation gave us a joint research grant in 1956–1957. We received an offer to be directors of the Peace Corps in a major non-Western area—as a team. So what was originally an oddity has come to be accepted.

At home we preserve a certain European tone to the household. Lloyd is not as responsible for household chores as I am, or perhaps even as much as the "usual" American husband might be. The English girl who moved in with us to take care of our new daughter, Jenny, and I manage most of the household. Lloyd does "men's work", moving, heavy gardening, gourmet salads. One major area in which Lloyd participates actively is the raising of daughter Jenny. She gets taken care of much of the day, while we are out, by her nurse, but Lloyd and I always have done all the night care and feeding. When I first had Jenny, he took what we came to call the heroic feeding at two A.M. every morning because I resumed my teaching right after she was born, and needed all my strength for that. When she went on a more regular schedule, we alternated the six A.M. feeding. This not merely as a matter of consideration towards me, but because of what we read in Doctor Spock. He claimed that most young babies, about the time that they started feeling shy of strangers, were apt to treat their father as such. Lloyd was determined this would not happen to him. I might add, that since we are late parents, our enthusiasm for Jenny is such that even if Doctor Spock had not given Lloyd an excuse, we might both pay as much attention to her as we do.

Finally, it seems to me that from what I can see in Academia, there will be many more couples like us coming along over the next ten or twenty years. Graduate students are increasingly marrying girls who are also graduate students, and the attempt to manage some kind of team work increases accordingly. I remember that when I was at Sarah Lawrence, and first becoming interested in Indian studies, I went to speak to Mrs. Gardner Murphy, who had recently returned from a trip to India with her husband. I asked her what kind of advice she might give me in order to speed me on my way as an India specialist. She said, "Think about the kind of man you might marry who would make a career in Indian studies possible." At the time I was outraged at this advice. It seemed totally irrelevant to an Indian career. In retrospect, I see that her remarks had much wisdom— that I have been able to do what I then wanted has depended to a large extent on the fact that I found a husband whose interests are not only compatible with mine, but whose collaboration has made my chosen area of work more satisfying.

Scholar, Mother, and Wife [37]

At this stage in my life, I am in the final throes of my thesis for a Ph.D. in Far Eastern languages and history and will teach a course in Far Eastern history at Wellesley College this fall. Looking back over the years that have brought me this far, I consider that the experience has been very satisfying and, at times, even exhilerating. So many people have asked me, "Haven't your children been neglected?" "Doesn't your work suffer?" "Hasn't your husband objected?" To all of these questions, I think I can answer in all sincerity, "Not at all." In fact, I believe that my children, husband and perhaps even my subject have gained rather than suffered because of my combining a family with a career.

The results, I feel, have benefited everyone involved because they were carried out under a most favorable combination of circumstances and evolved naturally out of my own situation. First of all, I was drawn to a life in the academic community because my husband was in that area. Moreover, preparing for an academic career is not like having a job which has to be carried out at certain specific hours and at one particular place. Its schedule can be molded to the individual's own needs. The flexibility of my schedule was helped along by the fact that my adviser at Harvard and my husband had been able to browbeat the Dean at Radcliffe into allowing me to go to graduate school part-time. Until then, a student had to be full time. That was an enlightening experience for me, because it made me realize that rules in academic institutions could be changed to the individual's own requirements if he went to the top authorities and fought for what he wanted.

The opportunity to go part-time was crucial to my going on to graduate school. It has taken me ten years instead of six or seven to complete my degree. Whereas this length of time might disturb my male colleagues who must worry about supporting a wife and family, it never disturbed me to have to write down "9th year graduate student" on my registration, because I didn't care if I made a living or not (I had a husband to support me) and my attraction to the field was motivated primarily by interest. Fortunately, when I was going to classes we were living in Cambridge, so that I could leave while my children were napping or be away for such short periods they hardly knew that I left. Also I managed to take mostly reading courses (Harvard's branch of the Sarah Lawrence conference system) and seminars. For the latter, I received permission to take journals out of the library and work on them at home, another privilege for which I had to go to the top authorities, but which made it possible for me to do most of my work at home instead of at a stall in the library.

The question which inevitably follows now is, "But how can you work with three children scampering about and clamoring for your attention?" Actually I have no answer to this except to say that with time one adjusts. Somehow, my concentration became so trained that unless the children were pulling one another's hair out, I was oblivious to the commotion. Likewise, my thoughts became accustomed to interruption. Now, I've not only learned to stop writing in the middle of a sentence, but even in the middle of a word without losing trace. In fact, it has become fun to be called away from my typewriter to tie a shoe or give out cookies to the neighborhood children and to return to find "Sally sees Dick, Jane helped Sally," right in the middle of some complicated sentence. After my initial annoyance, I've come to welcome these interruptions. They have taken the tedium out of thesis writing. I look on them as nothing more disturbing than the chiming of our cuckoo clock.

In all honesty, I must admit that I don't keep the household and my work going all on my own. After a few years of experimentation, I have acquired a devoted retinue of helpers. There is Mary, our cleaning lady, who takes four buses to come to our home now that we live in Wellesley and has never failed me unless public transportation stops running. I have a baby sitter, Lowell, who comes for a short time in the late afternoon about four times a week and helps with the dinner and the children's baths. Finally, this year we have Peggy, who comes in every morning for an hour after the whole family leaves for school. She puts the breakfast dishes in the dishwasher, does the beds and the laundry and then disappears. When the children and I return at noon, the house looks as if it never went through the breakfast and rush-to-school hour. That is the worst time of day in our home, but would be no matter what I was doing. Similarly, I have an expert typist who can read the scribbly drafts of my chapters so that I save many hours having to type out final versions. Clearly, our household would not run so efficiently, in fact it would not run at all and my degree would have taken much longer than ten years if it hadn't been for the wherewithal, moral and material help from our parents, and these devoted assistants to help it along.

My biggest helpers, however, have been my children and husband. Strange as it may seem I do not believe I would have gone on further in graduate school if it hadn't been for them. In my opinion, the life of a graduate student, like all work, can at times be wearisome and restricting. After a few hours of reading weighty Chinese documents or writing about the intellectuals in Communist China, the subject of my thesis, I truly welcome the diversion of my children and hope they will interrupt me. As for the impact of my work on them, they seem to be unconcerned. When I told them that I would be teaching next year, they were thrilled at first, but slightly disappointed after they learned I wouldn't be "teaching little kids" as they put it. While they're not too concerned with what I'm doing, how I do it affects them. On a rainy day, when none of his friends are around and his sisters are playing with dolls, my son frequently takes a book to his desk and announces to all that he's doing "research." Also, my oldest daughter learned to write Chinese characters before English words. "They're more fun," she says.

Best of all, my husband has always given me moral support. Outside of the fact that he wants me to do what I enjoy, he has, I believe, more selfish motives. At the time we were married, he was in the midst of preparing for his Ph.D. exams at Harvard. With the pressure on, his every moment, including Saturdays and Sundays, was spent at his books. With me settled in a similar pursuit, he could devote himself to his work, with less qualms of conscience and less complaints on my part. Although the pressure has relaxed, his life of research and teaching is still time consuming and does not shut itself off at 6:00 p.m. Consequently, with such a regime in our house, my similar though far less intense routine, makes life more harmonious. Perhaps even more important, though we are in different fields, he an economist, I an historian, our fields overlap enough so that we are able to add something to each other's work. For example, each of us edits each other's writing. At first, this lead to acrimony. Several times, as I was editing one of his articles, he would stamp out of the house swearing he would never show me any of his work again. However, with time, we figured out a system by which we would write our comments rather than speak them. Ever since we have been able to take each other's suggestions not as personal affronts, but as constructive criticism. I think our work, as well as our relationship, has benefited immeasurably.

As for my own feeling about this life of many hats, I find it extremely enjoyable, but I think it has some short-comings. To do a good job in my field and to give proper care to the affairs of my family, I have had to limit the range of my interests. Paradoxically, the more engrossed I have become in my work, the less time I have had to read books other than those directly related to my study. Hence, when I was recently with a group of my old Sarah Lawrence friends who were discussing J. D. Salinger and referred to several characters expecting me to have an opinion, my admitted ignorance truly shocked them. When they then turned to James Baldwin, they were frankly disturbed to find that my only acquaintance with him had been through the *New York Times* and *Time* magazine. Outside of these publications, my awareness of happenings going on in other fields such as literature, science and psychology has come purely from conversation with others. Furthermore, I have had to refuse to participate actively in certain community activities and the League of Women Voters. Also, I must confess that entertaining for me is more of a chore than a pleasure because I keep thinking of all the time that its preparation takes away from my own work. Still, despite these drawbacks, I have found that the joy of going deeply into a particular area of knowledge, of being able to shed some new light on it, of engaging in the stimulating exchange of ideas with my colleagues, and of experiencing the feeling of accomplishment more than compensates for these shortcomings.

Table 15/1 Average Number of Children of Radcliffe Ph.D.'s by Pattern
of Employment *

Pattern of Employment	Number of Women	Average Number of Children
Full-time	31	.84
Part-time	29	.90
Intermittent	32	1.4
Nonworkers	41	1.7

* Radcliffe College, *Graduate Education for Women: The Radcliffe Ph.D.* (Cambridge: Harvard, 1956), p. 73.

APPENDIX A ❊ ACADEMIC
WOMEN AND THE TRAINING OF
SOCIAL WORKERS

Two distinct strands—one academic and one agency-oriented—can be traced in the history of the training of social workers in the United States. The academic one was "masculine," the agency-oriented one, "feminine." In the second and third decades of the twentieth century the two strands began to come together, as more and more colleges and universities assumed the responsibility for training social workers and as more and more independent professional schools sought academic sponsorship. As late as the 1930's, the importance of academic affiliation was still a matter of discussion,[1] and to this day the relationship between the university and the agency remains an issue among those interested in the professional preparation of social workers.

For centuries, overseeing the poor, administering the poor laws, and operating institutions for dependents, delinquents, and defectives had been the work of men. By the nineteenth century, old methods of alms-giving or institutionalizing were recognized as grossly inadequate. "The nineteenth century had already begun the process of transforming simple relief into 'friendly visiting,' by the experiments of Thomas Chalmers in Glasgow, by the development of the Elberfeld Plan, by the rise of the Charity Organization Society."[2] All these approaches envisioned some sort of treatment or therapy, at least for those who were "worthy."

The actual face-to-face dealing with poor families came, in time, to be done primarily by women. Just as the spread of public school education a generation earlier had opened up the profession of schoolteaching to young women, so the need to minister to the victims of urbanization and industrialization in the middle and end of the nineteenth century opened up the new profession of "social case work" to them.

It was not felt, however, that a great deal of training was actually necessary to prepare them for this work. Until the end of

242

the nineteenth century, therefore, what training there was came in the form of an apprenticeship system. Young women learned in agencies, usually private agencies, on the job. Their teachers were not academic women but social work supervisors or administrators who taught them how to interview applicants for help, how to plan family expenditures, and how to dispense charity if necessary. The programs were quite independent of the colleges and universities. So long as social work consisted primarily of "friendly visiting" or even of "investigation" of the applicant—whether to prevent chiseling, to protect donors from imposition, to separate the worthy from the unworthy, or to supply information for a proper "diagnosis"—this apprenticeship training under gifted masters was adequate.

As urban problems became increasingly complex—with immigration, rural-urban migration, and industrial conflict complicating the already overwhelming problems of industrialization—the apprenticeship system broke down. As the enormous complexity of the social-work function became clearer and clearer, the inadequacy of complete reliance on on-the-job training alone became obvious. Social workers had to be and know more. Efficiency in administering help was, of course, still important, but "misery and its causes" [3] came to be seen as part and parcel of a vastly complex social system and had to be viewed in perspective.

Even when the necessity for formal and systematic training became recognized, such training was still not viewed as an academic function. The pattern that actually developed—unlike that of home economics which almost from the beginning found an academic home in the land-grant colleges—was one of independent professional schools. In the summer of 1898 the New York Charity Organization Society offered the first formal instruction in social work. Sometimes, to be sure, there was academic sponsorship, as when the Boston Training School for Social Workers was founded in 1904 under the auspices of Simmons College and Harvard University. But for the most part the academic ties were slight. The great teachers of social work were not academic women. During the first decade of the century there were important schools of social work in New York City, Chicago, St. Louis, Boston, and Philadelphia. So firmly established was the practice of having independent schools that as late as the 1930's four major schools of social work—New York, Pennsylvania (1908), Jewish (1926), and Atlanta (1920)—were still not affiliated with universities.[4]

The "masculine" strand in the training of social workers was oriented not around the training of "friendly visitors" or case workers, who were women, but of public administrators, especially of institutions, who were men, and of researchers. The prevention of pauperism, punishment of crime, care of delinquents, dependents, and defectives were among the many topics usually covered in courses called Social Science.

As early as 1891, President Andrew D. White of Cornell was arguing that schools of social work, that is, "for the study of the science of charity" then being urged by John Graham Brooks, "can only be made most effective when they are organized in connection with great institutions which bring together the active-minded young men of the country,—the men who are to become the future managers of public institutions, and the future benefactors of humanity." [5] Such schools would amplify the work then being taught under the rubric "Social Science," including American Charities, Charities and Corrections, Dependents, Defectives, and Delinquents, and the like.

A sexual division of labor had thus evolved in the field of social work over the years which was reflected in the training of professional workers. Administrative and policy positions which demanded a broad background in the social sciences were filled by men trained in "Social Science" in the universities; [6] positions which demanded face-to-face confrontation of social worker and family were filled by women trained in the independent professional schools.

In the second decade of the twentieth century the independent professional schools began to merge with academic institutions to form schools (usually graduate) of social work, and more and more academic institutions began to assume responsibility for training social workers.

The story at the University of Chicago illustrates trends both with respect to the independent school and its absorption by a university. The University of Chicago was also the home of two outstanding academic women in the field of social work education, Sophonisba Preston Breckinridge and Edith Abbott.

In 1898, the College of Commerce and Administration of the University of Chicago was organized to prepare practical men for business, consular and foreign commercial service, journalism, public service, and "philanthropic and charitable work." This was the masculine strand, preparing administrators, not case workers.

At about the same time, though, there was developing, as an extension course, the Chicago School of Civics and Philanthropy along the current pattern of independent schools of social work. Edith Abbott directed this school from 1908 until 1920. It had been known as the Chicago Institute of Social Science from 1905 to 1908.

A third stream that was finally to eventuate in a Graduate School of Social Service Administration at Chicago was in the Department of Sociology and Anthropology, where Marion Talbot, assistant professor of sanitary science, was giving the Ellen Richards type of courses—Sanitary Science; House Sanitation; Sanitary Aspects of Water, Food, and Clothing; and The Economy of Living. By 1906, Marion Talbot's courses, though still listed in the Department of Sociology and Anthropology, were given separate listing in a Department of Household Administration. In addition to Miss Talbot, there were now two other women, one of them Sophonisba P. Breckinridge. Among the purposes was the preparation of "social workers in institutions whose activity is largely expressed through household administration" as well as teachers of home economics.

Miss Breckinridge's courses in the Department of Household Administration included Organization of the Retail Market, essentially a consumer economics course but including also "the legal and economic position of women." The State in Relation to the Household was another composite type course which included "the relations between the householder and the public, as represented by federal, state, or municipal authority. The law requiring the head of a family to furnish support, and legislation tending to maintain the unity of the family. . . . Regulations concerning the food supply, the materials used in clothing and funishings, and the structure and care of the building will be studied, in order to formulate the principles upon which a proper degree of individual freedom may be adjusted to the necessary evil of public control." Finally, as though there might be some spot on the social-welfare waterfront not covered by the first two courses, there was one on the Legal and Economic Position of Women, "a study of the status of women with reference to their property; the effect of marriage; their share in the control of the children; their opportunities as wage-earners and producers; their function as householders and consumers."

By 1919, Miss Talbot had six courses and Miss Breckinridge, ten. The course on The State in Relation to the Household had been dropped, but there had been added: Care of Needy Families in Their Homes; Modern Care of Families in Distress; Family Expenditures; Public Aspects of the Household; Child and State; Problems in Household Administration; Modern Methods of Child Care; and Cooperative Buying. Miss Breckinridge was, in fact, more than half of a two-woman department of home economics and school of social work.

The next year the Graduate School of Social Service Administration was organized. It was the successor to the Chicago School of Civics and Philanthropy and also to the Division of Philanthropic Service of the School of Commerce and Administration referred to above. The Chicago School of Civics and Philanthropy, as noted earlier, had begun in 1905 as an extension series, known as the Chicago Institute of Social Science and in 1908 assumed the name of the Chicago Institute of Social Service. It had remained an independent professional school, in the current manner, until 1920. All three units—the Talbot-Breckinridge Department of Household Administration, the School of Commerce and Administration's Division of Philanthropic Service, and the Chicago School of Civics and Philanthropy—combined to form the new Graduate School of Social Service Administration under the deanship of an academic economist, Leon C. Marshall. The staff consisted of eleven men—sociologists, economists, political scientists, jurists—plus Miss Breckinridge and Edith Abbott. The Talbot-Breckinridge Department of Household Administration continued.

In 1923, Edith Abbott, associate professor of social economy, became dean. She inherited a school in which men predominated. There were, for example, two preprofessional courses, both taught by men; sixteen courses in social treatment, seven taught by men and four by women; seven social research courses, one taught by a man and two by women; eight courses in administration, four taught by men, one by a woman; three courses in the history of social work, none taught by men, all by one woman; ten courses in economic relations, eight taught by men, one by a woman. The next year there were still twenty men and only five women on the staff of the new School, not counting summer faculty, fellows, and lecturers.

But by 1925, Miss Abbott had made almost a clean sweep. Fifteen of the men from other departments who had formerly been listed in the School, though still listed, were listed separately. In the staff proper of the new School there were ten women and five men. The three preprofessional courses were taught by two women and one man; the Social Treatment courses were taught by seven women and two men; the four courses in the history of social work were all taught by Miss Abbott. The fifteen courses in administration were still taught predominantly by men, the ratio being five to two; and the ten courses in Medical and Psychiatric Social Work and Adult and Juvenile Delinquency were taught by four men and one woman. In the remaining three areas—social research, community organization, and economic relations—the ratio of men to women was unity. By the time Miss Breckinridge retired, in 1929, the ratio of women to men was almost three to one—twenty-seven women to ten men.

Sophonisba Preston Breckinridge (1866–1948), of the Kentucky Breckinridges, was one of that dauntless generation of women who made women's rights a crusade. She received her undergraduate training at Wellesley, took a doctorate at the University of Chicago in 1901, and a doctorate in jurisprudence in 1904. She was a member of the Kentucky bar. She was a resident of Hull House from 1908 to 1920. She was, as noted above, in the Department of Household Administration from 1902 to 1925 and professor of social economy from 1925 to 1929.

Edith Abbott, ten years younger than Miss Breckinridge, had her undergraduate training at the University of Nebraska, receiving an A.B. in 1901, and her graduate training at Chicago, with a Ph.D. from that University in 1905. She was instructor in political economy at Wellesley for a year (1907–1908) before she became associate director of the Chicago School of Civics. Like Miss Breckinridge, she lived at Hull House from 1908 to 1920, and she returned to live there again from 1949 to 1953. She was a member of the faculty at the University of Chicago for forty years, from 1913 to 1953, and dean of the Graduate School of Social Service Administration for eighteen, from 1924 to 1942.

Both Miss Breckinridge and Miss Abbott were reformers of the nineteenth-century mold with respect to enthusiasm and drive, of the twentieth-century mold in their insistence on careful research preparation. They were feminists—Miss Breckinridge was vice-president of the American Women's Suffrage Association in 1911 —and resented defection of their trainees to marriage. There was so much to be done, so few people prepared to do it, that when their cherished products chose marriage and motherhood, they found it hard to take. These were women in the grand tradition of academic women.

At Bryn Mawr the outstanding academic woman in the field of

social work—or social economy as it was known until 1957, when it became social work and social research—was Susan Kingsbury. The Carola Woeris!offer Graduate Department of Social Economy and Social Research began with and tended to retain an approximately equal number of men and women. The Smith College School of Social Work, organized in 1918 to train psychiatric social workers, partly no doubt because of its emphasis on case work, tended to have a sex ratio slightly in favor of women.

As long as social work was almost synonymous with case work, and as long as case work was predominantly a woman's profession, the "feminine" strand in professional training remained strong. But the depression of the 1930's produced a revolution in the profession as it was then organized. Public welfare administration, which had been in the hands of political hacks—usually men—had a bad odor in the nostrils of the trained professionals, almost all of them in private agencies. But the New Deal programs, designed for a different clientele from that of the old local programs, required a large well-trained staff of administrators. The private agencies were raided, and the profession was almost taken away from women. There was a great influx of men, notably into the administration of programs but also into the schools which trained the personnel. The training of case workers was still for the most part in the hands of women, of community organization workers, in the hands of men. In the 1940's a policy of upgrading the profession was followed by special encouragement and recruiting of men. Little by little the deanships of the great schools were taken over by men.

Even today there is no complete accommodation between "professional education" and "staff development," between the academic institution and the agency staff.

> Social work education is not the exclusive responsibility of the academic schools and departments. . . . Academic social work education is concerned with general approaches to problem-solving. As such, it has to be fundamental and essential, and must leave to practice the development of educational content appropriate for specific practice situations.[7]

It is taken for granted that there should be academic affiliation, but whether social work should be part of a graduate school, part of a liberal arts college, or part of a cluster of professional schools is not a matter of consensus.[8] In any event, close contacts between social work faculties and their colleagues in related fields is advocated.[9]

Staff development is still a job for agencies. "Thus a division of labor should develop between social work practice and social work education which would make it possible for the agencies to build a curriculum for staff development, closely articulated with the basic curriculum of the schools of social work." [10]

The "masculine" component of social work education—inheritor of the old Social Science tradition—is beginning to find powerful advocates. Thus Evaline Burns urges instruction in social policy for those preparing for work in community organization. "Too frequently in the past," she points out, "the teachers of subject matter that is related to social policy have been 'tolerated' as faculty members rather than accepted as an integral part of the social work educational family. Their subject matter has been the marginal claimant on the student's time. They have functioned in an atmosphere where prestige attaches only to practice, conceived of as the mastery of one of three (and often only two) types of method." [11]

Undergraduate departments of social work are likely to be administratively associated with departments of sociology, despite the disdain which many sociologists feel toward these practical courses. In some of the land-grant colleges, the social work courses train many of the public welfare workers whose job it is to determine eligibility rather than to do case work. The sociologists often profess to see little if any relationship between these courses and sociology. Nevertheless a large proportion, usually a large majority, of the undergraduate majors in departments of sociology are young women preparing for social-work jobs, if not careers, in contrast to the graduate students, who are overwhelmingly men. The academic women who teach the social-work courses are not in the same status-system as their male colleagues who teach sociology courses.

The teachers of the undergraduate social-work courses have another problem, another flank to protect. As home economists have widened their horizon and their conception of the role of women, they have come to see the necessity to prepare their students for participation in community programs. Just how their conception fits into the social-work concept of community work has not yet become clear. One solution proposed has been that the home economists should prepare women to serve in voluntary agencies as well-prepared volunteers, whereas the social-work departments should prepare them for graduate work in professional community organization.

Whatever the accommodation between the social-work teachers and the sociologists, this kind of academic woman keeps departments firmly anchored in the here and now and, in the process of supplying much-needed personnel for systems of public welfare, supplies a large proportion of the students for the classes of socologists.

APPENDIX B THE
PENNSYLVANIA STATE
UNIVERSITY STUDIES

Most of the material on which this book is based came from published statistical reports, research monographs, college catalogs,[1] and from the usual standard library sources. In addition, individual cases, either from biographical studies or from documents solicited especially for this study, were drawn upon. The following unpublished studies completed the resources used.

Four studies made at Pennsylvania State University have been useful as rough indexes of the success of academic personnel in role performance. One dealt with English composition, one with mathematics, one with sociology, and one with speech. Several criteria of success were used, including student and colleague ratings in the English composition study, student achievement in the English and the mathematics studies, and student reaction in the sociology and speech studies.

The English Study

This study, consisting of two parts, was only a pilot and was not intended as a definitive contribution. It was undertaken by the Committee on How to Recognize Good Teachers and Measure Teaching Ability, appointed by President Eric Walker in December 1958 and chaired by Otis E. Lancaster, Westinghouse Professor of Engineering Education at Pennsylvania State University.

The first part of this study used student and colleague ratings as criteria.[2] The results are shown in Table B/1. By and large student

251

ratings were higher than colleague ratings for the total number of teachers—eleven out of fifteen. But in the case of the four women teachers, only two were rated higher by students than by colleagues. In the case of three of the four women, however, the validity of at least one of the ratings was low because of the small number of responses. Not much can be learned from these data except that, by and large, the women tended to be in the middle ranks.

The colleague ratings of the four women on the opinionnaire deserve a word of discussion. Because the academic woman is so frequently in the status of a fringe benefit, not really thought of as a member of the department, she is less likely to be known to her associates. In the above colleague ratings, for example, only four of the eleven men were so little known to their colleagues that "insufficient information" was checked in more than ten percent of the possible checks; three of the four women instructors were that little known.[3]

It was also perhaps because of their status as fringe benefits that the women were less highly thought of than the men by their colleagues. Only half as many women as men received the highest colleague ratings; about one-fifth more women than men received poor ratings.[4]

As compared with the men, the women did best on a question of fairness. In answer to the question, "Does he (she) adhere to the principle that rights and rules apply equally to all?" of those who knew the subjects well enough to make a judgment, 40 percent said "almost always" in the case of the women, 33 percent in the case of men. The women made their next best showing on the question: "Does he (she) stimulate students to think, evaluate information, and substantiate conclusions?" Here two-thirds as many women as men received the "almost always" rating. About half as many ratings of the women as of the men, proportionately, were in the "almost always" category for the question: "When you think of this teacher in comparison with others teaching under similar conditions, do you think of him (her), in general, as a good teacher?" With respect to competence, between three and four times as many of the ratings of the men as of the women were high; with respect to interest shown in students as persons—this was surprising—five times as many of the men's as of the women's ratings were high. None of the women's ratings, as contrasted with 17 and 18 percent of those of the men were high in questions dealing with techniques and with communication with students on their own level.

In general, despite the fact that colleague ratings of women tended to be better than student ratings of them, still the colleague ratings tended to be lower for women than for men. This can be explained in part at least by less information on the teaching of the women.

The second part of this English study dealt with student achievement in both a given course and in a subsequent one rather than with either student or colleague ratings. There were only four subjects, however, and only one of these was a woman. Of the four, she was next to the best on both student and faculty ratings. Her students did worst of all on the common examination in the course she taught, but they did next to the best in a subsequent course.

In general, so far as both student and colleague ratings were concerned, the women were judged inferior to the best but superior to the worst teachers. With respect to achievement of students, the woman instructor was the least successful of the four so far as the course she was teaching was concerned, but more successful so far as the achievement of students in a subsequent course was concerned. Neither best nor worst appears to be a fair judgment here.

The Mathematics Study

In this study, the criterion for evaluation of teaching performance was the amount that students learned as measured on final examinations. It was planned originally to measure the relative effectiveness of television and of large and small face-to-face classes, but since 6 of the 23 small classes were taught by women, the general results were applicable to the problem here under consideration, namely a comparison of the relative success of men and women teachers.

All the experimental subjects were engineering students. Most of them were men; sex was controlled by random assignments to sections in a specific mathematics course. All were given a common examination at the end of the term, and all examination papers were graded by a common committee. There was available also an aptitude test score for each subject, based on a college aptitude test taken at admission to the University and presumably a rough measure of student ability to do university work.

The average mathematics grade for the six sections taught by women was 69.7; for the seventeen taught by men, 74.2. A similar result was found when grades were compared on an individual rather than on a grouped or class basis. The average grade for the 124 separate students taught by women was 70.0 and of the 393 individuals taught by men teachers, 72.6. These differences, though statistically significant because of the large number involved, were fairly small.

There was greater variance among the classes taught by men than among those taught by women—59.11 as compared with 34.69. The classes taught by women tended to approach the average. None of their classes did as well as that of the best male teacher (84.6) nor, on the other hand, as poorly as that of the worst male teacher (56.6).

The picture of the women teachers is somewhat less favorable, however, if student aptitude is taken into account. The average aptitude score of the students of the women teachers was 20.4, of the students of the men teachers, 19.3. On the average, the students of the women teachers had done slightly better on the aptitude test at admission than had the students of the men teachers. For all sections, the rank correlation between aptitude scores and achieved scores was 0.13. This figure, however, concealed the existence of two contradictory relationships. For the 17 sections taught by men, the rank correlation between aptitude and achieved scores was 0.33; for the 6 sections taught by women, it was −0.46. The relationship for classes taught by men, although small, was in the expected direction; the sections with good aptitude scores did better than those with poor scores. But for classes taught by women, the relationship was in the opposite direction; the sections with poor aptitude scores did better than those with good predicted scores. Apparently the women worked harder with the poorer sections (as measured by the aptitude score) than they did with the better sections. They were more likely to be patient than stimulating.

If aptitude score is held constant, the bright students of the women (aptitude scores of 20 or more) had lower achievement scores than the bright students of the men; but the less bright students of the women (aptitude scores less than 20.0) tended to average somewhat higher (median 74.2) than the less bright students of the men (median 70.2). Table B/3 summarizes these results.

The conclusion appears to be warranted that as measured by student achievement in tests, the women were about as good on the average as the men teachers; their classes tended to show less variance than those of the men, more nearly approaching the average. The women were not as good as the best nor as poor as the worst of the men teachers. The women tended to be relatively more successful with the less able students, as measured by college aptitude tests, than with the abler ones. They were relatively better than the men with students of average aptitude, but not as good with the superior students.

In all these evaluations it should be borne in mind that there is no record of how many, if any of the women teachers, were in the status of fringe benefits.

The Sociology Study

Success in role performance rests on the responses made by those in complementary roles. People in any role have to "look the part" or "fit the part" in order to perform it well. The brilliant but deformed man has less chance to perform adequately as head of an enterprise than a less able man who looks like the head and therefore calls forth the suitable responses from others. Appearance, accent, and mannerisms all contribute to role performance. This aspect of ability is a purely social phenomenon; it resides not in the individual himself but in the "field" or in the relationship between him and others. This kind of ability is less likely to be present in persons performing in unconventional or nontraditional roles. A woman in the role of professor is in a position usually assigned to men. It is more difficult, therefore, for her to perform well, not because she has less intellectual ability but because it is harder for others to respond to her in the appropriate manner.

The following experiment, not as well designed or controlled as those just reported, nevertheless offers some insights into the role-related handicaps of academic women, especially in controversial areas of knowledge which do not have the weight of established tradition behind them.

Two young people from the speech department at Pennsylvania State University, one a young man and one a young woman, were selected by the department as being of about equal competence in communication skills. They were given two written lectures to deliver to sections of Sociology 1. One lecture was taken from Samuel Lubell's *Future of American Politics,* analyzing the effect of the maturing of the second-generation immigrants in urban environments on political party alignments, especially during the New Deal. The second lecture was taken from Robert Bierstedt's chapter on sex differences in his introductory text. Presumably the first would be a more "masculine" type of subject, the second a more "feminine" one. Both young people were given the lectures in advance, and they agreed on how to interpret all major points in their presentations, which were to be identical. One spoke to each section and a week later each spoke to the other section. There were about seventy-five students in each section.

The question raised was: Do students learn more from one sex than another, holding contents and, hopefully, communication skills constant? Does the sex of the learner make a difference? Does the material dealt with make a difference?

The students were told they were to be examined on the lectures. They were examined very simply. They were asked to write briefly and cogently what they considered to be the major points made by the speaker. The amount of factual information retained by the students seemed to be about the same with both lecturers; neither the sex of the student [5] nor the materials made much difference.

As it turned out, the questions originally asked of the experiment proved to be of less interest than a serendipitous finding, namely the nature of the impact made by the two speakers on the students. The young woman had less impact than the young man. Many more of her listeners gave neutral or impersonal résumés of the talk when tested. The young man evoked much more reaction. About one-fourth of his listeners accused him of prejudice or bias or made other hostile comments; only two percent of the young woman's listeners reacted in this way. There was little if any sex difference among those who gave hostile responses. A tentative conclusion was that whether or not the students learned more from the young man they were at least more emotionally involved in his presentation.

Equally, if not more, interesting was the nature of the neutral responses. Papers were judged to be neutral if they merely reported on the lecture without expressing an attitude toward the speaker. But even among these neutral responses there were interesting differences. Some reported the contents of the lecture with a minimum of interpositions of "he said" or "she pointed out." These were the true neutrals; they apparently accepted the lecture material at face value; these were the facts. The teacher was a tool.

Others, however, reported on what "he said" or what "she stated." They, in effect, were not committing themselves. If you want to know what he, or she, said, they implied, here it is; but I'm not saying that it's true. Fewer of the young man's listeners than of the young woman's hid behind the "he said" dodge. They accepted what he said as fact. This was true of relatively more of the men students than of the women students. The implication is that material presented by a man is more likely to be accepted at face value than material presented by a woman; it seems to have more authority; it is more impressive.

One experiment involving only one man and one woman and two classes is by no means definitive. Replication is certainly called for. But the results are suggestive of a possible handicap faced by the academic woman in performing an academic role.

The Speech Study

Evaluation of courses by the Division of Instructional Services at Pennsylvania State University is available to all departments which request it. The head of the speech department, Robert T. Oliver, asked for such an evaluation of the basic required course in the winter of 1963.[6] Some 911 students in 56 sections were asked to fill in a five-page questionnaire at that time. The first part consisted of a forty-question attitude scale concerning the course as a whole, requesting the student to indicate whether he strongly agreed, agreed, was uncertain, disagreed, or strongly disagreed. The second part—24 questions—dealt with specific teaching activities—group discussions, term projects, and the like—which the students were to rate as extremely valuable, highly valuable, of uncertain value, of slight value, or a waste of time. The remaining questions were more general and are not discussed here. The questionnaire was administered at the end of the course by a person other than the instructor of the class. Since the purpose was not to evaluate individual teachers, no identification was made except for sex. It would be possible, therefore, for a teacher—man or woman—with many sections or students to weight the data by sex either favorably or unfavorably, according to whether or not he or she were a superior or an inferior academic performer. There were 18 men and 12 women involved; 36 of the sections were taught by men, 20 by women.

A composite score was derived for each section; the higher the score the better the student evaluations. These overall scores for the 56 sections are summarized in Table B/4. Unlike the mathematics study, this one showed sections taught by women as somewhat more variable than those taught by men. But the differences between the sections taught by men and by women were slight; the median of the scores for classes taught by men was 8.63, for those taught by women, 8.83.

Results for a sample of specific questions are shown in Table B/5. Again, differences were very small, but they tended to favor the women.

Contrary to popular opinion, more of the students taught by women (24 percent) than of those taught by men (21 percent) agreed or strongly agreed that the teacher graded too severely; more (53 percent) of the women-taught students than of the men-taught (48 percent) disagreed or strongly disagreed. When the question was phrased in reverse form, again more of the women-taught students (87 percent) than of the men-taught (85 percent) disagreed or strongly disagreed with the statement that the grading was too lenient. Not the magnitude of these differences, but their consistency is interesting.

It is interesting to note that more of the women-taught than of the men-taught students gave enthusiastic replies. Almost half (46 percent) of the women-taught students but only about two-fifths (39 percent) of the men-taught vehemently disagreed with the statement that the course was poorly taught; more than one-fourth (27 percent) of the women-taught and slightly less (23 percent) of the men-taught vehemently agreed that the instruction was very good.

Replies evaluating specific teaching techniques again favored the women. For all four of the selected items, more of the women-taught than of the men-taught students found them extremely valuable. For some of them, though, the differences were less than for others. The women-taught students, for example, found the instructor's written comments extremely valuable only 17 percent more often than did the men-taught students. They found the instructor's criticisms of speeches extremely valuable only 21 percent more often than did the men-taught students. Almost one-third more (30 percent) of the women-taught than of the men-taught students found the lectures or lecture-discussions extremely valuable. But 56 percent more of the women-taught (25 percent) than of the men-taught (16 percent) students found conferences with their instructor extremely valuable.

This extraordinary difference persisted even when those who rated their teachers "highly" as well as "extremely" valuable were included. The differences between the women-taught and the men-taught students who said instructor's criticisms of their speeches were highly *or* extremely valuable were practically zero (80 and 79 percent); with respect to written comments, again minor (73 and 71 percent, favoring the men); for lectures or lecture-discussions, small again (53 and 49 percent). But for conferences with instructor, 63 percent of the women-taught students, as contrasted with 51 percent of the men-taught students, reported them as highly valuable or extremely valuable. The implication is very strong that it was in these face-to-face, personal meetings in which the teacher could express interest and concern and tailor his or her contribution to the exact needs of the student that the women were especially strong. Here, rather than in lectures or lecture-discussions, her relative superiority was most apparent.

Table B/1 Evaluation of English Teachers by Faculty and Students

Subject	Student Rating	Faculty Rating		Combined Student and Faculty Rating
		With Opinionnaire	Without Opinionnaire	
1	3.65	4.08*		
2	4.28	3.15	11	7.43
3	3.06	3.29*		
4	3.81	3.21	7	7.02
5	4.04	3.32	6	7.36
6	3.54	3.10	10	6.64
7†	4.00*	3.36	9	
8	4.29	3.74	3	8.03
9	3.91	3.74		7.65
10	4.06	4.28	1‡	8.34
11	3.19	3.47	5	6.66
12†	3.85	3.37		7.22
13	4.13	4.00	2	8.13
14	3.86	3.43	4	7.29
15	3.43	3.19	8	6.62

* Too few responses to make valid rating.
† Women.
‡ Number 1 is the highest rank.

Table B/2 Evaluation of Four English Teachers on Basis of Four Specified Criteria

Instructor Code	Student Rating	Faculty Rating	Common Examination	Subsequent Course
			Criteria	
04	3.8*	3.2	3.2	3.6
06	3.5	3.1	4.5	3.0
10	4.1	4.3	3.5	4.5
12†	3.9	3.4	3.0	3.3

* The larger the rating the higher the evaluation.
† Woman.

Table B/3   Average Achievement Scores of Classes in Mathematics Taught by Men and by Women, by Aptitude*

Aptitude Score	Average Achievement Scores of Classes Taught by Women	Average Achievement Scores of Classes Taught by Men
22.0–22.4	60.1	71.8, 80.0, 82.4, 84.6
21.5–21.9		
21.0–21.4	69.3	72.2
20.5–20.9	67.9	81.5
20.0–20.4		72.6, 74.7, 76.6
19.5–19.9	74.2, 78.1	58.3
19.0–19.4		66.7, 69.5, 78.7
18.5–18.9	68.4	
18.0–18.4		79.0
17.5–17.9		
17.0–17.4		56.6, 85.8
16.5–16.9		70.8

* *Tables B/1, B/2 and B/3* are based on a study by Otis E. Lancaster, The Pennsylvania State University.

Table B/4   Distribution of Overall Attitude Scale Responses for 56 Sections in Speech, by Sex of Teacher

	Men		Women	
Score *	No.	Percent	No.	Percent
7.00–7.49			2	10
7.50–7.99	3	9	1	5
8.00–8.49	9	25	2	10
8.50–8.99	13	36	9	45
9.00–9.49	9	25	5	25
9.50–9.99	2	5	1	5

* The higher the score the better the evaluation.

Table B/5 Distribution of Responses to Selected Questions, by Sex of Teacher

Part I (N=911)

Question	Sex of Instructor	Num-ber	Percent Responses *				
			1	2	3	4	5
Graded too severely	Men	531	06	15	31	38	10
	Women	379	08	16	23	41	12
Poorly taught	Men	526	02	05	09	45	39
	Women	374	03	03	07	41	46
Graded too leniently	Men	529	00	00	15	60	25
	Women	370	00	01	12	58	29
Instruction very good	Men	539	23	46	18	11	02
	Women	351	27	42	17	10	03

Part II (N=911)

Question	Sex of Instructor	Num-ber	Percent Responses *				
Lectures or lecture-discussions	Men	508	13	36	39	10	03
	Women	366	17	36	37	08	01
Instructor's criticism of speeches	Men	528	33	46	14	05	02
	Women	383	40	40	11	08	01
Conferences with instructor	Men	425	16	35	31	14	04
	Women	312	25	38	22	09	06
Instructor's written comments	Men	514	29	44	20	06	01
	Women	364	34	37	20	08	02

* For Part I: 1=strongly agree; 2=agree; 3=uncertain; 4=disagree; 5=strongly disagree. For Part II: 1=extremely valuable; 2=highly valuable; 3=average value; 4=slight value; 5=waste of time.

APPENDIX C ❃ THE MATCHED
SCIENTISTS STUDY[1]

Hypothesis

The Matched Scientists study was based on the hypothesis that the reported productivity of academic women was a function of their disadvantaged position in the communication system of their disciplines, especially so far as personal channels of communication were concerned. That position of scientists in the communication system is an important variable in getting information and in stimulation has been documented in a number of studies.[2]

Variables and Instruments

On the basis of comments made by subjects as reported in the Radcliffe study,[3] a so-called "stag effect" was posited which had the effect of cutting women off from many of such interpersonal sources of communication. It was not hypothesized that there was a deliberate conspiracy on the part of the men to shut women out; it was, however, hypothesized that women would be in less favored positions to have the fruitful contacts and that talk would be more inhibited and "bull sessions" less free whenever women were present. The independent variable, then, was position in the communication system and the dependent variable was productivity. The first was studied by means of a questionnaire based on the one used by Herbert Menzel in his study of Columbia scientists[4] and the second by means of published work.[5]

Design

In designing the project it was important that factors known to be associated with productivity be controlled. These were: (1)

discipline; (2) doctoral university; and (3) institutional affiliation. In addition, of course, length of professional career would have to be held constant.

Discipline was controlled by selecting all subjects from the same field. Since data on scientists are more available than data on other disciplines, a science was selected; and since biology is a favored science for women, it was selected.

Doctoral university and institutional affiliation were controlled by matching. Because the career patterns of men and women are so different, perfect case-by-case matching for all the women proved impossible,[6] but approximately precise matching was achieved.

Length of professional career was controlled by selecting all the subjects from among those who received the doctorate during the same period of years.

Subjects

The subjects, then, included 28 men and 28 women zoologists. They were (1) all the women who received the Ph.D. in zoology during a given period of time who were in academic and related positions ten to fifteen years later and who were willing to cooperate and (2) men matched with respect to the specifications listed above.

Technical Problems of Interpretation of Differences

Because of the design of the project, problems of interpretation of differences were puzzling. Were there any logical tests to apply to them? Did the data conform to the specifications of any tests of significance, parametric or nonparametric?

The women subjects, for example, were not a sample; the men were, but far from a random one. Indeed, the effort to make the sample of men identical to the set of women with respect to four variables known to be related to productivity was deliberate. These circumstances violated the conditions required for most tests of significance.

The solution finally arrived at was to conceive of the women as representing the theoretical norm, since they included the entire number of available subjects, and to interpret the tests as indicating whether or not the men scientists came from this same statistical universe.

As indicated above, however, there were limitations in the selection of the matched men. Thus even the above concept of testing was inadequate. Some of the men were unique, being the only ones who were available who matched the specifications established. But for other cells in the population of women scientists there were several men available. The choice was (informally) random. What the tests say, therefore, is only that if a different selection of men from among the few available had been made, differences of the same magnitude as or larger than those actually found would have had a given probability of occurring. The null hypothesis, thus, was: In a given set of scientists, nearly identical with respect to doctoral university, institutional position, subject, and length of postdoctoral career, academic men do not deviate from the theoretically expected norms (the productivity of academic women) to an extent great enough to warrant concluding that they come from a different productivity universe.

The question still remained of what extent of "difference" was "great enough"? Even very small differences, and hence large probabilities, should probably be viewed as significant. The probability used for rejecting a null hypothesis should be large, perhaps as high as 0.10 or even 0.15. If the probability of getting a certain difference is as large as even one in ten, it should be viewed as significant, given the planned near-identity of the universe with respect to the related variables. A 0.10 level of significance was therefore taken as the standard for accepting or rejecting the null hypothesis.

Nonparametric rather than parametric tests were used because, as the discussion of productivity types in the text suggests, the assumptions basic to most parametric tests did not seem acceptable for the data. In view of the probable presence of several subsets in the distribution, nonparametric tests which did not make any assumptions with respect to distributions seemed more appropriate. Chi square and the Mann-Whitney one-tailed U test seemed most suitable.[7]

Results

Nothing in the findings contravened the following conclusions about scientists with the characteristics of those in this study:

1. There appeared to be a sexual "division of labor" with respect to areas of productivity based, presumably, on interest. Some kinds of publication were favored by men, others by women. In the set of scientists discussed here, publications addressed to publics of several kinds seemed to be the domain of men; those having to do with the work of the laboratory, of women. Articles, "notes" and short articles, and abstracts were contributed by men and women scientists in proportions close enough to conclude that differences were not significant.

2. There appeared to be at least two types or populations with respect to productivity of articles, chapters, and papers some ten to fifteen years after the doctorate, one with a mode of about 0–4 and the other averaging around 16. The first was composed largely of college scientists with, presumably, a major interest in teaching rather than research. The second was composed largely of university scientists. The sex composition of the two populations was similar. Both men and women scientists showed the same double-universe.

3. In general, contrary to findings reported in other studies, the men and women scientists seemed to belong to the same productivity universe so far as articles, chapters, and papers were concerned. When enough factors known to be related to productivity were controlled, apparently, differences in productivity between the sexes were minimized. The importance of institutional position was highlighted by the finding that university women came from a more productive universe than that of college men.

One equivocal result appeared, however. If one is willing to accept the null hypothesis on the basis of probabilities somewhat above 0.05, then the men and women scientists in universities may be thought of as belonging to the same productivity universe. In view, however, of the near-identity of the two sets of subjects with respect to productivity-related variables—along with the consistency if not the size of differences in favor of the men scientists (except with respect to abstracts) and with the results of earlier studies—the null hypothesis was not accepted for these sets of subjects; it was concluded that the university men did not belong to the same productivity universe as that of the women.

Although the relationship between position in the communication system, as revealed by means of a questionnaire, and productivity could not be pinpointed, it was found that the most productive scientists (the men in universities) were in the most favored position with respect to access to scientific information by face-to-face and interpersonal contacts and the women scientists in the colleges in the least favored. In view of the selective processes distributing scientists institutionally, however, as described in Chapter 5, both productivity and position in the communication system are probably related to a common third variable associated with the career choices of the scientists themselves.

Table C/1 Productivity of 1947–48 Recipients of the Doctorate, by Subject*

Subject	No Publications	One or More Titles	One or More Titles Other than Thesis	Average Number Publications	Publications with Single Authors
Chemistry	11	89	87	6.1	17
Biology	14	86	77	5.7	30
Physics	18	82	77	4.9	33
Psychology	23	77	72	5.4	53
Mathematics	32	68	61	4.0	85
Philosophy	37	63	59	2.8	95
English	39	61	57	2.2	97
Education	44	56	51	2.4	80
History	66	34	19	0.5	96

* Bernard Berelson, *Graduate Education in the United States* (New York: McGraw-Hill, 1960), p. 55.

Table C/2 Productivity of Doctorates by Doctoral University*

Doctoral University	Percentage of Recipients Who Published	Average Number of Publications per Recipient
Doctorates from Top Twelve Institutions	77	4.8
Doctorates from Next Ten Institutions	73	4.3
Doctorates from Remaining Institutions	66	3.5

* Berelson, *Graduate Education in the United States*, p. 128.

Table C/3 Number of Authors in Major Learned Journals, 1958, per 100 Faculty members *

Institutional Class	Authorship Rate
The Top Twelve Universities	12.0
The Next Ten Universities	5.5
Other AGS Universities (Plus Others)	5.2
Other Universities	2.5
"Best" Colleges	2.6
"Better" Colleges	0.7
Other Colleges	0.3

* Berelson, *Graduate Education in the United States*, p. 127.

Table C/4 Doctoral University and Institutional Position of Subjects of Present Study

Institutional Position	Doctoral University								Total	
	Top Twelve		Next Ten		AGS and Other		Other			
	Men	Women	Men	Women	Men	Women	Men	Women	Men	Women
Top Twelve	1	1							1	1
Next Ten	1	—	1	1	1	—			3	1
AGS and Other	1		1	1					2	1
Other Universities	4	5	2	2	1	2	2	2	9	11
College	2	2	2		3	4	2	2	9	8
Other*	2	3	1		1	3			4	6
	11	11	7	4	6	9	4	4	28	28

* Includes research laboratories, wildlife stations, museums, and the like. There were no bibliographical data for two of the women scientists in this category.

Table C/5 Acceptance or Rejection Levels of Null Hypothesis with respect to Sexual Differences in Productivity in Three Bibliographical Categories *

Sets of Scientists	Bibliographical Category		
	Articles	"Notes" and Short Articles	Abstracts
Men–Women	Accept H_0, p=.15	Reject H_0, p=.04	Reject H_0, p=.04
University–College	Reject H_0, p=.0005	Reject H_0, p=.03	†
University–Other	Accept H_0, p=.40	Reject H_0, p=.01	Accept H_0, p=.19
University Men–University Women	Reject H_0, p=.07	Reject H_0, p=.07	Accept H_0, p=.23
College Men–College Women	Accept H_0, p=.30	Accept H_0, p=.15	†
Other Men–Other Women	Accept H_0, p=.16	†	†
College Men–University Women	Reject H_0, p=.04	Accept H_0, p=.44	†
University Men–Other Women	Accept H_0, p=.43	†	Reject H_0, p=.06

* Based on Mann-Whitney One-Tailed U Test. Null hypothesis rejected at any level up to and including 0.10. Alternate hypothesis, H_1, always in direction indicated in Table 10/5.

† One set, or both, had fewer than three cases.

APPENDIX D ❋ THE BIOLOGICAL
SCIENCES COMMUNICATION PROJECT
STUDY OF LABORATORY
BIOSCIENTISTS[1]

The Subjects

The presence of two career-types—college and university—in the Matched Scientists study confused the picture. Fortunately a study of 673 laboratory bioscientists, 68 of whom were women, undertaken by the Biological Sciences Communication Project of George Washington University under Dr. Charles W. Shilling,[2] became available to shed some light on communication practices among men and women scientists as related to productivity. These were not primarily academic men and women, although many of the laboratories were in universities. Research and research guidance constituted their major activity; teaching was decidedly secondary.[3]

The 68 women were found in all kinds of laboratories, but more were in the private research institutes than in any other single type—industrial, public or private university, or governmental.

Taken as a whole, they were slightly older than the men (40.4 and 37.1 respectively). They were also somewhat less well trained, fewer having the doctorate. But those who did had received them from universities of the same quality as those from which the men had received theirs. The overall productivity of the women was somewhat less than that of the men, but productivity varied from one category to another (Tables D/1 and D/2).

Informal Communication

One of the most relevant findings, however, had to do with the nature of the communication practices of the men and the women. In line with current interest and concern about informal communication by way of interpersonal contacts and discussion—which, because of the slowness of formal media, must bear the burden of communicating the results of much recent research—the study asked about (1) opportunities for such informal communication, about (2) discussion with colleagues at the home laboratory and at scientific meetings, and about (3) communication networks.

Opportunities for Informal Communication: Laboratory Policy

So far as opportunities for informal communication which depended on laboratory policy were concerned, there was little or no evidence of discrimination against women (Table D/3). The laboratories they were in had about the same policies as other laboratories with respect to payment of expenses to scientific meetings, programs of visiting scientists, use of telephone for long distance calls, restrictions on travel, availability of paid consultants and assistants, and the like. There were differences among laboratories but little if any evidence that women had fewer opportunities provided by laboratories for informal communication than men.

Opportunities for Informal Communication: Self-Initiated

There were differences in opportunities for informal communication which depended on the initiative of the bioscientists themselves (Table D/4A) or on invitation from or election by fellow professionals (Table D/4B). Fewer women, proportionately, belonged to professional societies, and the average number to which they belonged was slightly smaller than that for the men. The proportion of women who went to no professional meetings at all (23 percent) was twice as large as the proportion of men who went to none (11 percent). Those who attended meetings attended fewer on the average. The proportion who visited other laboratories was smaller for women than for men, and the average number of laboratories they visited was smaller as well.

Opportunities for Informal Communications: By Invitation or Election

Women were less likely than men to be invited to participate in situations making for opportunities for informal communication. Fewer women than men—about one-fifth as many—had had temporary appointments away from their own laboratories. Fewer women than men were editors, associate editors, or members of professional panels and committees which would bring them into contact with confreres from other laboratories. As a result of these differences based on invitation or election, the average number of days the women were absent from their office or laboratory on professional work was smaller than in the case of men.

The picture which emerged was one of a more sedentary bioscientist whose face-to-face contacts with bioscientists in other laboratories were more restricted than those of men, not by laboratory policy but by lesser initiative and less frequent invitation or election by others to participate.

Face-to-Face Discussion

Since fewer women than men tended to go to scientific meetings, it was understandable that discussion at meetings of scientific societies was less important as a source of scientific information to them than to men; but discussion at home laboratories with visiting scientists and with laboratory colleagues was just as important to them as to the men (Table D/5). Discussion as a source of research ideas—as distinguished from information—was more important to women than to men. There is an implication here that the uses women made of discussion may have been somewhat different from those men made.

The proportion of women and of men who discussed their work with others and the proportion who belonged to discussion groups were about the same, although the median number of persons with whom the women discussed their recent research was smaller than the number with whom the men did. This seeming greater selectivity on the part of the women might be related to the slight sex differences in discussion as a source of research ideas.

The impression that comes through is that when discussion

opportunities were brought to the women, when they did not have to go out actively to seek them, they availed themselves of the opportunities to about the same extent as the men; when such opportunities required seeking, women were inclined to be less aggressive than the men.

Communication Networks

So far as communication networks were concerned—the systems by which scientists pass on to one another data useful to their research—the women were as active as the men with respect to those which depended on communication by mail, that is, sending reprints or preprints (Table D/6). But, on the receiving end, fewer women than men were on the mailing lists of other bioscientists, and those who were on such lists were on fewer. The impression is one of minimal differences between the sexes. The differences in aggressiveness appeared to be far less with respect to network behavior than with respect to face-to-face discussion. Much of the network communication is by way of mail rather than by direct confrontation as in discussion; here the women did not appear to be at a disadvantage, especially with respect to organized exchange groups.

Results

There was no direct evidence of a relationship between scientific productivity and informal communication practices, but it is interesting to note that "lucky accidents," that is, unexpected and unanticipated learning of research important to one's own work, were reported by slightly more men (24 percent) than women (21 percent). More importantly, none of these "lucky accidents" reported by women came by way of informal discussion, whereas 6.1 percent of those reported by men did. Slightly more women (32 percent) than men (27 percent) reported problems in obtaining scientific information, and of those reporting such problems, the women were far less likely (36 percent) to report successful solutions than the men (66.1 percent).[4] The information problems reported by the women (9 percent) were less likely than those reported by men (13 percent) to be those of delay.[5]

To the extent, as yet indeterminate, that productivity is related to informal communication, the differences in productivity between men and women scientists may be related to differences in communication practices between the sexes. The differences found between university and college scientists in the Matched Scientists study may be related to the greater intellectual isolation of the college scientists. The greater productivity of the university women as compared with the college men may be related to the greater opportunity for informal communication in the university. The greater productivity of the university men as compared with the university women may be related to their greater aggressiveness and initiative in actively seeking opportunities for informal communication.

Implications

It is not implied here that barriers are deliberately erected to discourage initiative among women scientists in actively seeking out opportunities for informal discussion of research with fellow scientists. There is, in fact, a deliberate effort to include women in some programs. Nor is it implied that women are not interested in actively seeking out opportunities for discussing work with fellow scientists. The barriers are doubtless of the subtle kind embedded in the mores which regulate the interpersonal relations between the sexes and still discourage overt aggressiveness in women in initiating contacts with men. Especially in a young, attractive, unmarried scientist, seeking out fellow scientists to discuss research problems might easily be interpreted as "making advances."

Table D/1 Productive Laboratory Bioscientists, by Sex *

Proportion Who Reported They Had:	Men (605)	Women (68)
Given Papers in Last Year	50.7	27
Published Articles	87.3	88
Written Chapters in Books	28.7	23
Written Books	14.5	4
Written Technical Reports	33.9	15

* Jessie Bernard, Charles W. Shilling, and Joe W. Tyson, *Informal Communication among Bioscientists* (Washington: Biological Sciences Communication Project, 1963).

Table D/2 Median Productivity of Laboratory Bioscientists, by Sex *

Median Number of:	By Men †	By Women †
Papers Given in Last Year	.56	.64
Articles	16.3	14.7
Chapters in Books	2.3	2.8
Books	.8	3.5
Technical Reports	4.2	5.0

* Source: See Table D/1.
† Number varies by category.

Table D/3 Opportunities for Informal Communication Related to Laboratory Policy, by Sex

Nature of Opportunity	Men	Women
Have Fellow Workers in Same Specialization	72%	72%
No Restrictions Reported on Use of Telephone for Long Distance Calls	73%	77%
No Restrictions Reported on Travel	21%	44%
Expenses to Conventions Paid Only If Participating	19%	19%
Assistants Available	72%	63%
Paid Consultants Available	20%	18%
Laboratory Had Regular Visiting Lecturers	57%	58%
Working in a Group Project	47%	43%
Median Size of Work Project Group	5	4

Table D/4 Opportunities for Informal Communication Related to Professional Activities and Participation, by Sex

A. *Self-initiated Opportunities*

	Men	Women
Proportion Belonging to Professional Societies	94.3	91
Median Number of Professional Memberships of Those Holding Memberships	3.9	3.6
Proportion Attending Professional Meetings	89.0	77
Median Number of Meetings Attended of those Attending Meetings	2.4	2.1
Proportion Visiting Other Laboratories	72.6	55
Median Number of Laboratories Visited by Those Visiting Other Laboratories	3.1	1.9

B. *Opportunities by Election or Invitation*

	Men	Women
Professional Duties (Member, Officer of Professional Panel, Editor, Associate Editor)	33	23
Proportion Having Temporary Appointments Elsewhere	11	2
Median Number Days Absent from Laboratory on Professional Work of Those Absent for Such Work	13.4	10.6

Table D/5 Informal Communication by Face-to-Face Discussion, by Sex

Form of Discussion	Men	Women
Proportion Who Discuss Work with Others	97.0%	98%
Median Number Persons with Whom Recent Research Discussed	2.3	1.8
Proportion Who Are Members of Discussion Groups	57.5%	57%
Discussion as Prime Source of Recent Research Idea	8.9%	12%
Discussion as Source of Information:		
Discussion with Colleagues in Laboratory	43.3%	46%
Discussion with Visiting Scientists	74.6%	70%
Discussion as Source of Significant Information at Meetings	43.7%	30%
Discussion as Prime Source of Information at Meetings	23.9%	25%
Received Comments on Work at Meetings	46.0%	30%

Table D/6 Communication Networks, by Sex

Nature of Network		Men	Women
Inside Laboratory:	Pass on Information	76.0%	72%
	Receive Information	77.8%	76%
Outside Laboratory:	Pass on Information	33.4%	28%
	Receive Information	38.4%	40%
Inside Laboratory:	Pass on Information	5.1	4.0
	Receive Information	4.6	3.8
Outside Laboratory:	Pass on Information	3.7	4.5
	Receive Information	3.5	3.9
Belong to Preprint or Reprint Exchange Group		5.7%	9%
Median Number Involved		9.2	9.3
Send out Reprints and Preprints:			
Reprints		79.6%	88%
Preprints		3.1%	4
Both		16.2%	——
Have Regular Mailing List		27.8%	24%
Median Number on Mailing List		6.7	5.7
Bioscientists on Regular Mailing Lists		33.7%	22
Median Number of Mailing Lists Bioscientists Are On		5.1	3.6
Network Includes "Greats" of Specialty		91%	92%

NOTES

Prelude

1. Emily James Putnam, *The Lady: Studies of Certain Significant Phases of Her History* (New York: Sturgis & Walter, 1910), p. 71.
2. Mary Beard, *Woman as a Force in History* (New York: Macmillan, 1946), pp. 251–258.
3. Myra Reynolds, *The Learned Lady in England, 1650–1760* (Boston: Houghton Mifflin, 1920), p. 23.
4. *Ibid.*, p. 28.
5. See Chapter 5 for some speculations with respect to these trends.

Chapter 1

1. Mabel Newcomer, *A Century of Higher Education for American Women* (New York: Harper, 1959), pp. 14–15.
2. No original research was done for the seven vignettes presented here. The material on Maria Sanford is from Helen Whitney, *Maria Sanford* (Minneapolis: Univ. of Minnesota Press, 1920).
3. Whitney, *Maria Sanford*, p. 9.
4. *Ibid.*, pp. 204–205.
5. *Ibid.*, p. 297.
6. *Ibid.*, p. iii.
7. Carolyn Louisa Hunt, *The Life of Ellen H. Richards* (Washington: American Home Economics Association, 1958), pp. 1–2.
8. *Ibid.*, p. 35.
9. *Ibid.*, p. 38.
10. *Ibid.*, p. 57.
11. *Ibid.*, p. 68.
12. *Ibid.*, p. 69.
13. *Ibid.*, p. 77.
14. *Ibid.*, p. 91.
15. *Ibid.*, p. 151.
16. *Ibid.*, p. 326.
17. *Ibid.*, p. 171.
18. *Ibid.*
19. *Ibid.*, p. 235.
20. Florence Bluemel, *Florence Sabin, Colorado Woman of the Century* (Boulder: Univ. of Colorado Press, 1959), p. 17.
21. *Ibid.*, p. 23.
22. *Ibid.*, p. 25.
23. *Ibid.*, p. 41.
24. *Ibid.*, p. 43.
25. George Herbert Palmer, *Life of Alice Freeman Palmer* (Boston: Houghton Mifflin, 1924), p. 27.
26. *Ibid.*, p. 45.
27. *Ibid.*, p. 50.

28. *Ibid.*, p. 119.

29. *Ibid.*

30. Edith Finch, *Carey Thomas of Bryn Mawr* (New York: Harper, 1947), p. 1.

31. *Ibid.*, p. 20.

32. *Ibid.*, p. 26.

33. *Ibid.*, p. 29.

34. *Ibid.*, pp. 30–32.

35. *Ibid.*, p. 31.

36. *Ibid.*, p. 57.

37. *Ibid.*, pp. 152–153.

38. Vida Scudder, *On Journey* (New York: Dutton, 1937) p. 19.

39. *Ibid.*, pp. 181–190.

40. *Ibid.*, p. 179.

41. Margaret Mead, ed., *Anthropologist at Work: The Writings of Ruth Benedict* (Boston: Houghton Mifflin, 1959), p. 122.

42. *Ibid.*, p. 129.

43. *Ibid.*, pp. 119–120.

44. *Ibid.*, pp. 138–139.

Chapter 2

1. Office of Education, *Summary Report on Faculty and Other Professional Staff in Institutions of Higher Education, 1959–60*, OE–53014 (Washington: GPO, 1961).

2. Talcott Parsons and Robert F. Bales, *Family, Socialization and Interaction Process* (Glencoe: Free Press, 1955), p. 23.

3. Jessie Bernard and L. L. Bernard, *Origins of American Sociology* (New York: Crowell, 1942), chap. 3; also Jessie Bernard, *Social Problems at Mid-century* (New York: Dryden, 1957), pp. 167–174.

4. Proponents of higher education for women were not necessarily proponents of women's rights, as the story of Ellen Richards illustrates, but many of them, such as Florence Sabin and M. Carey Thomas, were.

5. Florence Converse, *Wellesley College: A Chronicle of the Years 1875–1938* (Wellesley: Hathaway House Bookshop, 1939), p. 87.

6. *Ibid.*, p. 103.

7. Vida Scudder, *A Listener in Babel* (Boston: Houghton Mifflin, 1903), pp. 51–52.

8. *Ibid.*, p. 53.

9. *Ibid.*, pp. 50–51, 57.

10. Henry Noble MacCracken, *The Hickory Limb* (New York: Scribner's, 1950), p. 90.

11. Vida Scudder, *On Journey* (New York: Dutton, 1937), p. 186.

12. The elitist women's colleges—but not the nonelitist ones—rejected the home economics orientation. Wellesley was specific about this: it wanted to conform to the male pattern and therefore opposed the introduction of business and home economics courses. It would take long enough for the women's colleges just to catch up with the European universities in sustaining and fostering creative scholarship for its own sake; they could not take on other responsibilities (Converse, *Wellesley College,* p. 88). Lucy Maynard Salmon, of Vassar, published a book called *Domestic Service* in 1897. It was based on replies to some five thousand questionnaires which she had sent out to both employers and

employees in domestic service. In the best academic tradition and the only important contribution in the field, it was a theoretical rather than a service-oriented study, although it did have reformist implications. It was Miss Salmon, a warm friend of Ellen Richards, who furnished the inspiration for the Euthenics program at Vassar, an elitist women's college version of home economics, with special emphasis on child development. Smith College also inaugurated an institute for the coordination of women's activities which at least recognized some of the problems educated women were going to have to face.

13. Even the establishment of the Carola Woerschaffer Graduate Department of Social Economy rocked the Bryn Mawr faculty; "the schism was wide and perhaps never healed between the new school and the older wholly academic departments" (Edith Finch, *Carey Thomas of Bryn Mawr* [New York: Harper, 1947], p. 255).

14. This change in orientation is credited by one author to the establishment of the nonacademic Merrill-Palmer School in Detroit and the leadership of Edna Noble White. See American Home Economics Association, *Home Economists: Portraits and Brief Biographies of the Men and Women Prominent in the Home Economics Movement in the United States* (Washington: American Home Economics Association, 1929), p. 36.

15. For example: Alice F. Blood, who became director of the School of Household Economics at Simmons College, earned a Ph.D. in physiology at Yale in 1910; Katharine Blunt, who became chairman of the Department of Home Economics at the University of Chicago, had a doctorate from Chicago; Margaret M. Justin, who became dean of home economics at Kansas State Agricultural College in 1923, had a doctor's degree from Yale; Louise Stanley, who taught at the University of Missouri from 1907 to 1923, earned a doctorate at Yale in 1911; and Anna E. Richardson, dean of home economics at Iowa State from 1923 to 1926, had a doctor's degree from the University of Chicago.

16. There was—and still is—a wide separation between academic women in home economics colleges who taught the theoretical aspects of their subject and those who taught the applied. The doctorate has become almost the *sine qua non* for the higher positions.

17. The women's colleges were not supplying many faculty members in the 1950's and 1960's. A study of the undergraduate institutions which contributed college teachers, made by Allan O. Pfhister in 1961, showed that the University of California was at the top of the list of sixteen major college-teacher producing institutions. Sheer size might be invoked to explain the absence of women's colleges from the list except that Oberlin College ranked among the top sixteen.

18. Scudder, *On Journey*, pp. 299–300.

19. Women in the professional schools of social work were now becoming academic women. See Appendix A.

Chapter 3

1. Stanley Budner and John Meyer, "Women Professors," based on data gathered for the Lazarsfeld-Thielens study of the academic mind, to be published in a forthcoming volume.

2. Office of Education, *Total Enrollment in Institutions of Higher Education, First Term, 1959–60* (Washington: GPO, 1962), pp. 4, 5.

3. "Masculine" and "feminine" subjects will be further discussed in later

chapters and in Appendix A. Chapter 5 views subject-matter interests as indexes of "personality"; in Chapter 8 "masculine" and "feminine" teaching areas are examined in functional, as well as personal, terms: that is, an attempt is made to explain why, for example, the social sciences are "masculine" teaching subjects.

4. Total academic enrollments, graduate and undergraduate, are available by sex (Table 4/5). The proportion of women students has fluctuated from almost one-half, after wars, to about one-third.

5. Florence Converse, *Wellesley College: A Chronicle of the Years 1875–1938* (Wellesley: Hathaway House Bookshop, 1939), p. 81. The change in policy was probably functional. Vida Scudder's mother sent her to Smith rather than to Wellesley because she wanted her daughter taught by men as well as by women. Vida Scudder herself felt she got more from her men than from her women professors. See Vida Scudder, *On Journey* (New York: Dutton, 1937).

6. Frances L. Clayton, "A Source for College Faculties," *Pembroke Alumna*, 27 (Oct. 1962), p. 5. The eight colleges studied were Bryn Mawr, Connecticut College For Women, Goucher, Mills, Smith, Sweet Briar, Vassar, and Wellesley.

7. For a sociological discussion of competition, see Jessie Bernard, *American Community Behavior* (New York: Holt, Rinehart & Winston, 1962), chap. 5.

8. There are several other dimensions of competition. It may be crescive or contingent, the first reflecting rates of growth, the second, rivalry. It may be interactional or noninteractional. For a discussion of these dimensions of competition, see Bernard, *American Community Behavior,* chap. 5.

9. Within the institution, autonomous competition may also come into play. This point is discussed in greater detail in Chapter 9.

10. Theodore Caplow and Reece J. McGee, *The Academic Marketplace* (New York: Basic Books, 1958), pp. 160ff.

11. Peter M. Blau, J. W. Gustad, R. Jessor, R. S. Parnes, and R. C. Wilcock, "Occupational Choice: A Conceptual Framework," *Industrial Labor Relations Review*, 9 (1956), pp. 531–543.

12. Maria Sanford's manner of dress was a great handicap to her professionally. It was, as she realized late in life, a mistake. Her disregard for her appearance antagonized many of her students both at Swarthmore and at Minnesota. She would have been more successful as a teacher if she had been more conventional in her dress (Helen Whitney, *Maria Sanford* [Minneapolis: Univ. of Minnesota Press, 1922], pp. 89–90). The subjects of the study of Radcliffe Ph.D.'s gave as one of many reasons for their inferior productivity as compared with men that they had to give more time to their appearance than did the men (Radcliffe College, *Graduate Education for Women: The Radcliffe Ph.D.* [Cambridge: Harvard Univ. Press, 1956]).

13. Caplow and McGee report that compatibility as a criterion is used in inverse ratio to the prestige of the department (*Academic Marketplace*, pp. 160–163.) Home economists, however, include it among their standards for staff: "Certain similarities are essential . . . , including sufficient agreement as to ideals and purposes to work together happily, sympathetically, and effectively for the good of students, the department, and one another" (Gladys Branegan and others, *Home Economics in Higher Education: Criteria for Evaluating Undergraduate Programs* [Washington: American Home Economics Association, 1949], p. 96). Lindsey Harmon, in another context, states that "we have strong evidence from our follow-up studies of the importance of personality traits in on-the-job achievement, and suggestive evidence that our 'academic ladders' over-emphasize verbal abilities to the neglect, perhaps, of some social-emotional qualities that are significant for actual working performance" ("Progress and Potentiality: Career Determiners of High-Level Personnel," a paper given at the Utah Creativity Conference in June, 1962).

14. The dean may have underestimated the tax officers. Prejudice is often more verbal than behavioral, the result rather than the cause of discrimination. Words are often far more frightening than facts. Thomas Mann, in an impressive short story, "Disillusionment," showed how words are often more emotion-arousing than the phenomena they refer to. The description of a fire fills the protagonist with terror; viewing an actual fire leaves him unmoved. In a similar way, the idea of hiring Negroes in a plant may shock the workers, and they vote against it; the actual presence of a Negro worker, introduced without words, may be taken in stride. The idea of a woman tax economist might be rejected by the county tax officers, but the woman economist herself might be accepted without protest.

15. David V. Tiedeman, Robert P. O'Hara, and Esther Matthews, *Position Choices and Careers: Elements of a Theory* (Cambridge: Harvard Graduate School of Education, 1958), p. 119.

16. Margaret Mead, ed., *Anthropologist at Work: The Writings of Ruth Benedict* (Boston: Houghton Mifflin, 1959), p. 119.

17. Milton Eisenhower, president of Johns Hopkins University, has been quoted to the effect that it costs his university some $200,000 to train each full-time professional woman biologist, a figure arrived at, no doubt, by charging her for the cost of training all the women who leave the profession.

18. Dael Wolfle, *America's Resources of Specialized Talent* (New York: Harper, 1954), p. 236.

19. Mead, *Anthropologist at Work,* p. 429.

20. Mary Ellen Chase, *A Goodly Fellowship* (New York: Macmillan, 1939), p. 285.

21. The relative proportion of award-winners to applicants varied from one field to another, however, being higher, for example, in the life sciences and lower in other areas. In the life sciences, 24.4 percent of the awards went to women, whereas only 20.8 percent of the applicants were women. In the physical sciences, 10 percent of the awards went to women, 11.4 percent of the applicants were women. Relative negative disparities occurred in the field of general science, where 15.1 percent of the applicants were women, but only 3.5 percent of the award winners were, and in the area of "selected social sciences," where 6.8 percent of the awards went to women, while 10 percent of the applicants were women. See National Science Foundation, *Women in Scientific Careers* (Washington: GPO, 1961), p. 7.

22. Letter to the author.

23. Even with the careful selection of candidates by the Woodrow Wilson Foundation fellowship program committee, only 13 percent of the women elected between 1953 and 1956 had received the doctorate by 1961; 19 percent of the men had (*Report on Activities, 1957–1961* [Princeton: Woodrow Wilson Found., 1961] p. IV-45). Because of the high attrition rate, the policy of the Foundation has been to recruit most vigorously among male college seniors. "On the other hand, the critical shortage of college teachers is bound to bring about a change in the traditional attitudes towards women professors. The Foundation will therefore continue to encourage women to compete for fellowships and will support outstanding women students in graduate schools" (*Ibid.,* p. IV–43). An attempt is made to hold the proportion of women at about one-fourth. (*Ibid.,* p. IV–7). This is considerably higher than the proportion of Ph.D.'s who are women, which tends to fluctuate around 10 percent.

24. Robert Hampden Knapp and Joseph J. Greenbaum, *The Younger American Scholar: His Collegiate Origins* (Chicago: Univ. of Chicago Press, 1953), p. 72.

25. James A. Davis, *Great Aspirations*, Volume One: *Career Decisions and Educational Plans during College* (Chicago: National Opinion Research Center, 1963), p. 499.

26. Susan B. Riley, "New Sources of College Teachers," *Jour. Amer. Assn. Univ. Women*, 54 (Mar. 1961), p. 133.

27. International Labour Organization, *Problems of Women Non-Manual Workers* (Geneva: Inter. Labour Org., 1959), p. 18.

28. Minnie M. Miller, "Women in University Teaching," *Jour. Amer. Assn. Univ. Women*, 54 (Mar. 1961), p. 153.

29. International Labour Organization, *Women Workers*, p. 18.

30. Susan Riley, for example, in the article cited above, speaks of "the low percentage of women on college faculties." Cora Dubois has asked why there are so few women professors at the best universities ("The Accomplishment and the Challenge," *Jour. Amer. Assn. Univ. Women*, 54 [Oct. 1961], p. 23).

31. "All things being equal, fifty percent of the professors in the total of colleges and universities ought to be women." (Barnaby C. Keeney, president of Brown University, "Women Professors at Brown," *Pembroke Alumna*, 27 [Oct. 1962], p. 8).

32. Denis F. Johnston, *Educational Attainment of Workers, March 1962*, Special Labor Force Report No. 30, United States Department of Labor, Bureau of Labor Statistics (Washington: GPO, 1963), table B.

33. *Ibid.*

34. *Ibid.*

Chapter 4

1. M. Carey Thomas, *Address*, Bryn Mawr College Fiftieth Anniversary (Bryn Mawr: Bryn Mawr College, 1935), p. 50.

2. L. Clark Seelye, *The Early History of Smith College, 1871–1910* (Boston: Houghton Mifflin, 1923), p. 55.

3. *Ibid.*, p. 150.

4. *Ibid.*, p. 54.

5. National Science Foundation, *Women in Scientific Careers* (Washington: GPO, 1961), p. 4.

6. This was the conclusion of a survey by the American Association of State Universities and Land Grant Colleges covering its ninety-four members, published in June, 1961. Other factors operating in favor of the young men were better vacation and school-year earning potential and larger scholarship grants in the fields of athletics and engineering.

7. Paul H. Jacobson, *American Marriage and Divorce* (New York: Rinehart, 1959), p. 80. The corresponding figure for men is 3.4 percent.

8. Paul Heist, "The Motivation of College Women Today: A Closer Look," *Jour. Amer. Assn. Univ. Women*, 55 (Oct. 1962), p. 17. Margaret Mead has some interesting comments to make on the reasons why young women have such a high dropout rate in college; as usual what she has to say is stimulating if not always demonstrable. "The academic world is fundamentally hostile, by tradition, both to those aspects of femininity which involve child bearing and to those aspects of masculinity which involve the use of large muscles and the whole body. . . . The girls must . . . take an interest in intellectual concerns, whose style was set first by monks and now by intellectual men. . . . The teaching, the thought processes, the ethos of the physical sciences [are] more narrowly modeled on the male who is neither interested in his own body nor in human relations. . . . Almost the whole of the intellectual apparatus with which college students are expected to operate was devised by men. . . . To the extent that thought processes depend upon bodily metaphor, the imagery and figures

of speech that are most meaningful for males are opaque and difficult, like a strange tongue, to the girls. For a girl to learn to use any formal symbolic language which has been devised by men, is at least as difficult as for a Japanese to take a classics degree in a western university. . . . So girls find the world of learning, a world almost entirely shaped by men, a difficult one to enter. If they are to succeed they not only must learn to understand the traditional male style, but must also invent their own version of this style without the benefit of a tradition for doing so" ("Gender in the Honors Program," *Newsletter of the Inter-University Committee on the Superior Student*, May, 1961, pp. 2–5).

9. Of female nineteen-year-olds, 21.3 percent married during the year 1948; of twenty-year-olds, 22.6 percent; but of twenty-one-year olds, 30.1 percent (Jacobson, *Marriage and Divorce*, p. 80).

10. *Wall Street Journal*, February 1, 1962.

11. *Ibid.*

12. National Science Foundation, *Education and Employment Specialization in 1962 of June 1951 College Graduates* (Washington: GPO, 1955), p. 6.

13. *Ibid.*

14. Woodrow Wilson Foundation, *Report on Activities, 1957–1961* (Princeton: Woodrow Wilson Found., 1961), p. A–IV–20.

15. *Ibid.*, pp. A–IV–18, 19

16. *Ibid.*, p. A–IV–24. Follow-up study revealed that young women from the smaller colleges were often overwhelmed and discouraged, handicapped by lack of adequate training in working on their own.

17. Bernard Berelson, *Graduate Education in the United States* (New York: McGraw-Hill, 1960), p. 143. Berelson was struck by the lateness of the decision to get the doctorate. "Perhaps the most significant fact about the decision to go on to the doctorate has to do with when it is made. It is made late; only 35 percent by the end of college, 65 percent after that (and most of them only after the Master's). It is made especially late in the humanities and the professional fields." Women are likely to constitute a larger proportion of the Ph.D.'s in the humanities than in other areas, suggesting that they are slower than men in arriving at the decision to get the doctorate.

18. George Leonard Gropper and Robert Fitzpatrick, *Who Goes to Graduate School?* (Pittsburgh: American Institute for Research, 1959), p. 57.

19. Jewel Cardwell Field, "Factors Associated with Graduate School Attendance and Role Definition of the Women Doctoral Candidates at the Pennsylvania State University" (Master's thesis, Pennsylvania State Univ., 1961).

20. Logan Wilson referred to this possibility also in *The Academic Man* (New York: Oxford Univ. Press, 1942), pp. 16–18.

21. Woodrow Wilson Foundation, *Report on Activities, 1957–1961*, pp. A–III–10–11.

22. James A. Davis, *Great Aspirations, Volume One: Career Decisions and Educational Plans during College* (Chicago: National Opinion Research Center, 1963), p. 499. Among the brightest students who were going on for graduate study, only 18 percent of the men but 41 percent of the women did not apply for stipends. Of those who did not apply for stipends, 47 percent of the brightest men were not going on to graduate school for financial reasons, 38 percent of the brightest women (*Ibid.*, pp. 330, 331).

23. *Ibid.*, p. 361. The differences in motivation between men and women in the arts and sciences were greater among the brighter students than among the less bright ones. Thus among those not continuing in graduate study for motivational reasons, the proportion among the less bright women was about twice that among the less bright men; it was more than three times greater for the brightest students (*Ibid.*, p. 358)

24. *Ibid.*, p. 404.

25. The reasons for the rise have been analyzed in detail by Betty Friedan in *The Feminine Mystique* (New York: Norton, 1963). She attributes it to a misapplication of Freud's teachings, disseminated by such books as Lundberg and Farnham's *The Lost Sex*, to the functionalist school of sociology, to miseducation of young women, to exploitative advertisers and mass media, etc.

26. Mabel Newcomer, *A Century of Higher Education for American Women* (New York: Harper, 1959), p. 204. The median age at first marriage for women has been: 1940, 21.5; 1950, 20.1; 1959, 20.2; and, projected for 1980, either 19.5 or 20.4, according to what kinds of assumptions are made (Paul C. Glick, David M. Heer, and John C. Beresford, "Family Formation and Family Composition: Trends and Prospects," in Marvin B. Sussman, *Sourcebook in Marriage and the Family* [Boston: Houghton Mifflin, 1963], p. 37). The existence of large families is attested by the more than doubling of the birthrate of third, fourth, and fifth children between 1940 and 1960. The data for white women are:

	Third Child	Fourth Child	Fifth Child	Child Sixth-Seventh	Eighth and Higher Order
1940	10.5	5.9	3.6	4.1	3.5
1960	22.7	14.1	7.5	6.1	2.8

"Births of 4th and higher orders now represent 30 percent of the total compared with only 21 percent a decade ago" (National Office of Vital Statistics, *Natality, 1960* [Washington: GPO, 1961], pp. 1–6). Between 1950 and 1960, fourth order births increased 58.7 percent, fifth order, 72.9 percent, and sixth-seventh order, 61.7 percent.

27. Lindsey R. Harmon and Herbert Soldz, *Doctorate Production in United States Universities 1920–1962* (Washington: National Academy of Sciences-National Research Council, 1963), p. 53.

28. *New York Times*, January 15, 1961.

29. Wilson, *Academic Man*, p. 16.

30. Bernard Berelson has summarized a number of studies dealing with this point. One study, dated about 1900, reported 70–80 percent of those with Ph.D.'s in college and university posts. In the late 1920's, a study of a sample of doctors from seven major universities showed 70–75 percent. By the 1930's, the proportion was down to 65 percent, and in 1958, a study of all doctorates by the National Research Council found only 60 percent in academic positions. The proportion varied by field. The 1958 study, for example, found that 82 percent of those with doctorates in the humanities were in academic posts but only half that many—41 percent—of those in the physical sciences. Among the social scientists, 67 percent were academicians, among the biologists, 61 percent. (*Graduate Education in the U.S.*, pp. 50–51). About 42 percent of Radcliffe Ph.D.'s were or had been in academic positions (Radcliffe College, *Graduate Education for Women: The Radcliffe Ph.D.* [Cambridge: Harvard Univ. Press, 1956], p. 24).

31. In 1950, 12.6 per cent of employed women were in professional occupations; in 1960, 13.8 per cent were. *Women Workers in 1960*, Women's Bureau Bul. 284 (Washington: GPO, 1962), p. 16.

32. Dael Wolfle, *America's Resources of Specialized Talent* (New York: Harper, 1954).

33. Radcliffe College, *Graduate Education for Women*, p. 53.

34. Wilson, *Academic Man*, pp. 20–22.

35. John Gustad, *The Career Decisions of College Teachers* (Atlanta: Southern Regional Research Board, 1960).

36. Berelson, *Graduate Education in the U.S.*, p. 143.

37. Ruth E. Eckert and J. E. Stecklein, *Job Motivation and Satisfactions of*

College Teachers: A Study of Faculty Members in Minnesota Colleges (Washington: GPO, 1961), pp. 57–58.

38. Field, "Graduate School Attendance and Role Definition," p. 65.

39. *Ibid.* In this set of women, those in the physical sciences anticipated prejudiced discrimination in only slightly larger proportion—81 percent—than did those in the social sciences—79 percent. In education, however, only 17 percent did.

40. A study of 82 women biologists and 40 women chemists found that 10–15 years after receiving their Ph.D.'s, 24 percent of the biologists and 21 percent of the chemists were not listed in *American Men of Science.*

41. Stanley Budner and John Meyer, "Women Professors," based on data gathered for the Lazarsfeld-Thielens study of the academic mind, to be published in a forthcoming volume.

42. "The student bodies on most campuses today represent a relatively new species. . . . Students are different and they are differently related to faculty and administration than they have been in the past. . . . There is increased diversity and increased sophistication in college student bodies which add to the burden of forming adequate relationships on the campus. Relatively few colleges and few college presidents these days make the approach to developing loyalty in students which was so common 30 years ago, simply because student bodies have rejected these more obvious approaches. . . . Student bodies are more splintered in their loyalties than they were in the past. They have retained much more directly their ties with their local communities and with groups outside the college." (W. Max Wise, in Frank C. Abbott, ed., *Faculty-Administration Relationships* [Washington: American Council on Education, 1957], p. 27.)

43. These tension-creating trends, which have transformed or are in process of transforming the academic professions, have been summarized by York Willbern, in Abbott, *Faculty-Administration Relationships*, pp. 59 ff.

44. Daniel J. Boorstin, "Veritas or Mishmash?" *Book Week*, Nov. 3, 1963, p. 24.

Chapter 5

1. In 1954 the number of female full professors on arts and sciences faculties at the top universities was: Berkeley, 19; Chicago, 18; Wisconsin, 6; Columbia, 2; Harvard, 2; Michigan, 2; Johns Hopkins, 1 (Radcliffe College, *Graduate Education for Women: The Radcliffe Ph.D.* [Cambridge: Harvard Univ. Press, 1956]). These figures do not include women on professional school faculties. In 1963, there were 6 women professors on the Harvard faculty (*Washington Post*, Mar. 24, 1963).

2. Subject matter introduces bias. Of the 8,654 employed women on the National Register of Scientific and Technical Personnel in 1956–58 (33 percent of whom had the doctorate), almost half (47.4 percent) were in college or university posts, but the proportion varied with subject matter. Two-thirds of the astronomers were in college or university positions, but only 5.0 percent of the geophysicists (National Science Foundation, *Women in Scientific Careers* [Washington: GPO, 1961], p. 11).

3. Bernard Berelson reported about 60 percent of Ph.D.'s in 1958 were going into academic positions (*Graduate Education in the United States* [New York: McGraw-Hill, 1960], p. 51). In the Radcliffe study, about 42.4 percent of the women went into academic positions.

4. About 40 percent of those in university positions and about 37 percent of those in four-year colleges had the Ph.D. in the late 1950's. Newly appointed personnel were less likely to have the doctorate, 31.4 percent in 1954–55 and as few as 23.8 percent in 1958–59. See National Education Association, *Teacher Supply and Demand* (Washington: NEA, 1959), p. 21. In 1960–61, the proportions ranged from 17.1 percent in geography to 51.9 percent in psychology (Woodrow Wilson Foundation, *Report on Activities, 1957–1961* [Princeton: Woodrow Wilson Found., 1961], p. A-III-18).

5. Logan Wilson, *The Academic Man* (New York: Oxford Univ. Press, 1942), pp. 19–20.

6. George Leonard Gropper and Robert Fitzpatrick, *Who Goes to Graduate School?* (Pittsburgh: American Institute for Research, 1959), p. 38.

7. *Ibid.*, p. 37. See footnote #8.

8. *Ibid.*, p. 40. It should be pointed out here that the analyses Gropper and Fitzpatrick made of their data were designed to highlight a different phenomenon from that discussed here. They compared the proportion of men and women with different class backgrounds who planned to enter graduate work and concluded: "The relationship between father's education and advanced education plans was not significant for females," "the relationship between father's income and advanced education plans was not significant for females," "the influence of family status on the advanced education decision is not as clear cut [as its influence on going to college in the first place]," and "status is related to the men's decision, but not to the women's" (p. 34). These conclusions do not, however, invalidate the conclusion, from the same data, drawn in this chapter.

9. James A. Davis, *Great Aspirations, Volume One: Career Decisions and Educational Plans during College* (Chicago: National Opinion Research Center, 1963), p. 386. The analyses made here are not the same as those made by Davis. As in the Gropper-Fitzpatrick study, socioeconomic status was not related to plans for graduate study among women. The reason the *graduate* school population of women comes largely from high socioeconomic backgrounds lies in the fact that more *undergraduate* women than men tend to come from such backgrounds. Davis found that "among the total groups of whites, 44 percent of the high status students are female in comparison with 35 percent of the low status students. Attrition during college may play a part in this differential, but our guess is that the disproportion is due to the fact that high status families value and can afford higher education for all their children, lower status families value and can afford it for children who 'need it,' more often a son than a daughter" (p. 41).

10. Radcliffe College, *Graduate Education for Women*, p. 95. A study of 440 men and 440 women psychologists who received the Ph.D. between 1921 and 1940 reported the same trends: "The parents of the women, as a group, reached a somewhat higher educational level than did the men's parents. . . . More of the women's fathers are in the professional and managerial classes and fewer engaged in skilled labor than is the case with the men's fathers." (Alice I. Bryan and Edwin G. Boring, "Women in American Psychology: Factors Affecting Their Professional Careers," *American Psychologist*, 2 [Jan. 1947], pp. 5, 6.)

11. Berelson, *Graduate Education in the U.S.*, p. 133. Father's occupation as reported by Berelson was distributed as follows: professional and executive, 27 percent; small business and technical, 21 percent; clerical, sales, service, 21 percent; skilled, 14 percent; unskilled, 6 percent. Father's education: more than

college graduate, 13 percent; college graduate, 13 percent; some college, 12 percent; high school graduate, 17 percent; some high school, 9 percent; less than high school, 32 percent; foreign and other, 4 percent. Berelson comments on the evidence of graduate school as "a giant step in the career mobility of young people from what can fairly be described as lower-middle-class homes" (p. 134). By way of contrast, the Radcliffe study reported that 44 percent of the fathers of graduate students were professional men, 30 percent were in business, and 26 percent in miscellaneous occupations, half in clerical or governmental (p. 95). Granted that it is not valid to compare Radcliffe Ph.D.'s with all Ph.D.'s and that a better comparison would be between Radcliffe and Harvard Ph.D.'s the differences are still impressive.

12. Ruth E. Eckert and John E. Stecklein, *Job Motivations and Satisfactions of College Teachers: A Study of Faculty Members in Minnesota Colleges* (Washington: GPO, 1961), p. 57.

13. These findings are based on a study made by Lindsey Harmon. His overall findings are reported in "The High School Backgrounds of Science Doctorates," *Science*, Mar. 10, 1961. The analysis by sex was made especially for the present study. The college, as well as the high school, superiority in grade-achieving ability is documented in great detail in Davis, *Great Aspirations, Vol. One*, pp. 44, 46, passim.

14. It is an interesting testament to the gallantry of men that measures of intelligence always begin with the assumption that the intelligence of both sexes is, by definition, equal. Tests which result in assigning a higher IQ to one or the other sex are discarded. All tests must end by equating the average IQ of both sexes at 100. Thus tests in which boys tend to be superior must be balanced by tests in which girls tend to excel, and vice versa. Implicit in this policy, however chivalrous in intent, is the unconsciously arrogant assumption that recognition of differences would mitigate against women; women are worthy only as they resemble men. For the necessity of taking sex differences in mental tests into account, see L. J. Terman and Maud A. Merrill, *Measuring Intelligence* (Boston: Houghton Mifflin, 1937).

15. National Science Foundation, *Scientific Careers*, pp. 4–5.

16. Gropper & Fitzpatrick, *Who Goes to Graduate School?*, p. 31.

17. *Ibid.*

18. Davis, *Great Aspirations, Vol. One*, p. 344.

19. "Women appear to be less influenced than men by their high grades in deciding *in favor of* advanced education. But they are more influenced than men by their low grades in deciding against advanced education" (Gropper & Fitzpatrick, *Who Goes to Graduate School?*, p. 57).

20. Stanley Budner and John Meyer, "Women Professors"; Eckert & Stecklein, *Job Motivations of College Teachers*, p. 570.

21. There are still older academicians who bemoan the increased support for graduate study. They look back to the good old days when graduate students paid more of their own way and feel there is something unseemly in the support not only of students themselves but also of their dependents. Not only policies with respect to student support, but other issues also distinguish the academic generations. Many novels of academic life are built around the conflict between the conservative Old Guard and the rebellious Young Turks.

22. Radcliffe College, *Graduate Education for Women*, p. 30.

23. Budner & Meyer, "Women Professors."

24. C. P. Snow, *The Two Cultures and the Scientific Revolution* (New York: Cambridge Univ. Press, 1959).

25. An interview study of 30 humanists and 31 physical scientists at Pennsyl-

vania State University in 1961–62 by Richard A. Rehberg reported that: "Scientists and humanists do not hold negative stereotypes of each other. However, while scientists are confident that they are not viewed negatively by humanists, humanists suspect that they are viewed somewhat negatively by scientists; (2) both conceive of themselves as pursuing similar ends: the acquisition of truth, knowledge, and understanding . . . (3) scientists tended to have significantly more informal contacts with humanists than vice versa and scientists also tended to read a significantly greater number of books related to the humanities than did the humanists read books related to the sciences . . . and, finally, (4) with respect to their orientation to the other profession and disciplines, considerable diversity was found among both scientists and humanists." The author concludes from the last finding that "such diversity warrants the caution that generalized statements about the 'schism' of knowledge and communication between the 'two cultures' are apt to be somewhat tenuous and perhaps misleading" (Abstract from a Master's thesis, Pennsylvania State University, 1962).

26. Adapted from Carl Bereiter and Mervin B. Freedman, "Fields of Study and the People in Them," in Nevitt Sanford, *The American College* (New York: Wiley, 1962), p. 579.

27. Davis, *Great Aspirations, Vol One*, pp. 447 ff.

28. For example, in the six nonprofessional areas which showed more than half of their graduate students to be women, four were unconventional (languages, other humanities, English, and fine arts) and two (biochemistry and microbiology) were conventional. The four graduate subjects which had 42–46 percent women showed three to be unconventional (physiology, sociology, and other social sciences) and only one (biology) to be conventional (Davis, *Great Aspirations, Vol. One*, pp. 429, 523).

29. Anne Roe, *A Psychological Study of Eminent Psychologists and Anthropologists, and a Comparison with Biological and Physical Scientists* Psychological Monographs No. 352 (Washington: American Psychological Association, 1953).

30. "What is more impressive in Roe's findings . . . is the ubiquity of the contrast between a concern with people and a concern with things. It appears in the scientists' recollections of childhood and adolescence and in their adult social lives. It also appears in their Rorschach test responses. The social scientists report many more human figures than do the natural scientists, who on the other hand report more abstract patterns. Evidence of a lack of close interpersonal relationships in the lives of natural scientists was also given in a projective test study by Clifford (1958); and evidence for the lesser sociability in childhood of natural scientists is provided in Terman's longitudinal data (1954). There seems to be here a very clear-cut example of a difference in choice of fields of study reflecting a more basic and pervasive difference in way of life" (Bereiter & Freedman in Sanford, *American College*, p. 579). "All biologists are more like other biologists than they are like physicists or social scientists. [But] the anatomists are generally the least intellectually controlled; the physiologists seem to show more free anxiety and more concern with immediate personal problems than do the others. The botanists appear to be a generally rather well adjusted group, and rather placid, with no particular deviant tendencies. The geneticists are a more colorful group than the others, with somewhat more emotional dominance, but this is of a sort different from that shown by the anatomists" (Anne Roe, *Psychology of Occupations* [New York: Wiley, 1956], p. 218). There will be more about anatomists in Chapter 8. "If we examine the persons in experimental and physiological psychology as a group we find that they were considerably less attracted by opportunities for working with individuals or groups, and for the application of psychological techniques than were other psychologists, but were somewhat more influenced

by hearing or reading about research in this field. Clinical psychologists reverse this picture, being attracted to psychology less by research reports than by prospects for working with individuals or understanding themselves. . . . There are very marked differences in preferences for activities among the various psychological specialties. . . . The largest differences occur on the 'Helping Individuals' scale, with the clinical psychologists getting very high scores, with persons in general, experimental, and physiological psychology getting very low scores." (Kenneth E. Clark, *America's Psychologists: A Survey of a Growing Profession* [Washington: American Psychological Association, 1957], pp. 149–153). Clinical psychology is a preferred subspecialty of women. Differences in religious background were also noted among the different psychological specialists.

31. Concern for people as contrasted with concern for things has also been found to be related to signs of psychological disturbance, unconventionality, and awareness of psychological problems (Bereiter & Freedman, in Sanford, *American College*, p. 579).

32. Evelyn Goodenough Pitcher has summarized her work on children in the March 1963 issue of the *Atlantic Monthly*. Using games, picture drawings, and stories, she found that as early as the age of two, sex differences were pronounced, the girls already showing greater interest in people and the boys in things. Although she found parents emphasizing these differences, she recognizes that it is impossible to determine the extent to which the differences are cultural and genetic.

33. Lindsey Harmon, *Science*, Mar. 10, 1961.

34. See Chapter 4.

35. See Chapter 4.

36. Gropper and Fitzpatrick, *Who Goes to Graduate School?*

37. Interest as manifested in area of specialization for advanced degrees does not always reflect the subjects women will be teaching. That is, the areas in which academic women have contributed most significantly as teachers do not necessarily correspond with the areas in which they achieve degrees, for reasons to be discussed in greater detail in Chapter 8.

Chapter 6

1. Office of Education, *Opening (Fall) Enrollment in Higher Education: Institutional Data* (Washington: GPO, 1961), p. 3.

2. Differences in geographic location often involve other differences. As Riesman and Jencks have noted, "colleges in Massachusetts and California are nearly as different as the climate, geography, economics, and politics of the two states" ("Viability of the American College," in Nevitt Sanford, *The American College* [New York: Wiley, 1962], p. 159). Geographic location is also related to prestige. When, for example, in the 1920's, a young man was called to head a department in a middle western university, he wondered if he could afford to leave his position in a women's college in the East for an "inferior" academic position in the Midwest.

3. Logan Wilson, for example, was interested in "the mode of organization found in the central or major universities" such as Harvard, Chicago, Columbia, Yale, California, Wisconsin, and others that rank high (*The Academic Man* [New York: Oxford Univ. Press, 1942], p. 7). Theodore Caplow and R. G. McGee limited their researches to a similarly elitist set of institutions and warned their readers not to forget that their "sample includes only liberal arts

departments in major American universities. The universe of higher education is far wider than this" and that therefore "the title of this volume . . . is something of an exaggeration. We are dealing only with one row of booths in the academic marketplace, although, by nearly general consent, the most important" (*The Academic Marketplace* [New York: Basic Books, 1958], p. 17). Bernard Berelson was also preoccupied with the top-ranking universities (*Graduate Education in the United States* [New York: McGraw-Hill, 1960]).

4. Office of Education, *Statistics of Higher Education 1955–56; Faculty, Students, and Degrees* (Washington: GPO, 1958), pp. 39–40. These computations were based on the number of different individuals involved, not on full-time equivalents.

5. Stanley Budner and John Meyer, "Women Professors," pp. 10–11. A study of 262 sociologists—37 of whom were women—achieving the doctorate in the years 1946 to 1949, inclusive, reported the same situation. The women were not attached to the major universities in proportion to their numbers (Nicholas Babchuk and Alan P. Bates, "Professor or Producer: The Two Faces of Academic Man," *Social Forces*, 40 [May 1962], pp. 341–348).

6. "Certainly the better schools attract the better students (who then get to associate with a better group of students, for the stimulation and instruction that in itself provides) so their products should be better by that fact alone, even if their training were equivalent. At least this much can be said, I think: the better institutions get better students to start with, so that they are far ahead in turning out a superior product" (Berelson, *Graduate Education in the U.S.*, p. 125).

7. *Ibid.*, pp. 109, 110-113.

7a. Caplow & McGee, *Academic Marketplace*, p. 225.

7b. Berelson, *Graduate Education in the U.S.*, p. 125.

8. Even for men, the Wilson-Caplow-Berelson principle is far from accurate in detail. Many graduate students are remarkably naive. Their image of the status system among graduate schools is vague. They know that some rate higher than others, but often the department where a favorite professor secured his degree gets weighted disproportionately. Since the relative status position of departments varies from time to time, ratings may become obsolete. Thus students may be judging departments in terms of status ratings of a decade earlier rather than in terms of current position.

9. Berelson, *Graduate Education in the U.S.*, pp. 109 ff. At the Top Twelve, in 1958–59, 337 Ph.D.'s were awarded to women and 2,965 to men; at the Next Ten, the numbers were 204 and 1,607 respectively.

10. James A. Davis reported that 29 percent of women graduate students in liberal arts were married (*Stipends and Spouses* [Chicago: Univ. of Chicago Press, 1962], p. 175).

11. The best universities might be attracting more married students. In a set of 14 married zoologists who had received the doctor's degree at the Top Twelve, 9 were married at the time they secured the degree and one was married the same year. In a set of 5 married chemists who had received their degrees at the Top Twelve, 2 were married at the time of receiving the degree and one was married in the same year.

12. Dropouts were defined as all those who were not listed in *American Men of Science* (1960) and for whom no information was available from the alumni office of their university or from their last address. In the case of men they were often foreign scientists who had apparently returned home after securing their degrees.

13. The overall proportion of those in college positions as reported by Berelson was about 20 percent (*Graduate Education in the U.S.*, p. 52).

14. In 1935, M. Carey Thomas pointed out that "men professors who fill most of the important teaching positions in graduate schools seldom if ever recommend women scholars unless they are specifically told that a woman and not a man is wanted" (*Address,* Bryn Mawr College Fiftieth Anniversary [Bryn Mawr: Bryn Mawr College, 1935], pp. 54–55).

15. To those oriented toward the elitist institutions it seems incredible that anyone might prefer some position other than one in the "major league" universities. One can almost hear the contempt in the Budner-Meyer statement that it is difficult to determine how much discrimination there is in the hiring of women and hence in their institutional distribution "in view of the lower qualifications of the women and the possibility that they may *want* [emphasis the authors'] to teach at the kinds of schools which are willing to hire them" ("Women Professors," pp. 10–11).

16. Vida Scudder, *On Journey* (New York: Dutton, 1937), pp. 179–180.

17. Mary Ellen Chase, *A Goodly Fellowship* (New York: Macmillan, 1939).

18. Riesman and Jencks have commented on the crisis in women's colleges: "It may be hard for the best women's colleges to maintain their present enviable standards of academic instruction, particularly as the ablest Ph.D.'s increasingly want to teach in the big universities and don't need to begin their careers as talented teachers of girls. Thus the long-run future of the separate women's colleges, especially outside the Catholic fold, or possibly even within it, appears as unpromising as that of the colleges set up initially for other disadvantaged groups" (Sanford, *American College,* p. 97). This conclusion also reflects the elitist bias.

19. Compare with Caplow & McGee, *Academic Marketplace,* p. 74.

20. Henry Noble MacCracken, *The Hickory Limb* (New York: Scribner's, 1950), p. 70.

21. Caplow & McGee, *Academic Marketplace,* pp. 54–55.

22. Ruth E. Eckert and John E. Stecklein, *Job Motivations and Satisfactions of College Teachers: A Study of Faculty Members in Minnesota Colleges* (Washington: GPO, 1961), p. 57.

23. Caplow & McGee, *Academic Marketplace,* p. 53. Berelson also comments on this point.

Chapter 7

1. Budner and Meyer reported almost half (49 percent) of the women in their sample of social scientists were in women's colleges. See "Women Professors," p. 8.

2. "Shortages and Projected Needs in Important Areas of Home Economics," *Jour. Home Economics,* 51 (June 1959), p. 416. Academic women constitute a very small proportion of the home economics profession. In 1955, for example, only 3,443 out of 63,927, or about 5.4 percent, of professionally employed home economists were college teachers, administrators, or research workers, and of course not all of them were women. See Josephine Hemphill, "Home Economics Unlimited," *Jour. Home Economics,* 47 (Nov. 1955), p. 655.

2a. A study of the undergraduate background of those securing the Ph.D. degree in home economics 1936–50 shows a large number from the less prestigious institutions. Since 1946, the median time lapse between the baccalaureate and the doctorate has been longer for home economics students than for all doctors. See National Academy of Sciences, *Baccalaureate Origins of Doctorates in the*

Arts, Humanities, and Social Sciences Awarded in the United States, 1936–1950 (Washington: National Research Council, 1956), tables 6 and 10.

3. As noted in Chapter 5, social scientists tend to be more liberal politically than physical scientists.

4. When the elitist women's colleges did make a bow in the direction of home economics aims, it came in a modified form. Vassar was giving courses on the application of chemistry to food and sanitation in the first decade of the century, and its Euthenics program of the 1930's was an elitist version of trends then current in home economics colleges, especially its emphasis on child development.

5. Indeed, the vocational aspect of work in colleges of home economics sometimes runs away with the whole enterprise. Thus some nine faculties with fewer than two members were, in the fall of 1959, preparing students for professional employment in as many as four vocations; seventeen others, with two or three members, prepared students for as many as five vocations. The best faculties, of course, were large enough—thirty-four or more members—to prepare students for as many as eight vocations. See Office of Education, *Home Economics in Degree-Granting Institutions 1959–1960* (Washington: GPO, 1960), p. 31.

6. Howard S. Becker and others, *Boys in White* (Chicago: Univ. of Chicago Press, 1962).

7. At Pennsylvania State University, which boasts one of the best of the colleges of home economics, in 1960, 73 percent of the staff in child development and family relations had doctor's degrees, primarily in psychology and sociology; 70 percent of the staff in foods and nutrition and 60 percent of those in home economics education had doctorates, but in the more applied areas, less than half did.

8. In February, 1951, an exploratory conference was called by the Home Economics Education Service of the United States Office of Education to consider such problems and plans for solving them. The conference, attended by twenty-one representatives from fourteen universities, discussed, among other related topics, policies governing doctoral programs in home economics education. At that time fourteen institutions were offering the doctorate and three more were planning to do so in the near future.

.9. "Degrees in Home Economics," *School Life*, Oct, 1961, p. 26. The major degree-awarding university in home economics in 1959 was Columbia Teachers College, granting 15 in that year. Pennsylvania State University was next with 10, followed, in order, by: Michigan State, 9; Cornell, 8; Florida State, 5; Wisconsin, 4; Minnesota, 3; Texas Woman's University, 3; New York University, 3; Ohio State, 3; Purdue, 2; Iowa State, 2; University of Iowa, 2; and Syracuse, California (Berkeley), and Oregon State, each 1.

10. These are the areas in which doctoral programs in the college of home economics at Pennsylvania State University are offered. The "general home economics" program is designed "for teachers in secondary schools or small colleges," among others.

11. Office of Education, *Titles of Completed Theses in Home Economics and Related Fields in Colleges and Universities of the United States, 1959–60* (Washington: GPO, 1960).

12. One notable tenure case of the American Association of University Professors had to do with gaining tenure rights for a number of women who had been blanketed into a university faculty during the war as an emergency measure. They were former high school teachers. On the face of it, they might have appeared to be in fringe benefit status. Actually they were professionals so far as commitment was concerned.

13. Women constitute about 6 percent of the scientists in the National Regis-

ter but 12.3 percent of scientists not employed full time (National Science Foundation, *American Science Manpower, 1956–58* [Washington: GPO, 1961], p. 88).

14. For example: "Mary came to our town as a bride. She had had a successful career in industry. She was immediately recruited for community activities. After a year or so she decided they were not enough of a challenge. If she were going to invest so much of herself in outside activities, she wanted to be doing something more interesting. She went back to graduate school and got a doctorate. She was immediately hired as an instructor." This particular academic woman ended up as a professional.

15. The situation is by no means clarified by the fact that there are several patterns of academic participation by women in fringe benefit status. The Radcliffe study distinguished two: one they called the part-time worker and one the intermittent worker. Most of the part-time workers—19 out of 29—were married to academic men, as contrasted with only 7 of the 31 full-time married workers (Radcliffe College, *Graduate Education for Women: The Radcliffe Ph.D.* [Cambridge: Harvard Univ. Press, 1956], p. 63). But the same woman may be in both categories at different times. She may work only part time when her children are small; she may later work full time for a term or two; she may then, finally accept full-time work on a more-or-less permanent basis.

16. Some women in the status of fringe benefits belong to the category which Berelson calls ABD—"all-but-dissertation"—people (Bernard Berelson, *Graduate Education in the United States* [New York: McGraw-Hill, 1960], p. 171). He estimates that there are more than 10,000 ABD's who intend to secure the degree and about 3,300 who do not. The ABD's are a greater problem to social science faculties (40 percent) than to science and engineering faculties (15 percent).

17. Budner and Meyer suggest a possible, if not very feasible, index of commitment in their concepts of *permissiveness, vulnerability,* and *apprehensiveness.* In general, commitment would be measured in terms of permissiveness toward political deviants and deviant ideas, and the vulnerability which often accompanies such permissiveness, with consequent apprehensiveness. The implication in the present context, is that social science professionals *care* more, political ideologies *mean* more to them. It is an interesting idea.

18. Reference is made to the Radcliffe study referred to above which reported that 19 out of 29 part-time workers were married to academic men.

19. George H. Huff, reported in Eleanor F. Dolan and Margaret P. Davis, "Antinepotism Rules in American Colleges and Universities: Their Effect on the Faculty Employment of Women," *Educational Record,* Oct. 1960, pp. 285–295.

20. *Personnel Practices in Colleges and Universities* (Champaign: College and University Personnel Association, 1958), cited *ibid.*

21. Dolan & Davis, *Educational Record,* Oct. 1960, pp. 285–295.

22. *Ibid.*

23. *Ibid.,* p. 293.

24. *Ibid.*

25. The effect of career on family is discussed in Chapter 15.

26. These points are discussed in the Radcliffe study, pp. 73–74.

27. See Chapter 12 for further discussion of status inconsistency in academia.

28. Margaret Mead, ed., *Anthropologist at Work: The Writings of Ruth Benedict* (Boston: Houghton Mifflin, 1959), pp. 342–343.

29. *Ibid.,* p. 347.

30. This difference was not noted in a smaller set of chemists.

31. This difference was not noted among the chemists; about the same proportion—54 percent and 57 percent—received their doctorates at the Top Twelve.

32. This difference was not noted among the chemists; about the same number of professional memberships were reported for both academic and nonacademic women, 1.6 and 1.7 respectively.

33. This difference *was* noted among the chemists; half of the nonacademic women were married, but only 15 percent of the academic women. They were probably in nonacademic positions because they were married rather than the other way round.

34. Of all women in colleges, three were married. One was a Negro scientist and not included in the analysis here. The other two taught in junior colleges and belonged to the mixed-career category.

Chapter 8

1. It is becoming difficult for all these services to be performed by the same institutions. Students get in the way. There is beginning to develop a new kind of institution, such as the institutes at Princeton and at Stanford, in which scholars and scientists can think without distraction.

2. From the point of view of the student, in addition to offering teaching and training, universities and colleges confer the status symbol required for success, the academic degree; they serve as channels of upward social mobility and allocate talent to the several areas of learning by offering a wide choice of alternative careers. Much as some might deplore the fact, the modern academic institution serves also as a mating agency.

3. Office of Education, *Summary Report on Faculty and Other Professional Staff in Institutions of Higher Education, 1959–60* (Washington: GPO, 1961), table 3.

4. Franz Adler, "Toward a Sociology of Creative Behavior," p. 6.

5. *Ibid.*, p. 10. It would take us too far afield to relate in detail the comparative success of women as scholars in the Middle Ages and Renaissance to the above analysis. Reference is only made to the idea that where the major function of the man-of-knowledge is primarily one of conserving and transmitting knowledge, as in the case of sacred knowledge, women can perform well if they wish to. There is no problem of innovation, no problem of convincing reluctant colleagues, no problem of application. Such a conserving and transmitting function, characteristic of the monasteries and convents of the Middle Ages, does not preclude women. This might help explain why, according to historical account, they did so well. During the Renaissance, although the contents of learning changed from sacred to secular, again the function of the man-of-knowledge was a conserving and transmitting one. Again, this was something women could do well. Classics and rhetoric, it will be noted, were the subjects taught by the academic women in the Renaissance. When, with the beginning of the modern era, knowledge became more technological and scientific, however, other functions had to be performed by the man-of-knowledge, including the far more aggressive one of creating knowledge and fighting for its acceptance. This new function was less consonant with traditional feminine roles. It was one thing to be knowledgeable about religious tradition and the classics, a passive role; it was something else again to create new ideas and new knowledge, an active, even aggressive, role. This attempt to relate the nature of knowledge with women's contribution to it, based on Florian Znaniecki's analysis, is meant only to be suggestive, certainly not definitive. Too many other factors and forces were also at work to produce the situations described

by the historians to make any one wholly adequate. Not until the sociology of
the role of the woman-of-knowledge is written will all the elements become
clear.

6. Caplow and McGee report that in the physical sciences professors disclaim
the existence of "schools" of thought. That professors of science in different
universities emphasize different aspects and approaches to their subjects is,
however, clear from the work that issues from their laboratories.

7. Florian Znaniecki, *The Social Role of the Man of Knowledge* (New York:
Columbia Univ. Press, 1940), pp. 154–155.

8. Emerson Shuck, "Teacher's Role Book," *AAUP Bulletin*, 46 (Sept. 1960),
p. 269.

9. *Ibid.*

10. About 35 percent of the women in a sample of college teachers in Minnesota had come to their present positions from a job in a lower school and
hence, presumably, they were more inured to the exigencies of serving as a
moral model for the young (Ruth E. Eckert and John E. Stecklein, *Job Motivations and Satisfactions of College Teachers: A Study of Faculty Members in
Minnesota Colleges* [Washington: GPO, 1961], p. 59).

11. Znaniecki here uses the terms science and scientific in their broadest
sense, referring to any systematic body of learning.

12. At Vassar, only one of the nine professors was a woman; all but one of
the twenty-two teachers were women, and the one exception was an instructor.
The proportion of professors who were women remained low until the 1920's
and 1930's, reaching a high point in the 1930's and declining thereafter.

13. L. Clark Seelye, *The Early History of Smith College, 1871–1910* (Boston:
Houghton Mifflin, 1923), p. 54.

14. See Appendix A.

15. Mainly they came in interstitial positions such as associates in research
or research fellows.

16. Three women out of 108 held the rank of associate professor: one in
library science, one in anatomy, and one in personnel management and economics. There were eight with the rank of assistant professor out of 231, one of
whom was a research associate, one an assistant custodian in a specialized
library, two in piano, one in library science, one in pharmacology, and two in
psychology. Of the 360 instructors, 30 were women, including one in economics
and two in sociology.

17. The long struggle between the theoretical and the practical approaches
to learning has been reviewed by Znaniecki: "practical people for the last
seven or eight centuries have been continuously complaining about all that
useless knowledge which candidates for professional roles had to acquire in
academic schools before they were allowed to participate in active life. No
doubt, practical people are right in a way; for the systematic organization of
knowledge as taught in learned schools is radically different from that which a
man must acquire to be occupationally efficient. But if practical people had
their way, professional instruction would have remained in the stage of medieval
apprenticeship" (*Social Role of the Man of Knowledge*, p. 163).

18. Scientists on the faculties of professional schools have lower status in their
professions than those on faculties granting the Ph.D. degree, according to one
group of informants.

19. Howard S. Becker and others, *Boys in White* (Chicago: Univ. of Chicago
Press, 1961), pp. 132–133.

20. John B. Parrish, "Women in Top Level Teaching and Research," *Jour.
Amer. Assn. Univ. Women*, 55 (Jan. 1962), p. 102.

21. In her autobiography Alice Hamilton recounts an interesting example of

status inconsistency: "Nor did I embarrass the faculty by marching in the Commencement procession and sitting on the platform, though each year I received a printed invitation to do so. At the bottom of the page would be the warning that 'under no circumstances may a woman sit on the platform,' which seemed a bit tactless, but I was sure it was not intentional" (*Exploring the Dangerous Trades* [Boston: Little, Brown, 1943], p. 253).

22. See Appendix A for further discussion of this topic.

23. Since 1951, the number of women getting Ph.D. degrees in the social sciences has consistently exceeded the number getting degrees in arts and humanities; since the middle of the 1950's the number in the social sciences has approximated that in the physical and biological sciences.

24. Caplow & McGee, *The Academic Marketplace* (New York: Basic Books, 1958), pp. 87–89.

25. This is especially true in economics and political science, and it is precisely in these fields where women are most likely to be under-represented. In 1960, only 4.8 percent of those in economics were women; 2.8 percent of those in political science.

26. The important relationships in modern societies tend to be those centering about power, and the observations and reports of women do not seem to have as much cogency and immediacy as those of men in this area. By way of contrast, the observations and reports on preliterate societies made by women are accepted; the kinds of phenomena—family, kinship—which are basic in the organization of such societies are the kinds which women may even have an advantage in interpreting. Women are therefore listened to more readily in anthropology.

27. Faculties, by and large, tend to have the traditionally-defined "liberal" orientation; students often come from conservative backgrounds. Faculties tend to be Democratic; students in many colleges are predominantly Republican. Logan Wilson, Paul Lazarsfeld, and Seymour Lipset have all commented on these points.

28. Lucy Salmon's treatise on domestic service was, in a way, a social critique.

29. At one time, for example, nine out of ten of both professors and instructors in language and literature at Vassar were women. The highest proportion of women professors and instructors in the social sciences and history—in the 1940's—was only 71 percent (Table 9/3). The same contrast characterized the situation at Smith where women have equalled if not excelled men in language and literature, but have been sparsely represented in history and the social sciences. Swarthmore presents a similar picture, despite the fact that Maria Sanford taught the social sciences there in the earliest years. Of the land-grant colleges, Kansas State showed little difference between the sexes at the instructor level, but the usual difference at the higher levels. The contribution of women in the fields of the sciences and mathematics seems to have varied from school to school. In the early years at Vassar about half of the professors in these fields were women. At Smith the contribution of women in science and mathematics was second only to that in language and literature. With the exception of one woman in science and mathematics at Swarthmore in the nineteenth century, however, there have been none in that field there. The land-grant colleges have not used women extensively in this field either, except at the lower levels. At Harvard there were two astronomers in the 1930's. At the University of Michigan women were instructing in anatomy, geology, roentgenology, physiological chemistry, astronomy, botany, and the like. At the lowest levels, as assistants, they were contributing in pediatrics and bacteriology at Harvard and very considerably at the University of Michigan in the medical and dental schools and laboratories.

Chapter 9

1. Address, Bryn Mawr College Fiftieth Anniversary (Bryn Mawr: Bryn Mawr College, 1935), p. 55.

2. Henry Noble MacCracken, *The Hickory Limb* (New York: Scribner's, 1950), p. 25. Vida Scudder, whose mother sent her to Smith rather than to Wellesley because she wanted her to be taught by men, reported that "it was mostly the men at Smith who meant anything to me" (*On Journey* [New York: Dutton, 1937], p. 68). She illustrates how bad the teaching by women could be by two cases: "The first lady placed over us in the Literature classes was chosen, I surmise, because she had Published a Book—rarer distinction then than now. . . . Her caliber may be inferred from the remark with which she introduced Milton: 'Young ladies, the chief work of this poet is an epic called 'Paradise Lost' (note-books in order). I shall not expect you to gain great familiarity with it, for it is difficult to read. I have read every line of it myself, on a bet with my gentlemen admirers. They bet me a diamond ring that I couldn't read the poem through, and I won the ring. Here it is'—waving her hand. Yes, that is what she said. She stayed, I hasten to add, only a short time. . . . Our next teacher was an exquisite southern lady, a widow and tender-hearted. I can still see her little crossed feet as she sat, helplessly scared, on the platform. 'I do not know what you would like to study, dear young ladies. There is much—that would most wisely be left unread. I would suggest one work almost every line of which you might read without hesitation: 'The Idylls of the King,' by our poet laureate. I commend to you in particular the beautiful story of Geraint and Enid, because it presents a perfect image of wifely fealty, on which'—gentle, significant hesitation—'you would do well to brood.' Needless to say, 'wifely fealty' became a joyous by-word among the girls. . . . The little lady had no further suggestions; and at her request a friend and I planned out a course of study. . . . Our plan was gratefully received by the teacher." (pp. 68–70).

3. Compare, for example, Vida Scudder's judgments with those of Dr. Thomas and Dr. MacCracken.

4. Maria Sanford, for example, was recalled by an admiring Swarthmore student in this way: "The door opened and there swept in a presence, a power, a force which might have been called violent except for its control and direction—in the shape and person of Maria Sanford. I, and every student in the room, became instantly and vividly alert and expectant. The following hour seemed incredibly short. Miss Sanford opened a new and wonderful field to eyes eager to see, but till then blind." (Helen Whitney, *Maria Sanford* [Minneapolis: Univ. of Minnesota Press, 1922], p. 86).

5. "He was promoted over me and I have a much longer bibliography than he has" or "he got a raise and I'm a much better teacher than he is" are commonly heard comments on any campus. See the satirical sketch by Jack Swing, "A Real Find in 146," *AAUP Bulletin*, 48 (Sept. 1962), pp. 257–259. "In many institutions personnel policies are obscure. It is very difficult even to find out how personnel decisions are actually made." (John W. Gustad, "Policies and Practices in Faculty Evaluation," *Educational Record*, July 1961).

6. Richard H. Sullivan, in Frank C. Abbott, ed., *Faculty-Administration Relationships* (Washington: American Council on Education, 1957), p. 31.

7. In one department, while the accolade of "best teacher" was bestowed on a popular man teacher, it was a woman teacher into whose classes faculty members tried to have their own sons and daughters assigned.

8. One study of mathematics teaching during World War II at The Pennsylvania State University showed that the grades given by women correlated higher

than those given by men with the actual achievement of the students as measured by objective tests (reported by La Verne Krall from memory; the records of this experiment have been destroyed). In the early years of the elitist women's colleges one of the problems was to convince the men professors to impose high standards on the young women and not to be indulgent (Virginia Gildersleeve, *Many a Good Crusade* [New York: Macmillan, 1954], p. 105).

9. An analogous situation with respect to race was reported by a southern woman: "I was once rushed to an emergency hospital in a northern city. The physician assigned to me was a Negro. I just couldn't take him seriously. When I was well enough to be sent home I went to my family physician. He told me exactly the same things the Negro had told me. I believed them when he said them."

10. When the experiment was over the students were asked which of the two young people they would prefer as their regular teacher if they had a choice. The women said they would prefer the young man; the men students expressed no preference. Both were better than they were accustomed to. Virginia Gildersleeve tells of a woman student's rejection of women teachers: "A few days ago [December 1952] I asked a young woman who was a junior with top marks at one of our best universities whether she had any woman professor. 'No,' she answered, 'I haven't. I never thought of a woman professor. I don't believe I should like to study under one'" (*Many a Good Crusade*, p. 109). A young man at Princeton is reported to have said that "he didn't think he could take the authority of a woman; he couldn't even take assignments from a woman" (Jessie Bernard, "Breaking the Sex Barrier," *Princeton Alumni Weekly*, Sept. 23, 1961, pp. 5–6). David Riesman interprets refusal to learn from women as male vanity culture, arising from a fear of homosexuality (*Ibid.*, p. 3). But since even women may reject women as teachers there is probably more to it than that. See also Vida Scudder's statement above on her preference for her men teachers at Smith.

11. C. Michael Lanphier, Pennsylvania State University.

12. By Louise P. Thurber, Pennsylvania State University.

13. These arguments could not, of course, be used against women as models for women students, but others could. One banker, already noted in Chapter 1, in the 1920's declared he would never send another daughter to Wellesley to be subverted by the radical women professors there. Edith Hooker's students at Goucher followed her "as she strode along in the [suffragist] parades" (Elinor Bluemel, *Florence Sabin, Colorado Woman of the Century*, [Boulder: Univ. of Colorado Press, 1959], p. 64). Margaret Mead has argued for the presence of at least some women on campuses to serve as models for the women students ("Gender in the Honors Program," *Newsletter of the Inter-University Committee on the Superior Student*, May 1961, p. 5.

14. Among the objections to coeducation in the 1920's and 1930's were "the election by college women of the humanistic subjects in such numbers as to drive the men from these courses on the ground that they were 'feminine stuff,' thus depriving men of the liberal culture they greatly need" (Willystine Goodsell, "Coeducation," *Encyclopaedia of the Social Sciences* [New York: Macmillan, 1930], III, p. 616). Dr. Goodsell replied that "if men are driven from the humanistic courses by the presence of women in the classes the solution of the difficulty would seem to lie, not in banishing women, but in educating young men to accept association with women in college, as in life, as a matter of course."

15. Caplow & McGee, *The Academic Marketplace* (New York: Basic Books, 1958), p. 83.

16. *Ibid.*, p. 93.

17. *Ibid.*, p. 226.

18. *Ibid,* p. 111.

19. Caplow and McGee have made a perceptive analysis of what they call the disciple-ship, likening the attitude of colleagues toward it to their attitude toward a love affair. In both cases the relationship must be unobtrusive and protected from public observation. Those "in the know," however, and the participants themselves may enjoy it among themselves (*Ibid.*, pp. 71–72).

20. Cora Dubois, "The Accomplishment and the Challenge," *Jour. Amer. Assn. Univ. Women,* 54 (Oct. 1961), p. 24. Margaret Cussler has suggested that women have an important contribution to make to the creativity of industrial corporations by their emphasis on primary group values (*The Woman Executive* [New York: Harcourt, Brace, 1958], pp. 157–158).

21. At the undergraduate level this takes the form of rejection of counseling. If the student is having a rough time with personal problems, for example, the feeling is that struggling through by himself makes for strength. Help, even if it saves a year—or a life—is weakening. At the great public institutions which must be less discriminating in their admissions policies, counseling has been developed to a much higher degree; they cannot afford to reject a nurturing program.

22. Bluemel, *Florence Sabin,* p. 84.

23. *Ibid.*, p. 85.

24. Margaret Mead, ed., *Anthropologist at Work: The Writings of Ruth Benedict* (Boston: Houghton Mifflin, 1959), p. 347.

25. *Ibid.*, p. 85.

26. *Ibid.*

27. *Ibid.*, pp. 436–437.

Chapter 10

1. Lindsey Harmon, "Progress and Potentiality: Career Determiners of High-level Personnel," paper given at the Utah Creativity Conference, June 1962.

2. Bernard Berelson, *Graduate Education in the United States* (New York: McGraw-Hill, 1960), p. 55.

3. The classified nature of much research done for government agencies and the secret nature of much research done for pharmaceutical laboratories further complicates the problem of measurement.

4. "Women Professors," chapter in a forthcoming volume, p. 11.

5. Sylvia Fleis Fava, "The Status of Women in Professional Sociology," *Amer. Sociol. Rev.,* 25 (Apr. 1960), pp. 271–272. In 1952, although women constituted 14.6 percent of all professionally employed sociologists, they constituted only about 9 percent of those participating in annual professional meetings. The range in proportion of all papers contributed by women, 1949–58, was between 5 and 9 percent.

6. Radcliffe College, *Graduate Education for Women: The Radcliffe Ph.D.* (Cambridge: Harvard Univ. Press, 1956), p. 26.

7. *Ibid.*, pp. 44–45.

8. Nicholas Babchuk and Alan P. Bates, "Professor or Producer: The Two Faces of Academic Man," *Social Forces,* 40 (May 1962), pp. 341–348.

9. Ruth E. Eckert and John E. Stecklein, *Job Motivations and Satisfactions of College Teachers: A Study of Faculty Members in Minnesota Colleges* (Washington: GPO, 1961), p. 58

10. "Women Professors," p. 16.

11. *Graduate Education for Women*, p. 45. For a discussion of the relative competitiveness of academic men and women, see Chapter 12.

12. *Ibid.*, pp. 45–49.

13. James A. Davis, *Great Aspirations, Volume One: Career Decisions and Educational Plans during College* (Chicago: National Opinion Research Center, 1963), pp. 429, 523. Some of those going into the "masculine" subjects—history, philosophy, the earth sciences—were also low on research interest.

14. Alice I. Bryan and Edwin G. Boring, "Women in American Psychology: Factors Affecting Their Professional Careers," *American Psychologist*, 2 (Jan. 1947), p. 13.

15. *Ibid.*, pp. 16, 17.

16. These are discussed in greater detail in Chapter 15.

17. See Appendix C.

18. See the discussion of the technical problems of testing, Appendix C.

19. Before leaving the subject of productivity a word should be said with respect to the productivity of competent librarians. The recognition which so many scholars give to librarians—usually women—in their acknowledgements is by no means an empty ritual. As the late Professor Faris of Chicago used to note, librarians are among the few professionals who go far beyond the call of duty in performing their services—without exacting enormous fees. In one great laboratory the impending retirement of the librarian who had held the position for some thirty years all but disorganized the work of the whole staff. She had contributed enormously, but anonymously, to the productivity of everyone. The contribution of the librarian becomes increasingly—rather than decreasingly—important as the storing and retrieval of data become mechanized.

20. Bryan & Boring, *American Psychologist*, 2 (Jan. 1947), pp. 15, 16.

21. If men and women scientists are graphed separately, similar but, because of fewer cases, less symmetrical distributions result. If two women in the 9–13 bracket had been men, the second distribution of both sexes would have been symmetrical.

22. Data from other sources suggest that there might be a third type also, with productivity ranging up to a hundred or more items at a somewhat older age than the Matched Scientists. These cases were found in highly productive laboratories in a study of communication by the Biological Communications Project under Dr. Charles W. Shilling.

23. Survey Research Center, *The Attitudes and Activities of Physiologists* (Ann Arbor: University of Michigan, 1954), p. 139.

24. Lawrence S. Kubie, "Problems of the Scientific Career," *American Scientist*, 41 (Oct. 1953), pp. 605–606.

25. Jacques Barzun in *The House of Intellect* (New York: Harper, 1959) suggests sex as an achievement drive, pp. 255–256.

26. Bryan and Boring, *American Psychologist*, 2 (Jan. 1947).

27. *Ibid.*

28. The relative noncompetitiveness of women as revealed in statistical studies is discussed in Chapter 12.

29. The "stag effect" was hypothesized on the basis of comments reported in the Radcliffe study, namely: "There are still difficulties for a woman in getting the kind of experience that is necessary to be 'tops' in physics"; "In my earlier years, when there were fewer women in the field, we were made to feel not quite 'acceptable' and rather 'de trop' at scientific meetings"; "No doubt there are social arrangements, like clubs and stag dinners, that if they have any value could be stated as barriers"; "Professional societies ignore the women members"; and finally, "Men here have an advantage, because . . . there is much to be

gained from the easy social contacts possible for men at meetings of learned societies and elsewhere." (*Graduate Education for Women*, pp. 26–28).

30. In a pioneering paper on "Planned and Unplanned Scientific Communication," Herbert Menzel introduces some interesting concepts and raises some interesting research questions in the area of personal—as contrasted with impersonal—channels of communication among scientists (*International Conference on Scientific Information* [Washington: GPO, 1958]). He suggests that personal channels of scientific communication perform somewhat different functions from those performed by published channels. For scientists who know what they are looking for, he suggests, conventional channels of communication are adequate. But "when it comes to bringing scientists together with information the significance of which to their work they have not anticipated; when it comes to pushing out the frontiers, it may be that the system of informal and 'accidental' means of communication, inefficient though it may be, is as reliable a mechanism as one can get." Sir Alfred Egerton has noted, in fast-moving sciences, "of the total information extant, only part is in the literature. Much of it is stored in the many brains of scientists and technologists. We are as dependent on biological storage as on mechanical or library storage" (*Ibid.*, p. 308). It is to this source of information—the brains of fellow scientists—that access may be more limited for women than for men.

31. See Appendix D for a more detailed report on this study.

Chapter 11

1. Dr. Donald W. MacKinnon, Director of the Institute of Personality Assessment and Research, University of California, was quoted in the *New York Times* of October 22, 1961, as saying that their "most creative subjects haven't been grade-getters. . . . Many don't have the academic record that would get them admitted to most graduate schools today. By our methods of academic selection in graduate schools we are missing some of the individuals with high creative potential."

2. This is not to deny that more than sheer intellectual ability is required in academic creativity as well as in other areas of creativity. The argument is only that intellectual ability is probably relatively more important in academic than in other areas of creativity. For psychological discussions of creativity, see: Jacob W. Getzels and Philip W. Jackson, *Creativity and Intelligence* (New York: Wiley, 1962); Howard E. Gruber, Glenn Terrell, and Michael Wertheimer, eds., *Contemporary Approaches to Creative Thinking* (New York: Atherton, 1962); Eleanor E. Maccoby, "Women's Intellect," in Seymour M. Farber and Roger H. L. Wilson, eds., *The Potential of Woman* (New York: McGraw-Hill, 1963), pp. 24–39.

3. It has been suggested that there may be an inverse relationship between the qualities demanded for the doctorate and for creativity, at least for some persons, especially women. "The candidate working on his thesis is no longer a student; he is a scholar, elbowing his way into the professional market-place and hawking the products of his research in competition with wares of more experienced scholars. To the confident and resilient candidate the process may provide the stimulus to a lifetime of scholarship. To the uncertain and the inflexible, the years spent in preparing a thesis may stifle the creative intellectual drive or limit its ultimate productivity" (Radcliffe College, *Graduate Education for Women: The Radcliffe Ph.D.* [Cambridge: Harvard Univ. Press, 1956], p. 23). Bernard Berelson sought to test this position. He asked his subjects

whether they agreed or disagreed with this statement: "The rigors of doctoral study tend to discourage the brightest, most imaginative students in favor of the conscientious plodders." Practically all (91 percent) of the graduate deans disagreed; almost as many (85 percent) of graduate faculty members disagreed; and a large majority (81 percent) of recent recipients of the Ph.D. also disagreed (Bernard Berelson, *Graduate Education in the United States* [New York: McGraw-Hill, 1960], p. 138). Such statements do not, of course, tell us anything about the actual creativity of doctors of philosophy. There is no way of knowing, short of actual comparisons, whether the most creative work is being done by those with or those without the doctor's degree when training, experience, position, and ability are held constant. And there are certainly differences as among fields of research. Berelson's findings may be relevant with respect to the allegation that the very docility of young women, which makes them better grade-getters, also makes them less successful in the more aggressive creative function, discussed in greater detail below.

4. Vida Scudder felt that creativity in women expressed itself in statesmanship and in civic work. She was impressed by the inferior record of her talented students in the arts: "Many embryo poets and a few painters have passed under my eyes. . . . Yet except for the novel, which is essentially a social document, few women in any of these lines reach the front rank" (*On Journey* [New York: Dutton, 1937], p. 65).

5. Kenneth E. Clark, *America's Psychologists: A Survey of a Growing Profession* (Washington: American Psychological Association, 1957), p. 72.

6. *Graduate Education for Women*, p. 49.

7. Clark, *America's Psychologists*, p. 72.

8. Mabel Newcomer, *A Century of Higher Education for American Women* (New York: Harper, 1959), p. 200. In line with Vida Scudder's comments above, it is interesting to note that women have done relatively better as writers than as research scholars (*Ibid.*, pp. 204 ff.).

9. Margaret Mead, "Gender in the Honors Program," *Newsletter of the Inter-University Committee on the Superior Student*, May 1961, p. 5.

10. Otto Sonder, doctoral dissertation, Pennsylvania State University, 1964. In another study, 16 subjects were correct 66 percent of the time in identifying the sex of professional bioscientists on the basis of comments made on a questionnaire. The comments were not, however, on scientific matters but on attitudes toward teaching and research. Not thought-ways but role definitions were involved.

11. "Women don't mind your asserting that there their psyches *are* different; they mind your asserting that their psyches *have* to be different. It is almost as if they don't mind their lot; they merely mind the assertion that there is no escape from their lot" (David V. Tiedeman, Robert P. O'Hara, and Esther Matthews, *Position Choices and Careers: Elements of a Theory* [Cambridge: Harvard Graduate School of Education, 1958], p. 37).

12. Mirra Komarovsky has made a brilliant analysis of the reasons why college girls do not wish to be intellectually outstanding in terms of their role relations both to their parents and to young men (*Women in the Modern World, Their Education and Their Dilemmas* [Boston: Little, Brown, 1953]). The present discussion assumes they have overcome this original hurdle and have actually become scientists.

13. Znaniecki here uses the term science in a broad sense, as describing any systematic field of knowledge.

14. Florian Znaniecki, *The Social Role of the Man of Knowledge* (New York: Columbia Univ. Press, 1940), pp. 164–165.

15. *Ibid.*, pp. 173, 174.

16. Bernard Barber has distinguished at least six sources of such resistance to

innovation, namely: substantive concepts, methodological concepts, religious ideas, status differences, specialization, and rivalries among schools of thought ("Resistance by Scientists to Scientific Discovery," in Bernard Barber and Walter Hirsch, eds., *The Sociology of Science* [Glencoe: Free Press, 1962], pp. 539–556). The special case of resistance in the field of medicine has been documented by Bernhard J. Stern in "Resistances to Medical Change," in *Historical Sociology* (New York: Citadel Press, 1959), pp. 345–385.

17. Thomas S. Kuhn, *The Structure of Scientific Revolutions* (Chicago: Univ. of Chicago Press, 1962), pp. 171–172.

18. *Ibid.*, p. 65.

19. F. Reif, "The Competitive World of the Pure Scientist," *Science*, Dec. 15, 1961, p. 1959. This intense competition performs the function of enormously stimulating effort. But its very intensity may have dysfunctional aspects also. There has crept into the scientific community a hesitation to discuss work with fellow scientists for fear of "giving ideas away." One naïve newcomer on an intensely competitive campus was warned not to talk so freely at parties or someone else would write his book.

20. Eponymy is "the practice of affixing the name of the scientist to all or part of what he has found. . . . In this way, scientists leave their signatures indelibly in history; their names enter into all the scientific languages of the world" (Robert Merton, "Priorities in Scientific Discovery: A Chapter in the Sociology of Science," in Barber & Hirsch, *Sociology of Science*, p. 459). The highest level of eponymy is one in which a whole age is named after a man: the Newtonian epoch, the Darwinian era, or the Freudian age. High also is the level which names new sciences after great founders, thus: Morgagni, father of pathology; Cuvier, father of paleontology; Faraday, father of electrotechnics. On the next level a particular form of a discipline is named for a great innovator: Hippocratic medicine, Aristotelian logic, Euclidean geometry, Boolean algebra, Keynesian economics. "In rough hierarchic order, the next echelon is comprised by thousands of eponymous laws, theories, theorems, hypotheses, instruments, constants, and distributions such as the Brownian movement, the Lorenz curve, the Spearman rank-correlation coefficient" (*Ibid.*, p. 460).

21. Anne Roe, *The Making of a Scientist* (New York: Dodd, Mead, 1952), pp. 235–236.

22. *New York Times*, Oct. 22, 1961.

23. Lawrence S. Kubie, "Problems of the Scientific Career," *American Scientist* 41 (Oct. 1953), p. 605.

24. Jacob W. Getzels and Philip W. Jackson, *Creativity and Intelligence* (New York: Wiley, 1962), pp. 49, 51, 53.

25. The story of Newton and the apple is almost certainly apochryphal; it might just as well have been about a maid or wife who commented, in passing, while dusting in the study, that the earth in his model of the solar system looked like an apple pulling a big ball, the sun.

26. Anne Roe was convinced that "there is a sex difference [in the intensity of the needs associated with innovation in scientists], that such needs are stronger in men than in women," but she was not sure "whether this is a biological or a cultural phenomenon" (*Making of a Scientist*, pp. 235–236). She was, however, convinced that it was related to the paucity of creative women in science.

27. Experimental research has established the functional necessity of at least two roles in a task-oriented group, namely the so-called "idea-man" or instrumental role and the emotional-expressive role. The question is not why they are needed but why they are allocated as they are—the instrumental almost universally to men and the expressive to women. This allocation is probably related to childbearing. "In our opinion the fundamental explanation of the

allocation of the roles between the biological sexes lies in the fact that the bearing and early nursing of children establish a strong presumptive primacy of the relation of mother to the small child and this in turn establishes a presumption that the man, who is exempted from these biological functions, should specialize in the alternative instrumental direction" (Talcott Parsons in Parsons & Bales, *Family, Socialization and Interaction Process* [Glencoe: Free Press, 1955], p. 23). The experience of the Kibbutzim of Israel illustrates this logic. They began with an ideological equalitarianism which rejected the old division of labor along sexual lines. Yet as time passed they found that a conventional division of labor did emerge; the women tended to take over traditionally feminine occupations. It is not necessarily true that women are gentler, more tender, more loving than men; many men could probably do a better job of childrearing than many women. But there is a certain logic in this childrearing assignment to women. Even if there were no difference in parental attitudes on the part of men and women, it would still be strategically sound to assign the rearing of infants to women.

28. Robert Merton, in Barber & Hirsch, *Sociology of Science,* p. 469.

29. "I take great comfort in the very fact that I have always played a subordinate role. One source of serenity and happiness in these later years is recognition that I have worked in obscure ways, and that even in the fine if small group enterprises in which I have had a share, my part has never been that of an acknowledged leader. I have been at the birth of valuable and inspiring enterprises; but in none have I been called to take a leading part" (*On Journey,* pp. 430–431).

30. "This sensitiveness with respect to her own position led sometimes to an extreme modesty. Only last spring she was at first, out of pure bashfulness, unwilling to accept a doctor's degree of letters offered her by the University of Michigan. Her researches upon the newspaper were halted at one time because she did not think her materials important enough to warrant publication in two volumes" (Henry Noble MacCracken, *Address at the Memorial Service for Lucy Maynard Salmon* [Poughkeepsie: Vassar College, 1927], pp. 30–31).

31. "Miss Salmon does not shout her conclusions nor turn the spotlight on her own originality" (Henry Osborn Taylor, *Ibid.,* p. 12).

32. Franz Adler, "Toward a Sociology of Creative Behavior," p. 15.

33. Thomas S. Kuhn, reports the following incident from J. J. Strutt, *John William Strutt, Third Baron Rayleigh.* "Lord Rayleigh, at a time when his reputation was established, submitted to the British Association a paper on some paradoxes of electrodynamics. His name was inadvertently omitted when the paper was first sent, and the paper itself was at first rejected as the work of some 'paradoxer.' Shortly afterwards, with the author's name in place, the paper was accepted with profuse apologies" (*Structure of Scientific Revolutions,* p. 152).

34. Margaret Mead, *Newsletter of the Inter-University Committee on the Superior Student,* May 1961, p. 5. It might be argued that the enormous recognition accorded to her own work is a vivid refutation of her thesis. But it so happened that her work was in an area in which the opinions and observations of women have been accorded recognition, as noted earlier in this book.

35. "There was a young girl of nineteen in a small town of north Germany with a strong bent for research, but when her brother went to the University of Goettingen she, according to the customs of her country, remained at home. Agnes Pockels had observed the streaming of currents when salts were put into solution and, by attaching a float to a balance, had found that salts increased the pull of the surface of the fluid. In other words, she had discovered surface tension. This was in 1881. She did not know whether anyone else had ever observed this phenomenon, but, through her brother, she brought her work to

the attention of the Professor of Physics at Goettingen. It was, however, new and he failed to grasp its significance. For ten years she went on studying the properties of solutions quite alone in her own home. Then the renowned English physicist, Lord Rayleigh, began to publish on this subject, and so she wrote to him about her work. With a fine sense of honour he sent a translation of her letter to the English journal, *Nature*, asking that it be published. He wrote that the first part of her letter covered nearly the same ground as his own recent work and that with very 'homely appliances' she had arrived at valuable results respecting the behaviour of contaminated water surfaces. It is interesting to note that it is this same 'homely device' that is still used to measure surface tension. Lord Rayleigh then added that the latter part of her letter seemed to him very suggestive, raising, if it did not fully answer, many important questions. Then for a few years he arranged for the publication of all of her work in English, until the Germany of another era (1898) was proud to accept her discoveries for publication in her own language" (Florence Sabin in *Bryn Mawr College Fiftieth Anniversary* [Bryn Mawr: Bryn Mawr College, 1935], p. 69).

36. Thus, for example, when Nettie Stevens, a researcher at Bryn Mawr, discovered the X-chromosome at the same time as Edmund B. Wilson, it was he who first won recognition for it (*Ibid.*, p. 67).

37. One academic woman said, without rancor, even with humor, in a discussion of this point, "My former students often write to me appreciatively of my work, but they do not find it necessary to cite it in their own." A male reader of this book has commented on this point, however, that "women professors are ignored by their colleagues or students . . . not because they are women, but because of the slovenly scholarship that prevails in many academic fields today, especially the social sciences. References are made to the famous, but frequently not to many other worthwhile scholars who are publishing in relevant fields. This has nothing to do with sex."

Chapter 12

1. Comment from an academic woman in a commoner field, with no monopoly on her skills: "My clients always act hurt and abused when they get my bill. They act as though it's my duty as a woman to help them. I shouldn't have to be *paid* for what a woman does just naturally. At least not so much." A non-academic woman, whose salary was less than that of her male peers, explained her status this way: "At the crucial point in the bargaining situation I never have the heart to push my demands through. I feel guilty when I demand what I am entitled to. I finally back down because the extra pay just isn't worth the emotional effort needed to establish my superiority in the bargain. It would set up a barrier as long as I worked there. I suppose I buy 'affection'—Karen Horney!—or goodwill by giving in."

2. Clark Kerr discusses the nature of modern "multiversities" in his recent book, *The Uses of the University* (Cambridge: Harvard Univ. Press, 1963).

3. There is, of course, also the "social" system in the popular or entertaining sense. Here the status of a married woman is dependent on her husband's, and that of an unmarried woman, as the Radcliffe study noted, is uncertain. In addition, most campuses have at least one elite "gentlemen's club" whose members are "in," but these are always stag and academic women have no part in them.

4. Blaine E. Mercer and Judson B. Pearson, "Personal and Institutional Characteristics of Academic Sociologists," *Sociology and Social Research,* 46 (Apr. 1962), p. 266. "It was hypothesized that female sociologists will have experienced greater promotional difficulties than male sociologists. Academic folklore seems to support such an hypothesis. However, the Chi Square yield for the contingency distribution, in which the sex of the respondents is cross-classified against rapidity of occupational ascent, is not significant at the .05 level, nor even at the .20 level of significance. The cell weightings are in the hypothesized direction, but only slightly so."

5. National Education Association, "Salaries Paid and Salary Practices in Universities, Colleges and Junior Colleges, 1959–60," *Research Report, 1960* (Washington: NEA, 1960). See also Sylvia Fleis Fava. "The Status of Women in Professional Sociology," *Amer. Sociol. Rev.,* 25 (Apr. 1960), p. 273.

6. The concepts "competitiveness" and "level of aspiration" are social-psychological rather than, strictly speaking, sociological concepts. People may be "in competition" with one another without being at all "competitive" (Jessie Bernard, *American Community Behavior* [New York: Holt, Rinehart, and Winston, 1962], p. 66).

7. Thus, for example, Mrs. Barbara Bates Gunderson, a civil service commissioner, has stated: "I have found that a large number of keenly intelligent women shun responsibility of advancement. . . . These women are sociologically sold on the idea that . . . a woman . . . may not compete with a man in the working world but content herself with the role of handmaiden. Some Federal career women shun production not because they fear responsibility or masculine resentment in the office, but because it would put them in an income bracket superior to their husbands. . . . Such women turn the new job down without regret, feeling that they have proved their womanliness and virtue as wives" (*Civil Service Journal,* quoted in the *New York Times,* Feb. 19, 1961). Ruth Shonle Cavan makes a similar assessment of the situation. "If the woman is in the lower level of a profession or business occupation, it is frankly because she has chosen to remain there" ("The Status of Women in the Professions relative to the Status of Men," *Quart. Amer. Interprofessional Inst.,* Winter 1956–57, p. 9). Susan B. Riley points out that "often women who do secure college appointments are caught permanently on a low professorial rank by a net of trivia and devotion to routine, which they use as a justification for giving up the more arduous struggle for a doctorate and for engaging in research, scholarly writing, and similar activities leading to academic growth and recognition" ("New Sources of College Teachers," *Jour. Amer. Assn. Univ. Women,* 54 [Mar. 1961], p. 134).

8. Results of a series of experiments with strategic games led John R. Bond and W. E. Vinacke to characterize male strategies as exploitative and female strategies as accommodative. They found men more competitive; they strove harder to win. (Incidentally this strategy was self-defeating in the games as set up; the women won more.) The exploitative or masculine strategy was characterized by a struggle to defeat the rivals, to engage in whatever tactics promised the best deal. The accommodative or feminine strategy was more often a coalition of all three players rather than two-against-one, or no coalitions at all; it was more often one of dividing rewards equally; it was—contrary to popular cliches—one of little bargaining; it was one which included altruistic offers when a player suggested that a coalition be formed against another. The authors do not imply that these differences are biologically based; Micronesian male students show accommodative strategies. But there are differences based on personality: Those high in achievement-orientation tend to follow exploitative strategies; those high in nurturance, accommodative. See W. Edgar Vinacke,

"Sex Roles in a Three-Person Game," *Sociometry*, 22 (Dec. 1959), pp. 343–360;
John R. Bond and W. E. Vinacke, "Coalitions in Mixed Set Trends," *Sociometry*, 24 (Mar. 1961), pp. 61–75; and Thomas C. Uesugi and W. Edgar Vinacke, "Strategy in a Feminine Game," *Sociometry*, 26 (Mar. 1963), pp. 75–88.

9. Dael Wolfle, *America's Resources of Specialized Talent* (New York: Harper, 1954), pp. 234–236.

10. Jewell Cardwell Field, "Factors Associated with Graduate School Attendance and Role Definition of the Women Doctoral Candidates at the Pennsylvania State University" (Master's thesis, Penn. State Univ., 1961).

11. Bernard Berelson, *Graduate Education in the United States* (New York: McGraw-Hill, 1960), p. 135.

12. James A. Davis, *Stipends and Spouses* (Chicago: Univ. of Chicago Press, 1962).

13. Alice I. Bryan and Edwin G. Boring, "Women in American Psychology: Factors Affecting Their Professional Careers," *American Psychologist*, 2 (Jan. 1947), 12. It should be pointed out that not all the subjects were academic women. Unfortunately there was no breakdown by type of employment.

14. *Ibid.*

15. *Ibid.*

16. *Ibid.*

17. *Ibid.*

18. *Ibid.*, p. 13.

19. Money, in the experience of one department chairman, was more of a competitive lure than status among the women he dealt with: "The women as a group are more willing to work without the special rewards of promotion and other kinds of status-stimulation. So far as material rewards are concerned, however, I have not found them notably less interested in salary increases than are their male competitors."

20. Bernard, *American Community Behavior*, p. 75.

21. The teaching-research polarity is one of the oldest in academia, as old, no doubt, as the university idea introduced at Johns Hopkins. Research, it is popularly felt, has garnered the highest prestige rewards. Published research brings acclaim to the institution from the outside world; teaching serves only the students and its contribution to the fame of the school seeps out into the community only by way of its alumni, slowly and unspectacularly. Still, a study of one profession—sociologists—found that the research channel was not disproportionately rewarded as measured by speed of ascent in the academic hierarchy. It did not substantiate "the belief that the royal road to promotion is research activity. The Chi Square analysis reveals no significant relationship between rapidity of ascent and concentration upon research" (Mercer & Pearson, *Sociology & Social Research*, 46 [Apr. 1962], p. 267). There was, however, a hint that those who really went in for research, spending three-fourths or more of their institutional time on it, did have a somewhat higher ascent rate. But the converse was not true, namely that devotion to teaching was rewarded by faster promotion. "The view that those spending less institutional time upon teaching are promoted more rapidly seems to be justified by the analysis of the responses" (*Ibid.*, p. 268). The bewildered neophyte might well ask, how *should* he spend his institutional time if he is interested in rapid ascent? (The amount of institutional time spent in administrative activity was not related to rapidity of ascent.) Too much time on teaching will slow his ascent, but increased institutional time on research won't hasten it, unless it becomes almost exclusive.

22. The relative denigration of teaching which, whether it actually exists or not, seems to characterize academia has, according to one sociologist, had the effect of lowering the quality of university teaching below that of high school

teaching (Neal Gross, in a paper before the American Sociological Association, 1961).

23. As a matter of fact, departments need the proper "mix" for the functions they are performing. They need at least a minimum of teaching performed. They also need "names" to give them prestige. Professors are rarely hired for the teaching work; they are more likely to be hired to add lustre to the department, to help in the recruitment of good students and colleagues. Even researchers who study the profession think it anomalous that professors "are, in essence, paid to do one job, whereas the worth of their services is evaluated on the basis of how well they do another," namely, publish (Caplow and McGee, *The Academic Marketplace* [New York: Basic Books, 1958], p. 82). Professors are not really hired to perform the teaching function. They are hired to be masters of their field, perhaps to lecture, or even to "give" courses. Women are likely to be hired to do teaching.

24. The above statement was pieced together from local newspaper accounts of the death of Dr. Harriet Harvey, of the University of Oklahoma, in September, 1962.

25. Everett C. Hughes, "Dilemmas and Contradictions of Status," *Amer. Jour. Sociol.*, 50 (Mar. 1944), pp. 353–359; Gerhard E. Lenski, "Status Crystallization: A Non-verbal Dimension of Social Status," *Amer. Sociol. Rev.*, 19 (Aug. 1954), pp. 405–413 and "Social Participation and Status Crystallization, *Amer. Sociol. Rev.*, 21 (Aug. 1956), pp. 458–464; G. H. Fenchel, J. H. Monderer, and E. L. Hartley, "Subjective Status and the Equilibration Hypothesis," *Jour. Abn. and Soc. Psych.*, 46 (Oct. 1951), pp. 476–479; Erving W. Goffman, "Status Consistency and Preference for Change in Power Distribution," *Amer. Sociol. Rev.*, 22 (June 1957), pp. 275–281; and Elton F. Jackson, "Status Consistency and Symptoms of Stress," *Amer. Sociol. Rev.*, 27 (Aug. 1962), pp. 469–480.

26. Seymour Martin Lipset, *Political Man* (New York: Doubleday, 1959), pp. 322–324.

27. An interesting example of compounded status inconsistency was uncovered in the Matched Scientists study. Here it was an inconsistency between the status of a woman as a scientist and her status as a Negro. In reply to the question dealing with telephoning fellow scientists, she said: "Whenever I am writing and need access to journals at the white university in our community, I call the librarian's secretary, who checks the books out for me. I pick them up and return them to her. The library does not permit Negroes to check out journals." With respect to informal contacts with fellow scientists: "I am in a peculiarly isolated position as a scientist, but a Negro scientist. I do not want to make my white colleagues uncomfortable by being seen in their laboratories. . . . I *could* visit, but the consequences would vary with the degree of barbarity of those observing the visits."

Chapter 13

1. Bernard Berelson, *Graduate Education in the United States* (New York: McGraw-Hill, 1960), p. 217.

2. See Appendix A for the case of social workers.

3. For a discussion of the nature of sociological and social-psychological conflict see Jessie Bernard, *American Community Behavior* (New York: Holt, Rinehart, and Winston, 1962), chap. 6.

4. Florian Znaniecki, *The Social Role of the Man of Knowledge* (New York:

Columbia Univ. Press, 1940), pp. 117–163. The six types are: discoverers of truth, systematizers, contributors, fighters for truth, eclectics and historians of knowledge, and disseminators of knowledge.

5. This is the way faculty meetings looked to George Santayana at Harvard in the early years of the century: "The Faculty meetings were an object lesson to me in the futility of parliamentary institutions. Those who spoke spoke badly, with imperfect knowledge of the matter in hand, and simply to air their prejudices. The rest hardly listened. If there was a vote, it revealed not the results of the debate, but the previous and settled sentiments of the voters. The uselessness and the poor quality of the whole performance were so evident that it surprised me to see that so many intelligent men—for they were intelligent when doing their special work—should tamely waste so much time in keeping up the farce" (*The Middle Span* [New York: Scribner's, 1945], II, pp. 160–161.

6. For an unflattering picture of the academic man as colleague see George Williams, *Some of My Best Friends Are Professors* (New York: Abelard-Schuman, 1958), pp. 69 ff.

7. Henry Noble MacCracken, *The Hickory Limb* (New York: Scribner's 1950), p. 74.

8. *Ibid.*, pp. 68–69. Although Maria Sanford was the only woman professor at Swarthmore in the 1860's, there were other women teaching and "one of them disliked Miss Sanford . . . and became little short of a persecutor, and she made no secret of her enmity" (Helen Whitney, *Maria Sanford* [Minneapolis: Univ. of Minnesota Press, 1922], p. 97).

9. MacCracken, *The Hickory Limb*, p. 69.

10. *Ibid.*, pp. 69–70.

11. *Ibid.*, pp. 66–68.

12. *Ibid.*, p. 70.

13. Virginia Gildersleeve, *Many a Good Crusade* (New York: Macmillan, 1954), p. 52.

14. That such conflicts exist cannot be denied, but they differ only in degree, not in kind, from those of men. Any career demands choices and choices involve costs, hence conflict. Women have to choose between family and career demands on their time, as do men. True, the consequences are more important in women's choices than in men's and to this extent they are different.

15. Some of the early academic women knew only one way of being successful, and that was to perform their roles the masculine way. M. Carey Thomas, who never smoked on campus, nevertheless when "Bryn Mawr could no longer be harmed by it . . . determinedly smoked, and urged other women to do so, puffing gingerly a certain number of cigarettes a day, making great play with holder and ash dish, going to remarkable lengths to procure her favorite 'Ward's Russians'—all in order to prove women's emancipation" (Edith Finch, *Carey Thomas of Bryn Mawr*, [New York: Harper, 1947], p. 302). Vassar's psychologist, Margaret Washburn, was "intrepid enough to invade the sacred precinct of the men's smoker at psychological meetings. Marching uninvited into its midst, she had sat down and lighted a cigar. None questioned her privilege to enjoy a smoker thereafter" (MacCracken, *Hickory Limb*, p. 70). Attempts to look pretty and to dress becomingly were rejected by some of the early academic women. Maria Sanford made no concessions in this area, refusing to dress becomingly, or even femininely. This, as she realized late in life, was a mistake. Her disregard of her appearance antagonized some of her students, both at Swarthmore and later at Minnesota. "Although Swarthmore is a Quaker college, and the people were accustomed to plain dress, even Miss Sanford's warmest admirers bemoaned the fact that she would not dress more becomingly. Two men fifty years later spoke of the ugly congress gaiters she wore. She never

changed her style of dress as long as she taught. The severity and simplicity saved both time, thought and money, that she believed she could use to better advantage in other ways. But she was heard to say after she was eighty years of age that if she had her life to live over again she should do differently about dress. Without doubt she might have smoothed some rough paths for herself if when she was younger she had dressed more nearly in the accepted fashion" (Whitney, *Maria Sanford*, pp. 89–90.). Ellen Richards' contempt for fashion and finery were noted in Chapter 1. Many of the women who were so aggressively in favor of women's education were not themselves notably sympathetic to women or the feminine role; they were, in some cases, almost non-women. As a result, despite the fact that the portraits of many of the early great academic women—Carey Thomas, for example, and Alice Freeman—project strikingly beautiful faces, and despite recent changes in orientation toward appearance, the popular image of the appearance of academic women has tended to be unflattering. As late as 1961, for example, in a novel set in England, a young man asks why academic women have to look like haystacks (Iris Murdoch, *A Severed Head* [New York: Viking, 1961], p. 8).

16. This statement has been translated into sociological terms.

17. Talcott Parsons and Robert F. Bales, *Family, Socialization and Interaction Process* (Glencoe: Free Press, 1955), chap. 6.

18. There is a status aspect to the talker-listener relationship also. Listening belongs to the lower status; talking to the higher. The fact that a psychiatrist or clinician listens to a client is itself a therapeutic act, but people have to pay for the privilege of talking about themselves to these professionals.

19. One woman who left a university to return to a women's college explained her move as follows: "I got tired of having to yell to make myself heard."

20. For a sociological analysis of direct action, see Bernard, *American Community Behavior*, pp. 404–405.

21. Gildersleeve, *Many a Good Crusade*, p. 98.

22. Cases of male homosexuality are usually known on large campuses. Whenever unmarried academic women choose to live together in order to make a stable and attractive home, it is sure to arouse at least an occasional leering reference by hostile persons. Kinsey and his associates reported a higher incidence of homosexuality among women with graduate education than among less well-educated women (*Sexual Behavior in the Human Female* [Philadelphia: Saunders, 1953], pp. 459–461).

23. *Hickory Limb*, p. 41.

24. Such information is useful strategically, however, if an administrator wishes to get rid of one of his faculty. It is almost the only way a tenure faculty member can be dismissed without having the American Association of University Professors on campus the next morning.

25. There was a kind of hazing of the women medical students at Johns Hopkins in the late nineteenth century. "Some of the professors made biological jokes in class, and one outraged 'hen medic' spluttered to Florence about it. 'Why pay attention?' she asked with her disarming smile. 'You know they aren't told to embarrass us, but to illustrate a point' " (Elinor Bluemel, *Florence Sabin, Colorado Woman of the Century* [Boulder: Univ. of Colorado Press, 1959], p. 45). One wonders.

26. Stanley Budner and John Meyer, "Woman Professors," to appear in forthcoming volume, p. 22.

27. "One . . . a bold lass made a pass, on a bet, as I learned later. I was too dumb to notice it, she told me later, with chagrin" (MacCracken, *Hickory Limb*, p. 41). Women are more likely than men to try to use sex appeal in wangling grades.

28. The heroines in Robert Herrick's *Chimes* (1926), in Iris Murdoch's *The Severed Head* (1961), and in John W. Aldridge's *The Party at Cranton* (1960) are anthropologists. (And so, incidentally, was the academic woman in the television program, "Dobie Gillis.") Honor Klein in *The Severed Head* has an incestuous relationship with her half-brother. She is ugly, demoniacal, frumpy. The significance of her profession, anthropology, is relevant to the story. It endows her with the kind of knowledge and understanding that makes all behavior essentially amoral; she also understands symbolism. The "good" heroine is an economist at the London School of Economics. Dorothy, an anthropologist in *The Party at Cranton,* is practically an alcoholic. Conversely, the academic women in May Sarton's *The Small Room* (1961) have genuine moral concerns about the pressures on students that result in plagiarism; they are humanists. The women in Mary McCarthy's *The Groves of Academe* show up better than the men as they do also in Kingsley Amis' *Lucky Jim* and Bernard Malamud's *A New Life.*

Chapter 14

1. The Radcliffe study found the proportion married to be nigher among the younger than among the older women, as did Budner and Meyer. In the study of women scientists, it was found that whereas almost one-half (47 percent) of those born in 1920 or later were married ten to fifteen years after receiving the doctorate, only one-third of those born before 1920 were.

2. George Herbert Palmer, *The Life of Alice Freeman Palmer* (Boston: Houghton Mifflin, 1924).

3. L. Clark Seelye, as noted in Chapter 4, complained that it was hard to keep faculty at Smith; they left when they got married (*The Early History of Smith College 1871–1910* [Boston: Houghton Mifflin, 1923], p. 55). In the Fall of 1959, only 20 percent of the women who were administering home economics programs were married (Office of Education, *Home Economics in Degree-granting Institutions, 1959–1960* [Washington: GPO, 1960], table 31.

4. A study of over 700 college teachers in 32 colleges in Minnesota reported only 46 percent of the women to be married, as contrasted with 83 percent of the men (Ruth E. Eckert and John E. Stecklein, *Job Motivations and Satisfactions of College Teachers: A Study of Faculty Members in Minnesota Colleges* [Washington: GPO, 1961], p. 57). Lindsey Harmon's analysis of scientific doctorates, a large proportion of whom were in academic posts, revealed 46 percent of the women and 76 percent of the men to be married. The study of biologists showed less than one-half of the women (42 percent) but most of the men (92 percent) to be married ten to fifteen years after receiving the Ph.D. degree. A study of 440 men and 440 women doctors in psychology, 1921–40—not all of them in academic posts, however—found that in 1944 almost one-half of the women (43.2 percent) were single but only 5.3 percent of the men (Alice I. Bryan and Edwin G. Boring, "Women in American Psychology: Factors Affecting Their Professional Careers," *American Psychologist,* 2 [Jan. 1947], p. 14).

5. Among women physicians, 69 percent were reported to have been married in one study ("Survey of Women Physicians Graduating from Medical School 1925–40," *Jour. Med. Edcn.*, March, 1957, part 2). Of social workers over thirty years of age, more than 60 percent were found to be married ("Social Workers in 1950," *Amer. Assn. Soc. Workers* [Washington: GPO, 1951], data prepared by the United States Bureau of Labor Statistics). Of professional and managerial

women, only 38 percent were unmarried in 1950 (*United States Census of Population: Vol. IV, Special Reports, Occupational Characteristics* [Washington: GPO, 1954], table 8); editors and reporters, 46 percent (*Ibid.*); buyers and department heads in stores, only 32 percent. Only women executives (Margaret Cussler, *The Woman Executive* [New York: Harcourt, Brace, 1958], p. 29) and women in higher-level positions (Women's Bureau, *Women in Higher-Level Positions* [Washington: GPO, 1950]) with 53 and 55 percent respectively unmarried show marital status comparable to that of academic women.

6. In order to take into account the fact that marital status among academic persons appears to be related to area of specialization. Both men and women in the behavioral sciences (psychology and anthropology) tend to have a slightly higher marriage rate than those in the biological and physical sciences. Lindsey Harmon reported 81 and 50 percent of the men and women in the behavioral sciences married; in the biological sciences, 79 and 44 percent; and in the physical sciences, 72 and 42 percent. The Budner-Meyer study found 57 percent of the women social scientists to be single, compared with only 8 percent of the men; 43 percent were married, widowed, or divorced, compared with 92 percent among the men.

7. Margaret Mead, "Gender in the Honors Program," *The Newsletter of the Inter-University Committee on the Superior Student*, May 1961, pp. 4–5.

8. Palmer, *Alice Freeman Palmer*, pp. 172–173.

9. It has, however, been suggested that the proverbially low pay of even academic men performed the function, in effect, of enforcing a monastic style of life.

10. A study of 4,500 college teachers in 93 Catholic women's colleges, reported that 82 percent were women; 63 percent were religious (Sister M. St. Mel Kennedy, O.S.F., "The Faculty in Catholic Colleges for Women," *Catholic Educational Rev.*, May 1961, pp. 289–298).

11. A strong nonmarriage orientation shows up among some women graduate students even in this day and age. Among the women in one study of graduate students, 71 percent were single as compared with 51 percent among the men. The proportion married declined with age. The author concludes that both the interests of the women and dropping out at marriage accounted for his findings: "After age 23, marriage percentages do not increase so steadily as in the case of men, and from 22 on the women have lower proportions married than do the men. Possibly graduate school disproportionately attracts women who are not tempted by matrimony, but, equally possible, women students who marry are likely to quit school. Single women were asked, 'During the first five years after you finish graduate work, which of these would you prefer: marriage only, marriage with occasional work in my field, combining marriage with a career, or career only?' Of the single women, 20 percent of 361 chose the last or anti-marriage alternative. Similarly, when the marital expectations of single men and women are compared, up to age 34, single women are more likely to expect marriage in the immediate future than are single men. These indirect pieces of evidence suggest that the low marriage rates of the women come from attrition among the recently married rather than high spinsterhood" (James A. Davis, *Stipends and Spouses*, [Chicago: Univ. of Chicago Press, 1962], p. 31). There is no necessary incompatibility between the two interpretations. Among the women in this study, 16 percent were mothers; among the men, 30 percent were fathers.

12. Seelye, *The Early History of Smith College*, p. 55.

13. She was 38 years old at the time; the man she loved was married. She struggled with herself for five years and then resigned her position. "My resignation was the fierce grasp of one drowning after something stable, the attempt

for mastery of one whose brain was reeling. But that awful struggle was the crisis, and it brought me peace. There are still moments when I give way, but calm reason is sure to triumph" (Quoted by Helen Whitney in *Maria Sanford* [Minneapolis: Univ. of Minnesota Press, 1922], p. 107). The relationship between Miss Sanford and the man continued by correspondence for twenty years. She sympathized with his sorrows; she advised him about his children. But when marriage finally became possible, at the age of 60, she refused. In 1876 she had written a memorandum to guide her in this relationship: "I thank thee, oh my God, for light. 'Till death us part' it shall be true. I can work for him, seek his happiness, live for him; and receive no sign. Shall I not then be his good angel? That will not be coldness, but the fullness of unselfish love. O God help me! My heart shall not grow cold for I will keep it warm with sympathy and love for others. I will throw my whole soul into my profession. Oh it is hard but it is the rugged path that leads upward always. . . . The book is sealed" (p. 104). She had been guided by it.

14. Elinor Bluemel, *Florence Sabin, Colorado Woman of the Century* (Boulder: Univ. of Colorado Press, 1959), p. 44.

15. Edith Finch, *Carey Thomas of Bryn Mawr* (New York: Harper, 1947), p. 318.

16. Vida Scudder, *On Journey* (New York: Dutton, 1937), pp. 212 ff.

17. Virginia Gildersleeve, *Many a Good Crusade* (New York: Macmillan, 1954), p. 108.

18. Even among graduate students, about 49 percent of those aged 27 to 29 planned to marry (Davis, *Stipends and Spouses*, p. 171). All of the unmarried women graduate students working for the doctorate interviewed at Pennsylvania State University would like to be married (Jewell Cardwell Field, "Factors Associated with Graduate School Attendance and Role Definition of the Women Doctoral Candidates at the Pennsylvania State University" Master's thesis, Penn. State Univ., 1961).

19. *Op. cit.*, p. 108.

20. The resulting anomalies of status of the unmarried academic woman was recognized in the Radcliffe study: "There is no doubt that single women are in some sense an unattached group in academic society; they may feel themselves to be 'outsiders' even though their number is large. Their interests are not the same as those of their male colleagues. They have a special problem of social adjustment" (Radcliffe College, *Graduate Education for Women: The Radcliffe Ph.D.* [Cambridge: Harvard Univ. Press, 1956], p. 51).

21. Helene Deutsch, *The Psychology of Women: A Psychoanalytic Interpretation* (New York: Grune & Stratton, 1944), p. 290.

22. Tiedeman, O'Hara, and Mathews, *Position Choices and Careers: Elements of a Theory* (Cambridge: Harvard Graduate School of Education, 1958), p. 42.

23. In the Matched Scientists study, comments by the married women tended to dwell more on their husband's careers, with which they identified themselves, than on their own.

24. Paul Popenoe and R. H. Johnson, *Applied Eugenics* (New York: Macmillan, 1934), pp. 103, 236.

25. The effects of these processes were documented in the mental health survey of central Manhattan, where it was found that the unmarried women had the lowest degree of mental health impairment, the unmarried men, the most (Leo Srole and others, *Mental Health in the Metropolis: The Midtown Manhattan Study* [New York: McGraw-Hill, 1962], pp. 177–178).

26. Davis, *Stipends and Spouses*, p. 43.

27. *Ibid.*, For many of the married women in the Matched Scientists study who took the doctor's degree—before or after marriage—it was, indeed, a luxury

and not part of a planned professional career. They were not active scientists ten to fifteen years later.

28. The same general differences were also found in a younger set of chemists, but they were of somewhat lesser magnitude.

29. In a study of 440 men and 440 women psychologists receiving the Ph.D. degree between 1921 and 1940, it was reported that the unmarried women spent more time on the average (6.2 hours per week) than did the married women (5.4 hours) in professional reading; but there was no difference between them in amount of time spent in professional research and writing (3.3 hours per week). Unfortunately there is no way of knowing how many of these women were in academic positions (Bryan & Boring, *American Psychologist*, 2 [Jan. 1947], pp. 16–17).

Chapter 15

1. This point is made also by Charles D. Bolton in a letter to the editor of the *American Sociological Review*, Dec. 1962, pp. 903–905.

2. A documented elaboration of this theme as it has shown up in several aspects of the lives of women is presented by Betty Friedan in *The Feminine Mystique* (New York: Norton, 1963).

3. Guy Irving Burch, *A Revolution in Birth Rates* (Washington: Population Reference Bureau, 1949).

4. Several respondents in the Matched Scientists study listed their husbands as among the most stimulating of their intellectual contacts.

5. See the document on the Rudolph family below.

6. More employed than nonemployed mothers are reported to have considered divorce and more employed than nonemployed are actually divorced (F. Ivan Nye and Lois W. Hoffman, *The Employed Mother in America* [Chicago: Rand McNally, 1963], p. 272).

7. Alice I. Bryan and Edwin G. Boring, "Women in American Psychology: Factors Affecting Their Professional Careers," *American Psychologist*, 2 (Jan. 1947), p. 14.

8. These data are from Paul H. Jacobson, *American Marriage and Divorce* (New York: Rinehart, 1959), p. 159.

9. Among the psychologists, 22 of the divorced men had remarried, 8 of the divorced women had (Bryan & Boring, *American Psychologist*, 2 [Jan. 1947], p. 14).

10. It is an interesting commentary on academic marriage that in one divorce the major settlements had to do not with ordinary property, which presented no problem, but with joint research materials: who was to get the research notes, the tables, the interview transcriptions.

11. Bryan & Boring, *American Psychologist*, 2 (Jan. 1947), p. 14.

12. *Ibid.*

13. *Ibid.*

14. *Ibid.*, p. 15.

15. *Ibid.*

16. *Ibid.*

17. See Nye and Hoffman, *Employed Mother in America*, chaps. 15–20.

18. See Nye and Hoffman, *Employed Mother in America*, chaps. 4–14.

19. Virginia Gildersleeve was one of the first college administrators to see the logic of allowing maternity leave with pay for women, since men were al-

lowed to leave with pay for illness (Virginia Gildersleeve, *Many a Good Crusade* [New York: Macmillan, 1954], p. 108).

20. One academic woman reports that her students in a women's college were very protective of her, expressing concern about her high heels during pregnancy. Another, in a coeducational institution, reports that no attention at all was paid to her condition by either students or faculty. Everyone was so accustomed to pregnant women in offices, in libraries, and in laboratories as graduate students' wives, as secretaries, and as laboratory assistants that one more pregnant woman at the classroom lectern attracted no special attention.

21. Compare with Mrs. Murphy's advice to Dr. Rudolph in the Rudolph document below.

22. Bryan and Boring, *American Psychologist*, 2 (Jan. 1947), p. 15.

23. There is no explanation for the apparent inconsistency of fully employed women giving children as the chief factor in the abandonment of a career. Either the abandonment was temporary or the present employment is not professional.

24. *Ibid.*, p. 16.

25. *Ibid.*, p. 18.

26. *Ibid.* The corresponding figures for men are: 23.9 percent, 15.0 percent, and 2.8 percent.

27. Dr. Alberta Siegel's search of the literature with regard to her research on professional women and their children turned up an unpublished doctoral dissertation at Yale University in 1954 on "The Effect of Employment of Married Women on Husband and Wife Roles: A Study in Culture Change," by Deborah Kligler. This study suggested that "the difference in the importance and affect assigned to the mother and homemaker roles is striking. The special sanctions against neglect of the former function in favor of other interests are extremely powerful" (p. 154). Kligler also found that her working mothers exhibited some guilt about possible neglect of their children, but displayed little comparable concern about neglect of other tasks traditionally associated with homemaking. Both working wives and their husbands were significantly more willing to admit a decline in performance in the homemaker role than in the mother role. Lawrence Dennis notes: "If society accords a special and primary significance to the mother role, it would seem possible that academic women-with-children are caught in the conflicting role-expectations. It may be that it is not the children per se who mitigate against a productive academic career, but the internalized societal pressures which dictate that 'of course' the children shall have first call on her time. By the same token, little comparable pressure exists which compels her to attempt to be the best housekeeper in the block."

28. D. R. Miller and G. E. Swanson, *The Changing American Parent* (New 'ork: Wiley, 1958).

29. One woman whose husband sometimes left parties she was giving to return to his study to work remarked that she hoped her daughter would not marry a professor. Other men, she said, devoted only 7, 8, or even 10 hours a day to their professions; but professors were at it almost every waking moment. And even when her husband was cajoled to spend time with her and the children he soon became edgy and bored, anxious to get back to his work. Industrial tycoons also show a consuming absorption in their work. A study by Stanley Talbot, reported in *Time*, Nov. 10, 1952, p. 109, found that the tycoon clearly preferred his work to his family. The family life of ministers has also been subject to study, and here again the demands of profession have been found to impinge heavily on time budgeted for family. Much of the research on the suburban family is, in effect, a study of the junior executive as husband and father, and here too the exhorbitant demands of job are

emphasized. In the study of psychologists, noted in Chapter 10, 42.1 percent of the men and 26.9 percent of the women stated that "work contributes more than any other interest," and 19.0 percent of the men and 10.6 percent of the women reported that "professional work is major source" of satisfaction (Bryan & Boring, *American Psychologist*, 2 [Jan. 1947] p. 13).

30. One woman stated that she was glad for the distractions her children supplied: "I'm really glad my family makes demands on me. If I didn't have them to balance me I would become a hermit, studying all the time. It's good for me to be called back into the world to supply clean linen, shoe replacements, to take my turn at the car pool, make cookies for the PTA etc."

31. The following reply was made to the parents of a child who complained of too-high standards imposed on him by teachers because his mother taught at the college. "Quite the contrary. I had Billy as a student for two years in high school. So far from imposing too-high standards on him, we actually demanded less of him than of other children. We assumed he was brighter than the other children, an assumption that wasn't warranted, as it turned out. And he charmed us into passing him on his superficial appearance of knowing the material, because he could talk well. He never really mastered any of the fundamentals. He read superficially; he didn't know the multiplication tables; he mis-spelled words; he couldn't put a composition together; he could not speak Spanish (his foreign language), he had no specific grasp of history. He got by because his background gave him the kind of advantage that fools even good teachers."

32. James Spangenberg has found certain hazards among college students whose fathers are ministers. Unpublished doctoral dissertation, Pennsylvania State University, 1964.

33. One professor of family sociology whose children on a departmental picnic behaved no better—or, of course, worse—than the children of graduate students, remarked, when this fact was called to his attention, that his children hadn't read the books yet.

34. Bernard, Buchanan, and Smith, *Dating, Mating, and Marriage* (Cleveland: Howard Allen, 1958), pp. 100–101.

35. Ellen Richards was making this point decades earlier.

36. "I took another leave of four months last spring after the birth of our third child. . . . The three children thrive and change and we continue to adjust our schedules to each other. I feel most fortunate that my work and my husband's continuing collaboration allow this to be possible."

37. Merle Rosenblatt Goldman, "On Being Something Other Than Mother and Being Mother Too!" *Sarah Lawrence Alumnae Magazine*, Fall 1963, pp 14–16.

Radcliffe College, Graduate Education for Women: The Radcliffe Ph.D. (Cambridge: Harvard, 1956), p. 73.

Appendix A

1. J. E. Cutler and M. R. Davie in *A Study in Professional Education at Western Reserve University: The School of Applied Social Sciences* (Cleveland: Western Reserve Univ., 1930) in 1930 still felt called upon to justify the university's taking over the School of Applied Social Sciences. They argued that social workers needed contact with the fundamental pure sciences, that a university was a liberalizing influence, that research was best done under

university conditions, and that the university setting offered protection against propaganda (pp. 12–14).

2. Jessie Bernard, "Social Work" in *Contemporary Social Science*, ed. by P. L. Harriman, J. S. Roucek, and G. B. deHuszar (Harrisburg: Stackpole, 1953), I, p. 354.

3. This was the title of a book by E. T. Devine in 1918.

4. This was in line with Continental practice but in contrast to British practice; in Great Britain all schools of social work were closely tied to universities.

5. Jessie Bernard and L. L. Bernard, *Origins of American Sociology* (New York: Crowell, 1942), p. 625.

6. See *Ibid.*, Chapter 44, for a history of the courses in Social Science in colleges and universities.

7. Werner William Boehm, *Objectives of the Social Work Curriculum of the Future* (New York: Council on Social Work Education, 1959), pp. 167–168.

8. *Ibid.*, pp. 216–217.

9. *Ibid.*

10. *Ibid.*, p. 222.

11. *Ibid.*, pp. 273–274.

Appendix B

1. The catalogs, at ten-year intervals, of a selected sample of colleges and universities were canvassed to determine the proportion of the faculties who were women. The institutions selected were: Vassar, Smith, Wellesley, Swarthmore, Kansas State University, University of Michigan, and Harvard University. The data were broken down by subject matter, by rank of personnel, and by date. The results were reported in the body of the text.

2. *"Student Ratings.* A selection of 236 students was made which constituted all of those who took both English Composition 1 and English Composition 5 with some one of these instructors. . . . With one exception, all of these students had a different one of these instructors for English Composition 5 than they had had for English Composition 1. The objective was to get a rating of the instruction in English Composition 1. All of these students were mailed a copy of the first 'Opinionnaire on Teaching Effectiveness.' . . . Within a month to six weeks the forms had been returned by 83 percent of the former freshmen students. . . . The average score on all items was obtained and the 15 instructors given a numerical rating."

"Faculty Ratings. Eight members of the English faculty gave an ordered set of ratings of eleven of these fifteen instructors. They did not feel that they could rate the other four. . . . The English Department obligingly used . . . opinionnaires also to give a rating of the same instructors" (*Evaluation of Teaching Effectiveness* [University Park: Penn. State Univ., 1958], pp. 14–15).

3. There were 6 raters for 8 of the men and 1 of the women teachers, 5 raters for 3 of the men and 3 of the women. There were 7 questions and 6 possible answers to choose from for each question, one of which was "insufficient information." If all raters had checked "insufficient information" there would have been 35 such checks or 42, according to whether there were 5 or 6 raters. For the men the figures were: 3/35; 5/42; 1/42; 4/42; 15/42; 21/42; 3/42; 3/42; and 4/42. For the women they were: 4/42; 7/35; 8/35; and 6/35.

4. Highest ratings were assigned to men in 21 percent of all ratings, to

women in 10 percent. Medium ratings were assigned in 34 percent of the ratings of men and in 38 percent of the ratings of women. Low ratings constituted 44 percent and 52 percent of the ratings of men and women respectively.

5. After the experiment was over, the purpose was explained. Then, just as a matter of interest, the subjects were asked which of the two lecturers they would prefer as instructors. The men divided fairly evenly; the young women preferred the man.

6. This study was done by John K. Brilhart of the speech department and Richard Spencer of the University Division of Instructional Services.

Appendix C

1. This study was supported by National Institute of Mental Health Grant #MH–0651501.

2. A study of 157 applied scientists found that informal contacts with others in the field ranked about as high as consulting relevant reports as sources of information (I. H. Hogg and J. Roland Smith, "Information and Literature Use in a Research and Development Organization," *Proceedings of the International Conference on Scientific Information* [Washington: GPO, 1958], p. 188). Another study at Harwell, England, in the Atomic Energy Research Establishment, based on diaries kept by 63 scientists, found that "personal recommendation" was the second most common method by which research workers found information (R. M. Fishenden, "Methods by Which Research Workers Find Information," *Conference on Scientific Information*, pp. 168–174). Bentley Glass and Sharon H. Norwood reported a high incidence of learning by way of interpersonal contacts among 50 scientists at Johns Hopkins University *(Conference on Scientific Information*, p. 196). Face-to-face contacts with colleagues constituted one of the three most important tools for getting information among 500 medical scientists; they also rated highly as a source of stimulation (Saul Harner, "The Information-Gathering Habits of American Medical Scientists" *Conference on Scientific Information*, pp. 280–281). Of special relevance was Herbert Menzel's "Planned and Unplanned Scientific Communication." On the basis of a constantly restructured question-naire-interview, he studied 77 scientists in residence during the spring of 1957 at Columbia *(Conference on Scientific Information*, p. 199). He views his subjects as constituting a communication *system*, including not only the scientific literature, not only the formally established meetings and conferences, but also the informal, person-to-person modes of communication like corre-spondence, visits, and corridor conversations (p. 201). Menzel suggests that what looks like an "individual accident" in coming upon new information may constitute "aggregate regularity," for "while there is only a small likelihood that any accidentally obtained piece of information will be of use to the individual scientist who obtained it, the likelihood that it will be of interest to at least one of his departmental colleagues is much larger" (p. 206). Among the research questions Menzel suggests are these: (1) Does any significant part of information about current scientific developments fail to appear in the literature? (2) Why were specific published items of scientific news missed by scientists? (3) In what fields is published information most likely to be missed in the course of scanning? (4) What are the forms of personal communication which bring relevant scientific news to those who have access

to them? (5) What is the present opportunity for scientists in varying positions to have access to the fruitful forms of personal communications? In connection with the last question, Menzel states "it is important to know how much access to such communication scientists in various institutions, professional positions, and geographic locations now have, if plans are to be made to have more of them 'hooked up' in useful ways with the network of informal information flow" (p. 220). It was in the last-named area that the Matched Scientists study falls. It was designed to explore the effect of type of institution (college, university) and of sex on access to channels of scientific communication.

3. See Chapter 10.

4. *Conference on Scientific Information.*

5. See Chapter 10 for method of coding published items. No attempt was made to weight for single or joint authorship. Any system of weighting would involve judgment, and the resulting weights would not necessarily be any more valid than equal weighting. I am indebted by my colleague, Dr. Jack Sauer, himself a distinguished scientist, for help in arriving at this decision.

6. There were, for example, no men wth doctorates from the Top Twelve who were teaching in junior colleges, as in the case of two of the women, or in a teachers college, as in the case of a Negro scientist. For some women, on the other hand, there were several men from among whom matching subjects could be selected. In such cases the selection was random. It will be noted that there were more men than women among both university and college scientists. This resulted from the fact that when a scientist did not reply to the request for cooperation, another was substituted for him. In some cases the first scientist did later cooperate.

7. Sidney Siegel, *Nonparametric Statistics for the Behavioral Sciences* (New York: McGraw-Hill, 1956), chap. 6. The one-tailed test was used because the alternative to the null hypothesis was always one assuming a directed difference in a given direction.

Appendix D

1. This study was supported by the National Science Foundation through Grant No. NSF–G23975–Use of Communication Channels in Biology.

2. Jessie Bernard, Charles W. Shilling, and Joe W. Tyson, *Informal Communication among Bioscientists* (Washington: Biological Sciences Communication Project, 1963).

3. *Ibid.*, p. 29.

4. *Ibid.*, p. 39.

5. *Ibid.*, p. 38.

INDEX

A

Abbott, Edith, 244, 246, 247
Abbott, Frank C., 287, 299
Academic momism, 131, 142–143
Academic professions,
  as proportion of labor force, 29
  functions of, 29–30
  number in, 29
  sex roles and, 30
Academic quietism, 35, 97
Academic women,
  academic rank of, 180, 189, 190, 297
  alternative careers of, 63–64, 72, 73
  appearance of, 312
  as "analytics," 194
  as colleagues, Chapter 12, Chapter 13
  as "creatives," 194, 195, 196
  as graduate student mentors, 140–145
  as models, 137–138
  as mothers, 219–227
  as proportion of academic personnel,
    38, 40, 51
  as returnees, 228–231
  as teachers,
    at elementary level, 121
    effect of sex on acceptance of, 129–
      130, 255–257
    evaluation of,
      by colleague ratings, 319
      by student achievement, 129
      by students, 128, 130–131, 255–
        257, 299, 300, 319
    in humanities, 125, 126, 191
    in professional schools, 122–123,
      242–250
    in social sciences, 123–124, 126, 191,

298 (see also Budner, Stanley,
  and Meyer, John)
  rank of, 121, 126, 180, 189, 190
  as wives, 215–219
ascribed versus achieved status of,
  187–188
at top universities, 287
children of, 220–226, 241
  average number of, 241
  effect of, on career, 220–222
  effect on, of career, 222–226
class background of, 77–78, 288–289
compared with academic men, Chapter 5
  in age, 80–81
  in career patterns, 87–91
  in class background, 77–78, 288–289
  in institutional affiliation, Chapter
    6
  in marital status, 81
  in "personality," 81–83
  in position in scientific communi-
    cation system, 157, 182, 220, 263
  in test-intelligence, 78–80, 84
compared with nonacademic women,
  in age, 109, 113
  in doctoral university, 109, 113
  in marital status, 109, 113
  in memberships in professional or
    ganizations, 109, 113
creativity among, reasons for lower
  level of,
  166–176 (see also Creativity)
"damaged feminity" of, 210–211
decline of, as proportion of academic
  personnel, 37, 40, 41
  reasons for, 41, 62